The
Abused
Child

**A Multidisciplinary Approach
to Developmental Issues and Treatment**

The Abused Child

A Multidisciplinary Approach
to Developmental Issues and Treatment

edited by
Harold P. Martin, M.D.

foreword by
C. Henry Kempe, M.D.

Ballinger Publishing Company • Cambridge, Massachusetts
A Subsidiary of J.B. Lippincott Company

 This book is printed on recycled paper.

Library of Congress Cataloging in Publication Data

Main entry under title:
  The abused child.

  Includes bibliographical references and index.
  1. Child   abuse—Addresses,   essays,   lectures.   I. Martin,   Harold   P.
[DNLM: 1. Child abuse. 2. Child development. WA320 A167]
HV713.A28   362.7'1   76-11766
ISBN 0-88410-218-1

International Standard Book Number: 0-88410-218-1

Library of Congress Catalog Card Number: 76-11766

Printed in the United States of America

Contents

Foreword

C. Henry Kempe, M.D.

It is a fascinating question to consider why it is that during the past seventy years of active protective services work on behalf of troubled families, the focus of treatment, and indeed of diagnosis, has been upon the mother rather than on each member of the family, but it is not surprising. For one thing, the mother was more readily available to a social worker who was beginning to provide diagnostic and treatment services to a family while the father was at work during the time the social worker was available. Moreover, the philosophy of protective services for the past fifty years has been very much geared to the feeling that if a mother could be helped to be more competent or more loving to her child, or able to stabilize her marriage, even though the father might be the primary abuser, that good things would of necessity happen in regards to the abused child and the other children in the family. It is not surprising, therefore, that while there is an extensive literature on case work with mothers, there is much less on work with fathers and virtually nothing on the abused child.

Most studies have been retrospective, that is starting out in juvenile detention homes, prisons and psychiatric clinics and hospitals. The very high incidence of child abuse of individuals in these institutions was often remarked upon but it is fair to say that the abused child was not dealt with either from a diagnostic or a treatment point of view until he was known to be deviant either by failing kindergarten and primary school, or requiring many foster home placements because of personality difficulties, or later on because of adolescent deviant behavior such as truancy or delinquency. On the other hand, all of us who have dealt with abused children over the past twenty years have been struck by the very massive emotional disturbance often found in these children even in the very first year of life. Our own ability to focus on the child involved in child abuse from the earliest time of our contact perhaps was delayed by our need first to know more about the psychodynamics of the adults involved in child abuse, and the development of numerous modalities of treatment in addition to case work in trying to help both abusive parents. We know that lay-therapists, backed up by crisis nurseries, parents groups including self-help groups such as Parents Anonymous, family learning centers or family residential centers and therapeutic day schools for abused children can supplement case work to provide a range of therapeutic modalities which is not only more effective but can very often speed the decision-making process in child abuse when relinquishment or termination are considered.

We now know that unless both parents receive active intervention with combinations of the above modalities, they will not easily tolerate treatment of their child. Indeed, when children are placed in therapeutic nursery schools and are moved from "frozen watchfulness" to awareness and then to personal creativity, parents view such a change almost invariably as a worsening of the child's behavior which is often intolerable to them and results in termination of such treatment. On the other hand, if the parents themselves receive what they perceive to be useful and consistent support from lay-therapists or from other parents in self-help or parents groups and therapeutic nursery schools, they can work through these feelings and tolerate changes in the child.

It is now possible to turn from the well-established approaches to the parents for the parents' needs to the less well established approaches to the child. Diagnosis of the emotional damage to the physically abused, sexually abused, or seriously neglected child is imperative if reasonable treatment approaches are to be evaluated. But regardless of the amount of psychological and intellectual damage that has occurred, it is now clear that all such children, and indeed all their siblings, require some kind of outreach help from early on. Any child protective service department that fails to recognize the needs for therapeutic intervention on behalf of the child is simply failing to do an adequate job. Moreover, the erroneous notion that placing a child in foster care necessarily represents treatment must be overcome. Foster care can be therapeutic, but regrettably, it often is not. This is so because some of the children involved are not easy to care for, and the child may fail foster care very much as he fails kindergarten and primary school later on. Further, the violent and abrupt separation from the parent is in itself traumatic to the abused child who invariably feels abandoned and often responsible even at very young ages. The abused child in foster care cannot understand why he can only see his mother for an hour a week in a strange place and under difficult circumstances and usually cannot see his father at all. Not only is visiting by biologic parents in foster homes discouraged or disallowed, but, further, foster parents often do not want to have the abused child attend a therapeutic day care center. When the child is compliant, as so many of these children are when they are first placed, the foster family may want to keep him just that way.

While detailed experience with the diagnosis and treatment of physically abused children is a recent development, it is already very clear that the needs of these children are enormous; that these needs represent a developmental emergency; and their diagnosis and treatment by encouraging emotional growth and development and providing a safe and supportive curative environment must be initiated at once when the diagnosis of physical abuse has been made. Children are on a time table of their own, and emotional growth and development of a child cannot tolerate a situation where the child is placed in an emotional deep freeze waiting for the time when, in one way or another, the parents have been made better, six or twelve months hence. The time involved in improving parents is so enormous if considered in terms of a child's emotional growth and development that it is little wonder that the child suffers grievously in the interim.

The dilemma of welfare departments is clear. If they are to be totally safe in terms of reinjury, then foster care separation may seem the only approach. And yet foster care separation has been abused by its prolonged nature; the cruel separation from the family when the child is thought to be eligible for return; and the selection of foster families who do not allow the parents ready access to the child in a safe environment. All these negative results could be overcome by the development of family learning centers where the children would live in small groups of five or seven with a stable and loving small staff and the granting of ready access of the parents to their children on nights and weekends and by the mother during the day. By providing an accurate early diagnosis of the severity of emotional damage done to the child who has been abused or severely neglected, it is also frequently possible to identify those families where relinquishment or termination are the only means to ensure the child's chances for emotional survival. All these determinations are far better made when the child and the parents are available to each other and to helping people. Current foster home practices are not consonant with this approach.

It is indeed heartwarming to see the great improvement made by many children who are remaining at home, but who do develop through a therapeutic nursery setting the ability to grow up emotionally and to heal their scars. They then can move into regular nursery school and into regular school, but they will probably always have to have a part of their life supplemented by love from relative strangers since they quickly perceive that as far as their own parents are concerned love is episodic, punishment is harsh, and understanding is minimal.

The child quickly learns that there can be three lives: the sleeping life, the happy life in nursery school or school, and a more difficult but tolerable life with parents who only gradually develop their own feelings of self-esteem and appreciation of some of the qualities of the child. In any event we have learned that we cannot wait until the parents are better, because this may take years and they may not be all that much better when they are done. Rather we must view intervention on behalf of the child in terms of his medical care as only the very first step in assessing his other needs. It is a challenge for the already overworked departments of child protection in our 3362 counties to develop programs in collaboration with private and volunteer agencies in their communities on behalf of these very needy children. That such effort will be rewarding in human and financial terms cannot be in doubt. The emotional cripples of today are the abused children of yesterday. Through some of the experiences presented in this book, suggestions for the evaluation and treatment of the child involved in abuse are now possible.

Preface

The contributors to this book have all worked in the area of child abuse for many years. With the exception of the two British authors, Dr. Lynch and Mr. Appleton, all of the other contributors are affiliated with the National Center for Prevention and Treatment of Child Abuse and Neglect in Denver. The Denver group, under the guidance of C. Henry Kempe, have been heavily involved in child abuse from the early 1960s. While most of the authors have written in numerous places about their experiences and findings concerning child abuse over the years, there has been an increased interest in the dilemma of the child himself in the past five years. There has truly been a contagion of interest, concern and care stemming from the pioneer and current efforts of Dr. Kempe. Under his influence, we have all wanted to help fill a gap in our state of knowledge concerning child abuse, that is, by sharing with the reader our findings and experiences with the victims of this syndrome, the abused children.

Several studies and programs for abused children have developed at the National Center in recent years. Most of this book is taken from our experience with such programs. A preschool for abused children was opened in the Fall of 1974. Shortly thereafter a crises nursery for abused children was established here. A residential treatment program for abusive families similarly was begun which included a child care unit as part of this program. Along with these programs, more detailed studies of abused children in a variety of settings have been undertaken, such as a systematic study of children at the time of hospitalization for physical abuse.

Interest in the abused child has reached beyond the boundaries of the National Center *per se.* Several faculty and staff from the John F. Kennedy Child Development Center at the University of Colorado Medical Center have become involved in trying to understand these children's problems. Indeed, anyone interested in the effect of aberrant parenting on the development of children finds the area of child abuse keenly interesting. The interest of the authors then has stemmed not only from a very personal and humanistic concern for the mistreated child, but also from an interest in child development.

Appropriately, this book is multi-authored and is multidisciplinary in nature. The contributors come from the fields of pediatrics, social work, clinical psychology, child psychiatry, child development, speech and language pathology, occupational therapy, early childhood education, and law. As we have learned in the field of child development, the skills and understanding of many disciplines are needed to adequately understand the effects of the abusive environment on these children.

In a sense, this book is a collage—a collection of systematically obtained research data, clinical impressions gained from years of work with abused children, and descriptions of treatment programs which have developed at the National Center to try to obviate the effects of the abusive environment on abused children. Impressionistic data, hypotheses to explain behavior of these children, and exposures to the struggles we have endured are also included.

It is our hope that this book about abused children will serve as a catalyst for others to similarly focus their attention on the many developmental issues of importance to understanding and helping the abused child.

Harold P. Martin, M.D.

Acknowledgments

By tradition, acknowledgments designate those people and agencies who have made a work possible. To truly acknowledge all of the people and agencies would clearly be impossible. To be fully honest and complete in this endeavor, I would need to mention every important friend, relative, teacher and colleague from over an entire life span. From a developmental viewpoint, one must be aware of the importance of all of these people throughout infancy, childhood, and maturity. And so I start from the premise that any listing of people to whom one is indebted will be incomplete and quite selective.

It seems very important to acknowledge and extend gratitude to those people whose financial support has been essential in this work. They have been courageous, generous, and farsighted to support such efforts. The staff at The National Center especially thank the Grant Foundation for the support of our research efforts, and the Commonwealth Fund, and the Robert Wood Johnson Foundation for their unstinting and almost complete fiscal support of the diagnostic, treatment, and educational programs at The National Center. The Office of Child Development, HEW, is further mentioned as their recent professional and fiscal support has been essential in our work. Maternal and Child Health division of HEW, through their support of Grant #926, has enabled the JFK Child Development Center Staff to study the abused child and his development. These foundations and agencies are not mentioned out of obligation; rather, from a genuine gratitude for their support of our efforts to understand and help abused children.

Dr. C. Henry Kempe must be acknowledged. As the Director of the National Center, he has made this work possible. He has served in many capacities, to inspire, support, and to develop the efforts of most of the contributors. Many of the programs described herein, as the residential treatment program for parents, the preschool for abused children, and the crisis nursery were conceptualized and directed by him. His efforts to help abused children and abusive parents have been extensive and truly monumental. And from a more personal vantage, I wish to dedicate this book to three different groups of people to whom an immense amount of gratitude and affection flow. These are the very special people who have helped me personally and professionally.

I first and foremost dedicate this book to Delores, Lyn, and Marcus who have helped me understand love and loving.

I also dedicate this book to Henry who has helped me understand abused children.

Finally, I dedicate this book to Herb and Sam, who helped me understand myself.

Harold P. Martin

The Abused Child

A Multidisciplinary Approach
to Developmental Issues and Treatment

 *Chapter 1*

Introduction

Harold P. Martin

This is a book about abused children, it is not a book about child abuse. It is a book about the various wounds of the child—psychological, developmental, and neurologic wounds. The child who has been assaulted and mistreated is identified because of his physical wounds. The physical injuries may be devastating and lethal. Over the years, the child's psychological and developmental injuries may be every bit as devastating and debilitating. The authors have wanted to call attention to these wounds, as they are not so visible as physical injury. We have tried to note and understand the various ways in which the abusive environment has affected the child. Armed with that understanding, the next step has been to determine how those wounds can be treated or cured.

It seems ironic that the victim of child abuse has had so little attention in the literature. This attention has been paid the child primarily in two areas. First has been the overriding concern with keeping the child from being killed or seriously maimed. Other efforts to help the child have been more indirect, e.g., legislation; establishing systems for managing this syndrome; dealings with the perpetrator, whether they be punitive or rehabilitative in nature; trying to understand the dynamics of the abusive adult; development of innovative and successful treatment modalities directed towards parents; and teaching and training various professionals and lay persons.

There have been a few reports on abused children.[1-14] In 1964, Morris *et al.*[15] described what she considered to be unusual behaviors that were frequently seen in abused children when they were hospitalized. Elmer and Gregg were truly pioneers in focusing interest on abused children. In 1967, they published both a book and a paper in the medical literature describing 52 children presumed to be abused.[16,17] Their discouraging summary noted that of the 52 children, at follow-up twelve were either dead or in institutions for the retarded. (Parenthetically, it is of interest that they chose to combine those two groups of children.) Of the 33 children seen for evaluation, the morbidity was 88 percent judged by the rather gross parameters of mental retardation, emotional disorders of significance, serious speech problems, or marked physical defect. Early in 1974 a review of the literature[7] pertaining to the development of abused children found only a few investigations and reports. David Gil's book[18] is an epidemiological survey rather than a clinically or psychologically oriented document. Fontana's book[19] deals mainly with medical diagnosis and medical, social and legal intervention, saying little about the effects of abuse on the child or what sort of treatment methods were necessary for the child. Elmer and colleagues have recently completed an eight-year follow-up of seventeen abused children.[20] Although there was an attempt to obtain an adequate control group of children, it appears as if many of the control group were also neglected and perhaps physically mistreated. This may be why so few differences were noted between the identified abused children and the control group. Certainly Sandgrund's recent research[21] clearly shows differences between children who have been abused, a neglected group of children, and a control group who came from quite low socioeconomic families.

Other treatises on child abuse often deal very minimally and superficially with the child. Leavitt's 1974 selected readings[22] devotes very little space to an understanding of the abused child. One short chapter[23] describes observations of abused children in the hospital. Papers which by title suggest they are addressing services to children, deal almost exclusively with services for abusing parents. Franklin's 1975 book[24] has one six-page chapter by MacKeith on the abused child. Its tentative nature is inherent in the title, "Speculations on Some Possible Long-Term Effects." Ebeling and Hill's valuable and innovative book[25] has one chapter inappropriately entitled "The Physically Abused Child." The first sentence of this chapter states, "This chapter focuses on personality factors found in the parents who physically abuse their child." Even Newberger and Hyde's recent contribution[26] to the pediatric clinics of North America says little about the effects of the abusive home on the child.

The works cited above and the contributions of other scholars in the field have been tremendously important and valuable. Abused children in this country have benefited greatly from the investigations of model legislation, systems for dealing with the abusive syndrome, treatment approaches for parents, and the like. I in no way mean to deny the theoretical and pragmatic value of our early efforts in identifying and dealing with child abuse. Rather, I am pointing out that much less has been done in assessing the broader and long range effects of the abusive environment on the children; and little has been done, until recently, to scrutinize the needs of these children and discover how they can best be met. This book is an attempt to begin to fill that gap, and hopefully to catalyze interest in the abused child, as well as in child abuse.

One might ask why there has been so little work done in studying the abused child. Clearly the early and sustained interest in the syndrome of abuse was motivated largely by concern for the victims. The clinical compassion of men and women like Kempe, Steele and Helfer for these ravaged children was what diverted their professional interest from other areas of medicine to spend years of work in helping abused children. Why, then, the paucity of information on what these children are like and what types of intervention they need? The answer is not simple, but it is multifaceted.

First, one must have a perspective on the history of investigation into this syndrome. The history of the work undertaken to understand and eradicate this syndrome parallels the history of attack on other diseases. It must be pointed out that much of the early work in this area was embedded in the field of medicine—work by radiologists, pediatricians, psychiatrists. It was from the matrix of medicine that society in this country was forced to recognize and acknowledge that child abuse is a not uncommon phenomenon that may result in the death or permanent maiming of children. Early approaches were focused on diagnosis, pathogenesis, and etiology; and their primary concern was on saving the lives of the victims of this "disease," the abused children. The mortality rate of this syndrome was alarming and demanded first priority in starting to conquer this disease. Medical diagnosis and treatment of the child's physical injuries were undertaken. It was recognized that to save the child one first had to diagnose the syndrome and that traditional medical examination alone was not sufficient. Hence, professionals in the behavioral fields were drawn in to help with identification and diagnosis. This pathway led to understanding the dynamics of the abusing adult. To assure the survival of children, alternatives to living with abusing parents were developed; and involved child protection agencies and the legal systems, courts and police. They also required a critical examination of the legal status of abused children and parents; and the rewriting of state laws to deal optimally with this syndrome, a process that is still going on.[27-34]

A second basis for the minimal attention given to abused children lies in the erroneous attention upon physical abuse as the cause or etiology of this "disease," rather than in the understanding that child abuse is a syndrome. So long as one focuses only on the physical trauma to the child, one will necessarily focus on the medical consequences of that trauma—death, brain damage, mental retardation, physical handicap. This is the most distressing and the most critically important aspect of this syndrome. However, physical attack upon the child is but one piece of the composite of child abuse. Early on we recognized that we could prevent reinjury to the child by separating the child from the remainder of the family; so foster placement was undertaken as a treatment modality for the child. Even currently, with high priority given to maintaining family integrity whenever possible, with good treatment approaches it is usually possible to return the child to his family with very minimal risk of reinjury. And yet we continue to see abused children, no longer being physically attacked, who continue to show the neurological, cognitive, and personality scars of being in an abusive environment. Physical abuse of a child is a sign, an indicator of a complex dysfunctioning family and an unhealthy parent-child interaction.

When abuse is seen as a syndrome rather than as a disease, then one must consider not only the effects of the physical damage to the child, but also maternal deprivation, neglect (both medical and emotional), undernutrition, rejection, the effects of emotionally disturbed parents on children, and the chaos and dysfunction of the family unit. Even without the physical trauma *per se*, all of the above components of the abusive syndrome can and do, in and of themselves, have an effect on the development of children. Hence, to understand abused children, their development and their treatment needs, it is imperative to shift from a strictly medical model which considers *physical abuse* as the entire basis for harm to the child. One must shift to a broader base of viewing child abuse as a syndrome, with physical trauma perhaps the most critical and important, but still only *one* of a whole series of signs and symptoms of a dysfunctioning family unit. Physical abuse is not only a medical problem to be addressed but also a signal, a marker if you will, of a pervasive and complex syndrome which has serious consequences to the developing child.

If medicine has initially viewed child abuse as a disease and undertaken to solve this problem as the medical profession has traditionally dealt with disease, social agencies have likewise approached child abuse as they have approached other crimes. The parallels are too striking not to be obvious. How does society deal with such crimes as rape or theft? We develop ways to identify such crimes. We develop legal systems to remove the perpetrator from society and punish him. We even work to rehabilitate the perpetrator so he will not repeat his crime. We develop security systems to try to prevent crimes from occurring or recurring. And yet, we do not see societal systems dealing with the victims of such crimes. What of the person who has had his monies and valuables taken? What of the rape victim? What of the victim of assault? The legal, fiscal, emotional and personal effects of such crimes to the victim are not of much interest to our society. This same paradigm has been followed in child abuse. The abusing parent may be arrested, tried for a crime and jailed. With or without criminal prosecution, rehabilitation through a variety of treatment approaches may be offered the perpetrator. The child may be put in foster care to prevent recurrence of such a crime. I do not disparage such efforts. They are important, valuable and often critical. Yet the question must again be raised, what of the victim? Why do we turn away from him and deal exclusively with the criminal?

A number of facts and a body of data support the hypothesis that society has little concern for the victim. In child protection agencies, it is not uncommon for a placement worker to carry a caseload of from 40 to 60 abused and neglected children. Clearly with such a caseload, he or she can offer little to any of these children. When this large burden was pointed out to the legislature in

Colorado, the response was for them to consider a mandate that child protection workers must not enlarge their caseloads—i.e., the solution to keeping the caseload from growing was to insist that the protection worker must drop a child from her caseload every time she picked up a new child to be responsible for. This asinine approach only serves the purpose of keeping the statistics from looking worse than they presently do. In a recent attempt to contact a number of abused children, colleagues and I found that one large Colorado child welfare department had lost track of one of the children; they actually did not know where the child was or had been for the past year. The surrogate parents, the child welfare department, had simply overlooked and lost one of their legal dependents, an abused child who was in their custody. The approach of community agencies has followed the paradigm with which they are comfortable, e.g., apprehend the perpetrator, consider punishment or removal from society, rehabilitate him so he will not repeat his offense—all of which may be laudatory goals. Nonetheless, the victim of the offense—the abused child—may get lost in this legal and administrative shuffle. One wonders what are the dynamics that make it easier to deal with the offender than to endure the difficult and painful task of trying to understand and help the victim.

Finally, a fourth parameter of our disregard for the development of the abused child must be considered. This involves professionals looking at the harmful effects of their interventions and the failures of their efforts. This painful task is a tradition in conscientious medical societies. Medical students in training are admonished that the first rule of their profession is to "do no harm." And yet that naive, if well-meaning admonition, is not possible to incorporate completely. We know we cause pain and take risks every time we undertake surgery or give the simplest of medicines to patients. The pain, the risks and the potential harm of our treatment procedures must be recognized, acknowledged and, insofar as possible, minimized. Let us turn to treatment procedures for the abused child. What do we so frequently do? We further stress and traumatize the child by putting him in a hospital (even when no medical indications are present). We separate him from his parents. We force him to deal with separation, loss and erratic and inconstant parenting. We may refuse to allow his biological parents even to communicate with him by phone or letter. He is in the midst of legal proceedings where he is the center of emotional and legal storms. In a follow-up study of 58 abused children, colleagues and I found that over 20 of the children had had from three to eight home changes in a mean time span of 4.5 years. It has been a common experience for us to see abused children suffer repeated changes of foster homes while parental rights were not severed for so many years that the child was no longer, in a pragmatic sense, a good candidate for adoption into a permanent home. We recently reviewed the case of a six-year-old little girl who had been physically abused at twelve months of age. Since that time she had had thirteen home changes, including one unsuccessful attempt at adoption. The consequences of a skull fracture and other assorted injuries at one year of age are still present, but are only mildly handicapping. We protected this little girl; we removed her from her mother. We treated her injuries and made sure she was never physically reinjured. A treatment success! But look again. It took 4.5 years before parental rights were severed. Through mismanagement of placement we now have a bright little girl who is seriously emotionally handicapped; without the capacity of attaching to any one person; a learning-disabled, acting out, unhappy little girl whose future will undoubtedly hold a continued series of unsuccessful home placements. Our treatment and management have crippled this abused child more seriously than the skull and tibial fractures of five years ago.

My point is that as we have the courage and interest to care about the development of abused children, the consequences of the abusive environment, and the needs of these children, *we shall be forced to critically assess the problems raised by our treatment procedures* and find ways to minimize those problems and help children deal with our interventions. When we sit at a child abuse team meeting, we shall ask the questions: What does this child need; in what ways will our treatment planning provide new problems for the child to deal with; what are the aspects of the family apart from physical abuse which are detrimental to the development of the child, and what can we do about them? We shall heed the advice of Goldstein, Freud and Solnit[35] to choose the "least detrimental alternatives" in planning for the child.

This is, therefore, a book about abused children. The contributors have attempted to describe what abused children are like, what the abusive environment does to them, how they cope and what the children in an abusive environment need in the way of treatment and help. It is our hope that the reader will become as interested in abused children as he is in child abuse. Our goals are for professionals to view abuse as a syndrome and consider the various factors in that syndrome, in addition to the physical trauma, as potentially detrimental to the children.

It is hoped that we can go beyond the initial critical concern with mortality and medical morbidity to encompass concern for the child's subsequent cognitive, emotional and social development. The concentration of interest in the perpetrator of the physical abuse must be augmented by a primary concern with the child caught up in this devastating syndrome. We are presumptious enough to dream that this book may ignite interest, investigation and inquiry into the many unexplored questions surrounding sound management for the welfare of abused children.

References

1. Kempe, C.H., Silverman, F., Steele, B., Droegmueller, W., Silver, H., "The Battered Child Syndrome," *Journal of American Medical Association*, 181:17-24 (July 1962).

2. Kempe, C.H., Helfer, R. (eds.), *The Battered Child*, University of Chicago Press (1968, 1974 2nd ed.).

3. Kempe, C.H., "Paediatric Implications of the Battered Baby Syndrome," *Archives of Diseases of Childhood*, 46:28 (1971).

4. Kempe, C.H., Helfer, R. (eds.), *Helping the Battered Child and His Family*, Philadelphia: J.B. Lippincott Co. (1972).

5. Kempe, C.H., "A Practical Approach to the Protection of the Abused," *Pediatrics*, Vol. 51:804 (April 1973).

6. Martin, H., Beezley, P., Conway, E., Kempe, C.H., "The Development of Abused Children, Part I: A Review of the Literature; Part II: Physical, Neurologic and Intellectual Outcome," *Advances in Pediatrics*, Vol. 21: 25-73 (1974).

7. Schmitt, B., Kempe, C.H., "Neurological Aspects of the Battered Child Syndrome," In Vinker, P.J., Bruyn, G.W. (eds.), *Handbook of Clinical Neurology*, North Holland Publishing Co., Amsterdam (1974).

8. Schmitt, B., Kempe, C.H., "The Battered Child Syndrome," In Kelley, V.C. (ed.), *Brennemann-Kelley Practice of Pediatrics*, New York: Harper & Row Publishers, Inc. (1974).

9. Schmitt, B., Kempe, C.H., "Neglect and Abuse of Children," In Vaughn, V.C., McKay, R.S. (eds.), *Nelson's Textbook of Pediatrics*, 10th ed., Philadelphia: W.B. Saunders Co. (1974).

10. Schmitt, B., Kempe, C.H., "Child Abuse—The Battered Child Syndrome," *A Folia Traumatologica* monograph, Ciba-Geigy, Ltd., Basle, Switzerland (1974).

11. Schmitt, B., Kempe, C.H., "Child Abuse," *The Encyclopedia Americana* (1974).

12. Schmitt, B., Kempe, C.H., "The Battered Child Syndrome," In Gellis, S.S., Kagan, B.M. (eds.), *Current Pediatric Therapy*, 6th ed., Philadelphia: W.B. Saunders Co. (1974).

13. Schmitt, B., Kempe, C.H., "The Pediatrician's Role in Child Abuse and Neglect," *Current Problems in Pediatrics* monograph, Yearbook Medical Publishers, Inc., Vol. 5(5), Chicago (1975).

14. Martin, H.P., Beezley, P., "The Personality of Abused Children," *Developmental Medicine and Child Neurology* (Accepted for publication 1976).

15. Morris, M.G., Gould, R.W., Mathews, P.J., "Toward Prevention of Child Abuse," *Children*, 11:55-60 (March-April 1964).

16. Elmer, E., *Children in Jeopardy*, Pittsburgh: University of Pittsburgh Press (1967).

17. Elmer, E., Gregg, G.S., "Developmental Characteristics of Abused Children," *Pediatrics*, 40:596-602 (1967).

18. Gil, D.G., *Violence against Children—Physical Child Abuse in the United States*, Cambridge, Mass.: Harvard University Press (1970).

19. Fontana, V.J., *The Maltreated Child*, Springfield, Ill.: Charles Thomas Publisher (1974).

20. Elmer, E., "Panel Presentation on Abused Children," Presentation at American Psychiatric Association, Anaheim, California (Spring 1975).

21. Sandgrund, S., Gaines, R.W., Green, A.H., "Child Abuse and Mental Retardation: A Problem of Cause and Effect," *American Journal on Mental Deficiency*, 3:327-330 (1975).

22. Leavitt, J.E., *The Battered Child—Selected Readings*, New York: General Learning Corporation (1974).

23. Galdston, R., "Observations on Children Who Have Been Physically Abused and Their Parents," In Leavitt, J.E. (ed.), *The Battered Child—Selected Readings*, New York: General Learning Corporation (1974).

24. Franklin, A.W., *Concerning Child Abuse*, New York: Churchill Livingstone (1975).

25. Ebeling, N.B., Hill, D.A.. *Child Abuse: Intervention and Treatment*, Acton, Mass.: Publishing Sciences Group (1975).

26. Newberger, E.H., Hyde, J.N., "Child Abuse: Principles and Implications of Current Pediatric Practice," *Ped. Clinics of North America*, Vol. 22, 695-715, Philadelphia: W.B. Saunders Co. (August 1975).

27. Fraser, B., "Legislative Approaches to Child Abuse," A compilation (looseleaf), The National Center for the Prevention and Treatment of Child Abuse and Neglect, Denver, Colorado (1973).

28. Fraser, B., "A Pragmatic Approach to Child Abuse," *American Criminal Law Review*, 12:103 (1974).

29. Fraser, B., Fine, A., "The Battered Child," *The Colorado Lawyer*, 3(6):33 (April 1974).

30. Fraser, B., "Toward a More Practical Central Registry," *Denver Law Journal*, 51(4):509 (1974).

31. Fraser, B., "Legislative Status of Child Abuse Legislation," In Kempe, C.H., Helfer, R. (eds.), *The Battered Child*, University of Chicago Press, 2nd ed. (1974).

32. Fraser, B., "Child Abuse and Neglect: Alternatives for State Legislation," Education Commission of the States, *Report No. 44* (December 1974).

33. Fraser, B., "Pediatric Bill of Rights," *South Texas Law Review*, 16(3): 245 (1975).

34. Fraser, B., Besharov, D., "Child Abuse and Neglect, Model Legislation," Education Commission of the States (September 1975).

35. Goldstein, J., Freud, A., Solnit, A.J., *Beyond the Best Interests of the Child*, New York: Free Press (1973).

Section 1

Developmental Issues

Chapter 2

The Environment of the Abused Child

Harold P. Martin

This first section of this book addresses the question of what abused children are like. Later chapters will describe these children from a variety of facets and perspectives. To be emphasized of course is that they are children. They are more alike than dissimilar from any other nonabused child. The reader who is interested in knowing what abused children are like would be advised initially to know what children are like, i.e., infants, toddlers, latency age and adolescents. It is beyond the scope of this book to review normal child development. And yet it is essential to have a knowledge of normal child development to understand this special group of children, abused and neglected children. For only with such a backdrop can one appreciate how abused children differ and do *not* differ from other children. For those who have had little experience with normal children, several references are included on normal child development.[1]

In addition to describing abused children's characteristics, there is also a need to explore the factors which have led the abused child to being who he is. Four separate factors will be considered in various chapters:

1. The characteristics of the child which may have increased the likelihood of his/her being abused. Chapters Three and Four address this question in some detail.
2. The physical abuse *per se*. The type, nature and severity of the physical trauma does affect the child's development, especially when the injury involves the central nervous system. The effects of the trauma will be addressed throughout Section 1 with special attention to this in Chapter Six.
3. A third factor which has drawn insufficient attention is the effect of the various interventions which take place after abuse has been identified. The

effects of our intervention schemes must necessarily be considered in each of the chapters in Section 1, but will be given special attention in the second section on treatment approaches for abused children.

4. Finally, the area of concern which is addressed in this chapter, the environment of the abused child.

The initial chapter of this section deals with the environment of the abused child because of the professional bias of this author. In my view, the environment of the abused child is the most important factor in the child's life which has impact upon his growth and development. The importance of understanding the complex and multifaceted environment of the child is embedded in the importance of seeing child abuse as a syndrome, not as a single disease or social problem. To avoid the possibility of this being a trite jargonistic statement, it is essential to explore the meaning and implications of viewing child abuse as a syndrome. Hence, a diversion seems relevant as the implications are important and perhaps critical to this author's perspective on abused children.

A syndrome is a group of symptoms, signs and phenomena which when considered together constitute a specific condition or circumscribed entity. The term has been especially useful in medicine when a single exact cause of a condition is unknown. Let us consider an example—rheumatic fever—which may then be used as an analogy. Until quite recently the cause of rheumatic fever was not known. And yet it was a very specific and undeniably identifiable condition. There were various consequences of this syndrome—fever, swollen joints, heart murmur, fatigue, abdominal pain, nosebleed, subsequent heart disease, nodules under the skin, a skin rash, and others. No patient who suffered this syndrome necessarily had all of these symptoms. In each case there were slight differences in the course of the patient. Some patients had no nosebleed, others no abdominal pain, still others had no heart disease. And yet they all had rheumatic fever. The most dangerous aspect of this syndrome was the heart disease, the one aspect which put the child at greatest risk of death. For good reason, then, the first priority was treatment of the heart condition. And yet we could not ignore the fever or painful joints or fatigue. Sometimes treatment of one symptom made some other symptoms worse. For example, large doses of aspirin given to reduce the fever could make nosebleeds more prominent.

Ultimately all analogies break down, so before that point arises, let us consider how child abuse might be understood differently from this perspective. Child abuse also is a syndrome. Our first and most important concern is to protect the child's life, which requires diagnoses and treatment of the physical trauma and intervention to assure that subsequent trauma does not recur. The physical trauma is not the cause of the syndrome, but only a very prominent and dangerous symptom. Deprivation and neglect are also symptoms of this syndrome. Psychopathology of parents may exist as well as serious dysfunction of the family unit. And so on. One perspective is to consider the child as the patient—the victim of this syndrome. The parents may have serious social and emotional problems, the family may be dysfunctional, the community may be outraged and offended. But the child is the victim. Our efforts, whether directed towards the parents or siblings or family unit should have the purpose of helping the abused child. To understand the syndrome requires that we examine all of the symptoms and signs, especially those embedded within the environment of the child.

It is acknowledged that the environment of the abused child is complex and has many facets. One might look at family social conditions, relationship to siblings, geographical considerations or health factors. In this chapter we shall focus primarily on the parents of the child, for two reasons. First is the predominant role parents play in the child's growth and development, more important than any other single environmental factor. And related to this is the awareness that it is the parent who must help any child negotiate the special conditions of his environment. The effect of poverty or wealth, or of rural versus urban life, will largely be shaped by the manner in which the parent of any child helps the child in his reactions and adaptations to those varying types of environment.

To understand the environment of the abused child, we will use two different approaches. The first will be to review what is known about the parent of the abused child, the second will be to try to view the family from the child's position.

The literature is replete with articles, books and treatises on the abusing parent. Rather than listing and reviewing each, I should like to touch briefly on the works of five different groups who have differing data and perspectives on the abusive parent.

The most helpful data for me have been found in the work of the "Denver group" with various works by Steele, Pollock, Helfer and Kempe. Steele and Pollock, psychiatrists for adults, described their findings and impressions of 60 abusive families in Kempe's 1968 book on *The Battered Child.*[2] Since that original contribution, Steele has had continued extensive experience with abusing parents and has appropriately altered and modified his understanding of such patients. A very nice summary of his experience can be found in the 1975 booklet published by the Office of Child Development.[3] Therein he lists and discusses eight characteristics of abusing parents. They are listed but not discussed here.

1. Immature and dependent. The dependence may be on the child or on a treatment setting or on the therapist.
2. Social isolation.
3. Poor self-esteem.
4. Difficulty seeking or obtaining pleasure.

5. Distorted perceptions of the child. This is primarily discussed in terms of Morris and Gould's treatise on the role-reversal phenomenon.[4]
6. Fear of spoiling the child.
7. Belief in the value of punishment.
8. Impaired ability to empathize with the child's needs and to respond appropriately. I would go further and suggest that most abusive parents are only minimally able to empathize with anyone other than themselves; their children, spouse, friends, employers, etc. This relates, I believe, to these people's seriously impaired concept of object constancy, a hypothesis which will be addressed later.

Steele has primarily focused on the intrapsychic dynamics of the abusing parents, although he has not ignored the multiple factors in the life of the adult which affect his behavior. He has made no pretense of studying a necessarily representational group of abusing adults. However, experience with a wide variety of abusing families, including various ethnic groups, differing socioeconomic groups, rural and urban families has tended to corroborate the features Steele and Pollock first identified. At any rate, his formulations empirically have stood the test of time and experience from most workers around the country and in other Western countries.

A second approach could be highlighted by the work of Gil. His book appeared in 1970, and while it is quite different in orientation, it is of considerable value to any serious student of child abuse.[5] He surveyed a large number of abusing families, a group of over 12,000 abused children, from 1967 to 1968. His data are largely demographic and statistical. He has taken a more sociological view of this syndrome. For him, the cultural attitude permitting the use of physical force in childbearing is the common core of all physical abuse of children.[6] For Gil, child abuse must be viewed, if not exclusively at least primarily, in terms of the environmental factors in which it is embedded. Gil reports he found most abusive families to come from low income, poorly educated urban families. Fifty-five percent of the parents had not finished high school, 48 percent of the fathers were unemployed, 43 percent of the parents had a history of deviancy in social and behavioral functioning, 29 percent of the families had no man in the home.

Lystad has reviewed the literature and focused on social and cultural aspects.[7] And yet, to consider social phenomena such as violence or crime or alcoholism only on the basis of the cultural matrix in which it is primarily found has not been a terribly helpful approach for the clinician facing a patient with such a problem. And further, his data are open to question on the basis of not being adequately representational of abusive families. Most experts comment on the propensity for middle- and upper-class families not to be reported to official agencies and on the fact that most studies of abuse are done in medical or social agencies which by definition serve the lowest socioeconomic classes.

And while Gil's data are extremely valuable and helpful, I would be remiss if I did not acknowledge my serious disagreement with his statement "Physical abuse is by and large not very serious as reflected by the data on the extent and types of injury suffered by the children in the study cohort." Or, "Even if allowance is made for underreporting, especially of fatalities, physical abuse cannot be considered a major cause of mortality and morbidity of children in the United States" (p. 138).

In contrast to Gil's work, Newberger and Hyde point out very nicely in their 1975 paper that when public awareness campaigns highlight the importance of reporting abuse and systems are developed to facilitate reporting, the increase in recognized abuse and neglect may be astronomical.[8] Take for instance the fact that in 1968 in California there were approximately 4000 reported cases of abuse and neglect—and that in 1972 there were over 39,000. Or the Florida experience, where the number of reported cases of abuse and neglect rose from only 10 cases in 1968 to almost 30,000 in 1972; or in Michigan where the reports rose from 721 to 16,000 in those same four years (p. 707). It would seem clear then that there has been an underestimation of the pervasiveness of this syndrome. Further, one will undoubtedly minimize the consequences of child abuse if only the physical damage to the child is considered; whereas, the toll the children pay in terms of mental retardation, learning difficulties, unhappiness and emotional conflict is immense.

A third report on abusive families deserves our attention. That is the work of Smith, Hanson and Noble.[9] In their paper *Parents of Battered Children: A Controlled Study*, they imply they have a representational group of abusive parents in Britain, although this claim is of questionable validity. Nonetheless, they studied the parents of 134 battered infants and children under five years of age and of 53 control children admitted to hospital as emergencies. They found the psychopathology and sociopathy of the abusive parents impressive. For instance, they found 76 percent of the abusive mothers and 64 percent of the fathers to have abnormal personalities in comparison with only 14 percent of the control parents. While only 3 percent of the abusive parents were viewed as psychotic, they found 14 percent of the mothers and 37 percent of the fathers as having severe personality or psychopathic disorders. They found that one-half of the abusive mothers had intelligence scores in the borderline or defective range. It is difficult to know how to explain this last piece of data as this has not been the experience of most investigators. It certainly raises the possibility, in my mind, that many of those parents who score low in I.Q. tests have reasons other than impaired intelligence for their low scores, i.e., poor education, anxiety, depression, etc.

Smith, *et al.* also found that 29 percent of the fathers and 11 percent of the mothers had criminal records. In the control group none of the mothers and only two of the fathers had a criminal record. Smith's conclusions and general attitude towards treatment of the parents are pessimistic. He emphasizes that "the tendency to perpetuate child abuse in successive generations is not diminished by supplying extensive medical and social help to battering parents." He quotes Skinner and Castle as showing that 60 percent of children who are returned home are rebattered. I would remind the reader that such conclusions are not shared by many and especially not by the experience of the Denver group. Rather, I would suggest that if such poor results are occurring, that the quality and type of treatment should be critically examined—and that rather than giving up and removing the child from the custody of the parents, improved and more extensive types of intervention should be sought and provided. Further, as will be discussed in more detail later, the effects on the child of being permanently separated from parents for whom he has attachment, love and familiarity, provides a whole new set of potentially harmful and traumatic events for the child to adapt to.

There is still another kind of valuable data on abusive parents from the work of Lenoski. Unfortunately, his work has not been published, so little detail can be included here and critical analysis of his methodology and results is not possible. However, it is of note that he has interviewed 674 abusive families and 500 controls who came to a California hospital. He highlighted the social isolation of these families by noting that while 88 percent of the control group had a listed telephone, only 10 percent of the abusive parents did. The majority of the abused children were wanted and were born to married couples—indeed there were more illegitimate births among the control group. The abusive mother was more likely to have delivered a premature baby, and there was six times greater probability that she named the baby after herself or her husband. Unlike Smith, Lenoski found the abusive families better educated than the control parents, although in keeping with Steele he found them to have been poorly reared themselves as children, and as adults to be socially isolated with a distorted expectation as to what the child would mean to themselves and their family function.

I have wanted to point out the four types of information on abusive families noted above, inasmuch as they are all founded in different approaches to understanding such families, and furthermore, in my view, all have important and valuable information and implications for the clinician. Clearly it would be impossible to review the work of many more contributors, many of whom have also made extremely valuable contributions to understanding the milieu of the abused child. Rather than undertake that extensive task, which would be of limited value to the reader, I direct the reader to one more bit of literature, a 1972 paper by Spinetta and Rigler, *The Child-Abusing Parent: A Psychological Review.*[10] In this valuable review, Spinetta and Rigler very nicely review the important work done to that point. They indicate that most of the experts in the field agree on three points: (a) that abusive parents were themselves abused or neglected, physically or emotionally as children; (b) that abusive parents share common misunderstandings with regard to the nature of childrearing and look to the child for satisfaction of their own parental emotional needs; (c) that only a few of the abusing parents show severe psychotic tendencies. The disagreement among various investigators and clinicians comes in describing the source of the aggressive impulses. The two authors of this review emphasize that all abusing parents are not the same and are particularly impressed with Merrill's attempt to develop a typology for abusive parents.[11] Merrill found abusive families falling into one of three clusters. Very briefly they are as follows:

1. Parents with continual and pervasive hostility and aggressiveness, sometimes focused and sometimes directed at the world in general.
2. Parents with characteristics of rigidity, compulsiveness, lack of warmth, lack of reasonableness and minimal pliability in thinking and belief. There was considerable rejection of the children. These are the types of parents who feel self-righteous and defend their right to act as they had in abusing their child.
3. The third group shows strong feelings of passivity and dependence. Many were unassuming, reticent and very unaggressive. The parents often competed with the child for the love and attention of their spouses. Generally depressed, moody, unresponsive and unhappy, they are immature people.

The Child's Perspective

I turn now from this brief foray into investigations of abusive parents to attempt to view these families from the eyes of the infant or child. For specific attributes and characteristics of the parents are relevant here only insofar as they affect the infant and child. For instance, the child does not really care if his parents have a listed phone number. The relevance is found if this is an indication that a child is being raised in a home where there is a mistrust of strangers, minimal contact with people outside the nuclear family, and if there is no modeling for the child as to find enjoyment and gratification from social contact with others. The religious affiliation of the abusive parent is a superficial piece of information to the child developmentalist, unless we can draw inferences from such data to understand the flexibility or rigidity of the parent, and some insight into superegos which will affect the growing child. And so we shall attempt to view the family as the baby might. We run the risk of adultapomorphisation in this controlled regression to speak for the nonverbal child. Nonetheless, it seems like a worthwhile exercise to try to empathize with the child in imagining and fantasizing what his/her environment is like.

From the beginning of prenatal life, the baby is apt to be in a suboptimal environment. As Lynch has demonstrated in Chapter Four, there is a greater likelihood of difficulties and complications of pregnancy which all have the potential to affect the prenatal child. It is even possible that the child in utero may have his first attack here as a number of mothers report being beat about the abdomen by their mates during pregnancy. The emotional milieu of the mother may or may not affect the developing baby. But certainly if the mother has had several babies and is living in poverty, the biophysiologic systems supporting the developing baby will be inefficient and inadequate. It is quite possible that the mother is looking forward to having a baby with extensive fantasies about what the baby will be like and how nice it will be to have the child. However, this mother is not thinking of how nice it will be to take care of a tiny dependent baby, nor the ways in which she will meet the baby's needs and help him/her to grow and develop. Rather she is more likely to be thinking of the satisfactions she will get from the baby, how the baby will love her and care for her and how good the baby will be.

The baby's separation from the mother's womb and entry into the world is likely to be a difficult time. He is at two to four times greater risk than other children of being born before a full nine-month stay in his mother's uterus or being underweight at birth. He is ten times more likely than other children to be delivered by Cesarian section than by the normal and healthy vaginal route. In the nursery, he is more apt to be sick or thrive less well than other babies. It is very likely that from the very beginning of extrauterine life, he is a disappointment to his mother. Like all babies, he recognizes no one, does not smile, is not really all that attractive. He certainly does not at all look like the Gerber ad baby. His sex may be just the opposite of what mother really wanted. His mother will want neither to hold him, nor touch him nor speak lovingly to him. He will probably not be breast fed. When he is brought to his mama, she will hold him awkwardly and clumsily. She may try to prop a bottle so as to not have to hold it and feed him herself. He may have to stay in the hospital nursery when his mama goes home, and neither mama nor daddy is apt to visit him much during this stay.

He finally comes home. Picasso's idyllic painting of mother and baby do not apply here. Feeding, bathing, diaper changes are not experiences where he is held, talked to, touched or handled in a caressing loving manner. The early normal symbiotic relationship of mother and baby as described by Mahler is distorted. The mother is not getting to know him as a person. His needs are not met with alacrity and caring concern. His crying and discomfort are viewed as intrusions on the world of adults rather than as opportunity for the mother to administer to a dependent baby. He does not learn that certain behaviors of his, such as crying, will lead to a change from a state of non-pleasure to pleasure. Indeed, such a behavior as crying may lead to increased nonpleasure. He may be spanked or hit for crying or may be isolated by being put into a room by himself for many hours of his day.

As the baby grows older he continues to experience punishment or unpleasant experiences such as isolation for a variety of normal behaviors, e.g., crying, getting into things, exploring his world, not holding still when being diapered, etc. The responses of the adult people in his world are not consistent or predictable, so the child cannot know what to expect. His world is not a predictable stable world of cause and effect. This continues throughout his childhood. While he may be struck or otherwise punished on occasion for a particular behavior, at other times this same behavior is ignored or may be enjoyed and reinforced by the same adult people. There are even times when the child is encouraged or provoked to "misbehave" by his parents—after which they may enjoy the misbehavior or alternately may punish him/her and show their disappointment and disapproval of the very behavior they have overtly or covertly encouraged. This is a very confusing world for the child. He learns fairly quickly that the mood of the parent is the most critical aspect of the parent's response to him. When the parent is acting certain ways, or giving vibrations of certain mood states, the child knows that he is at high risk for disapproval and punishment, even for behaviors which he has never been taught are bad. To say, "I am hungry" may catalyze an emotional storm on certain days. The child then, to survive, and to try to assure a fantasied atmosphere of being loved, becomes quite expert in reading the environment. He develops an exquisite sensitivity to the mood and emotional status of the adult people around him. The more refined this sense in the child is, the less punishment and disapproval he receives.

The child lives in a world where his parents make demands and expectations on him that are not made on other children. The parents may expect him to be toilet-trained by six-to-twelve months of age. Speech is expected well before two years of age. "Lying" is not tolerated, nor masturbation, nor sassing. At age four he may be expected to babysit a younger sibling, to help with the washing or housecleaning, or to prepare and serve food to others. Some of these expectations are impossible, biologically and cognitively, to meet, leaving the child feeling worthless. He cannot do what his parents tell him he should be able to do. He is a failure, unacceptable and disappointing to the adult people. In other instances, he develops the mechanical skills to meet the parents' demands and expectations. He is not aware that he is precocious in any of his abilities. His successes and impressive skills are not a source of feeling good about himself, for they are what he feels are normal abilities and behaviors for children like himself.

The child is in an environment where he is expected to be sensitive to and responsible for much of the happiness of the adult people in his world. He is expected to comfort mama when she is feeling blue. He certainly is not to make life more difficult for the adult people by demanding, asking for or wanting things. One six-year-old boy accurately reported to us that when his mother was afraid or feeling sad, she would come to bed with him. He would hold her and snuggle up to her to help her feel better. The gift of blarney may well develop in the young child in his attempts to take care of his parents. The child's response to this environment is variable, but the parents in his environment are asking him—no, *expecting* him—to be a source of comfort and sustenance to them.

He is in a home where there are very few contacts outside his nuclear family. His parents rarely ever have friends come in. They do not go out to socialize or to have fun. Indeed, there is very little laughter in his home. People do not play games, especially not with him. His parents never laugh at themselves, nor see the humor in everyday events. He has very little contact with other children. As he grows older, he is made aware that his parents do not want him to develop relationships and liaisons outside the home—be they with peers or other adults. He has no opportunity to see how adult people other than his mother and father act and behave.[12] His parents fight a lot—he hears and sees verbal and physical hostility between the only adult people in his environment. They sometimes fight over him—and sometimes either one of them may get irritated or angry in a jealous fashion if he is nicer to the other. While he does not understand it, he continually gets put into "no win" situations. What he is increasingly aware of is the continual grinding frustration of his life. How he copes and adapts to this and other aspects of his environment may be quite variable, and this subject will be addressed in later chapters. But for here, a sense of the atmosphere in which he lives makes one uncomfortable and uneasy when one truly gets a feeling of what it is like. Indeed, we have been amazed that more of these children do not suffer thought disorders or outright psychosis.

Our imaginary friend, the abused child, is not expected to have any joy in life. Laughing and elation are disapproved of overtly or less obviously. Further, he does not see any modeling of true happiness and joy in his home. The adult people around him may be abrupt and angry, sad and depressed, distant and aloof, unfriendly and cold—but they are not happy zestful people. He is expected to enjoy being good, doing his chores, helping his mama, and just being around—but life to him is a difficult and serious business. Each day is a day to be gotten through with a minimum of trouble and hopefully without being struck for misbehavior. The child senses that the world outside his home is the same—a hostile demanding environment through which he must negotiate. Given a flower garden, the child sees the weeds to be pulled and the work that is required—he does not see the flowers to be smelled and enjoyed. Given a puzzle to negotiate, he sees a task to be solved, an expectation to be met—he does not see a fun game to be played.

He may be ignored—and his basic needs neglected. He may be in a world where the adult people pay no attention to him, so long as he does not make demands or provide intrusions into their lives. It is more likely that he is in a world where the adult people *do* pay attention to him—not in play or in joy—but in the sense that these adults are very interested in him acting right, acting his age and learning to be obedient. A high premium is put on his being good. And yet it is rarely clarified what good is. It usually means being cooperative and pliable to the demands of mom and dad. Acting his age does not in any way correspond with reality testing, but means acting the way his mama and daddy think a child of his age should act. Obedience is required. This is really what being good means—for he is not taught internal controls or an empathetic concern about others, but rather doing what others—the adult people—want and tell him to do. Violence, cruelty, and causing pain to others are not considered bad to him. Indeed, his parents have been violent and cruel and deliberately inflicted physical and psychic pain on him under the aegis of teaching him, helping him and controlling him. His developing sense of conscience is a distorted and tenuous thing.

It might be helpful to consider this child's world in terms of Mahler's conceptualization around the development of object constancy through the developmental tasks of individuation and separation.[13] She has very nicely described the first three years of life for normal children in the context of the developmental tasks of individuating from the primitive symbiosis with mother and separating from the early influential sphere of the mother. One of the basic measurements of a successful and adequate phase of separation and individuation is the development of a sense of *object constancy*. This is a concept that has been confused with the Piagetian concept of *object permanence* (p. 111). For our purposes, the concept of object *permanence* is a cognitive-perceptual level of development wherein the child early in his second year of life becomes aware that objects, animate or inanimate, exist in the world whether or not the child has perceptual clues as to their existence or whereabouts. It is not until that time that the child is aware that a toy, a utensil or a person has an existence outside his perceptual framework. Before then, out of sight, out of mind is the cognitive rule. Elaborate and interesting experiments can be conducted to show that before that time when a favored toy is covered with a cloth, the child does not seek it out—that for the child the toy has no meaning unless he can see, hear or touch it. Mahler's description of *object constancy* is another matter. It refers to the child's ability to appreciate the uniqueness and value of another person (the mother) even when the mother is absent; even when the mother is disapproving; and whether or not the mother is relating to the needs of the child. At this stage, people no longer exist solely in relationship to oneself. Mothers can now be appreciated apart from their mothering role with the child. The child can more objectively and without relationship to *self* appreciate qualities in the mother which do not necessarily have any advantage to the child, e.g., a mother's sense of humor, physical attractiveness, interest or skill in some craft or artform, etc. With this sense of object constancy, the child also has developed a hierarchy of values towards different adults—so that he is not indiscriminately affectionate to all adults—but has greater value and attachment to his parent even if at the time another adult is caring for him and his parent is absent. Adults are not valued exclusively on the basis of their ability to give sustenance to the child. This stage must be reached for the development of empathy, philanthropy, selflessness and altruism.

What does it take to attain this developmental stage? Mahler points out the vicissitudes of the anlage of object constancy. Certainly from early on the child needs a stable and permanent love-object available to him, offering a satisfactory degree of gratification for the child's biological and emotional needs. He needs a parent who is able to allow him to separate and individuate—who can encourage and support his fearful attempts to become his own person. It requires patience in the face of his early attempts at autonomy as they are usually couched in the important early verbalization . . . "No!" It needs the mother who not only will allow the child to go off on his own, but also will be available for the child to check back with her for security, the stage of rapprochement. And this is in a way saying it requires the beginning development of a sense of self by the child—a very difficult and complex task to understand and/or describe.

What does all of this have to do with the abused child and his environment? The child is in an environment where separation and individuation is not encouraged and often not allowed. The requisite "good enough mothering" is not present in early infancy. The beginning attempts at distancing from the symbiotic tie to the mother are not welcomed by the parent. Rather he is in an environment where the parents expect him to orient himself around supplying satisfaction and sustenance to the adult rather than the reverse. He is valued only when he is acting in relation to the parent's needs. Conversely, he is not able to value or cathect the parent except when the adult is relating to him—meeting *his* needs, or punishing him or attending to *him.* The parent models a paradigm where other adults are thought of only in terms of what they can or might do for or to the parent. The parent may have acquaintances, but they will be described only in terms of the joint activities of the parent and the acquaintance. This is even modelled in terms of the mother's and father's interrelationship, and is modelled in the parent's relationship with the child. The child is in an environment, then, where his parents neither model relationships built on a firm concept of object constancy, and where the parents do not encourage, support, or even allow adequate nondistorted individuation and separation by the child, and hence prohibit the acquisition of object constancy by the child.

After abuse has occurred and been recognized by some professional or agency, the environment of the abused child may well change, depending on the intervention strategies. The child is now in a home where his parents have been accused of maltreating him, and the evidence, if you will, for this mistreatment is the child himself. He is a liability, a concrete piece of evidence of the parent's failure in parenting, the basis for litigation and general hassle from society's representatives. The child is now in an environment where the parent's perception of him has changed somewhat. It may be anger, guilt or penitence that is engendered by his very existence in the home. Another alternative is for the child suddenly to be separated from his parents. This may involve being in a hospital—an environment which is inevitably frightening, confusing and terrifying, and which provides no opportunity for prophylactic re-parenting. The reactions of normal children to hospitalization speak to the traumatic environment by its effect on children. The environment may change by the child suddenly being put into a new home with new and different parent surrogates and possibly peers who are also strangers. In addition to dealing with an inexplicable loss of his "beacon of orientation," the child must now suddenly learn to negotiate a home wherein the daily rules of conduct and entire emotional atmosphere is quite different from his prior experience. He may further deal with periodic visits from his parents which are terminated without any understanding of why they are leaving again, and again and again. He may be thrust into a litigious environment, in or out of court, where he is the center of the litigations and accusations, and is too young to understand the sense of it all.

In the months and years to follow, his environment may improve little if any. He may return to the same environment where nothing is changed except that the severity of physical punishments is less. If he is not so lucky, he may find that his adult caretakers change every few months, requiring a readaptation. He has no opportunity for a sense of permanence and continuity to develop. How he adapts, what he thinks and fantasizes, how he copes—these will vary. But adapt he must and cope he must; and inevitably thoughts and fantasies of what this is all about and why life is this way must reverberate throughout his mind and soul.

Subsequent chapters will describe different aspects of the abused child. However, very briefly here it is noteworthy that many of his behaviors can be seen as obvious adaptations and reactions to his environment. The tremendous orality of these children who seemingly can never be satiated with food, affection, or attention is not surprising. The indiscriminate affectionate behavior with strangers is what would be expected. The child's hypervigilance and sensitivity to cues from the adults about him may well have been a critical survival function of the child's ego. His apathy, depression, opposition, and immaturity can all be viewed in terms of adaptation—or consequences to the environment.

As an author rereading the last few pages describing what it might be like to be in an abusive environment, I was impressed that the style of writing shifted—and in some ways paralleled the content—disorganized, boundaryless, and free-associative rather than logical and encapsulated. Perhaps this might be a form of experiential learning for the reader then—not only to cognitively consider what the environment of the abused child is like, but also to experience the sense of uncertainty, impermanence and disorganization in which the child lives. As one tries to feel what it is like for the abused child in his world, it indeed is common to lose one's perspective on reality and secondary process thinking. Insofar as this is true, it may well have implications for the reactions of professionals to the world of the abused child and the influence it has on his/her professional judgments.

Summary

Inasmuch as there is no one template for an abusing family, the task of describing the environment of the abused child cannot be succinctly and validly undertaken. Innumerable variations on several themes will be the rule. Some children live with psychotic parents, in a psychotic or schizophrenogenic world.

Some live with sadistic or alcoholic or drug-addicted parents. Some live with parents who, except for an occasional loss of impulse control, provide fairly normal healthy parenting. Some live in abject poverty, much like the families Polansky and others have described wherein the apathy and hopelessness of the bleak environment is perhaps the most important shaping aspect of the child's world.[14] Nonetheless, the environment of the abused child as described above is a common one, albeit not exclusive to abused children. It should be kept in mind that the environment may change as parents act and behave differently with children of different ages and developmental levels. Further, even in adults without special problems, growth and development of parents goes on so that 20-year-old parents are not the same people they are fifteen years later when they are in their mid-thirties. There is no more only one type of abusive environment than there is only one type of abused child. Yet, I refer you to the opening statements in this chapter in regard to the value of conceptualizing certain phenomena as syndromes. Despite differences and various emphases on different components of the situation, child abuse is a syndrome. There is value in understanding as much as we can about the usual, common, or frequent signs, symptoms and pathogenesis of the syndrome.

I remind the reader again of the purposes of this chapter. The physical assault to the child is but one of several harmful components of a mosaic of child abuse. The child's subsequent neurologic, cognitive and emotional development will in large part be more related to the abusive environment in which he has been developing than the effect of the physical assault *per se*. Hence, to keep a focus on the victim of this syndrome, the child, we must consider the entire syndrome if we are to understand and be able to help the patient, the abused child.

References

1. Readings in Child Development:

   a. Lewis, M.: *Clinical Aspects of Child Development*, Philadelphia: Lea & Febinger, 1971.

   b. Illingworth, R.S.: *The Development of the Infant and Young Child—Normal and Abnormal*, Baltimore: Williams and Wilkins, 1972.

   c. Stone, L.J., Smith, H.T., Murphy, L.B.: *The Competent Infant*, New York: Basic Books, 1973.

   d. Knobloch, H., Pasamanick, B.: *Gesell and Amatruda's Developmental Diagnosis—The Evaluation and Management of Normal and Abnormal Neuropsychologic Development in Infancy and Young Children*, New York: Harper and Row, 1974.

   e. Mussen, P.H., Conger, J.J., Kagan, J.: *Child Development and Personality*, New York: Harper and Row, 1974.

2. Helfer, R. and Kempe, C.H.: *The Battered Child*, 2nd edition, University of Chicago Press, 1968, 6:103-148.

3. Steele, B.F.: *Working with Abusive Parents from a Psychiatric Point of View*, DHEW Publ. #OHD 75-70, 1975, U.S. Gov't. Printing Office, Washington, D.C.

4. Morris, M.G., and Gould, R.W.: Role Reversal: A Necessary Concept in Dealing with the "Battered Child Syndrome," *Amer. J. Orthopsychiat.*, 1963, 33:298-299.

5. Gil, D.G.: *Violence Against Children*, Cambridge, Mass.: Harvard University Press, 1970.

6. Gil, D.G.: Unraveling Child Abuse, *Amer. J. Orthopsychiat.*, April 1975, 45:346-356.

7. Lystad, M.H.: Violence at Home: A Review of the Literature, *Amer. J. Orthopsychiat.*, April 1975, 45:328-345.

8. Newberger, E.H., Hyde, J.N.: Child Abuse: Principles and Implications of Current Pediatric Practice, *Pediat. Clinics of N. Amer.*, August 1975, 22:695-715.

9. Smith, S.M., Hanson, R., Noble, S.: Parents of battered children: A controlled study. In A.W. Franklin (Ed.), *Concerning Child Abuse*, New York: Churchill-Livingston, 1975.

10. Spinetta, J.J., and Rigler, D.: The Child Abusing Parent: A Psychological Review, *Psychol. Bull.*, 1972, 77:296-304.

11. Merrill, E.J.: Physical Abuse of Children: An Agency Study. In V. DeFrancis (Ed.), *Protecting the Battered Child*, Denver: Amer. Humane Assoc., 1962.

12. Bronfenbrenner, U.: The Origins of Alienation, *Scientific Amer.*, August 1974, 53-61.

13. Mahler, M.S., Pine, F., Bergman, A.: *The Psychological Birth of the Human Infant: Symbiosis and Individuation*, New York: Basic Books, 1975.

14. Polansky, N.A., DeSaix, C., Sharin, S.A.: *Child Neglect: Understanding and Reaching the Parent*, New York: Child Welfare League Publ. #618, 1972.

 *Chapter 3*

Which Children Get Abused: High Risk Factors in the Child

Harold P. Martin

There has been considerable interest in the types of parents who are likely to bash their babies and children. This has naturally evolved into an interest in being able to predict which parents may abuse as contained in such work as that of Kempe,[1] Helfer[2] and Schneider and Gray.[3] The original premise of the Denver group was that child abuse grew out of specific types of psychopathology of parents. Insofar as that hypothesis was valid, then naturally enough identification of those psychopathological characteristics would forewarn us of a family at high risk for abuse. This approach is valuable, but it was soon acknowledged that other factors would either heighten or diminish the risk of child abuse, given a certain set of parental personality characteristics. Sociological data became important, as Gil[4,5] has emphasized the role that "chance" sets of circumstances play in igniting the syndrome of abuse. One might argue that chance is not the correct term to use. For example, if a woman has certain personality characteristics placing her at high risk for abuse, that risk might be greater if she is married to a similar type of mate. And we so commonly see the poor choice of mates by abusing adults as to suggest that it is hardly chance that two potential abusers marry each other. Income level, unemployment, size of family, distance (physical or emotional) from family, and educational level are a few of the social factors which may alter the risk of abuse. Kempe and Helfer[6] pointed out several years ago that there are three factors needed for abuse to occur—a certain type of adult (the abusogenic parent), a crisis, and a special child. While this leaves out the role of sociological factors in favoring or diminishing the actuality of abuse, it does point to two other factors—a crisis—and the role of the child.

Little need be said here about crises, except to emphasize that the crises that the abusive parent reports may not be considered crises by most people. The important element is that the abusive parent may react to an event, however minor, as a major crisis or catastrophe. This crisis may be being tired, the breakdown of the washing machine, the husband being late for supper. In all fairness, the crisis may be more devastating in the hard light of reality—e.g., the loss of a job, an abortion, learning of a mate's infidelity. Nonetheless, the clinician must look for the adult's perception of a crisis rather than objective data that one has occurred.

Finally, we turn to the child. It has been suggested that only "special" children are abused. As with the role of crisis, the important element is whether the parent perceives the child to be abnormal. Nonetheless, the implication may be that abused children are often different, special, or abnormal—with examples given of mental retardation, brain damage or birth defects. While there are certain conceptual differences between this view and my own, the value of such a paradigm is to emphasize the characteristics and events in and around the child which do play a role in the abuse syndrome. Some children are more likely to be abused than others given the identical parents. It is the purpose of this chapter to examine the factors in the child which may place him at higher or lower risk of being abused. Dr. Lynch explores an aspect of this question in Chapter Four.

Let me hurry to clarify one point regarding the role of the child in the abuse syndrome. Children do *not* congenitally invite abuse. Abuse does not grow out of some biologically inherent masochism of babies.

The role of the child in the abuse syndrome shall be considered via six different facets. While it is readily acknowledged that there is considerable overlap in these different categories, it is deemed most helpful to start from a viewpoint of considering each separately.

1. *Attributes of the child making him more difficult to care for and/or less capable of reinforcing good "mothering" from parents.* Lewis and Rosenblum's recent book,[7] *The Effect of the Infant on Its Caregiver*, stresses what parents and clinicians have intuitively known for years, namely, that the infant has an effect on the behavior of his parents. As stated in this book, "Social interactions between the young and the parents involve the reciprocal exchange of behaviors with positive value. . . . The infant's responses that have positive values for the parent . . . are the contribution of the young to social interaction" (pp. 15-16). In the theoretical structure below,[8] the healthy state and loving behaviors of the child engender or reinforce normal parenting from the parent figure.

STRUCTURE A:

Average Expectable

PARENT ⸻⸻▶ Feelings and Behavior Toward ⸻⸻▶ CHILD

    1. Expectation of child
    2. Desire for child
    3. Capacity to give

4. Ego strength to adapt to stress
5. Ability to accept imperfections
6. Realistic fantasies of child

STRUCTURE B:

Engendering or

CHILD ─────────────▶ Reinforcing Normal ─────────────▶ PARENT

Parenting from

1. Absence of defects or imperfections
2. Matching of parent's expectations
3. Healthy state
4. Loving behavior (smiling, cuddling, thriving)

The issue then arises that there are babies who have limitations in their capacity to be "good" babies. The most striking example of this type of baby is the infant with very definite, but minimal dysfunction or delay in central nervous system function. This type of infant is particularly difficult for parents to relate to. Furthermore, professionals frequently overlook the subtle manifestations of CNS dysfunction. Even when identified as slightly different from other babies, an infant with such mild differences does not represent such a deviation from the norm that support systems come into play to assist and support the family. If a newborn is identified as sick, retarded or having congenital defects, then professionals, friends, relatives, and various agencies are in sympathy with the parents. In the latter case, the child is clearly identified as different, as a problem, and as a special set of circumstances with which to deal.

A newborn with mild CNS dysfunction or delay, however, engenders no such reactions and support systems. He is usually thought to be completely normal by professionals and friends of the family. He does not look different, no diagnoses or labels have been attached to him, and people assume that he is an average child requiring no special attention. And yet let us consider this hypothetical child. He is a difficult baby to parent. He eats poorly, chokes easily, does not mold well to the adults shoulder. He is difficult to diaper or manipulate physically. He may be quite irritable and fussy and difficult to console. Alternately, he may be apathetic and quiet, giving very little feedback to the parent. If he has persistent or strong primitive reflexes, such as the symmetric or assymetric tonic neck reflex, tonic labrynthine reflex, or startle, the physical handling and caring for the child are quite difficult for very obvious mechanical neuromuscular reasons.

At this Medical Center there is a Special Well Baby Clinic where children are seen for medical attention who have historical bases for considering them at high risk for neurologic damage of dysfunction. Babies who were born prematurely or who grew poorly during pregnancy; babies born of women with complicated pregnancies; babies who had special medical problems in the newborn nursery; these types of children are followed along in this Special Well Baby Clinic until it can be determined whether or not their neurological function is a special problem, or alternately that they are completely normal. Our experience in this clinic[9] corroborates the hypothesis that babies with very mild degrees of neurological immaturity or dysfunction greatly stress the ability of the mother to love and attend to them. With acknowledgment of the special difficulty such babies are to care for, and with helpful suggestions for how to more easily feed, hold, dress and care for these babies, most of their mothers are able to become much more affectionate and loving with their babies.

Let me clarify this issue a bit. I am not suggesting that children who are grossly different or unusual are necessarily at greater risk of being abused. Indeed, our experience and research studies have indicated that neither children who are congenitally mentally retarded, nor children with birth defects or significant brain damage, nor babies with special medical problems such as cystic fibrosis, hemophilia, or osteogenesis imperfecta, are more apt to be abused than their normal counterparts. Smith and co-workers[10] found in their recent study an unusually higher percentage of abused children with birth defects who were thought to be inherently mentally retarded. Sandgrund, *et al.*[11] report that upon identifying a group of abused children, an unusually high percentage of them were functionally retarded at the time of identified abuse. The implication is that these children may have been retarded pre-abuse; and a further implication is that the children might have been abused *because* they were retarded. And yet this has not been our experience. We have not found more than 2 to 5 percent of abused children with significant medical or developmental problems of a congenital nature. We do find that most abused infants and young children function retarded at the time abuse is identified. However, this is usually not an inherent retardation of intelligence and it improves with environmental improvement, be it foster placement, treatment of parents, or educational therapy in a preschool or day care setting. Furthermore, even if and when we detect signs of brain damage or mental retardation in an abused child, it must be kept in mind that 25 to 50 percent of children identified as physically abused have been seriously abused *before.* The hypothesis cannot be ignored that where we see true neurologic damage in the abused child, the cause of that damage or dysfunction may well be previous physical assaults from the parents.

The author of this book has worked in a child development center as a developmental pediatrician for the past nine years. In that center, the patient population is primarily children with mental retardation and other types of neurologic damage and/or dysfunction. It has not been my experience, nor that of experts in the field of mental retardation, that physical abuse is a common or frequent phenomenon. There are various ways that parents react and adapt to having a defective child,[12-18] and physical assault of the child is not a common reaction of such parents. Rejection of the defective child may well be an adaptation, with the most glaring example of this the institutionalization of the newborn by the parents, a procedure which, by the way, used to be recommended by most professionals, and unfortunately to this day is still recommended by some practicing physicians. The point to be made here is that the overt, obvious and significantly different baby is not at higher risk of abuse in our experience. Inasmuch as some investigators have conflicting reports, this issue needs to be addressed by other workers in the field.

However, the child who is different from other babies, but not in such a manner to make these differences obvious and not in such a manner to bring in support systems to the parents, may well be at higher risk of abuse. The child who is colicky, fretful and difficult to care for is not reinforcing parenting behaviors or loving affect. The very exciting work of Brazelton[19] in documenting subtle differences in babies—a logical extension of the original work of Chess, Birch, and Alexander[20]—establishes without question that some babies are more adaptable and are easier to live with and care for than other babies. Whether the basis for the individual differences are viewed as inherent differences in temperament, as Chess and others have done; or whether one looks at the differences in terms of inherent variations in the strength of impulses or drives or coping mechanisms as Freud[21] suggested many years ago; or whether the baby's behavior is a manifestation of some structural or biochemical delay or aberration in the tissue of the central nervous system; the result is the same. This is a child who is more difficult to live with, to care for, and to love. This is a child who, given a parent with a high potential to abuse *any* child, is at *greater* risk of abuse than a more compliant, adaptive and loving sibling.

There are some children, then, who seem completely normal to the usual examination and appear to be normal babies to parents and other adults and yet are more difficult babies to care for and are less capable of the kinds of behaviors which reinforce loving parenting behavior. Given a parent with tenuous capacity to relate adequately in a mothering way to any baby, this difficult baby adds an additional barrier to a normal child-mother interaction.[22] If and when such a child is born to a more adaptable and stable mother, this risk of impaired child-mother interaction is less relevant. On the other hand, when a child is born with obvious and significant differences, such as with medical disease, mental retardation, or birth defects, while the mother-child interaction may be seriously distorted, it is not common for that interaction to be played out in the form of child abuse.

2. *Chance events affecting mother-child relationship.* Dr. Lynch's work, reported in Chapter Four, points out various medical problems which are related to child abuse. Some of these problems may relate to the issue of attachment which is discussed below in point three. Yet others do not as easily fit into that category. For instance, Lynch has found that difficulties in the pregnancy are more common in the past history of battered babies than that of their siblings. This is to say, that given the same mother and similar sociological factors, when

an abusogenic mother has serious medical problems during the pregnancy, she is more apt to batter the baby of that pregnancy than her other babies. Similarly, there are events which may occur postnatally which increase the risk of abuse in certain mothers.

Why should these events be found more often in the child who is physically abused? Exactly how these events increase the propensity to batter a baby is unclear and open to conjecture. It may be, given a mother with a high probability to abuse a child, that any added stress during the pregnancy or early life of the child is that extra stress which, Helfer suggests, is needed to ignite abuse. Certainly among the factors that Lynch found more often in abusive mothers, all of these stresses were associated with the baby. "If it had not been for this baby, I wouldn't have had these troubles," may well be the thinking of the abusive mother. Anger and disappointment at medical complications may well be transferred to the child who in some way may be thought to be the cause of the medical illness or complication.

It is not only medical complications which intrude into the mother-child interaction. In a study of babies who were nutritionally neglected, Chase and I[23] found that many of the underfed children whose fathers had deserted the mother during the pregnancy had been named for the deserting father. This made it especially easy to see how this mistreated child must have been a constant reminder of the man who deserted the mother. When other social stresses such as this occur, it is not uncommon to see the mother blaming the infant. Babies frequently get blamed for mothers' sagging breasts or changes in the husbands' affectionate behavior to mothers. Resentment of the baby may well begin during the pregnancy as the developing baby in utero becomes part of a fantasy system of the mother. Such mothers express such fantasies when they declare that the baby is making them ill, or the baby is kicking them so hard, or the baby is why their husband left them. It seems simplistic, but perhaps valid, to assume that the anger and resentment the mother may feel is easily transferred to the baby who in some way is seen as the cause of the change in the mother's life with which she is so upset.

In addition to the specific behaviors of the child, then, chance events may be attributed to the baby and can increase the risk of physical abuse. Again, the core ingredient in the child abuse syndrome is a parent with the psychopathological factors which place her at a greater risk of abusing a child than some other parent. However, given this propensity, such chance events may be the extra stress required to ignite the actuality of child abuse.

3. *Disruptions in attachment.* Bowlby's classic works on attachment[24] have taken new dimension, given the recent research of Kennell and Klaus.[25-29] Klaus and Kennel suggest that there are claiming behaviors of the human mother, not unlike those of other animal species, which are required for optimal attachment of mother and child. They have demonstrated the striking effects of increasing the time that mother and newborn spend together in the first few

days of life and have further postulated that immediate physical contact between mother and newborn significantly effect the mother's behavior toward that child over many years. In a controlled study they showed that with the only variable being the amount of time the mother and baby spend together in the first few days of life, the growth of the child, the attending behavior of the mother at one year of life, and verbalization patterns of the mother to the child at two years of age are all affected in a positive manner.

How does this attachment concept relate to child abuse? To begin with, one might well consider that battered children are much more apt to be born prematurely than nonabused children.[8,30] Klein and Stern[31] suggest from their data that a delay in the mothering process, due to prolonged separation of mother and infant, is a prominent feature in the pathogenesis of the child abuse syndrome. This seems to be a reasonable explanation for the over-representation of prematures in any group of abused children. In our own studies, we have not found that the premature babies were organically damaged children, but we were unable in retrospective studies to document the significance of early separation of baby and mother.

In other studies at the National Center, there has been an attempt over the past few years to look quite closely at the behavior of the mother in the delivery room when the baby is presented to her as well as at feeding behaviors during the first few days. There are striking differences in the responsiveness of mothers to their newly born infants. While these studies are not completed, it is our contention that distortions in the early claiming behaviors of mothers are suggestive of subsequent distortions in mother-child interaction, including child abuse.

Many investigators over the past ten years have been interested in intervening in the usual nursery practices around premature babies because of our awareness that parenting is tenuous with such babies. Brazelton has been struck by the tremendous energy available in young parents for early attachment to their neonates,[32] and enjoins physicians to spend considerable time in helping cement this early relationship. Rutter's recent work on maternal deprivation[33] further explores the differences in attachment behavior and the more mechanistic "imprinting" first described by Lorenz (pp. 17-22).

Any phenomenon which may intervene in the early attachment of mother to child—such as prematurity, illness in newborn or mother, significant life events in the mother's life, psychological stress on the mother—may be an important contributor to the pathogenesis of child abuse. Here again the primary ingredient is the abusogenic adult. Whether that increased potential to abuse is acted upon or not may be greatly dependent on the early opportunities for attachment between child and mother.

4. *Mismatch of the child and the parents' expectations.* The abusing parent is likely to have considerable expectations of his child. It is often the case that precisely when the child is not meeting the expectations of the parent, is the

point at which he will be physically attacked. The expectations of the parents are often unrealistic. The parent may expect the child not to cry, and when the child does, his behavior becomes the catalyst for physical reprimand. The parent may expect the child to be toilet-trained at a very early age. One of our children had his legs broken at eight months for refusal to use the potty chair. Limitless examples of this phenomenon have been detailed in our work with abusive parents.

Terr's 1970 study of ten abusing families[34] is a most helpful account of the distorted perceptions, fears and expectations of abusing parents embedded in quite unusual and occasionally bizarre phantasies. Losanki's findings that abusing parents had more investment and desire for the child than nonabusive control families raises the issue of why they wanted these children and then battered them. What were their wishes, phantasies, expectations of the yet unborn child. In Anthony and Benedek's book on *Parenthood,*[35] two papers[36,37] point out that pregnancy is accompanied by considerable thoughts and expectations of what the baby will be in all parents. Further, many expectant parents review and sometimes revise their memories of their own childhoods. Given these background data, it is fair to assume that most potentially abusive parents, even during the pregnancy, have either unusual or distorted ideas of what the child will be like or have very intense feelings and phantasies of what the child will do for them. What happens, then, if and when the child does not meet these expectations? This situation will most assuredly happen if the parents' expectations are so unrealistic that no child could possibly meet them—as noted in the paragraph above. The parental expectations may not be unrealistic or bizarre, but may be very intensely cathected. Here, chance takes a part in determining whether the child will be able to meet the parents' wishes. The child may be a male when the mother desperately wanted a little girl. The parent may have phantasied a blue-eyed, blond-haired child who would be an active, zestful go-getter; unfortunately, the child may have none of these qualities. The disappointment and anger engendered by the frustration of those expectations may be a critical etiological component in the actualization of physical abuse.

This phenomenon is certainly more easily seen in the older child. Here it is easy to identify unrealistic expectations when the parent expects the two-year-old to have the coordination, social grace and verbal facility of a four- or five-year-old. Here we also see the parent whose expectations may not be so unrealistic or invalid but whose child may not possess the qualities that are valued. The parent may want and need a child who is superbly obedient and socially competent with peers or who has a certain level of competence in intellectual tasks; and the child just may not have the developmental equipment to meet those expectations. Surely this is a phenomenon not peculiar to abused children and abusive families; for the offices of pediatricians are full of parents whose concerns center around disappointed hopes and expectations, often unconscious to the parent. But given a parent with a greater than average potential to physically mistreat a child, the difference in whether or not abuse occurs may well reside in the capacity of the child to meet the parents' expectations. Whether or not the child will be capable of meeting those expectations may depend either on chance, i.e., whether or not the biologic equipment is adequate to the task; or may depend on the inherent and developed adaptability of the child, i.e., his capacity to meet environmental stresses and demands in a manner that minimizes the danger to him, either from other people, or from anxiety from within.

5. *The developmental level of the child.* This is a factor which has received too little of our attention. It is clear to most pediatricians or physicians who care for children, that in the normal patient population, many parents vary in terms of their ability to relate to children of different developmental stages. There are some of us who as adults are quite good at meeting the needs of helpless dependent infants, but who react in a variety of ways, to our discomfort, in adequately parenting the nonverbal, exploratory toddler. The verbal preschooler presents a whole different type of child to understand and try to love. Similarly, the latency age child or adolescent is received variably by different parents. Mahler pointed out some years ago the inability of some mothers to help their infants negotiate the difficult tasks of individuation and separation in the first three years of age. The emerging independence and autonomy of the child in the second half of his first year may be met with resentment and depression by the mother who has a need to continue the earlier symbiotic relationship of helpless newborn and mother. Mahler, Anthony and Kestenberg[38-41] have very nicely pointed out the stresses a child at different developmental levels places on parents.

Let us return to the abused child and family. We recognized early on that the younger the child is, the greater the risk of physical abuse. Perhaps this reflects the less mature capacity of adaptability in the infant. However, two other pieces of information suggest this is not always the case. For one, there are some children who are not abused until a later age. A graphic example of this involved a family where the firstborn child was physically abused at 2.5 years of age. He, at age 3.5, and his younger sibling at age 2 were enrolled in the JFK Preschool. The mother contrasted the two children, demeaning the older and idealizing the younger. However, over the ensuing year, she started reporting that the younger child was beginning to become more and more like the older child in his obnoxious traits. Upon talking with the mother and seeing the children regularly over the year, it became apparent that what this mother was complaining about were the emergence of normal behaviors of the two and a half to three-year-old child. Indeed, the second child was finally physically abused at age three. It seemed clear in this case that as the child started developing mastery with peer interaction and enjoyed this; as his cognitive skills and verbalizations increased; as more and more initiative was shown by the younger child, the mother could no longer tolerate the child and perceived him as bad, ungiving, unloving and despicable. We need to extensively investigate those children who are given adequate parenting until they reach certain developmental stages after which the pattern of physical abuse begins. Sexual exploration, and manifestations of a normal oedipal pattern in the child have been seen as triggers to child abuse in not a few parents.

The other piece of data which must impress us is the growing acknowledgment that there is considerable abuse among school-age children and adolescents. The medical profession especially has been ignorant or oblivious to this until the past few years. Much abuse may go unnoticed because school-age children are not examined by physicians or seen unclothed with the frequency of children under age five. Certainly, the experience of many school districts in the Denver area has been that when the school finds ways and means to facilitate the reporting of physical abuse by school personnel, the reporting rate climbs astronomically. There is a considerable and impressively high rate of abuse of children of school age, both latency age and adolescents. Here, too, while the homes may have been chronically suboptimal, still there is often no evidence of previous abuse of these children. As pointed out above, it may well be that certain parents can tolerably meet their obligations to younger children, but, given the stresses of their children during the normal processes of developing into elementary age children or into adolescents, the pattern of physical abuse explodes into reality.

Certain developmental stages and age-appropriate behaviors may be especially likely to result in physical assault from the parent. Hence, the developmental stage of the child may be that characteristic or aspect of the child which is feeding or fueling the abuse syndrome. I am suggesting that the adept child may well inhibit certain of his behaviors as a survival mechanism, much as Anna Freud[42] suggested over 40 years ago that children might. When one is considering then the ingredients or prerequisites of a child-abuse incident, in addition to considering the type of parent, the particular stresses the family is undergoing, and the type of child or how he is perceived, one may well also consider the developmental tasks and behaviors of the child as abusogenic.

6. *The child invites abuse.* In 1964, Milowe and Louri[43] suggested that some children invite abuse. One cannot help but be impressed that this two-page report of comments made by these two scholars has been quoted and referred to in multiple papers and treatises on child abuse; and yet to my knowledge this issue has never been adequately studied in an abused population. Green[44] reported a significant relationship between physical abuse and self-mutilation in a group of schizophrenic children. This at least suggests that in a group of seriously disturbed children who had been physically abused in the past, there was a need or impulse to cause physical pain and damage to themselves.

And so at this point we are left, as is so common, with anecdotal material, personal experience, and hypothetical statements. And yet, it is without apology that it is stated that there are a number of children, abused in the past, who deliberately or unconsciously, covertly or quite overtly, provoke anger, irritation and even physical trauma from adults. All of us at the Denver National Center have noted this in some children, especially when they are seen in their homes. Dr. Steele poignantly describes children who, after some misbehavior, bring their parents a paddle for a spanking. Early in my experience with abused children, I was shocked at the nursing staff reacting to a few abused children in hospital with anger and protestations that, "No wonder that child got abused; I'd hit him too if I had to live with him." More subtle has been the provocation of some children during testing and developmental evaluations in my office. In a study of the behavioral characteristics of abused children, colleagues and I were initially at a loss to explain the large number of children who had provocative behaviors which clearly got them into conflict with their abusing parents. This seems so maladaptive of children in abusive homes. Formal research and in-depth studies of children with such provocative behavior have yet to be done. However, tentative hypotheses and clinical impressions deserve consideration, if for no other reason, to begin a dialogue concerning this phenomenon.

In some instances the provocative behavior of children in abusive families seems to be an expression of aggression through identification with the aggressor. Indeed, some of the abusive parents erratically support and reinforce aggressive behavior in such children, while responding to it with physical punishment at other times. In other instances, especially with the younger child, it seems that the provocative behavior may be the most ready method the child has of getting some attention from his parents. It is as if the child may be equating punishment with love. Perhaps this indeed is the genesis of masochism. It certainly brings to mind the propensity of abusing mothers to marry men who are physically abusive to the wife. Perhaps in a very convoluted way, this early masochism of the child carries in it retaliation, inasmuch as there is often embedded in masochism a considerable degree of derision of the attacking person. And yet, for this clinician, faced with a child who has provoked anger and physical abuse from his parent, these explanations are too complex and convoluted for immediate help in understanding such a child. I must start with the more simplistic question: What is the child getting out of such provocative behavior? Taking a behavior modification paradigm, where are the reinforcers? How is such behavior adaptive, or in what ways can such behavior be viewed as the result of the family environment? Thinking in those terms, then, one begins to think that the child may have been told and treated for so long as if he were a "bad" child that the child incorporates this self-concept and behaves accordingly. The parent may well need the child to misbehave and may reinforce such behaviors even though complaining about them and occasionally physically attacking the child. Perhaps the child is in some manner equating the reaction to his provocative behavior as caring responses—i.e., better a response of anger than of apathy.

At any rate, when one is considering the pathogenesis of child abuse, this sixth parameter of the child must be considered. In looking to see which children get abused, one must respond that in some instances it is the child who has learned, for whatever reasons, to provoke the anger of abusogenic parents.

Summary

I start from the premise that all adults have some potential to abuse their children. However, it is helpful to see this as a gradient or spectrum, where some adults have a very low and other adults a very high potential for acting out their impulses to batter a baby or child. The components of this abusive potential are multiple. Certainly, they would include such factors as impulse control, level of frustration tolerance, tendency to *act* to solve conflicts, the presence of other stresses in one's environment, and the complicated issue of the ability of the parent to altruistically and empathetically see the child as valuable apart from the child's role of gratifying the parent.

We see completely normal children who are abused, regardless of their physical condition, neurologic integrity, sex, length of gestation, etc. Because of the factors within the parent and perhaps additionally the social conditions of the family, a child may well be abused regardless of his condition. Indeed, it is my belief that this is *usually* the situation in the child abuse syndrome. Nonetheless, there are some children who, without some special condition might never have been abused. This is the situation where the psychological makeup of the parent and cultural-social conditions place the child at slightly greater risk of abuse than the general population. However, some characteristic or aspect of the child may then be just enough to tip the balance and ignite abusive behavior from the parent. For example, most premature children are not physically abused by their parents. However, it sometimes happens that a parent who has never abused one of his or her children, given a premature child, does attack this particular child. In the face of a delay in attachment and bonding, or in the face of a neurologic dysfunction that interferes with the parent's ability to adequately care for the child, the potential for abuse is triggered and acted upon. When a child is not able to meet the parent's expectations, or when the child is going through a specific developmental stage of his life, it may be then that he is physically abused. The injury may be partly a response to a provocation of the child.

The victims of crimes are not to be considered as responsible for the commission of the crime. Yet they have played some part in inciting the act of the criminal. The child *is* part of the child abuse syndrome. There are conditions which make him more susceptible—at higher risk of being abused. Unfortunately, most of these conditions are not under his control, and yet they may serve as triggers to abuse.

As we turn to the task of preventing child abuse, one pathway seems to be our ability to predict abuse, or at least our ability to recognize those families wherein child abuse is more likely to happen. In such attempts, we have focused primarily on the psychopathology of the parent, to a lesser degree on those socioeconomic factors which may act as an added stress to the family. It is my contention here that to satisfactorily address the issue of prediction and prevention, we must further consider those factors in and around the child which increase the risk of abuse; given the psychopathological conditions of the family and a stressful environment. It is to this end that I have attempted to address the factors in and around the child which play some triggering role in the child abuse syndrome. It is clear that this is only a beginning but it will hopefully serve as a catalyst to review and investigations by others.

References

1. Kempe, C.H.: Studies in progress.

2. Schneider, C., Helfer, R.E., Pollock, C.: *The Predictive Questionnaire in Helping the Battered Child and His Family* (Kempe and Helfer, editors), Philadelphia: J.B. Lippincott Co., 1972.

3. Gray, J., Cutler, C., Dean, J.: Studies in progress.

4. Gil, D.: *Violence Against Children.* Cambridge, Mass.: Harvard University Press, 1970.

5. Gil, D.: Unraveling Child Abuse. *Amer. J. Orthopsychiat.*, April 1975, 45:346-356, 34.

6. Kempe, C.H., Helfer, R.E.: *Helping the Battered Child and His Family.* Philadelphia: J.B. Lippincott Co., 1972, pp. XIV-XV.

7. Lewis, M., Rosenblum, L.A.: *The Effect of the Infant on Its Caretaker.* New York: John Wiley & Sons, 1974.

8. Martin, H.P., Beezley, P., Conway, E.F., Kempe, C.H.: The Development of Abused Children. *Advances in Pediat.*, 1974, 21:25-73, p. 63.

9. Boggess, P. (M.D.), JFK Center, University of Colorado Medical Center. Attending physician for High-Risk Infant Clinic.

10. Smith, S., Hanson, R.: Battered Children: A medical and psychological study. *Brit. Med. J.*, 1974, 3:666-670.

11. Sandgrund, A., Gaines, R.W., Green, A.H.: Child Abuse and Mental Retardation: A problem of cause and effect. *Am. J. Mental Def.*, 1975, 3:327-330.

12. Martin, H.P.: Parental Response to Handicapped Children. *Devel. Med. Child Neurol.*, 1975, 17:251-2.

13. Martin, P.: Marital Breakdown in Families of Patients with Spina Bifida Cystica. *Devel. Med. Child Neurol.*, December 1975, 17:757-763.

14. Mandelbaum, A., Wheeler, M.E.: The meaning of a defective child to his parents. *Social Casework*, 1960, 41:360.

15. Olshansky, S.: Chronic Sorrow: A response to having a mentally defective child. *Social Casework*, 1962, 43:190.

16. Howell, S.E.: Psychiatric Aspects of Habilitation. *Pediat. Cl. North Amer.*, 1973, 20:203.

17. Richmond, J.B.: The Family and the Handicapped Child. *Clin. Proc. Child Hosp.*, 1973, 29:156-164.

18. MacKeith, R.: The feelings and behavior of parents of handicapped children. *Devel. Med. Child Neurol.*, 1973, 15:524-527.

19. Brazelton, T.B.: Neonatal Behavioral Assessment Scale. *Clinics in Devel. Med. #50,* Philadelphia: J.B. Lippincott Co., 1973.

20. Alexander, T., Chess, S., Birch, H.G.: *Temperament and Behavior Disorders In Children.* New York: New York University Press, 1968.

21. Freud, S.: *Heredity and the Aetiology of the Neuroses,* from *Standard Edition of Freud,* Vol. III, pp. 141-161, James Strackey, editor, London: Hogarth Press, 1962.

22. Ounsted, C., Oppenheimer, R., Lindsay, J.: Aspects of Bonding Failure: The Psychopathology, and Psychotherapeutic Treatment of Families of Battered Children. *Devel. Med. Child Neurol.*, August 1974, 16:447-456.

23. Chase, H.P., Martin, H.P.: Undernutrition and Child Development. *N. Engl. J. Med.*, 1970, 282:933-939.

24. Bowlby, J.: *Attachment and Loss; I: Attachment.* London: Hogarth Press, 1969.

25. Klaus, M.H., Kennell, H.J.: Mothers separated from their newborn infants. *Pediatr. Clin. North Amer.*, 1970, 17:1015.

26. Barnett, C.R., Leiderman, P.H., Grobstein, R., and Klaus, M.: Neonatal Separation: The maternal side of interactional deprivation. *Pediatrics*, 1970, 54:197.

27. Klaus, M.H., Jerauld, R., Kreger, N.C., McAlpine, W., Steffa, M., Kennell, J.H.: Maternal attachment: Importance of the first post-partum days. *N. Engl. J. Med.*, 1972, 286-460.

28. Kennell, J.H., Jerauld, R., Wolfe, H., Chesler, D., Kreger, N.C., McAlpine, W., Steffa, M., and Klaus, M.H.: Maternal behavior one year after early and extended post-partum contact. *Dev. Med. Child Neurol.*, 1974, 16:172.

29. Ringler, N.M., Kennell, J.H., Jarveila, R., Navojoski, B.J., Klaus, M.H.: Mother-to-child speech at 2 years—effects of early postnatal contact. *J. Pediatr.*, January 1975, 86:141-144.

30. Martin, H.P., Beezley, P.: Prevention and Consequences of Child Abuse. *J. Operational Psychiatr.*, Fall-Winter, 1974, VI:68-77.

31. Klein, M., Stern, L.: Low Birthweight and the Battered Child Syndrome. *Amer. J. Dis. Child*, July 1971, 122:15-18.

32. Brazelton, T.B., Koslowski, B., Main, M.: The Origins of Reciprocity: The Early Mother-Infant Interaction. In M. Lewis and L.A. Rosenblum (eds.), *The Effect of the Infant on Its Caregiver*, New York: John Wiley & Sons, 1974.

33. Rutter, M.: *The Qualities of Mothering: Maternal Deprivation Reassessed.* New York: Aronson, 1974.

34. Terr, L.: A Family Study of Child Abuse. *Amer. J. Psychiatr.*, 1970, 127:125-131.

35. Anthony, E.J., Benedek, T.: *Parenthood: Its Psychology and Psychopathology.* Boston: Little, Brown & Co., 1970.

36. Benedek, T.: The Psychobiology of Pregnancy. Chapter 5, pp. 137-152 in reference number 35.

37. Winnicott, D.W.: The Mother-Infant Experience of Mutuality. Chapter 9, pp. 209-244 in reference number 35.

38. Mahler, M.S., Pine, F., Bergman, A.: The Mother's Reaction to Her Toddler's Drive for Individuation. Chapter 11, pp. 257-274, in reference number 35.

39. Kestenberg, J.S.: The Effect on Parents of the Child's Transition Into and Out of Latency. Chapter 13, pp. 289-306, in reference number 35.

40. Anthony, E.J.: The Reactions of the Parent to the Oedipal Child, Chapter 12, pp. 275-288, in reference number 35.

41. Anthony, E.J.: The Reactions of Parents to Adolescents and to Their Behavior. Chapter 14, pp. 307-324, in reference number 35.

42. Freud, A. The Ego and Mechanisms of Defense. In Anna Freud, *The Writings of Anna Freud*, Vol. II. New York: International University Press, 1966.

43. Milowe, I.D., Louri, R.G.: The Child's Role in the Battered Child Syndrome. *J. Pediatr.*, December 1964, 65:1079-1081.

44. Green, A.H.: Self-Destruction in Physically Abused Schizophrenic Children: Report of cases. *Arch. Gen. Psychiatr.*, 1968, 19:171-197.

Chapter 4

Risk Factors in the Child: A Study of Abused Children and Their Siblings

Margaret Lynch

Child abuse can never be seen as simply "caused." Nor is it merely the inevitable consequence of a child being born into a violent and disturbed family.* In every case a sequence of interrelated events leads up to the final catastrophe. While the pedigree of the family generally sets the stage for abuse, the final outburst is a result of the interaction between parent and child.

Abuse is an extreme manifestation of bonding failure.[1,2,3] The formation and maintenance of a healthy bond is a two-way process, influenced both by attributes in the child and by the perceptions and expectations of the parents. Much has been written about the psychopathology of abusing parents; but little is known about the attributes in the child that are likely to provoke attack.

Intensive therapeutic work in Oxford[1,3,4] with families in which child abuse had occurred suggests that bonding failure in such families related in part to the difficult pregnancy, adverse perinatal experiences and early ill-health of the subsequently abused child.

The Critical Path

By laying out the events in sequence that lead up to the abuse a flow diagram or critical path can be constructed. The critical path (Figure 4-1) leading to Rachael's abuse is a good illustration of this bonding failure. At eleven weeks of age she was admitted moribund with bilateral subdurals, fundal haemorrhages, a recent fracture of one femur and an old fracture of one radius. The father had an ordinary upbringing, but mother, the dominant partner, came from a notorious problem family. When her parents finally separated in her early teens she became

*I thank Dr. Janet Lindsay, Dr. Jennifer Dennis and Jacqueline Roberts for advice, discussion and encouragement.

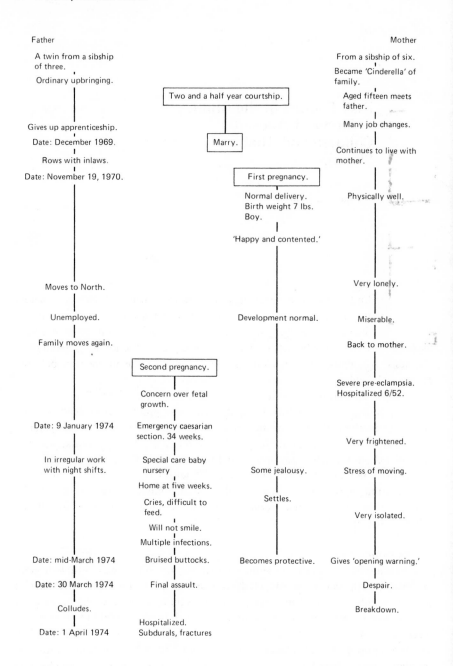

Figure 4-1. Critical Path of Rachael's Family

the "Cinderella" of the household, staying home from school to care for younger siblings. She met her husband when she was fifteen years old, and after a two and a half year courtship they married. A pregnancy quickly followed. They were living amid hostility in the maternal grandmother's house. However, the baby, born after a pregnancy in which mother was physically fit was "happy and contented." They moved to a distant town but because of unemployment soon were forced to return to maternal grandmother. A second pregnancy occurred. Mother became very ill with raised blood pressure and required hospitalization for six weeks, something she resented and blamed on the unborn child. There was great anxiety, among the obstetricians, over the foetal growth rate. Many investigations were performed culminating, at 34 weeks, in an amniocentesis which pierced the umbilical cord. Emergency Caesarean section had to be carried out to save the baby. Mother was horrified at being "cut open." The baby, Rachael, weighing five pounds six ounces, developed respiratory distress syndrome and remained in the special care nursery for five weeks. Mother felt strongly that the baby did not belong to her—"Just flesh and bone—with wires hanging out everywhere," (Mother's words). Ten days after mother had left hospital without her baby, she had the additional stress of moving into her own house. Her husband was now in regular work, but this entailed night shifts. It was difficult to visit the baby. When Rachael came home, no bond had formed between parents and child. She was difficult to feed, cried all the time and always had a cold. Her smile appeared late and was difficult to elicit. Advice with feeding and handling was regarded as interference by this defensive, isolated mother. However, on one occasion during a feeding battle, she bruised the buttocks and immediately called the family doctor. This open warning[3] was not read, mother receiving only reassurance. Two and a half weeks later the final outburst came and mother attacked the child. Forty-eight hours later the child was admitted almost dead to the hospital. This mother whose own upbringing and adverse circumstances increased her potential for abuse, had apparently successfully reared one infant. She was, however, unable to bond to her second child, the product of a difficult pregnancy and operative delivery, who had required care in a special nursery for five weeks. Each of these three sequentially occurring events put this baby at increased risk of abuse.

Abused Children and Their Siblings

In families where all the children are abused it seems likely that the psychopathology in the parents is such that they would abuse any child. In other families only one child, like Rachael, is abused, while the siblings remain at least physically unharmed. In a recent series of 50 families accepted for inpatient therapy at the Park Hospital, Oxford[5] because of actual or severe risk of abuse, 30 children had already been unequivocally injured. These children came from 28 families. Sixteen had only one child. The remaining twelve families had two or more children but only two had physically abused more than one child, in both instances twins. The parents of such families often claim the child they have abused is different and more difficult to rear than his brothers and sisters. This feeling is often shared by workers in the field, but there have been no detailed data to confirm this.

A separate study in Oxford compared 25 abused children with their 35 unharmed siblings.[6] The contrast between the abused and their siblings emerged with clarity. The use of this internal control group, instead of the usual matched controls or population figures, keeps parents' pedigrees, biographies and personalities constant, highlighting the importance of factors surrounding pregnancy, delivery and early life of the abused child. Statistical studies showed six factors to be highly significantly overrepresented in the proband biography as compared with the sibling group; abnormal pregnancy; abnormal labour or delivery; neonatal separation; other separations in the first six months; illness in the first year of life and illness in the mother in the child's first year of life.

To appreciate fully the impact a child has on a family, his biography must be followed from the moment of conception. Thus, the first five of these factors are all potential at-risk factors readily identifiable in the child's biography.

This study will be described and discussed in some detail.

Patients and Methods. All 25 children considered had been unequivocally abused, the injuries ranging from relatively minor soft tissue damage to life-threatening cerebral haemorrhage. The general characteristics of the families were consistent with the referrals to our service as a whole and descriptions given by Gil[7] and Steele and Pollock.[8] The families did not come predominantly from any one socioeconomic group. While there was a high incidence of illegitimacy within the families, it was higher among the non-abused siblings, of whom nearly a third were illegitimately born. More of the abused, it was claimed, were planned children. There were no significant sex differences either in the proband or the sibling groups. Half of the children were under one year of age when referred. The abused child could be anywhere in the sibship (Table 4-1). The majority were the youngest; but ten had one or more younger siblings.

In all cases, information obtained from the parents about the pregnancies and

Table 4-1. Risk Factors in the Child

Place in Sibship of Proband

1/2	2/2	1/3	2/3	3/3	1/4	2/4	3/4	4/4
4	11	0	3	4	0	2	1	0

Numerator: Birth order of proband.
Denominator: Total number of children in family.
E.G.: 2/4 = Proband was second of four children in family.

early life experience of the children was checked against obstetric, neonatal and paediatric records. Where appropriate, social work and family doctor records were also consulted.

The results were as follows.

Abnormal Pregnancy. Pollock and Steele[9] describe how an abused child may be the product of a difficult pregnancy. Poor antenatal attendance has also been recorded.[10] In the Oxford study abnormality in pregnancy was defined as: any complication requiring investigation and/or hospitalization before admission in labour or for induction. Pregnancies where the mother had severe emotional problems, concealed the pregnancy, refused antenatal care, or was refused termination were all also included. Preterm deliveries when the pregnancy itself was considered to be normal until the time labour commenced were excluded. Sixty percent of the proband and 20 percent of the sibling pregnancies were abnormal (Table 4-2). Taking only the pregnancies in which the mother required hospitalization before term, a fact that can be established without any doubt, 40 percent of the mothers required hospitalization with the proband pregnancies, while it was required in only three (8.6 percent) of the sibling pregnancies (Table 4-3).

Abnormal Labour and Delivery. This was defined as: prolonged labour last-

Table 4-2. Abnormal Pregnancy

	Abnormal	*Normal*	*Total*
Proband	15	10	25
Sibling	7	28	35
Total	22	38	60

$$\chi^2 = 8.40$$
$$p< = .01$$

Table 4-3. Mothers Admitted to Hospital During Pregnancy (Apart from Delivery)

	Admitted	*Not*	*Total*
Proband	10	15	25
Sibling	3	32	35
Total	13	47	60

$$\chi^2 = 6.74$$
$$p< = .01$$

ing over 24 hours; preterm labours resulting in deliveries of infants of 36 weeks gestation or younger and all operative deliveries except those described as easy lift-out forceps. Induction alone was not considered to be an abnormality. Not included were labours and deliveries which the mother (or father) described as horrifying or excrutiatingly painful, where no abnormality was recorded by the attendants. These significant observations, while they may be valuable in a prospective study are very difficult to measure retrospectively. Forty-eight percent of the abused group could be said to be the product of an abnormal labour or delivery. In labour with the siblings, these same women were notably free of complications. With only two of the 35 (5.7 percent) siblings were there abnormalities of labour or delivery (Table 4-4). In both cases Caesarean sections were performed. In the proband group there were three Caesarean sections, all resulting in infants requiring admission to the special care nursery. Only one of the two section siblings had to be so separated.

Neonatal Separation. In Oxford all healthy babies stay at their mother's bedsides. Only babies requiring special care, the small prematures, the small for dates and the sick are admitted to the special care baby nursery.

An increased incidence of "Prematurity" and low birth weight in abused children has been reported in several investigations.[11,12,13,14,15,16,17] An increased incidence of neonatal separation was mentioned by several of these workers and others.[10] Klaus and Kennell[2] saw the battered baby syndrome as the most dramatic evidence of a disorder of mothering in which prematurity or serious illness leading to separation was a precipitating factor, and Steele and Pollock[18] emphasize the distressing effect congenital abnormality and prematurity have in vulnerable families. The part the behaviour of such children might play in disturbed bonding is discussed by Martin and Beezley.[19] In the Oxford study neonatal separation was defined as 48 hours or more in a special care nursery. Many of these separations were caused by serious and lengthy illness, for example, the very preterm infant requiring assisted ventilation for respiratory distress. Forty percent of the abused group were separated with only two (5.7 percent) of the siblings requiring similar separation, (Table 4-5). Interesting comparisons can be made between the admission rates for the abused children,

Table 4-4. Abnormal Labour/Delivery

	Abnormal	Normal	Total
Proband	12	13	25
Sibling	2	33	35
Total	14	46	60

$$\chi^2 = 11.49$$
$$p< = .001$$

Table 4-5. Neonatal Separation (48 Hours or More)

	Separated	Not Separated	Total
Proband	10	15	25
Sibling	2	33	35
Total	12	48	60

$$\chi^2 = 8.68$$
$$p< = .01$$

their siblings and the general population of neonates born at our local maternity hospital in 1973 (Table 4-6). The proband rate is much higher than the general population, while their siblings were well below the expected. That is, unharmed children of parents who have abused are very healthy in the perinatal period.

Other Separations in the First Six Months. Included in the separated group were all children admitted to the hospital in their first six months without their mother. An increased incidence among abused children of early hospital admission due to congenital abnormality or serious illness has been cited previously.[9,10] In this present study five of the abused and one sibling required hospitalization. Hospitals in our area have facilities to admit mothers with their children. None of the mothers from these families seems to have availed herself of the opportunity, possibly an indication of hostility and fear of the hospital. Not all the separations were due to illness; others were due to fostering or the child being left with relatives or friends for more than two days, while mother herself was in hospital or otherwise away from home. One mother was in jail. Thirty-six percent of the abused children were separated from their mothers in the first six months compared with 5.7 percent of their siblings (Table 4-7).

Illness in the Child's First Year. Intercurrent illness is particularly distressing to parents with high potential to abuse.[8,16] An increased incidence of congenital abnormality has been found among abused children,[10,20] though other studies do not confirm this.[17] The Oxford study looked for all children whom

Table 4-6. Admission to Special Care Nursery

	Admitted	Not Admitted	Total
Proband	10 (40%)	15 (60%)	25 (100%)
Sibling	2 (6%)	33 (94%)	35 (100%)
Population	761 (15.5%)	4164 (84.5%)	4925 (100%)

Table 4-7. Other Separations in First Six Months

	Separated	Not Separated	Total
Proband	9	16	25
Sibling	2	33	35
Total	11	49	60

$$x^2 = 7.03$$
$$p< = .01$$

their parents or doctors reported as seriously or recurrently ill in the first year of life. Thus, both severe illnesses, requiring hospital admission and recurrent minor health problems were included. The abused group were found to be exceptionally ill children: pneumonia, bronchitis, viral carditis with congestive heart failure, pyloric stenosis, severe cleft palate and hare lip, cerebellar ataxia and convulsions were all found. In addition to this there was an abundance of irritating minor health problems. Three children had eczema, there were six with recurrent colic and vomiting, three with failure to thrive. In all, 60 percent of the abused children were significantly ill (Table 4-8). In direct contrast, their siblings were outstandingly healthy.

Adverse Factors. The total numbers of adverse factors in the proband and sibling groups are shown in Table 4-9. Nineteen (76 percent) of the probands had two or more adverse factors in their early lives while 25 (71 percent) of their siblings had none. When comparing each abused child with his or her unharmed siblings, it was found that in only three cases did a sibling have more adverse factors. It was rare to find factors positive in the sibling and negative in the

Table 4-8. Illness in First Year of Life

	Ill	Not Ill	Total
Proband	15	10	25
Sibling	3	32	35
Total	18	42	60

$$x^2 = 16.00$$
$$p< = .001$$

Table 4-9. Total of Adverse Factors In Abused Children and Siblings

Number of Adverse Factors	0	1	2	3	4	5	Total
Proband $N = 25$	4	2	7	5	5	2	61
Sibling $N = 35$	25	6	2	2			16

proband. It was also in the abused group that a sequence of events occurred, one adverse factor following another.

All the five factors described, abnormal pregnancy, abnormal labour or delivery, neonatal separation, other separations in the first six months and illness in the first year, usually bring the family into contact with the medical services and provide an opportunity for mutual recognition of potential child rearing problems. Preventive help can then be offered and in many cases a disaster averted.[1,21,22]

The Siblings. It would seem that the good health and development of the brothers and sisters helped to preserve them from physical harm, while a sequence of minor disasters preceded the battering of the abused. It must not be forgotten, however, that although free of apparent physical injury, the siblings are constantly exposed to the families' abnormal rearing pattern. It is unlikely that they will escape completely unscathed. Detailed ongoing studies into both probands' and siblings' physical, emotional and intellectual development are in progress.

Continuing Developmental Problems

In addition to the well-defined events described in the above study, it seems likely that any continuing medical problem in the child can contribute to the processes leading to abuse. One must always be alert to the possibility of undiagnosed illness in the abused child. Where its presence has been suspected by the parents, but not diagnosed by their medical advisers, the stress will have been all the more acute. One striking example of this was a child, congenitally blind and therefore unable to gaze fixate his mother, who was abused seven times before the underlying abnormality was appreciated.

Other examples presented to our service have included chromosome abnormalities, developmental retardation due to cerebellar ataxia and haemophilia.

Dramatic evidence of how a disease can interfere with the bonding process is given by a family where mother and child both had myotonic dystrophy. The potential for abuse in this family was high. Both parents were from unhappy and divided homes. The mother had a hostile dependent relationship with her own mother, while the father had suffered an uncompromisingly rigid upbringing. They were both very young; the mother just twenty, had had two Caesarean sections within thirteen months. After birth, her second son was very ill and required assisted ventilation for some days in the special care nursery, where he spent the first seven weeks of his life. During his stay the diagnosis of myotonic dystrophy was made, both in himself and his mother. It is likely that the elder sibling is also affected, although the effect on him was less marked.

On discharge home the new baby had a floppy, expressionless face; he made none of the grimaces and little noises a normal baby makes. He was even unable to cry effectively. His smile did not appear. Feeding was a distressing experience.

Much of his time he slept "like a dead baby." His mother was further handicapped by her own inability to use facial expression as a means of communication. It was almost inevitable that no bond formed between mother and child. Soon all those involved in the baby's care, including the mother herself, were fearful for the baby's safety, and help was sought from our service, before neglect or actual abuse had occurred.

These are extreme examples of illness interfering with the bonding process and in some families contributing to the final cataclysm of abuse. Because abusive parents have rich fantasies and high unrealistic expectations of their children, any minor deviation from accepted or expected "normal development," even just being the "wrong sex," which would provoke mild anxiety in any other family might well have catastrophic results. They are likely to see abnormality in their child as yet another criticism of themselves and their ability as parents. The clumsy, slow learning, enuretic child will compare unfavourably with a quicker, better coordinated dry sibling. These parents can also easily be driven to distraction by a very active child or one with a powerfully developed exploratory drive. Any child who steps outside the rigid criterion of what is acceptable in development and behaviour puts himself at risk. Many children try to save themselves from harm by quickly adapting their behaviour, the extreme examples being frozen watchfulness; described by Ounsted[23] and discussed in Peter Appleton's chapter in this volume.

The Older Child

The biography of Gerry and his family (Figure 4-2) illustrates how an older child who steps outside boundaries set by demanding and rigid parents may come to be abused.

Gerry was not severely injured until he was age six years eleven months old. His father lost control and beat him after he had been caught stealing from a local store. The subsequent injuries were discovered and reported by his school teacher. Once again we see a family with a typical biography. Father was reared in a hostile aggressive atmosphere. He chose to break completely with his family in his teens and joined the armed forces. Mother came from a strict home where physical punishment was frequently used. She met father when only fourteen, and they married following an extramarital conception three years later. The pregnancy was a difficult time emotionally; she had to live with her parents, and her husband was away with the military. She had one brief hospitalization before term. The delivery was normal, and the baby, Gerry, was healthy, weighing eight pounds. She found herself unable to breastfeed. The baby was initially good, but not overly responsive.

Soon after his birth the young family moved to a distant industrial town. The mother became very lonely. Soon, however, father was spending more time at home and mother began to settle to married life. A second pregnancy was planned; another boy was born who was successfully breastfed and soon showed

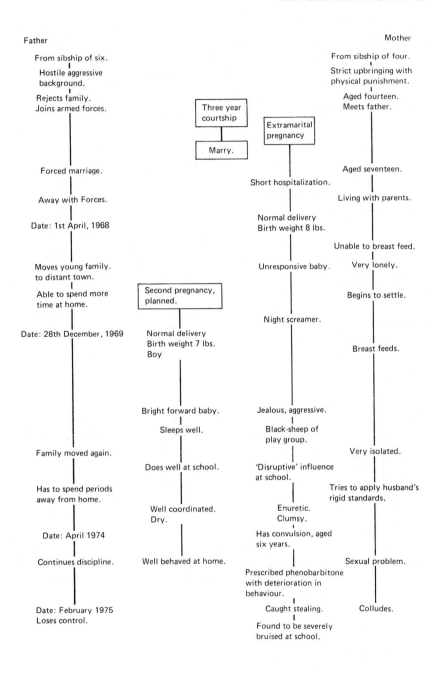

Father

From sibship of six.
Hostile aggressive
background.
Rejects family.
Joins armed forces.

Three year
courtship

Marry.

Forced marriage.

Away with Forces.

Date: 1st April, 1968

Moves young family.
to distant town.
Able to spend more
time at home.

Second pregnancy,
planned.

Date: 28th December, 1969

Family moved again.

Has to spend periods
away from home.

Date: April 1974

Continues discipline.

Date: February 1975
Loses control.

Extramarital
pregnancy

Short hospitalization.

Normal delivery
Birth weight 8 lbs.

Unresponsive baby.

Night screamer.

Normal delivery
Birth weight 7 lbs.
Boy

Bright forward baby.

Sleeps well.

Does well at school.

Well coordinated.
Dry.

Well behaved at home.

Jealous, aggressive.

Black-sheep of
play group.

'Disruptive' influence
at school.

Enuretic.
Clumsy.

Has convulsion, aged
six years.

Prescribed phenobarbitone
with deterioration in
behaviour.
Caught stealing.

Found to be severely
bruised at school.

Mother

From sibship of four.
Strict upbringing with
physical punishment.
Aged fourteen.
Meets father.

Aged seventeen.

Living with parents.

Unable to breast feed.
Very lonely.

Begins to settle.

Breast feeds.

Very isolated.

Tries to apply husband's
rigid standards.

Sexual problem.

Colludes.

Figure 4-2. Critical Path of Gerry's Family

himself to be a bright alert baby, forward in his development. Gerry, who had by now established himself as a night screamer, became very jealous and aggressive towards his rival. He was the "black sheep" of the local play group. The family was soon uprooted again and moved to an isolated base, where Gerry soon became "a disruptive influence" in his primary school. He was clumsy and occasionally enuretic. His younger brother in contrast slept well, was well coordinated and dry: he was a success from the first day at school. Father had rigid ideas on child rearing, his discipline was strict and mother, in his frequent absences, tried to conform to these standards. The family had no close friends.

Gerry was always the one in trouble. Then aged six, on the annual family holiday, he had a convulsion which precipitated his admission to the hospital. He was subsequently shown to have mild photosensitive epilepsy. This added acute anxiety over his future to the mounting tension within the family. To aggravate the situation further, the phenobarbitone prescribed worsened both his temper and behaviour. There followed some months during which the parents tried desperately to discipline their son and to get him to conform to their standards, their own relationship deteriorating drastically. Then Gerry was caught stealing; the final cataclysm occurred; father, with mother colluding, battered him.

Here we see a biography which, on several occasions, moves very close to breakdown. The parents' attitude to child rearing, their environment, isolation and marital difficulties all contributed to the final breakdown. However, it is likely that Gerry's deviation in development made him the target of the final aggressive outburst.

Conclusion

This chapter has deliberately concentrated on the high-risk factors identifiable in the child himself. In reality the events leading up to the final abuse form a stochastic process in which attributes in the child can play an important role. Many families are confronted with the problems minor and major described, some will have child rearing problems, a very few will abuse their child. All, however, can only benefit from a sensitive appreciation of parental reactions to developmental abnormalities or illness and to the effect these can have on a family's dynamics. By taking a holistic view of every child and his family, factors which in isolation are of little predictive value, become, in families with a high potential for abuse, valuable warnings. Only then can we hope to prevent a child saved from a life-threatening neonatal illness being sent home to be battered to death by alienated parents.

References

1. Ounsted, C., Oppenheimer, R., Lindsay, J.: Aspects of Bonding Failure: The Psychopathology and Psychotherapeutic Treatment of Families of Battered Children. *Dev. Med. and Child Neurol.*, 1974, 16:447-456.

2. Klaus, M. and Kennell, J.: Mothers Separated from Their Newborn Infants. *Ped. Clinics. N. Amer.*, 1970, 17:1016.

3. Ounsted, C., Lynch, M.: Family Pathology as Seen in England. *Child Abuse and Neglect–The Family and the Community*, edited by R.E. Helfer and C.H. Kempe. Cambridge, Mass.: Ballinger Publ. Co., 1976.

4. Lynch, M., Steinberg, D., Ounsted, C.: Family Unit in a Children's Psychiatric Hospital. *Brit. Med. Journal*, 1975, 2:127-129.

5. Lynch, M., Ounsted, C.: A Place of Safety. *Child Abuse and Neglect–The Family and the Community*, edited by R.E. Helfer and C.H. Kempe. Cambridge, Mass.: Ballinger Publ. Co., 1976.

6. Lynch, M.: Ill Health and Child Abuse. *Lancet*, 1975, 2:317-319.

7. Gil, D.G.: Incidence of Child Abuse and Demographic Characteristics of Persons Involved. *The Battered Child*, edited by R.E. Helfer, C.H. Kempe. Chicago: University of Chicago Press, 1968 (first edition), pp. 19-40.

8. Steele, B., Pollock, C.: Psychiatric Study of Parents Who Abuse Infants and Small Children. *The Battered Child*, edited by R.E. Helfer and C.H. Kempe. Chicago: University of Chicago Press, 1968, pp. 103-147.

9. Pollock, C., Steele, B.: A Therapeutic Approach to the Parents. *Helping the Battered Child and His Family*, edited by R.E. Helfer and C.H. Kempe. Philadelphia: J.B. Lippincott, 1972, p. 10.

10. Homan, R.R., Kanwar, S.: Early Life of the Battered Child. *Archs. Dis. Childh.*, 1975, (50)1:78-80.

11. Elmer, E., Gregg, G.S.: Developmental Characteristics of Abused Children. *Paediatrics*, 1967, 40:596-602.

12. Klein, M., Stern, L.: Low Birth Weight and the Battered Child Syndrome. *Amer. Journal of Dis. of Childh.*, 1971, 122:15-18.

13. Skinner, A.E., Castle, R.L.: *Battered Children: A Retrospective Study*. United Kingdom: National Society for the Prevention of Cruelty to Children, 1969, p. 5.

14. Weston, J.T.: The Pathology of Child Abuse. *The Battered Child*, edited by R.E. Helfer and C.H. Kempe. Chicago: University of Chicago Press, 1968, p. 83.

15. Smith, S., Hanson, R.: Battered Children: A medical and psychological study. *Brit. Med. Journal*, 1974, 3:666-670.

16. McRae, K.N., Ferguson, C.A., Lederman, R.S.: The Battered Child Syndrome. *C.M.A. Journal*, 1973, 108:859-866.

17. Martin, H.P., *et al.*: The Development of Abused Children. *Advances in Pediatrics*, 1974, 21:25-73.

18. Steele, B., Pollock, C.: Psychiatric Study of Parents Who Abuse Infants and Small Children. *The Battered Child*, edited by R.E. Helfer and C.H. Kempe. Chicago: University of Chicago Press, 1968, p. 129.

19. Martin, H.P., Beezley, P.: Prevention and the Consequences of Child Abuse. *Journal of Operational Psychiatry*, 1974, 1:68-72.

20. Birrell, R.C., Birrell, J.H.W.: The Maltreatment Syndrome in Children: A Hospital Survey. *Medical Journal, Australia*, 1968, 2:1023-1029.

21. Kempe, C.H., Helfer, R.E.: Innovative Therapeutic Approaches. *Helping the Battered Child and His Family*, edited by C.H. Kempe and R.E. Helfer. Philadelphia: J.B. Lippincott, 1972.

22. Kinnaird, D., *et al.*: A children's group and a mother's group for families

in which there is threatened abuse. Manuscript in preparation—Park Hospital for Children, Oxford, 1976.

23. Ounsted, C.: Biographical Science. An Essay on Developmental Medicine. *Psychiatric Aspects of Medical Practice*, edited by Mandelbrote, B. and Gelder, M.G. London: Staples Press, Ltd., 1972, p. 130.

✳ *Chapter 5*

The Abused Child at Time of Injury

Jane Gray and Ruth Kempe

Attention to the abused child has primarily focused on the details of medical injury or failure to thrive. This emphasis is understandable, for it is the physical injury that requires immediate attention. The importance of physicians identifying suspected inflicted trauma is essential to anything more being done to protect and help the child. However, it is also important to be aware of the abused child's behavior so that his emotional attitudes and his interactions with his parents, peers and medical personnel can be integrated into a total family diagnostic evaluation.

There have been a small number of reports of the handicaps and the personality of abused children, but most of these have been gleaned from observations made some time after the abusive incident. There have been few systematic observations of the children at time of entry into the hospital or emergency room. Morris, *et al.*[1] have one of the few early descriptions of the behavior of abused children in hospital. They have emphasized the tendency of normal children in hospital to turn to their parents for help and sustenance in contrast to the absence of this behavior in most abused children. Galston,[2] in his description of hospitalized abused children, emphasizes their marked fearfulness or apathy and makes suggestions for how hospital staff might respond to the demanding behavior of these children in later stages of hospitalization.

When the child presents at the hospital, he is reacting to the recent injury. However, one must also keep in mind that this child has been living in an abusive home for some time. We must therefore take into account the effects of that environment on the child *prior* to this particular incident. The first section of this book details a number of traits of these children, emphasizing both the developmental delays and deficits of so many abused children, as well as the impact of the abusive environment on the personality of the child.

57

The behavior of the child at the time of physical abuse will vary according to a number of factors. It is necessary to take into account the child's age and developmental level, the degree and type of injury, the period of time between the injury and the child's examination, how frequently the physical abuse has occurred, who has accompanied him to the emergency room, his general health status, and especially, the relationship between child and parent.

When children are *first* seen for physical abuse (in the emergency room, pediatric clinic or pediatric ward), the great majority have the same initial behavioral characteristics. In general, most are very frightened, withdrawn and extremely passive. They sit quietly and survey every move of the staff with wide-eyed, frozen watchfulness in an attempt to cue in on an unfamiliar environment and to the unfamiliar personalities of the staff. They rarely can be engaged in an enlightening dialogue about their present injuries, and attempts at conversations are met with a cryptic answer of one or two words or a mere shake of the head.

It should be noted that a medical setting realistically inspires fearfulness and withdrawn behavior in most children, especially when they do not have available to them immediate access to warm, sympathetic support from parents. The system often dictates that a law enforcement officer (a stranger to the child) brings the child to the physician (another stranger) in the medical setting (strange environment). This would inspire fear in most normal children; however, the abused child seems even more fearful and withdrawn than these circumstances would indicate.

The passive, frightened behavior will change a bit as the child begins to warm up and be more comfortable—although this is more commonly seen when the child is hospitalized. Even in the clinic where the child may be kept for several hours, one can see the beginnings of change in the child as his reactions to the new medical setting start to diminish and his more usual personality style begins to take over. Yet clinic staff notice that this tendency to become more comfortable and active is much slower in abused children than in others who will recover their vivacity within a brief period of waiting. As the child becomes more secure, his behavior will shift in one of several directions.

One useful way to categorize abused children is to divide them into those children who have, for the most part, tried to meet parental needs—the children who have "bought into the system," and those who have not bought into the system. Our estimates from the Child Protection Team at Colorado General Hospital suggest that approximately 75 percent of abused children fall into the category of those who are still trying to meet the demands of their parents.

These are the children who are overly compliant and hypervigilant to cues as to how to mold their behavior. They look to the professional staff at the Pediatric Clinic for cues as to how they should behave. Their compliancy is sometimes manifested by rather bizarre acquiescence. Lenoski[3] has even reported abnormal positioning in some of these children. When an extremity is raised and left in this abnormal position, the child between one and three years of age will continue to hold it there in an almost catatonic state. Typically passive behavior is seen at the time of a painful procedure, i.e., during blood drawing or during an injection. During these times the child may lie perfectly still with his arm outstretched. He may neither cry nor struggle as most children do. This type of behavior can also be seen when a child is being dressed after a physical examination. The abused child is apt to lie perfectly still with his legs abducted during diapering, where the normal child would be squirming and crawling away. We often see in those 75 percent of children who are trying to please their parents, a true role reversal—especially in the slightly older child when the injuries have not been severe enough to cause great pain or discomfort. They are mindful of the feelings of their parents. They may try to take care of their parents, bringing them magazines or an ashtray. They may busily straighten toys in the playroom, dust and clean up about the examination room. And yet, paradoxically, these care-taking children are usually quite indiscriminate in their seeming attachment to people. They separate from their parents easily and show no resistance to going with a nurse to a treatment room for a medical procedure. Although they are frightened, their behavior belies such a reaction.

At the other end of the spectrum are the other 25 percent of abused children. These are the children who are not compliant or withdrawn or trying to please. They are variously labeled as provocative, aggressive or hyperactive. These are the children who almost seem to provoke abusive behavior from adults, and one can easily see how abuse could occur. In the hospital these children are shifted from rooms near the nurses' stations to beds progressively further and further away. These are the children who will later "fail" foster care and be shifted from one home to another because of the foster parents' inability to handle them. Their provocative behavior estranges them from care-giving adults.

The behavior of the parents in the clinic is variable. They may be angry at the intrusion of police and welfare agencies and also at the physician or nurse who is interviewing them. They may be worried; however, rarely are they worried about the child, but rather about themselves. This is not the place to discuss at any length the behavior of abusing parents; the major point to be made here is that the parent is usually *not emotionally available to the child.* The parent does not show empathetic understanding and support for the child who is in this very frightening circumstance. And so, from the child's perspective, he does not have a parent to turn to for support and comfort. He must face the physician, the medical procedures and the possibility of separation from parents, all by himself.

In Hospital

The behavior of the child who is hospitalized because of abuse is very similar initially to that seen in the clinic. There are, however, some special aspects of hospitalization which deserve attention. For one, abused children who are hospitalized are a selected group. They usually have more serious and severe injuries. It may be that hospitalization is ordered only to buy time for the professionals to assess the safety of the child's home. In either case, the hospitalization itself is an additional stress for the child, compounding the stress of the injury and the abusive environment in which he has lived. When the child first arrives, he may be in considerable pain if his injuries are severe, particularly if he has much bruising or has sustained fractures. Hence, the initial behavior of the child may be caused by his pain and distress from the physical injuries. A note of caution should be inserted here, that the abused child may have learned to not demonstrate the intensity of his pain and suffering. In this case, the child may be relatively stoic in his reactions to what is obviously a painful injury. As will be pointed out repeatedly, the child's overt behavior may not be a true manifestation of his feelings—neither his physical nor his emotional inner state.

Hospitalization itself is a strange and often terrifying experience for any child. Most abusive families are isolated, and their children rarely have experiences outside the home. Many of them have had little, if any, medical care. Therefore, doctors, nurses, hospitals and clinics may be quite strange to them, and they have had little opportunity to know how they would be treated by medical personnel. It is, therefore, almost inevitable that a young child will be very frightened when he first comes to the hospital and will be in need of reassurance. If he is old enough to understand very simple terms, the pediatrician or nurse can do much to alleviate some of his anxiety by telling him what is going to be happening next.

The third aspect of hospitalization the child must deal with initially is his separation from parents. More commonly than not, children who have been abused show very little reaction to separation from their parents. Sometimes they do not seem to notice when the parents leave. The parents make little effort to explain to them what is to happen and often will make some kind of statement which is deliberately misleading. Possibly this is done so that the parents will not have to deal with the child's presumed anxiety. A few children will protest their parents' leaving. The parents may not respond supportively, or they may encourage the protest as if they are pleased by such demonstration of attachment to them. Therefore, the child gets little help and support in dealing with the hospitalization from his parents. This is, of course, augmented by the fact that the parents themselves are very frightened, anxious and concerned about what is going to happen *to them* and have little energy to spare for the child. There are some children who seem to react to the leaving of their parents with relief, and it is our impression that very many of them are ambivalent concerning the separation. They respond to the kindness shown them by the hospital staff and feel more comfortable with this. At the same time there is usually an underlying sadness and fear when separation takes place. This kind of ambivalence is frequently seen with abused children around other areas besides separation. In spite of the fact that they may have many angry and hostile feelings towards their abusive parents, they also may quite genuinely love the parents and look to them for whatever comfort and care they do get.

The specific behaviors of the abused child during his tenure in hospital will be similar to those seen in the clinic. One will see the majority of children being quite compliant and uncomplaining, sometimes being too cooperative with staff during frightening and painful medical procedures. A smaller percentage of these children, after becoming acclimated to the environment, will behave in a most provocative and oppositional way, with hostile aggressive behavior directed towards peers and hospital staff.

Rather than redundantly list the various behaviors of the abused child, three especially important issues for the child at the time of hospitalization for abuse will be noted.

First is the attachment patterns of the abused child in hospital. Most of these children are quite indiscriminate in their relationships. They may not distinguish between those adults who are with them a good deal and those whom they see only infrequently. Most are indiscriminately friendly, responding with appeasing behavior, smiling at inappropriate times (such as at the beginning of a medical procedure) to anyone who approaches them.

A three and one-half-year-old little boy who had been brought into the hospital with bruises and a basilar skull fracture, seeing a woman doctor walking towards his group in the ward, immediately began walking toward her with a big, somewhat empty smile, saying loudly, "I like you." He quickly attached himself to this new person and followed her down the ward, eager for attention, anxious to play with her and very inappropriately concerned about pleasing her and getting approval in return. On other occasions he was observed comforting his mother and offering to do things for her. Another four-year-old boy with several healing fractures, bruises and severe growth retardation was unable to play with toys or relate in a play interview. Instead he preferred to wander about the ward saying "Hi!" to everyone.

The second, and perhaps the most important issue to be kept in mind, is the disparity between the child's thoughts, feelings and fantasies and the overt behavior of the child. The abused child may not *show* fear and pain when it is appropriate, but he does *feel* them. The passive cooperative behavior of the child is not a reflection of indifference or a true working alliance, but rather is a learned coping mechanism to dangerous and anxiety-provoking situations. The disparity between overt behavior and the child's inner concerns has often been quickly and startlingly demonstrated in psychiatric play interviews.

One little boy of two and one-half years who appeared indifferent to separation from his mother and mildly provocative with the staff was seen in a routine play interview in the ward. Here he spent ten minutes repeatedly throwing the mother doll on the floor saying in a tone of desolation, "Dead! Dead!" over and over again. His own separation seemed to have reactivated his feelings on seeing his mother lying unconscious and ill on the floor months before (as was later brought out in the history).

One little girl of five who had been severely and repeatedly beaten by her mother's boyfriend seemed very compliant, uncomplaining and friendly with the staff. Yet, in a play interview she denounced the boyfriend with considerable anger. When asked what she wished to be when she grew up, she stated that she would like to be a boy. The reason for her wish to be a big boy was that then she could "fight little girls." This unhappy girl could see no safe outlet for her rage other than through identification with her aggressor.

A third issue of importance with the hospitalized abused child is the staff's inquiries around the events of the injury. The willingness and capacity to discuss the injuries and how they were inflicted varies greatly, not only with the age and verbal capacity of the child, but also with his relationship to the adult who has inflicted the injury. Some children are very willing, during the first few days following injury, to discuss what has happened and to describe the reasons for the injury insofar as they are able. Rarely does a child under two have the verbal capacity to respond to any questioning, but sometimes children between the ages of two and three are surprisingly capable of doing so. They may say, "Momma hit me" or "Daddy did it." When asked, "Why?" the child might respond, "Because I was bad." When asked why he was bad, he might say, "I wet." As a child becomes older, he becomes more verbally capable and more sophisticated in terms of understanding the significance of answering such questions. One can see the discomfort children have in being subjected to questioning. Some children will refuse to answer and simply ignore the questions. This is very frequent, particularly with questions which cause considerable anxiety. Other children will attempt to give the same explanation as given by the parents, presumably because of coaching. When confronted with the fact that the father or mother did injure them, some children will then discuss this and describe quite accurately how the injury occurred and the circumstances and reason for it. The willingness to describe the feelings about the injury and the response to the parents is also variable, but tends to be in inverse ratio to the permanence of the relationship to them. For example, if a child is injured by a recent boy friend of the mother's and the mother has indicated that she also blames the boy friend, then the child may feel quite free to accuse the man, to describe exactly what happened and to indicate anger and indignation concerning the injuries. If, however, the relationship between the parents, or the mother and boy friend, is of long standing and the "innocent" parent tends to cover up for the other parent, the child is in a dilemma and finds himself reluctant to make an accusation. If the parent who injured the child is the mother or biologic father, this dilemma increases further. Ordinarily, in this situation if the child describes the parents as punishing and having hit or injured him, the child is very apt to take some of the blame by indicating that it was a punishment for his misbehavior. An example of this is the following statement by a seven-year-old boy who had been whipped with a horsebelt buckle. He stated, "My daddy (step-father) didn't want to punish me but he had to because I messed my pants. He sort of liked to punish me when I did it and although he didn't want to he had to because I was bad. It was my fault that he had to and when I go home I am going to give him a present to make him feel better." Here is seen not only the reluctance to accuse the parent, but also the ready assumption of blame by the child who may genuinely feel that the punishment was appropriate, no matter how severe. He felt that parental expectations were appropriate and that his own behavior was bad enough to warrant such punishment. It has not been our experience that a child will make up a story which implicates any given adult; if a child gives a story at all, it is likely to be true. This statement, however, maintains the reservation that a child may give a story which is identical to that given by the parents but is untrue and the result of coaching by the parents.

Management Issues

The whole issue of making hospitalization as humane and unstressful as possible for any child has been addressed many times. Given the special issues surrounding the abused child in hospital, several specific management issues should be noted.

1. Maximize the consistency of the environment. The child should not be moved from room to room in hospital except for critical medical reasons. The deprived, neglected or abused child should have as much consistency of caretakers as is possible. The same nurse or aide should be assigned to the child for feeding, bathing, etc., from day to day. We have found great benefit in assignment of one or two foster grandparents to the abused child who visit and spend up to four hours daily with the child.

2. Do not be deceived by the behavior of the child which erroneously suggests that he has little affect about his injuries, separation or hospitalization. It is particularly important with the abused child to explain what is going to happen to him before any medical procedure. It will be helpful for the staff to verbalize to the child what the staff feel his reactions truly are. This child needs help in learning to identify his own feelings and thoughts. He also needs help and permission to express them.

3. Use the time in hospital for developmental evaluation. The frequent developmental delays and deviations in these children are discussed more broadly in other chapters of this book. While the child is in the hospital, it is our recommendation that neuro-developmental assessment and psychological consultation should be obtained.

4. Use this time of hospitalization to observe the coping mechanisms of the child. The reactions of the child (as described above) to stress, to peers, to play and to adults can be seen and noted with more clarity by hospital staff than by any professional consultant. This information regarding the personality of the child will be useful to foster parents, biologic parents and to the child protection agency. An understanding of the personality of the child should be helpful in anticipating problems which will be encountered by the child's subsequent caretaker. This information should be the basis for child-guidance counseling for biologic or foster parents.

5. Use the hospitalization to make observations regarding the parents' relationship to the child. Visiting patterns of the parents should be recorded. When parents do visit, their behavior with the child should be noted and recorded. In most instances, the rather significant element of neglect or deprivation will be noted, perhaps most easily seen in terms of the parents' inability and awkwardness in meeting the most basic needs of the child. It is common to see the parents ignoring their own child and relating to other children or parents on the ward. For example, the mother may hold her infant, but far away on the edge of her lap. She may hold her child but talk to someone else and pay no attention to the efforts of her own child to attract her attention. Or, she may sit beside her child or across the room and make no effort to play with him. Both parent and child sit looking awkward and uncomfortable as if they don't know how to interact. Discussions by the nursing staff of the progress of the child are usually met with an obvious need on the part of the parents to talk about themselves. When the parents are with their own child, such basic and fundamental behaviors as feeding the child frequently show considerable ineptness and an inability to relate appropriately to the child at his age.

These observations of parent-child interaction may be helpful in diagnosis and in disposition. Just as important, the hospital staff's observations of the parents should be most helpful to caseworker and therapists for the parents. Their support and therapy for the parents can be more adequately focused if they are privy to the observations of the staff concerning the parents' difficulties in relating to the child.

6. Psychological or psychiatric consultation should be considered for all abused children when hospitalized. This consultation can be helpful in understanding the child and his reactions to the stresses of injury, hospitalization, and having lived in an abusive environment. As noted above, the feelings, thoughts and fantasies of the child may be taped in play interviews and then be fed back to the hospital staff. The staff is better able to be helpful to the child in hospital if they know more about the child's inner psychic life. Psychological consultation may especially be helpful toward management when the child is provocative and aggressive, i.e., when his behavior is upsetting to ward staff. Staff are frequently uneasy about knowing how to deal with these children, and such consultation can be most helpful in establishing management guidelines.

In summary, we are suggesting that while hospitalization is indeed a stressful event for the abused child, it does give hospital staff the opportunity to help the child learn to master stress. The time in hospital can be used so that hospitalization is truly a therapeutic event for the child. It is a time when staff can learn to know and understand the child, his development, his reactions to stress, and his coping mechanisms. Staff can help the child identify and express his feelings and thoughts about himself and the many stressful events in his life. The child can learn in this setting that adults can be consistent and trustworthy. Hopefully, the child can use this experience to learn new ways to cope with stress and new ways to view himself and others.

References

1. Morris, Marion G., Gould, Robert W., and Matthews, Patricia J.: "Toward Prevention of Child Abuse," *Children*, Vol. II, No. 2, 55-60, 1964.

2. Galdston, Richard: "Observations of Children Who Have Been Physically Abused and Their Parents," *American Journal of Psychiatry*, 122:440-443, 1965.

3. Lenoski, E.F.: Paper presented at Seminar on Child Abuse, Denver, September 30, 1974.

General References

Elmer and Gregg, "Developmental characteristics of abused children," *Peds.*, 1967, 40:596.

Freud, Anna: "The role of bodily illness in the mental life of children," *Psychoanalytic Study of the Child*, 1952, 7:69-81.

Prugh, Dane, *et al.*: "A study of the environmental reactions of children and families to hospitalization and illness," *American Journal of Orthopsychiatry*, *XXIII*, 1953, 70-106.

Richmond, J.B., Eddy, E., and Green, M.: "Rumination: A psychosomatic syndrome of infancy," *Peds.*, 1958, 22:49.

Robertson, James and Joyce: "Young children in brief separation," *Psychoanalytic Study of the Child*, 1971, 26:264-315.

Solnit, A.J.: "A study of object loss in infancy," *Psychoanalytic Study of the Child*, 1970, 25:257-272.

 *Chapter 6*

Neurologic Status of Abused Children

Harold P. Martin

The medical consequences of trauma to a child are many and varied. Before addressing the neurological sequellae,[1] it must be emphasized that there are other important consequences of the trauma, from the ultimate tragedy of death of the child to scars, burns and the loss of limbs or various organs. These medical consequences have been addressed quite adequately elsewhere and so will not be discussed here. Two points will be made here inasmuch as I believe they have received too little attention, although people working with abused children are certainly cognizant of them. The first is to emphasize that medical and nutritional neglect of a child increases the risk of serious medical consequences to the abused child. When a physically traumatized child is in addition a child in a state of undernutrition or a child who has been chronically ill with poor medical care, his capacity to mend adequately is impaired. His recovery will be hampered by his poor nutritional and medical status. A child with subdural hematomas (hemorrhages under the skull with the potential to cause damage from pressure on the brain) will be more difficult to treat and slower to respond if the child is additionally anemic or protein deficient, or his restorative physiologic processes have been affected by repeated or untreated illnesses.

The second point to re-emphasize here is the impressive presentation of Dr. Caffey[2] which documents the damage to the brain that can occur from shaking a baby. Its special relevance is in realizing that a baby can suffer significant damage to his brain with no *outward* sign of damage to the head such as bruises or fractures of the skull. Similarly, blows to the abdomen with no or minimal external signs of injury may cause serious internal damage. It certainly raises the possibility that when abused children are first recognized as functioning in the retarded range of development, the retardation could be related to earlier undiagnosed and undetected central nervous system injuries such as those Caffey describes.

Neurologic Examination

Let us now turn to a consideration of the neurologic status of abused children. I do not consider it a digression to take up from the start a consideration of what is meant by neurologic status. Let me begin by admitting that that term has different meanings to different children's physicians and certainly other meanings to professionals from other disciplines. It is incumbent on the nonphysician to clarify what the child's doctor means when he speaks of neurologic status of the patient.

To most physicians, to speak of the neurologic status of a child is to refer to what that physician found on his examination of the neurologic system of the child. Therein lies our first dilemma, since physicians vary in the type of neurologic examinations they routinely and proficiently perform.

The most traditional view of a neurologic assessment should be considered first. Neurology started as a field which undertook to understand the neurologic problems of *adults*—which meant primarily the study of disease or dysfunction based on structural pathology. If an adult had a tumor, or a hemorrhage or a cyst or death of a portion of the brain from trauma, he had something wrong with the structure of the brain—and the neurologic examination was designed to clarify the effects of that structural pathology on the neurologic function. Further investigations, especially laboratory in nature, might help the neurologist divine the cause of the structural pathology. Later, infections of the nervous system, seizure disorders not associated with structural pathology (epilepsy) and even metabolic causes of brain damage fell under their area of expertise. The neurologic exam then, while requiring an examination of neurologic function, was based on finding evidence of structural damage. This type of neurologic exam is what is traditionally and usually taught to medical students. With such an orientation and examination, for example, it is not unusual to find the neurologic examination to be completely normal on a person who is mentally retarded. The mental retardation itself may or may not be considered evidence of neurologic damage or pathology. Certainly, an assessment of intelligence may not be included in a standard neurologic examination of a person. At best the intelligence may be cursorily assessed through intuition or a few brief questions to the patient. The examination, while varying from one physician to the next, focuses on eliciting knee jerks and other reflexes; testing muscle strength, coordination and bulk; seeing whether the subject is receiving sensations such as touch, smell, pain, sound; determining whether balance and coordination are adequate; special emphasis on whether things mentioned above are symmetrical and whether the twelve major nerves which supply sensation and muscles of the face (called the Cranial Nerves) are all functioning normally. Developmental issues are not considered. For one, there is little difference in what one expects to find in a 20-year-old and a 50-year-old. When a physician is limited to the traditional examination of the nervous system, there will be a large number of children who are reported out of his office as having a "normal neurologic examination" and yet who clearly have neurologic dysfunction and pathology. Even the adult who has behavior obviously representing a dysfunctioning nervous system, such as an adult with a seizure disorder, may have a "normal neurologic examination." The physician is not meaning to imply that the neurologic system of the individual is without problems or pathology, but only that on the examinations he did as a doctor, he found nothing abnormal. The difference may be subtle, and certainly is frequently confounding to the physician and the nonphysician alike.

The neurologic examination of children is quite another matter, especially for one who is developmentally oriented in regard to children. First is the fact that most neurologic problems of children are not caused by structural pathology that can be detected by the standard neurologic examination. Numerous neurologists have commented to their chagrin that their clinical tools of examination are so often not helpful in evaluating and clarifying the neurologic problems of children, especially newborns and infants. Consider for a moment the kinds of damage to the brain that might result, for instance, in retardation of intelligence. Lack of adequate oxygen to the brain (anoxia) during pregnancy, labor, delivery, or in the postpartum period will result in a diffuse damage not usually limited to a defined part of the brain. Similarly, diffuse bleeding from many small vessels results in damage in a scattered fashion in children, unlike the results of a massive hemorrhage from a large vessel as is seen in the stroke victim. Abnormalities of the chemistry of babies, or metabolic disturbances as exemplified by PKU, or low thyroid function all affect the brain, but not a discrete area of the brain. So, in assessing the neurologic system of children we are faced with factors almost idiosyncratic to children. First is that many of the types of pathology from which they may suffer are not circumscribed structural defects or discrete structural damage. In many instances, a traditional neurologic examination may fail to reveal any abnormality. Even when there are obvious abnormalities on the examination, such as in the case of children with significant cerebral palsy, the findings on examination may not correlate with a specific type of damage to a specific part of the brain.

The neurologic examination of children then must focus on function, not structure. What can and can't this child do? Can he walk, talk, name colors, turn over, hop, etc? We are not so much trying to divine what and where damage might exist, as we are looking to see how well and age-appropriately the nervous system of the child is functioning. And further, the key words here are *age-appropriately*. For in children, development is a confounding albeit an exciting additive factor. The neurologic functions of the four-month-old are quite different than those of the fourteen-month-old. The nervous system of the fourteen-month-old has different capacities than that of the 24-month-old, and so on through childhood.

The nonmedical professional frequently comes across the term, "soft neurologic signs," and is unsure of its meaning. Let me assure you that that same uncertainty is shared, perhaps less candidly, by medical doctors. There are various ways this term has been utilized. To my mind, there are two aspects of "soft" neurologic findings which may be helpful to keep in mind. The first is that such findings may refer to a physician's judgment as to the inferior quality of some function of the patient. As we look at the neurologic function of children, one component of our examination, for example, is to assess the motor (or muscle) development. One can artificially divide this into two areas. The first is to determine if the child has age-appropriate motor skill acquisition, e.g., can he sit, pull up, walk, hop, balance on one foot, etc. The second judgment has to do with the *quality* of those neuro-motor acts. Is the motor act (consider walking as an example) as coordinated, or as facilely performed as one expects for a child of that age. This latter statement requires a judgment on the part of the physician and is less quantifiable or objective, with a greater chance for poor inter-examiner reliability. Nonetheless, it is an essential bit of data concerning the neurologic system of the child. It is not enough to know if a child has mastered the skill of walking. One must further consider if the facility and gracefulness of the child's gait is appropriate to his age. If the child's motor acts are clumsy, dyssynchronous or awkward, this suggests that, for whatever reason, the neurologic integrity of the child is in question.

The second category of soft neurologic findings are those examinations which are not part of a *traditional* neurologic evaluation and are usually done only in children. Let me give some examples. Is the child able to perform motor acts across the midline, i.e., can his right hand be used to do tasks such as drawing with a crayon to the left of the midline of his body? This is a neurologic function which develops during the first few years of life. Is there overflow or mirroring? Only with neurologic maturation can a child use certain muscles and inhibit the movement of other muscles. One can have the child perform a variety of tasks, such as having him open and close a fist, or pat his hand on his thigh—and then look to see if the opposite hand or arm, or facial muscles are also being put in use when the child is asked to move only one limb. Activity level, distractibility, attention span, auditory memory span, ability to making increasingly sophisticated perceptual judgments are other examples of neurologic function which are developmental in nature, and inasmuch as they are less "objective" than looking at a knee jerk response are unfortunately called "soft." I would maintain this is a poor description of such neurologic findings, inasmuch as the term soft implies lack of certainty. When a physician who is experienced with children's neurologic function observes variations from the norm such as these, such findings are just as valid and "hard" as determination of reflexes or muscle strength. One must remember that even with such supposedly objective findings as determining the intensity of a knee jerk, no two physicians would necessarily agree in their judgment. Calibrated instruments are not used to

measure either the strength of muscles or the symmetry of the facial muscula-
ture. The physician is making a judgment, just as he does when he listens to a
patient's heart with a stethoscope.

At any rate, the nonphysician should keep these three things in mind. First is
that the physician's statement that the child has a "normal neurologic" probably
means that his examination failed to reveal any abnormalities, but does not
mean that neurologic functions which he may not have assessed are normal, e.g.,
thinking, remembering, articulating, etc. This suggests the second point, that the
nonphysician is entitled to know what the examination of the physician
included. This is valid for any professional assessment of a child. If a
psychologist sees a child and says the intelligence of the child is normal, one is
legitimately entitled to know what the basis of that judgment is. Was that
judgment made on the basis of talking with the parents; or based on clinical
intuition after seeing the child in a school; or based on some test that was given
the child? The judgment of the professional may be, and usually is, valid; but
nonetheless, others have an obligation to know exactly what the professional did
to come to his diagnostic conclusions. This seems particularly pertinent to the
neurologic examination. I certainly want to know whether the examination
included an assessment of the child's developing skills; the quality of his
function; or any assessment of cognitive or personal-social functions. Knowing
the nature of the neurologic examination, then, one may be more knowing in
considering what other areas of the child's neurologic function need to be
assessed. And finally the point is made that "soft neurologic signs" are not
neurologic findings of inferior quality, nor clinical hunches, but are valid
judgments of the examining physician concerning neurologic behavior which are
important signposts of neurologic maturation. They, like all of the neurologic
exam, require experience and judgment on the part of the physician.

Biologic and Psychological Interplay

One further aspect of the nervous system of humans must be considered to
interpret neurologic findings adequately. This is the very intimate and rich
interplay between psychological and biological parameters of neurologic function.[3] To explore this relationship, let us first consider the developmental task
of separation anxiety which starts around one year of age and while probably
never completely disappearing, rapidly dissipates so that its manifestations
should not be handicapping after two to three years of age. One might separately
consider what are the neurologic and psychologic prerequisites of such a
developmental task.

Separation anxiety of children implies that the child gets anxious only when
certain important people (usually the mother) separate from him. This requires
that the child must be able to differentiate his parent from other people, a
developmental task associated with stranger anxiety which starts at four to six
months of age. For this earlier developmental task to be negotiated, the child

must have the perceptual and cognitive maturation to recognize differences in big people; and to know that his mother looks, sounds, smells and tastes different from other large people around him. This requires perception, memory, recall and critical judgment. If those neurologic functions are delayed, so also will be the development of stranger anxiety.

Now given that the child can differentiate mother from other adults, the question then arises as to why he should become anxious when he and mother are not together. Again, first let us look at the biophysiologic aspects. Piaget and others have detailed quite nicely the development of *object permanence* in children,[4] starting in the second half of the infant's first year of life. Early on, the child is not able to comprehend that objects have any life or existence of their own. Things (including people) only exist in terms of their relationship to the infant. A favorite rattle only exists in the infant's reality when he can see it, shake it or chew it. Put the rattle under a diaper or paper, and the eight-month-old child will make no attempt to retrieve it—acting as if it no longer exists—and may even show some surprise when it is returned to his perceptual field. It is only with the development of object permanence that the child can recall in his mind the existence of some favored toy or person and search it out. This is a neurologic ability with tremendous implications. After the infant recognizes the permanent nature of objects, he can then take note that their existence is not *only* for his pleasure. Later with the more complex development of *object constancy*[5] (an important concept of Margaret Mahler), he can appreciate that important people around him (like his mother) have other things in their lives which please and motivate them other than just himself. With the development of object permanence, the child can now for the first time consider the possibility that a toy or a person who is out of sight, *may not be retrievable.* He can now miss something. He has now made the first step which will ultimately allow him to grieve for and mourn for people and objects.

Let us try to empathize with the anxiety of the child when he is separated from his loved ones by considering adult experiences. We have all had the experience of knowing that we keep a wallet or automobile keys in a certain place—a certain pocket or a specific nook or cranny in one's purse. Consider the panic one feels after consummating a very expensive meal when the wallet is not in the place we know it is always kept. We say, "My God, it's lost, where is it, is it gone forever, did I leave it some place, has it been stolen," etc. The psychologic component is there also—danger, not being able to meet the situation, embarrassment, panic, anxiety or whatever. It must be something very akin to this and yet monumentally more intense when the infant suddenly is aware that mother is not with him and displays acute anxiety. Fear, panic and confusion seem to be embedded in this anxiety reaction. Later, with time and maturation, the child will learn to trust in the mother's return—and be comfortable with his own autonomy and independence. Later reverberations of this primitive developmental task may be seen indeed throughout childhood and adult life.

I have tried to point out that neurologic maturation is a prerequisite for the development of stranger anxiety. Rather sophisticated and complex neural connections must develop involving perception, memory, recall, discrimination, thinking and perhaps early ability to fantasize or imagine events and people. This phenomenon of separation anxiety has also been described, almost exclusively so, in psychological terms. For separation anxiety to occur, the child must first have developed a significant attachment to the adult. This whole subject of attachment is an immense psychological concept, the work of Bowlby,[6] Kennell and Klaus[7] and others being exciting explorations into its inception and vicissitudes.

When one sees an eighteen-month-old who is oblivious to separation from a mother figure, one immediately raises a hypothesis. Is this child not truly attached to the adult? Has he had so many changes in mother surrogates that no one adult is any more important to him than any other? Has his behavior been shaped in such a fashion that he does not express his anxiety? Is his seeming apathy an analogue of the institutional child Spitz[8,9] described? Is he an autistic child who relates with humans no more intimately than he does with inanimate objects? Is he so frightened of the parents that he is relieved to be rid of them?

The point is that there are hosts of developmental tasks which require neurologic maturation and also require psychological development for them to develop. Most important, from a clinical viewpoint, when one sees deviations from the norm, one has to consider both components in explaining such deviations.

Consider hyperactivity. It may be due to anxiety or fear—or may be a result of the child's neurologic inability to inhibit motoric impulses and screen out the huge number of stimuli in his environment. Consider the child whose drawing of a person is quite primitive and simplistic for his chronological age. This may be secondary to poor motor coordination. Perceptual-motor dysfunction, or dyspraxia (impaired ability to conceptualize and carry out a motor task) can result in such a production. Some people have used the draw-a-person task as an estimate of the child's intelligence. It is just as possible, however, that the poor drawing of the child is a reflection of his diminished self-concept, or of a reluctance to do what is asked of him, or of a host of other psychological forces.

The inevitable and most valuable question man can ask must be on the reader's mind at this point . . . that is, so what? If the clinician is assessing the central nervous system of the child, the first step he must take is to indicate the absence or immaturity or distortions of the child's neurologic function. He will indicate that certain neurologic functions are deviant, e.g., the child's drawings of people are immature or primitive; the child is significantly hyperactive; the child has no signs of separation anxiety. His first task is to recognize that those are neurologically-based phenomenon. The second task of the clinician is to try to determine why the particular neurologic finding is there. Is the poor drawing a reflection of dyspraxia, or of an uncertain self-concept. Is the hyperactivity due to some chemical abnormality of the blood (such as occurs in PKU) or to behavior which has been reinforced by the child's family. Is the absence of separation anxiety secondary to delay in the development of object permanence (and perhaps reflective of a generalized retardation of intelligence), or a marker of impaired attachment to a mother figure with poorly negotiated sense of trust (in Erickson's epigenetic schema).[10] We deserve answers to such questions. And for the physician to try to answer them, he must first of all attend to such behaviors and consider them legitimate parts of the neurologic examination. To try to make a differential diagnosis in terms of understanding the reason for such deviations, he must have an awareness of the psychologic factors which can result in such neurologic abnormalities. And finally, he must be able to communicate with nonphysicians in a manner which clarifies his thinking and the limitations of his professional expertise.

What of the implications of the interweaving of nature and nurture to the nonphysician? The first consideration is to keep in mind the variation in the neurologic examinations of different physicians. And since most physicians will place some limitations on the extensiveness of their neurologic purview, it should be kept in mind that abnormal or immature neurologic development may coexist with a neurologic examination that indicates no abnormal findings. The second implication is that people other than physicians are needed to understand the neurologic integrity of the child. The child may be abnormally hyperative. Parents, teachers and behavioral scientists may be needed to understand the basis for this deviation from normal. The physician may report a neurologic finding, such as a delay in language acquisition. It is obvious that consultation from a language pathologist may be of help. What is not so obvious is that the observations by the child's teacher or caseworker may be essential to coming to an adequate neurologic diagnosis. The delay in language development may be a result of environmental or personality factors which require the expertise of those who are in contact with the child in more natural settings than the professional's office. The implication then is that the neurologic evaluation of a child may require a multidisciplinary team approach. Inasmuch as psychological factors, family environment, and biologic integrity all play into neurologic function, the experience and expertise of many are needed to adequately diagnose the child's neurologic status.

Neurologic Sequellae of Child Abuse
Finally, we turn to the neurologic consequences of physical abuse and of the abusive environment. The previous remarks seem essential as a backdrop for the reader to assess and make critical judgments about any reported neurologic data.

A number of studies of abused children are reviewed elsewhere in this book. Our own five-year follow-up study[11] of abused children found 53 percent of 58 abused children with some neurologic abnormalities, of which 31 percent were moderate to severe and handicapping the everyday function of the child. The 58 children we studied, while perhaps not a completely unbiased random sample of abused children, did have the advantage of representing less severely injured children than most other studies. Thirty-one of the 58 children had had only soft tissue trauma, with the other 27 having histories of head injury, burns or fractures. Selecting this group of children, then, seems to provide a more representative sample of abused children in general than focusing exclusively on children with fractures or those with medical conditions requiring hospitalization. The mean I.Q. of this group was 92, with a median score of 96.5.

The neurologic examinations of these children resulted in each child being assigned to one of four groupings.

Class 3. Serious and significant neurologic abnormalities including paresis, impaired cranial nerve function and focal signs.

Class 2. Less severe neurologic handicaps and abnormalities including deficiency in proprioceptive, tactile, kinesthetic or haptic perception; hyperactivity; dyspraxia and delay in motor skill acquisition.

Class 1. Mild neurologic findings sufficient for the child to be considered neurologically immature or to have "soft" neurologic findings, but not severe enough for him to show significant *functional* handicap or to warrant a diagnosis of brain damage. Examples include mild gross motor or fine motor incoordination, mild hyperactivity, mild perceptual or sensory distortions and mild dyspraxia.

Class 0. No neurologic dysfunction, immaturity or damage.

For comparing a number of pieces of data, we grouped Classes 2 and 3 together as moderate to severe neurologic dysfunction and Classes 0 and 1 together as no or insignificant neurologic dysfunction.

It should be noted that 43 percent of children with no history of head trauma manifested some neurologic dysfunction (classes 1, 2 or 3). Only in neurologic class 3, severe neurologic impairment, did the physical trauma explain the subsequent neurologic findings.

The eighteen children with moderate or severe neurologic dysfunction had a mean I.Q. of 78.4, while the 40 others in class 0 or 1 had a mean I.Q. of 98.6. On the Peabody Test[12] similar correlations were noted. Children with significant neurologic dysfunction had a mean I.Q. 22.1 points lower than those with no or minimal neurologic findings (p. 0.05). On the Beery[13] test of visual-motor perception, twelve of eighteen children with a history of head trauma, and twelve of fourteen children with moderate or several neurologic damage scored more than six months below their chronological age level. However, only 17 of 35 children in neurologic class 0 or 1 scored more than six months below their age level, with none of them functioning more than one year below age level. None of the fourteen children from neurologic class 2 or 3 were functioning more than two years delayed in visual-motor integration.

Another finding was that those children who had had failure to thrive at the time of abuse were at greater risk of neurologic dysfunction and impaired intellectual function than the better nourished. In an earlier follow-up study of

42 abused children by this author,[14] it was pointed out that failure to thrive occurred twice as frequently in the children who were functioning retarded at follow-up as in those with subsequent normal mental function. The basis for the more pessimistic neurologic prognosis in those undernourished children is not always clear. It is quite possible, of course, that neurologic damage resulted from calorie or protein deficiency. It has been adequately established that during early infancy, permanent irremediable damage to the nervous system can occur secondary to malnutrition.[15] It is just as feasible to consider those abused children who were also undernourished at the time of identification as children where there was considerable and pervasive neglect—both physical and medical neglect as well as emotional neglect or deprivation. Here, too, the literature is convincing that maternal deprivation[16] can result in neurologic damage and dysfunction in spite of adequate caloric intake by the child. At any rate, when an abused child has evidence of neglect, especially nutritional neglect, there is considerably greater chance of neurologic damage if there is no intervention in the deprivation-neglect component of the family.

It is, of course, no surprise that neurologic dysfunction may have been caused by head injuries with subsequent damage to the brain. Slightly over 50 percent of the abused children with neurologic findings had no history of head injuries, skull fractures or subdural hematomas. What was the basis for their neurologic dysfunction? It is possible, but not thought probable from their histories, that they had some neurologic damage on a congenital basis that was unrelated to the abuse or the abusive environment. It is further possible, in light of Caffey's work,[2] that brain damage was inflicted without *evidence* of head injury, or without the child being seen by a professional at the time of an injury. However, a third possibility must be seriously considered, that is that neurologic function is affected by the emotional milieu of the child.

Baron's provocative case report in 1970[17] suggests that neurologic findings of an exaggerated startle, hyperreflexia, and increased muscle tone were secondary to the abusive environment, and not secondary to structural CNS damage. This infant mimicked the picture of organic brain disease. This is a concept which has not been widely accepted, i.e., that environmental factors really can affect a variety of functions of the human nervous system. At best we give lip service to this phenomenon. We do acknowledge that hyperactivity of children may be due to psychological stress. We acknowledge that intellectual function may be inhibited by psychological stress. But it is less well established that psychological stress might affect such neurologic functions as reflexes, muscle tone, coordination, etc. In effect, though, we truly acknowledge that neural physiology is affected by psychological state when we see intellectual ability depressed by inadequate stimulation, maternal deprivation or anxiety. In our follow-up study, we found this to be the case. Those children with a history of head trauma and those with abnormal neurologic exams at time of follow-up were removed from consideration to compare children with minimal chance of organic damage to brain tissue across a number of social parameters. Two factors were seen to be significantly correlated with the I.Q.s of the children, keeping in mind that intelligence is a key neurologic function. There is a significant relationship in these abused children between the environmental factors of instability of the family and of punitiveness toward the child, and the neurological function of thinking and problem solving.

Depending on the type of injuries and depending on the subsequent home environment in which the abused child lives, the neurologic system will be variably handicapped in its functioning. It is certainly fair to say that in almost any group of physically abused children, from 20 to 50 percent of the children will have significant impairment of neurologic function, ranging from severe brain damage to mild but handicapping dysfunction. If the child survives the physical assault, it is the neurologic system which is most vulnerable and critical to subsequent consequences of both the physical assault *per se*, and the abusive environment, both pre- and post-abuse.

While data from a study of elementary-aged abused children is not yet completely gathered and analyzed, it is clear that abused children are at considerably greater risk of having learning disorders in school than their non-abused peers. School personnel have reported to us that children assigned to EH classes (educationally handicapped) are overrepresented by abused and neglected children. The basis for this phenomenon is at least dual. Many of these children have a variety of neuro-cognitive handicaps, including perceptual deficits, language lags and other types of neurologically-based educational handicaps. Some seem to learn poorly because of more strictly psychological factors. The whole issue of learning and cognition will be addressed in Chapter 8. But, it seemed incomplete to not mention this cursorily at this juncture, inasmuch as it is another type of neurologic consequence of abuse and an abusive environment.

I turn now to consider another source of data concerning the neurologic functioning of abused children. At the National Center in Denver there has been a preschool for abused children operative since November 1974. Children are eligible for admittance if they have proven physical abuse in the past six months and are between the ages of 2.5 and 5 years. The operation of this preschool will be discussed in other parts of this book. While considering the neurologic function of abused children, though, it would seem helpful to explore and discuss data gathered from neuro-developmental assessments of these children. The author has tested thirteen of the abused preschoolers. The Revised Yale Developmental Schedules are part of the neuro-developmental assessments. The Revised Yale is a developmental assessment tool made up of test items from the Gesell,[18] the Stanford-Binet[19] and the Merrill-Palmer.[20] It is divided, much as the Gesell Developmental Schedules, into five areas of development: gross motor, fine motor, language, adaptive and personal-social. The thirteen children were not tested immediately upon admission so as to give them some chance to adapt to the school, but were seen early in the course of their educational treatment program, all of them evaluated within the first six weeks of the preschool experience.

Some rather interesting results are being found in these children. I shall focus here entirely on the developmental test scores. The mean scores on this developmental testing at present are as follows.

Fine Motor	D.Q. 97.2
Adaptive	D.Q. 96.9
Personal-Social	D.Q. 95.4
Gross Motor	D.Q. 81.3
Language	D.Q. 81.1
Overall Developmental Quotient:	90.3

Time and time again the developmental functions in gross motor and in language areas were considerably below the child's abilities in the other three areas of the testing. The mean scores point this out nicely with the developmental quotients of gross motor and language being fourteen to sixteen points lower than the quotients in fine motor, adaptive and personal-social development. Eleven of the thirteen children had their lowest scores in either gross motor or language areas.

Observations of the preschool staff, speech and language testing by Dr. Florence Blager, and helpful consultation from Tobie Miller, OTR at the JFK Child Development Center corroborated these developmental profiles. Why gross motor and language? If structural damage to neural tissue was the explanation, why was gross motor delayed so much more than fine motor development? Why should language function be so much more difficult than nonverbal cognitive tasks.

The "traditional" neurologic examination did not help answer this question. No focal signs were noted. None of the children had cerebral palsy. Two of the thirteen had mildly increased muscle tone, and one was slightly hypotonic. Cranial nerves were all functioning well except for two children with mild strabismus. No cerebellar signs were noted. What one did see impressively on the standard neurologic examination was just what was noted on neuro-developmental testing, that is, that these children performed gross motor tasks poorly. They were both delayed in the acquisition of specific skills, such as balancing, hopping, skipping, riding a tricycle, etc., and just as impressively demonstrated very poor quality of gross motor tasks. They were poorly coordinated, maladroit, dyssynchronous, awkward. Even with tasks they could complete, there was more effort required to accomplish the large motor tasks than one would expect. The issue of the language development of these children will be discussed at length in Chapter 7. However, some impressions of this pediatrician may be similar to those of the reader.

I was quite surprised to find such low language scores in these children. As one sits with them, talks with them, plays games and examines them, one is impressed that they have quite good communication skills. A few had mild articulation problems, but no more impressively so than one might find in any preschool-age population. I usually felt I knew what the child was communicating to me, and was similarly being understood by him/her. The receptive language abilities of the child were superior to his/her expressive abilities. As I became aware that on formal testing the language area of the test was a significant area of weakness, I started becoming more critical of the spontaneous communications of the child. Three factors were noted. First was that the child was utilizing nonverbal communication abilities to augment his sparce verbal abilities. And second the very concrete abilities, such as naming pictures, were superior to the more abstract language tasks. For example, one test item asks the child for action agents, e.g., what swims, what flies, what cuts, what burns, what boils, etc. It was on this type of task that the children did quite poorly. On this latter task, there are few boundaries of thought. From hearing one word, the verb "burn" for example, the child has the universe from which to choose an answer. This is quite a different type of cognitive task than when he has a puzzle piece and must choose from ten places to put it. This is quite a different type of cognitive task than when he has a crayon and is asked to draw a shape identical to one he is shown. The third factor in these children's language with which I was impressed was the adaptive nature of some of their verbalizations. Some of the children reacted to the anxiety of leaving the preschool and being with me by immediately asking very personal questions, as if they were taking a genuine interest in me. They inquired as to how I got to work, what kind of car I drove, how many children I had, etc. They used verbalizations when testing tasks were difficult. Instead of refusing tasks, they often said things like, "I can do something different." When asked to imitate a block structure, one child said, "I can make something better." Some of them tried to reverse roles and control the situation by making a block structure or a drawing and then asking me, the examiner, to imitate their productions. In summary then, these children's language ability was not as good as casual assessment would indicate. Much of their communication was nonverbal. Concrete tasks, both verbal and nonverbal, were superior to the more abstract unstructured language skills. And some of their adaptive maneuvers to the testing situation and their anxiety erroneously suggested superior language abilities.

I am raising the hypothesis that the impressive weaknesses in gross motor and language neurologic function are to be understood in the context of the home environments of these children. One might consider these weaknesses in development either as reactions to the home environment or alternately, as modes of adaptations of these children. I am reminded of a much overlooked but classic paper by Coleman and Provence[21] published in 1957. They pointed out that the syndrome of hospitalism or anaclitic depression described by Spitz and others in children in institutions can also occur in children living in their own families. In their paper, the language and gross motor abilities of the children were delayed most impressively. This is a phenomenon we have seen not infrequently at the JFK Child Development Center in children in homes where adequate mothering is not available. This might be understood in terms of minimal stimulation or opportunities for practice. When a child has little verbal stimulation or feedback from his parents, he will show considerable delay in verbal facility. He needs language stimulation for language development to proceed. He needs practice and experience for either language or motor development to flourish. This is seen in infancy in the child kept in bed, playpen or crib. So, one way to consider the delays in gross motor and language development is to consider the absence of necessary environmental supports for adequate development to proceed.

A second way to consider these delays, and in no way mutually exclusive of the explanation offered above, is that for survival, to adapt to the abusive environment, the child inhibits (quite unconsciously) his language and gross motor skills. One is here reminded of Anna Freud's[22] defense mechanisms of children. She points out on pages 93-105 that in the face of external danger (that is, danger from outside the personality of the child himself, in contrast to the internal danger from one's own impulses), one adaptive mechanism of children involves the inhibition of certain ego functions. This is exactly what we are seeing in these children. Consider this quite simplistically. What is the child in an abusive family most likely to get punished for? He *is* likely to be in danger of punishment for getting into things—for running about, for being too active. This is what mothers complain about with children from two to five years of age. This is when pediatricians find mothers coming to them for drugs to dampen 'hyperactivity." Children from two or three years of age up to five also get into trouble for talking. Spitz[23] pointed out very nicely the critical stage when children first say that terribly important word—*no*. This is followed normally a few years later by that equally important word, frequently said in almost perseverative manner, *why*. The child in an abusive family gets hit for "sassing," for questioning things, for complaining about things, for expressing his feelings of aggression, anger or disappointment. For did some old sage not say, "Children are to be seen and not heard?" This old chestnut comes from the same adult-oriented page as "Spare the rod and spoil the child."

What I am raising as an hypothesis for the reader to consider is that the neurologic system of the abused child may at times be best understood if one considers how the particular child's function may be adaptive to his world. Lack of gross motor activity and speech and language development may have high survival value in the child's home. The reason certain neurologic signs are noted in an abused child may not be related to what areas of the brain received what type of biologic damage, but rather that the nervous system of the child is adapting to his environment. So, psychological and environmental factors may not only result in impaired thinking but may also be the basis for tremors, incoordination, impaired perception, delayed language abilities and perhaps even for abnormal muscle tone, hyperreflexia, impaired balance and equilibrium, etc.

Summary

To adequately understand any study of the neurologic consequences of abuse to a child, some understanding of how the central nervous system is evaluated is necessary. Some pertinent issues which frequently cloud and obfuscate an understanding of the neurologic status of children are explored. The interrelationship of biologic organic factors with environmental experiences is also explored insofar as they may each separately or conjointly affect the function and physiology of the central nervous system of the human. These two issues serve as a backdrop to a presentation of some of the findings concerning the neurologic function of abused children. The importance of a multidisciplinary approach to these children is stressed *vis-à-vis* understanding neurologic function. It is suggested that certain neurologic signs traditionally associated with organic damage may be altered by environmental experience. It is further suggested that rather than exclusively considering neurologic pathology as a consequence of environmental events, it may be more helpful to view these deviations as a child's adaptation to his/her environment.

The neurologic system of the child is considered in a very broad sense in this chapter, including many functions which are often considered psychologic or psychiatric issues only. A reminder of their basis in neurophysiology is based on this author's view that we shall best understand and serve our patients if we do not separate the child's personality and more traditional neurologic behaviors. Abused children are at risk for damage and dysfunction from the physical assaults they have suffered. The nervous systems of abused children are also at risk from the psychological and environmental stresses to which they are exposed.

References

1. Heiskanen, O., Kaste, M.: Late Prognosis of Severe Brain Injury to Children. *Dev. Med. Child Neurol.*, February 1974, 16:11-14.

2. Caffey, J.: On the theory and practice of shaking infants: Its potential residual affects of permanent brain damage and mental retardation. *Am. J. Dis. Child*, 1972, 24:161-169.

3. Kalverboer, A.F.: *A Neurobehavioral Study in Preschool Children.* Suffolk, England: Lavenham Press, 1975.

4. Burgner, M., Edgcumbe, R.: Some problems in the conceptualization of early object relationships. II: The Concept of Object Constancy. *Psychoanal. St. Child*, 1972, 27:315-331.

5. Mahler, M.S., Pine, F., Bergman, A.: *The Psychological Birth of the Human Infant: Symbiosis and Individuation.* New York: Basic Books, 1975, Chapter 7, pp. 109-120.

6. Bowlby, J.: *Attachment and Loss.* I: Attachment. London: Hogarth Press, 1969.

7. See References 25-29, in Chapter 3 of this book.

8. Spitz, R.A.: Hospitalism: An inquiry into the genesis of psychiatric conditions in early childhood. In the *Psychoanalytic Study of the Child*, Vol. I, 53-74. New York: International University Press, 1945.

9. Spitz, R.A., Wolf, L.M.: Anaclictic Depression: An inquiry into the Genesis of Psychiatric Conditions in Early Childhood. In *The Psychoanalytic Study of the Child*, Vol. II, 323-342. New York: International University Press, 1946.

10. Erikson, E.H.: *Childhood and Society.* New York: Norton, 1963.

11. Martin, H.P., Beezley, P., Conway, E.F., Kempe, C.H.: The Development of Abused Children. *Advances in Pediatrics*, 1974, 21:25-73.

12. Dunn, L.M.: *Peabody Picture Vocabulary Test.* Minneapolis: Amer. Guidance Service, 1965.

13. Beery, K.E.: *Developmental Test of Visual-Motor Integration, Manual.* Chicago: Follett Education Corp., 1967.

14. Martin, H.P.: The Child and His Development. In C.H. Kempe and R. Helfer (eds.), *Helping the Battered Child and His Family.* Philadelphia: J.B. Lippincott, 1972, 93-114.

15. Martin, H.P.: Nutrition: Its relationship to children's physical, mental, and emotional development. *Amer. J. Clin. Nutrit.*, 1973, 26:766-775.

16. Rutter, M.: *The Qualities of Mothering: Maternal Deprivation Reassessed.* New York: Aronson, 1974.

17. Baron, M.A., Bejar, R.L., Sheaff, P.J.: Neurologic Manifestations of the Battered Child Syndrome. *Pediat.*, 1970, 45:1003-1007.

18. Gesell, A., Amatruda, C.W.: *Developmental Diagnosis.* New York: Hoeber, 1947.

19. Terman, L.M., Merrill, M.A.: *Stanford-Binet Intelligence Scale, Manual for the Third Revision*, Form L-M. Boston: Houghton-Mifflin Co., 1960.

20. Stutsman, R.: *Guide for Administering the Merrill-Palmer Scale of Mental Tests.* New York: Harcourt, Brace & World, 1948.

21. Coleman, R., Provence, S.A.: Developmental Retardation (Hospitalism) in Infants Living in Families. *Pediat.*, 1957, 19:285-292.

22. Freud, A.: The Writings of Anna Freud, Vol. II, 1936, *The Ego and the Mechanisms of Defense.* New York: International Universities Press, 1971.

23. Spitz, R.A.: *A Genetic Field Theory of Ego Development.* New York: International Universities Press, 1959.

 *Chapter 7*

Speech and Language of Abused Children

Florence Blager and Harold P. Martin

Introduction

The speech and language of abused children is a neurologic function of special interest. It is a critical function of the nervous system of humans which is particularly sensitive to any fluctuations in the equilibrium of the child—organic or psychological.

Speech and language is a system of communication and hence not only reflects an aspect of brain function, but reflects the state of interpersonal relationships. While not the exclusive way in which we communicate, it is a primary and critical means of interpersonal communication. Given the psychological problems in abused children, especially in the area of object-relations, speech and language might be one area in which to study this psychological distortion.

Finally, while little detailed research has been done *vis-à-vis* the speech and language of abused children, there are scattered reports of significant delays in this area of function. Martin[1] and Smith and Hanson[2] have both reported delays in the language development of abused children. In Chapter 6 Martin has commented on the delays in both speech and language as well as gross motor function of preschool aged abused children. Even Elmer's recent study,[3] where she and her colleagues were unable to demonstrate many effects of abuse on a follow-up group of children eight years after abuse, does show that expressive language was lower in the abused children than in either of two comparison groups. Anecdotal and impressionistic data from a plethora of professionals who work with abused children all suggest that speech and language stands out as a major deficit in these children.

The basis for our impressions and conclusions about the speech and language of abused children comes from several sources. The senior author has done speech and language assessments in some detail on 23 abused children. Thirteen of these children also were evaluated after a period of therapy. In addition to the test data per se, some comments will be made regarding the behavior of the children during the testing. There are also data from speech and language obtained from less structured sources. One source of the data comes from spontaneous language samples collected by tape recording during the time the child was with the senior author. Less objective information comes from observations of these children in other settings such as in a preschool or a waiting room.

Methodology

The test data on 23 abused children actually must be subdivided as there were two separate groups of children, each of which should be briefly described.

Ten preschool children were tested, all of whom were enrolled in the preschool for abused children at the National Center in Denver. The mean age of these children was 43 months, ranging from two and one-half years to four years of age. All of these children had had documented physical abuse within six months prior to admission to the preschool. This is an important point to note, as these families were still in considerable turmoil. Child protection agencies and the courts were involved with all of the families, and there had been little time for much intervention for either the parents or the child.

The second group of children were thirteen children who were being seen for psychotherapy as part of a research study. Twelve of those thirteen children are described in Chapter 16. These children ranged in age from three years nine months of age to eight years two months, with a mean age at time of testing of five years three months of age. In addition to being an older group of children, there were some other important differences between this and the former group. This latter group of children was being evaluated several years after physical abuse had occurred. All of the parents of these older children had had some professional involved with them in therapy. The families were in less turmoil, although this is not to suggest that the parent-child relationships were normal. Formal abuse in the legal sense was not still operative in these families, while in the preschool children, there were several times when reports of recurrent suspected nonaccidental injury had to be made by the preschool staff.

The younger group of children were administered the Peabody Picture Vocabulary Test,[4] the Houston Test for Language Development,[5] and assessment of articulation.

The older group of children were also given the Peabody, but in addition were given the Templin-Darley Screening Test of Articulation,[6] the Illinois Test of Psycholinguist Abilities,[7] and a Developmental Sentence Score of spontaneous 50-word sentence language samples.

Results

Preschool Group—Almost all of these children were delayed in speech and language on all parameters measured. The Peabody measures receptive language and does not require a verbal response from children. Nonetheless, the ten preschool children averaged ten months below their chronological ages on this test. When those scores are changed to a derived I.Q. score, the mean derived I.Q. was 80 with a range from 65 to 104. It is important to note that this is not an adequate measure of intelligence, but rather only a reflection of single-word receptive language.

On the Houston Test, the child is required to name picture items rather than merely point to them and respond to spoken language on directions and questions. Here, too, the children had scores averaging nine months below their chronological ages.

The articulation of these younger children was quite poor for their age. While formal measurements of spontaneous language were not possible, their speech and language in the preschool showed clear deficits in quantity and in quality. They were able to communicate their needs and other messages either non-verbally or with a verbal form which communicated intent while still being quite deficient in syntax and vocabulary. Pointing, grunting and idiosyncratic verbalizations usually made it possible for adults to know what the child wanted to communicate. This is an important point, inasmuch as the ability to communicate meaning may confuse the adult as to the real deficits in speech and language which exist.

Psychotherapy Group—the test scores on these children were surprising to the examiner. Actual test scores on the Peabody, the Templin-Darley test of articulation, and on the more extensive Illinois Test of Psycholoinguistic Ability (ITPA) showed means at or slightly above average for their chronological age. And yet despite these scores, there were other indications of speech and language deficits which showed up on assessment of less structured language tasks.

The language sample that was taken was analyzed in terms of syntactic structure using the technique of Laura Lee.[8] When these data were scrutinized, it was seen that the thirteen children scored on an average of eleven full months below their chronological ages. The "natural" use of language of these children was somewhat like the findings in the younger children. They communicated meaning and intent quite adequately. These older children had "caught up" in many of the rudiments of language such as vocabulary, articulation, and other psycholinguistic components. And yet, when using language outside a testing situation, the form and complexity of their language was of a younger age. As Rodeheffer and Martin pointed out in Chapter 10, speech and language may be used very adaptively by children to escape difficult tasks, to ingratiate themselves with the examiner, and perhaps to stay out of harm's way. In other words, language was not being used as a means of transmitting ideas, feelings and knowledge. It was as if the language as a "communication" tool had not kept pace with the growth of language as an area of knowledge. The communication tool had remained less mature while language knowledge had matured to age level.

Another finding of note was discovered in analyzing the subtests from the ITPA. Perhaps a few words of description of that particular test are in order. The ITPA has ten different subtests. They are arranged so as to assess various functions which together make up one's psycholinguistic skills. Subtests are divided to look at very reflexive responses, somewhat automatic functions, and higher level intentional language skills. It also attempts to separate out visual, verbal and manual means of receiving or expressing meanings. Most basically, it looks at three separate processes of communication—that of reception of information; processing of that information; and an expressive response to the information the brain has taken in and processed.[9,10]

Eight of the thirteen children showed a marked scatter of abilities across various subtests of the ITPA, although no one pattern of strengths and weaknesses emerged at a statistical level of significance. The point to be made is that while the overall average scores on this test were quite within the normal limits, a closer analysis of the individual profiles of the subtest scores showed more scatter of abilities and disabilities than would be expected. This is somewhat analogous to what was found on developmental testing as described in Chapter 6. This is also analogous to the pattern on subtests of I.Q. measures (such as the Wecshler) in children with either organic brain damage or emotional disorders. This is also a pattern the senior author has found in children with a large emotional component in their language functioning. The other five children showed more normal distributions of subtest scores.

Behavior During Testing

Many of the same phenomena were noted in speech and language testing that have been described in Chapter 10. A few behaviors and impressions bear emphasis here.

It was very difficult to obtain test data on the preschool children. Language and speech are typically more difficult to elicit in children of this age than gaining their cooperation with manual games or gross motor play. With these abused children, this seemed even more so than with other children. The most striking behavior noted was that these children would simply stop—refusing any more cooperation—when they were faced with their first failure on the tests. Whether the child was asked to point to pictures or name things or whatever, he would respond until faced with the first request that was difficult. Even when the examiner quickly attempted to retreat to very easy test items, it was to no avail. It was as if the perceived failure completely disorganized the child. This required then a modification of technique whereby the children were then immediately dismissed, and a second, third or further session of short periods of time (often only five to ten minutes) was needed to complete the testing. Actually, the ability of the children to accept difficult items or failure did improve with subsequent sessions. It was felt this was probably due to a beginning tenuous trust in the examiner and an awareness that the examiner was neither going to get into a battle for power nor force responses from the child.

A second feature of the preschool children was noted after the examiner became aware of her almost intuitive use of basic reinforcers, such as food, with all of these children. This really bespoke the difficulty encountered in obtaining cooperation and interest from the children. After it was recognized, this technique of giving oral reinforcers for the feeblest of attempts at cooperation was used deliberately to facilitate the testing. The appeal of the tidbits of food never seemed to wane and was more effective than is usually the case in the examiners experience.

The older children were less obviously refractive to usual testing techniques. Their resistance was considerably more passive or disguised. It often took the form of roving about the room physically or verbally. What was discovered very quickly was the need these children had for very clear structures and limits from the examiner.

A second somewhat puzzling behavior of the older psychotherapy group was their inexplicable seeming attachment to the person who brought them to the testing room. These children were very often brought to the center by a stranger to them—someone who had been recruited to drive them in. Sometimes the children would cling to these persons as though they were very important people to them. They would ask to leave the testing room to go to see the driver. It was with some amazement that the senior author later discovered that the driver to whom the child seemed attached had never seen the child before that day. Perhaps this was manipulative behavior of the child, and it surely speaks to the indiscriminate affection of these children with distorted object-relations.

In general these older children were also very difficult to test. The evaluations of both groups of children required much more energy and alertness on the part of the examiner than is usual. They were manipulative, clearly distrustful, and passive-aggressive in their resistance to being tested.

In both groups of children there were considerable changes in the test behavior of the thirteen children who were retested six to twelve months later. This change in response to the examiner and the testing format itself was considerably more striking than any changes in actual test scores. They became much more likable, easier to test and more cooperative. There was less verbal barrage and manipulation and more appropriate person-to-person behavior.

Intervention

During this study the children in the playschool received intervention consisting of attendance in the play school and speech therapy, individually or in small groups, for work on articulation, vocabulary building, comprehension of spoken language and use of more age-level structures in language. The playschool staff was given program suggestions geared toward each child's specific problems to use in the playschool for speech and language stimulation. This intervention occurred over a six-month period. Each child received an average of four individual and six group speech therapy sessions aside from the stimulation in the playschool.

The older children received play therapy once or twice a week, and the mothers continued to receive counseling and therapy. No specific speech or language therapy was introduced. Each child received an average of 70 play therapy sessions during the year.

Six of the preschool children were retested. The younger children had improved noticeably in their overall communication. They were more spontaneously talkative. On formal testing, results were not as impressive, but some growth had occurred.

On the Peabody, there was a mean gain of seven months of language development in this six month interim. It appeared that the intervention and stimulation were successful in producing change in their speech and language. It is also probably safe to say that if the children had been seen after a longer period of intervention, more improvement would have been documented.

Seven of the thirteen children in psychotherapy were re-evaluated. These older children showed a different picture of change. On articulation the children had continued to improve. On the other language tests their scores were basically unchanged, still in the normal range, although slightly lower from pretest scores.

Individual psycholinguistic profiles continued to show two patterns. The children who had had widely scattered profiles were now more centered, and the children who had been more centered at the beginning had become slightly more splintered.

The developmental sentence scoring showed some confusing but interesting results. The four children whose splintered profiles had become more centered had improved in sentence scores. They had moved from being sixteen months below their chronological age to only four months below, a relative gain of twelve months. The three children whose profiles had become more splintered were also looked at separately; they showed a remarkable drop. They had dropped from eleven months below chronological age at the beginning and were now 37 months below at the end.

The play therapy for the children and counseling for the mothers seemed to have helped those children for whom the emotional component was reflected in their language (scattered profiles) and delayed spoken language structure.

Discussion

This was not a controlled study, so one must be cautious in interpretation of either the test data or our observations and impressions. More important than documenting the degree of difference between these children and the hundreds of non-abused children who have undergone the same procedures, is to try to raise hypotheses and explanations for the data and behavior which were seen.

The delay in speech and language which has been noted by others working with abused children showed up most noticeably in the preschool population. This indeed was what was expected. For one, these children were much closer in time to the turmoil of reported physical abuse with less time for intervention for parents or themselves. The families of these children were in more turmoil, and suspected non-accidental trauma was still occurring in many of the families. One would also presume that speech and language would be more delayed in younger abused children. As hypothesized in Chapter 6, speaking may be much more dangerous for these children—when the child is in his home—than for the older child where the influence of elementary school must be having an effect. And not only do we feel that not talking is valued in these families, but the behavior of the preschool children during the testing also impressed us with the fear and anxiety aroused by anticipated failure or mistakes. Not to respond at all may be a safer response than to respond erroneously.

The paucity of language stimulation among these children must further play a large role in their language delays. While we can only assume what the parent-child interaction had been earlier, certainly at this point the children were not talked to, sung to, read to or otherwise stimulated to enjoy verbal communication. Klaus and Kennel's[11] work comes to mind, as they were able to show significant differences in the style in which mothers talked to their two-year-old children when they compared mothers with varying degrees of early attachment and bonding to their neonates.

It should be further noted that the test data on the preschool children did not show as marked a delay or deficit as is usually reported in the literature. One very plausible explanation for this relates to the testing procedures used. If the examiner had used the usual format for evaluation, the performance of these children would have been simply miserable. Repeated testing, use of reinforcers and considerable efforts to assure the child were required for the data to be gathered. Perhaps one reason why others have found more impressive delays in speech and language is that these "parameters" of testing were not used. It also raises the possibility that the skills and abilities which the children did show during the testing are really not available to them in most social contexts—at home, at school, with strangers. This is another way of saying that these children will appear more delayed in most environments than they truly may be. This also relates to Drs. Rodeheffer and Martin's experience in psychological and developmental testing.

The older children from the psychotherapy study present other types of findings to explain. With these older children it seemed as if they may have learned that talking is no longer dangerous and even may be adaptive and desired by this time. However, despite their adequate performance on various language tests, they were delayed when their more natural spontaneous conversation was analyzed. It seemed that, even if they learn that talking is safe behavior, they may talk, but it shows up as an almost aberrational chatter. It is not the kind of "talking" that keeps pace with increased knowledge or with ideas and feelings. It remains separate from other language growth, and therefore remains delayed.

This may help explain why the older children in the play therapy group did not seem to show the classic delay of language described in abused children. They had learned substantive language. However, they had not learned communicative language. Spoken language is learned through practice, a particular kind of practice. A child speaks and his utterances are echoed and elaborated by the adults around him. He speaks and his utterances are corrected and expanded.[12,13] There must be enough safety to risk talking, and some significant adult with whom to identify.[14,15] If not, then the form of his language will remain at a less mature level. This is what seemed to be absent in the psycho-communication environment of abused children. That may be why substantive language was age-adequate, but spoken language structure remained delayed.

It was mentioned earlier that such wide scatter is seen in children with either perceptual deficiencies or in children with emotional disorders. It is thought that this latter explanation must be the operative factor. If the scattered profiles were truly reflecting problems in processing language, one would expect other evidence such as not understanding or remembering what had been said to them, giving inappropriate responses, or delays in their use of language in thinking. The entire picture they displayed was what the senior author has come to identify in other children with emotional conflicts wherein the language processing is being affected.

The data from re-evaluation deserves further comments. The preschool children not only had this educational experience seven hours per day for four days per week. They also had specific therapy for speech and language deficits. Each child received an average of four individual and six group speech therapy sessions over the six-month period. Perhaps more important was the general stimulation of speech and language from the preschool staff. This latter intervention required consultation from the speech and language pathologist and took the form of identifying the specific problems of each child with recommended procedures for remediation in the classroom. While these therapeutic maneuvers were only used for six months before the children were retested, there was noticeable improvement in their spontaneous language. Even on formal testing there was slight improvement with a mean gain of seven months of language development in the six months of preschool. This is particularly impressive, given the fact that these children were delayed in their speech and language and hence were showing evidence of "catching up." The retest data on the older children who had been in psychotherapy for a year were different. They had had no specific speech or language therapy. There was improvement in articulation, and on the formal test scores there was no significant change. The children showed slightly poorer scores, but were still functioning in the normal range.

However, those whose speech and language patterns seemed delayed on an emotional base did show improvement over the year's time; a less divergent scattered profile in the ITPA, i.e., at retest there was less divergence from subtest to subtest; and improved language structure.

Those children whose profiles were slightly more splintered showed a marked drop in their language structure. It was felt that these children were either showing increasing emotional interference or perhaps some language processing problems were just beginning to emerge.

Summary

We have reconfirmed the finding that speech and language is a particularly sensitive neurologic, social and emotional behavior, sensitive to structural central nervous system damage and to aberrations in parenting. The speech and language of abused children is typically delayed and distorted. Several factors apart from neurologic damage seem to be pertinent.

1. Age of the child. The younger abused child is apt to demonstrate more striking delays and deficits in speech and language.
2. Lack of experience. Especially with the younger abused or neglected child, lack of appropriate experience in language is of particular importance.
3. Reaction to testing. Modifications of usual testing procedures must be utilized to maximize the opportunity to see what the potential of the child might be. Without such parameters of usual technique, the results of testing for speech and language will be erroneously deficient scores.
4. Relationship to trauma. The older child is less impaired for several reasons. In these particular groups of children, a particularly germane issue was the amount and type of intervention which the parents and the child had received.
5. Type of intervention. Those children who received specific speech and language intervention improved in their function. For those children who received only intervention for emotional problems, the emotional components of their speech and language improved, but for continued language growth these children probably need more specific stimulation.
6. Adaptiveness of the child. As discussed in Chapter 8, where intelligence is seen to vary according to the adaptive modes of the child, so in speech and language. In some families and at certain ages of the child silence or a real paucity of talking may be quite adaptive and used for survival. In other families, and perhaps at older ages, talking is not only allowed but may be required for survival and adaptation. This may be a helpful way to try to understand the child's speech and language patterns, in addition to the usual assessment of amount and degree of language stimulation in the home.

The children studied did show delays in speech and language which have been previously described. The abused children did show particular areas of strengths and weaknesses depending on their age, how recently they had been placed in an intervening situation, what the type of intervention was, what their developmental potential seemed to be, and the amount of support or non-support there was in the psycho-communicative aspects of their environment. And the younger children showed improvement in speech and language through an educational therapy program with specific speech and language stimulation and therapy.

References

1. Martin, H.P., *The Child and His Development* in Kempe and Helfer (eds.) *Helping the Battered Child and His Family*, Philadelphia: Lippincott, 1972, pp. 93-114.

2. Smith, S.M., Hanson, R., 134 Battered Children: A Medical and Psychological Study. *Brit. Med. Journal*. 14 Sept. 1974, pp. 666-670.

3. Elizabeth Elmer and Colleagues, *Report of a Study of Abused Children*, presented at American Psychiatric Assn. meeting, Anaheim, California, spring, 1975.

4. Dunn, L.M., *Peabody Picture Vocabulary Test*. American Guidance, Inc. Circle Pines, Minnesota, 1965.

5. Crabtree, M., *The Houston Test for Language Development, Part I and Part II*. 10133 Bassoon, Houston, Texas, 1963.

6. Templin, M.C. and Darley, F.L., *The Templin-Darley Tests of Articulation, Second Edition*, University of Iowa, Iowa City, 1969.

7. Kirk, S.A., McCarthy, J.J., and Kirk, W.A., *Illinois Test of Psycholinguistic Abilities*. University of Illinois, Urbana, 1968.

8. Lee, L.L., *Developmental Sentence Analysis*. Evanston, Ill.: Northwestern University Press, 1974.

9. Kirk, S.A., and Kirk, W.A. *Psycholoinguistic Learning Disabilities. Diagnosis and Remediation*. Urbana: University of Illinois Press, 1971.

10. Paraskwopoulos, J.N. and Kirk, S.A., *The Development and Psychometric Characteristics of the Revised Illinois Test of Psycholoinguistic Abilities*. Urbana: University of Illinois Press, 1969.

11. See reference 25-29 in Chapter 3.

12. Brown, R. and Billings, V., Three Processes in the Child's Acquisition of Syntax, *Harvard Educ. Review*, 35:133-152, 1964.

13. Miller, J.F. and Yoder, D.E., "A Syntax Teaching Program," *Language Intervention with the Retarded*. (ed.) J.E. McLisn, D.E. Yoder, and R.L. Schiefelbusch. Baltimore: University Park Press, 1972.

14. Gray, G.W. and Wise, C.M., *The Bases of Speech*. New York: Harper & Brothers, 1959.

15. Mysak, E.D., *Speech Pathology and Feedback Theory*. Springfield, Ill.: Charles C. Thomas, Publisher, 1966.

 *Chapter 8*

Learning and Intelligence

Harold P. Martin and **Martha Rodeheffer**

Abused children are handicapped in learning and intelligence. At least an inordinate number of abused children are identified as having learning problems in academic settings and receive low scores on intelligence tests. This chapter shall explore what is known regarding this neurologic function of abused children. More important than merely reporting test scores and performance, however, is an attempt to understand why the abused child may be handicapped in learning.

The authors are using a broad definition of intelligence. We are speaking of the child's ability to understand things, solve problems, learn facts and to make sense of the world about him and act accordingly. "Intelligence tests" are but one way of measuring the child's intelligence and provide an incomplete evaluation at best. An intelligence test measures only selected abilities of the child on a specific day that could be observed by a particular person in a setting that is unnatural and unfamiliar to the child. We are not intending to minimize the importance and implications of test data. Standardized tests give us the opportunity to compare the individual child's performance with that of hundreds of other children in similar circumstances. These test data may also be highly predictive of the child's ability to master academic material. However, we want to stress that one must look at a wider repertoire of the child's abilities and behavior to understand his actual intellectual abilities adequately.

The child in an abusive family will have learned a number of ways of behaving which are adaptive and have survival value in such an environment. It will be pointed out in this chapter how many of these adaptive mechanisms (such as hypervigilance or silence) should be viewed from different perspectives. On the one hand, they bespeak to the intelligence of the child, as they reflect the ability of the child to realistically perceive and understand his world and adjust his

The work of these authors has been supported by Maternal Child Health, #926, H.E.W. and by the Grant Foundation.

behavior accordingly. These behaviors may also be seen as symptoms of conflict and anxiety. It is also essential to note that these adaptive mechanisms are impediments to learning—as they preempt activites of the child which lead to the knowledge and abilities needed to negotiate the world outside his abusive environment.

There are a few abused children who have not been so handicapped. Some understanding and explanation of why some abused children have superior intelligence will be explored. There is a great deal to be learned from focusing on the pathology in any group of children. There may be as much or more to be learned in understanding the smaller number of such children who have escaped such pathological outcomes.

Data from Formal Intelligence Tests and
School Performance

What little is available in the literature regarding the intellectual functioning of abused children is primarily data about how certain groups of abused children perform on standardized intelligence tests. There is also some data about school performance. Studies to date suggest that abused children, as a group, perform poorly on formal intelligence measures. Such children are also likely to exhibit learning problems in school, sometimes despite adequate intelligence as measured on intelligence tests. The effect of differing degrees and longevity of physical attack upon the cognitive development of children at different ages is not yet available in the literature. If physical attack on the child occurs for the first time during school-age years, it would be expected that the effect upon the child's intellectual development might be quite different from that occurring as a result of prolonged abuse during infancy and pre-school years.

The data on intellectual functioning of abused children must be interpreted with caution, avoiding over-generalizations from relatively small groups of children selected with a sampling bias that is not representative of the total spectrum of abused children. The major thrust for social action regarding child abuse came originally from hospital-based medical personnel observing primarily young children brought to the hospital for treatment of injuries which were often quite severe. With the recent advent of increased reporting by private pediatricians, neighbors and school personnel,[1] it has become evident that school age children and young children whose injuries are less severe are significantly under-represented in the early research on child abuse. Data regarding the intellectual development of children included in these studies is presented below along with results from a nationwide survey which provided information on the academic functioning of a broader spectrum of abused children.

Elmer and Gregg[2] reported that of a sample of 22 children who had suffered multiple bone injuries as a result of physical abuse, 57 percent were found to have I.Q.s below 80 upon examination in a follow-up study. In a normal population, approximately 11 percent would be expected to have I.Q.s below 80. In a subsequent study of children under thirteen months of age who appeared at the hospital for treatment of injuries, these same investigators[3] compared the intellectual development of 30 children whose injuries were believed inflicted, with the intellectual development of 83 children whose injuries were judged accidental or questionable accidents. They found that 42 percent of the abused children, as compared to 18 percent of the accident children, were retarded. The possibility of some commonalities between these two groups is suggested by the unexpectedly high incidence of retardation in both groups. Similar results were found by Morse *et al.*[4] who studied a group of 25 abused and/or neglected children who had been hospitalized three years previously for injuries or illnesses. Of these abused children, 42 percent were reported to be mentally retarded at the time of follow-up.

Martin[5] conducted a follow-up study of 42 physically abused children who had been referred for developmental evaluation three years previously at the time of inflicted injury. He reported that 33 percent of these children were functioning in the retarded range, with developmental quotients (D.Q.s) or intelligence quotients (I.Q.s) below 80. Of the thirteen children who had suffered skull fractures or subdural hematomas, nine (64 percent) were retarded in their functioning, and a lack of developmental improvement in seven of these children over a three-year period was attributed to neurological damage due to significant brain insult. Of the 28 children who were not retarded, 43 percent demonstrated language disabilities on formal testing.

In a subsequent follow-up study by the same investigator and his colleagues[6] the intellectual functioning of 58 abused children was evaluated. These were children identified from hospital records some four and one-half years previously for inflicted injuries. The injuries of this particular study group were considerably less severe than those reported in other studies, with 31 of the children having only soft tissue damage. Despite the observations that the performance of at least 25 of these children was hindered by resistance to test procedures and disturbed behavior, the group of 58 abused children obtained a mean I.Q. of 92. Still, 35 percent of these children (*N*=19) had I.Q.s below 85 as compared to the expected finding of 15 percent in the normal population. The sub-group of 21 children with the history of head trauma, however, obtained a mean I.Q. of 80. Brain damage, neurologic handicaps and the quality of the home in which the child was living independently affected their scores. Nine of 24 school-age children with no neurologic dysfunction or handicaps in intelligence, were identified by school personnel as having significant learning problems in school.

Sandgrund[7] studied 120 children to assess the impact of abuse on cognitive development. Twenty-five percent of the abused children (*N*=60) had I.Q.s below 70. This was compared to 20 percent on a matched group of neglected children who were not known to have been abused (*N*=30). A matched group of non-abused children (*N*=30), produced a more typical 3 percent retarded.

Investigators concluded that both abuse and neglect are strongly associated with mental deficiency and noted that it was impossible to assess the degree of neglect in the background of abused children.

Gil[8] conducted a nationwide survey of 13,990 identified incidents of child abuse reported in the Central Registries of the 50 states during 1967 and 1968. In a sub-sample of 1380 of this group chosen for more comprehensive study, it was discovered that 13 percent of the abused children of school age attended special classes for the retarded or were in grades below their age level. It was noted that another 3 percent of school age abused children had never attended school.

Test Data Interpretation

Test data as presented above are unsatisfactory in really understanding the abused child. Test scores reflect a sampling of what a child did on a certain day, under specific circumstances, with a particular person. Performance may be low because of illness, inattention, opposition or inability. Performance may be high because of a need to please, a need to avoid the shame of failure or a compulsive need to get things right. The really important question to be answered by the professional testing the child is *why* did the child perform as he did. This question will be taken up later in this chapter.

Chapter 10 examines the difficult task of interpretation of developmental test data on younger children. The same points are germane to intelligence test data. The examiner must consider how the specific behaviors of the child might interfere with test performance. It is important to note the degree of scatter on test performance, as abused children often show remarkable variation between subtests and may "fail" easy test questions while "passing" much more difficult problems. The considerable fluctuation of abused children's behavior in varying settings has been commented upon. It is especially important to note then whether the behavior of the child in the testing situation is an accurate reflection of his behavior at home, in school or in other settings.

Unless the examiner is willing and able to speak to the reasons why an abused child performed as he did on any test, we are suggesting not only that the child's test scores may be misleading but that it is a professional disservice to release those test scores to teachers, parents or other professionals. Too often test scores in the retarded range have been the basis for placing the child in classes for the mentally retarded when the test scores have not been a reflection of the child's intellectual ability or potential but a reflection of his maladaptive response to the testing situation. We must expect then from the professional examiner, a reporting of the test performance, a description of the child's behavior during the testing, and most important an interpretation of those results and behaviors. Let us turn now to an exploration of the various factors which will impact on the child's intelligence. We shall first look briefly at the impediments to learning resulting from damage to the nervous system and then deal with the psycho-social environmental handicaps to learning.

Deficits in Learning Due to Central Nervous System Damage

One of the most obvious reasons for limited intelligence is cerebral damage from the incident of physical abuse. Depending on the severity and types of injuries in children, one will expect at least 20 to 30 percent of abused children to demonstrate impaired mental ability. This will be higher when the children studied have had head injuries or fractures, and less prominent when those children have only histories of burns and soft-tissue damage. When sensory deficits in vision or hearing have resulted from the injury, learning will also be compromised. The relationship between intelligence and the type of injury has been commented on before.[6]

It is possible that some of the neurologic damage to the abused child may arise from events prior to the actual assault by the parent. Lynch has pointed out in Chapter 4 that medical problems in the pregnancy, labor and delivery or in the postnatal life of the child are more prevalent in those children who are later abused than in their non-abused siblings. While she focuses primarily on the attachment and bonding process, the effects of potential high risk events on the brain of the child cannot be overlooked. For example, one of the five significantly different events in the abused child versus his non-abused sibling was separation from the mother in the first 48 hours of life. In point of fact, that separation occurred when the newborn was having medical problems necessitating placement in the intensive care nursery. So the separation of baby and mother, while important in and of itself, was the result of a medical problem which had potential for damage to the newborn's central nervous system.

Another facet to be considered is the effects of neurologic handicaps, even when the overall mental ability as measured by intelligence tests is not impaired. In our broader definition of intelligence, we are considering the child's ability to learn and understand things which may not be measured by formal I.Q. tests. Perceptual deficits, diminished auditory discrimination, hyperactivity or distractability all interfere with the child's ability to learn. He learns and understands less, and with more effort, when handicapped by such neurologic distortions. So, in spite of obtaining a normal I.Q. score, children with such problems are handicapped in understanding the world about them. They may not adequately perceive the world. The ability of their cerebrum to process and make sense of what they perceive is compromised secondarily to structural damage to the brain. Hence, we find correlations between neurologic integrity of the child and his ability to learn, solve problems, know things and understand his world. This may partially account for the inordinately high percentage of abused children requiring special education classes for the learning disabled.

Psychosocial Impediments to Learning

Learning takes place in a social world; it is a neurologically based set of functions which requires social interaction and reinforcement. There are a number of characteristics common to the abusive environment which interfere with the child's capacity to learn and understand. We have chosen to touch briefly on six such factors and how they impede the developing intelligence of the newborn and young child. Undoubtedly there are other environmental factors which may be peculiar to an individual family or which are additive components in the stultification of learning.

1. *An Unpredictable, Non-Nurturing World.* In the normal course of events, the totally dependent infant is nurtured and stimulated by an adult, usually the mother, who has an intense commitment to the child's well-being and future development. The infant experiences a state of non-pleasure (hunger, cold, wetness), he cries, and the mother does something which results in a change to a state of pleasure (satiation, warmth, dryness). The infant learns that his own acts, in this case crying, can bring a desired response from other people. He learns to associate a change of state from non-pleasure to pleasure with his caretaker. He begins to learn that certain things are predictable, that there are cause and effect relationships, that the world is a reasonably safe place, and that he can cause things to happen. In the home of the abused child, where the parents are preoccupied with their own needs, the appearance of the parent may be quite independent of the child's discomfort and crying. When the infant's needs go unmet for long periods of time, he remains in a state of tension. The world can make little sense to the infant if there appears to be no predictable response to his crying. It will be even more chaotic and inexplicable if the parents' response varies between meeting the infant's needs, ignoring him, and at times inflicting pain on him. This inconstant erratic parental behavior does not provide the infant with a logical or rational world or a basis to develop sense of trust or security that someone will be there to care for him when needed. Elkind[9] has recently pointed out the need for a structured orderly world for normal perceptual development to progress in children. At older ages this same confusion and chaos persists. The child may be encouraged to behave in a way which is met alternately with approval, apathy or physical punishment. He has no way to know what the consequences of his behavior might be. There is no assurance his parents will be available, will meet his needs or will react in a reasonable fashion. In such an environment, there is little opportunity to relate to a constant, predictable world. There can be no development of a sense of trust in parents or in a logical world. Whatever the theoretical basis for learning that the reader wishes to use, such a world for the abused child can be seen to impede the development of learning.

2. *Restriction of Opportunities for Learning.* From the beginning the abused child is in an environment where exploration is minimized. To explore and investigate, to ask questions, to pursue how and why things work is dangerous in an abusive home. This is especially true in the home where neglect and deprivation accompany abuse. The child may be literally kept in a play-pen or

crib for hours or days on end. Sensory deprivation accompanies this neglect when the child is kept in a room with the door closed most of his waking hours. The exploration required during the early sensory-motor period of learning is viewed by parents as "getting into things," naughtiness or disobedience. The stages of initiative and autonomy will be seen as willfulness, and hence discouraged, or met with punishment. The acquiescence and obedience which are valued by the abusive parent inhibit exploration and learning. Clashes occur because of the young child's natural impulse to touch, taste, feel and manipulate objects. It is no wonder that the child develops the expectation that any of his behavior may be found unacceptable and that being observed by an adult may lead to sudden punitive action toward himself. Adults become not so much resources from whom to learn, but rather individuals from whom the child must protect himself. Learned inhibition of activities around adults results in lost opportunities to experiment and practice new cognitive feats. Thus, unnecessary delays in cognitive development occur.

3. *Inadequate Stimulation and Support.* Specific stimulation from adults is needed for many ego functions to develop. This is especially true of language development. For language to develop the child must have verbal input from others about him. The normal child is talked to and read to and encouraged to speak. Many games between child and parent focus on learning verbal communication. This play which serves as cognitive stimulation is lacking in the home of the abused child. The abused child's struggles when asked to express himself belie the fact that his parents do not encourage self-expression. The abused child appears confused and often produces responses that are only loosely associated with the question asked. The developing child benefits from the opportunity to practice verbalizing as well as from listening to adult input. Abstract thinking and expressive language skills are enhanced by opportunities to interact verbally. Thinking, which otherwise may remain vague and overgeneralized, is refined in the process of selecting words from the universe of those available to the child. As the child expresses himself aloud, the interested responses of other people are reinforcing and supportive. Corrective feedback, immediately available as the adult reflects back what the child has tried to say, further refines the cognitive processes of the child. This does not happen in the home of the abused child. The child, if encouraged to speak at all, is expected primarily to respond in a rote fashion to narrowly worded questions for which there is a "correct answer." Even bright children who have been abused often demonstrate difficulty with expressive language.

This social interplay is also seen with other tasks of older children, e.g., learning to tie shoes, ride a tricycle, dress one's self. These skills require help for the learning child and, as any parent knows, considerable patience and effort. Abusive parents are rarely capable of the patience and altruism required to teach their child such tasks. It may be argued that the parent simply does not know what is required of him to help his child learn. However, the authors feel this is a more complex dynamic, inasmuch as even abusive parents who are quite bright and knowledgable in child development act *as if* they did not know what they need to do. From the child's perspective it makes little difference why the help and stimulation he needs are unavailable. He is raised in an environment where there is minimal cognitive stimulation and certainly very little support for development.

4. *Danger of Performance and Non-Performance.* The abused child is caught up in a double bind around competence versus incompetence. On the one hand the adult expects much of the child, and the child's behavior is judged without consideration of his actual stage of development. Unrealistic and distorted expectations are the hallmark of most abusive parents. This gross distortion of age-appropriate behaviors guarantees that the child will have many failure experiences as he attempts to do things far beyond his level of development. He is punished if he does not meet those expectations. Approximations to the task are not accepted, only complete compliance and competence. If the child tries to do what the parents want and comes close but is not quite able to accomplish the task, he will be verbally or physically abused. If the child does not even try, the same consequence is forthcoming. The abusive parent is not child-oriented and does not accept normal developmental stages of the child. So, the child is at risk if he behaves like other children of his own age. Age-appropriate performance is not accepted— and non-performance is not accepted!

This dilemma is resolved differently by abused children. The most common response we see is the child not trying—not speaking, not understanding, not moving about and not exploring. The child says, "I can't"—and it is only with time and patience that one can get the abused child to risk trying.

5. *Energies Preempted by Survival.* Much of what is said above suggests that the abused child's mental energies are largely spent on survival tactics. It takes a great deal of mental energy to stay out of harm's way. The child is not only dealing with survival in a physical sense, but also emotionally. He must find ways to obtain nurturance and love from his parents. He is not only at risk of physical abuse, but he is also constantly exposed to verbal abuse and denigration. This means he must fear the loss of his parents as well as the loss of their love. He must *earn* whatever love and affection he can obtain from them for it is only given on condition. We have pointed out in Chapter 10 how the child's survival behaviors hinder learning. He must be constantly alert to his environment so that he will have some opportunity to know whether he is safe or in danger. Malone[10] has very nicely described this hypersensitivity to the environment in preschool children. One facet of the tremendous work expended to be safe and accepted is seen in the role-reversal[11,12] of the abused child. He literally takes care of his parents—sometimes in very concrete behaviors—and at other times by being sensitive to the moods and

feelings of the parent and "mothering" the parent. To those of us testing abused children, this characteristic stands out in bold relief, e.g., a pre-school-aged child notices a yawn and asks if the examiner is tired, and would like to take a break; a ten-year-old girl ties to comfort by sympathetically commenting that the examiner shouldn't feel bad because his drawings with pencil and paper were not very good. Efforts to entertain or comfort are numerous.

During developmental testing, the children frequently ask permission before touching toys—and keep looking to the examiner's face to see if things are still all right. This behavior takes priority over learning and exploring, as it is clearly seen as essential to the child to survive.

These behaviors which are really adaptations to a dangerous environment can be seen in the broadest sense as indications of intellectual ability—for they surely are evidence of the child's ability to quickly identify and accurately interpret sensory clues. They demonstrate his ability to know and understand the world of people. And yet, it is quite clear that when such social perceptions become rigid obsessive traits, they allow the child little freedom to learn other things, e.g., to learn of mastery of inanimate objects, to learn social intercourse with peers, to learn of one's self. Thus, by the usual criteria of intelligence, these traits handicap the child, while they are nonetheless signs of cerebral function which are hypertrophied for survival purposes.

6. *Anxiety.* A further dynamic of the abused child is what has been recognized for some time in the so-called neurotic learning disabled child. When the child is anxious, fearful or preoccupied with fantasy life, he has little energy and attention to give to learning. This may most graphically be seen in the compulsive child who consumes much energy in getting things "just right." Parenthetically, our follow-up study of abused children showed approximately 25 percent of the children demonstrating obsessive-compulsive traits. It should also be pointed out that learning is an aggressive act—a process wherein a person must actively manipulate the world—in the world of words, figures and people. We see two ways abused children have of dealing with aggression. The largest percentage of abused children are unable to discharge aggression directly—dealing with the world in an inhibited, passive-aggressive manner. A smaller percentage of abused children are noticeably aggressive, but this aggression takes the form of anger and hostility rather than being sublimated into more socially acceptable channels such as learning.

The preoccupation of these children with their fears, anxiety, and fantasy world is a paralyzing force which does not allow for mental energies to be spent in learning about the world.

Abused Child Who Achieves Academically

There remain a group of abused children who even by traditional criteria demonstrate superior intelligence. In our follow-up study[6] we found eight of 58 children with I.Q.s one or more standard deviation above the mean—their I.Q.s ranged between 115 and 131. This seems a paradox worth trying to understand. Why and how did these children escape intellectual handicap? What could explain their superior ability? They also came from abusive homes where there was inadequate parenting. According to all we know about child development, at first glance we cannot fathom how normal or superior intellect can develop when the abusive home provides such minimal stimulation and so few prerequisites for learning.

Two factors were noted in the families of these children. First is that these children were not emotionally neglected or deprived children. It is our very strong conviction that emotional and physical neglect or deprivation is much more harmful to the development of a child than physical abuse which occurs when there is considerable attention and investment in the child. The parents in these families were concerned about their children's behavior in a very active and often intrusive way. A second factor in these homes was that "being smart" was either highly valued by the parents or at least was tolerated and not seen as a basis for punishment. One of the brightest children seen was the son of a college professor. Book knowledge was highly valued in this family. In these families then, learning and knowing things was one way of meeting the expectations of the parents, or at least of placating them from their more usual critical stance.

Another factor to consider is that there may be a significant bias in those children who survive the abusive environment. As pointed out above, even those adaptive modes which interfere with and handicap learning in the traditional sense are to be viewed as evidences of intellectual ability. In a Darwinian sense we may be seeing the survival of the fittest. Those children with less able minds would appear to be less able to perceive and meet expectations and therefore be at greater risk of recurrent abuse and possibly of relinquishment and recurrent foster-home failure.

Learning, or knowing things, is a defensive mechanism for many normal children. It can be a very socially acceptable way of dealing with anxiety and stress. Anna Freud has suggested that learning is only possible because of anxiety and stress. When the family allows or encourages learning, what better escape for the abused child than to escape into the world of books and facts. The dynamics of this adaptation are not all that dissimilar to that of obsessive-compulsive behavior. That is, the more the child knows, the more he is able to understand the world, and the more accurately he is able to anticipate what will happen next. Learning, which may lead to recognition and achievement, is a common sublimated form of escaping from interpersonal relationships and channelling aggressions and one's needs for approval. When the drive for learning comes so intensively from such needs, one finds the child taking little real joy in his learning. The endless series of facts and store of knowledge of the child may not be usable in his everyday life. Children cannot live exclusively in a world of books, numbers or thoughts. The child lives primarily in a world of people.

Knowledge is to be used. It should be a tool for negotiating life more adequately. What one finds in the "bright" abused child is an inability to negotiate life with other people despite the store of facts and knowledge he has. It is as if what the child knows is quite separate from how he lives his life. The knowledge and information the abused child has is compartmentalized and not available to him to truly understand either himself or his surroundings. Faced with ambiguous situations, the abused child appears remarkably inept. This is especially striking in the abused child who demonstrates good cognitive strengths on standardized intelligence tests. This same child may perform in a very regressive anxious manner to the series of inkblots composing the Rorschach test, or the projective pictures of the Children's Apperception Test. There are "right answers" to narrowly structured clearly defined problems on intelligence tests; here the "bright" abused child excels. However, situations which demand creative solutions and a flexible approach to novel stimuli are not the abused child's forte.

Intellectual superiority of these abused children has not arisen so much from a delight and joy in learning or in mastery, but instead has arisen from an almost driven need to acquire information, to be seen as capable and to discharge into the learning situation their aggression and libidinal drives.

Summary

For most abused children, the development of intelligence is severely compromised and distorted. Mental retardation may result from injury to the brain of the child. Neurologic handicaps compromise learning. In addition to structural central nervous system damage, the development of various ego functions of the child are also affected by the home environment in which he lives. This should not be surprising to us as numerous studies since the landmark work of Spitz have documented the effects of maternal deprivation on learning and a variety of other neuro-developmental abilities.[6] Learning, competency, exploration, initiative, autonomy are not valued in most abusive homes; indeed, they may be the basis for physical assault by the parents. The fear of failure of most abused children is commented on. In our treatise on developmental assessment of these children (Chapter 10), we have pointed out how a variety of adaptive mechanisms of the child (such as hypervigilance and attention to various sensory input) which may have high survival value are quite handicapping to the child's learning. It has been pointed out that there is a small subset of abused children who demonstrate superior abilities on intelligence tests. Our experience with such children is the basis for several hypothetical explanations for this seeming paradox.

Intelligence is not just what is measured on intelligence tests. The child who has successfully survived in an abusive home has evidenced intelligence through his adaptive mechanisms, albeit they may be quite handicapping to him in more formal learning. Still, it is important to appreciate the ego's facility to adapt to an abusive home. This ability is not measured on formal tests of intelligence. This ability to adapt may be seen primarily in terms of psychopathology. Nonetheless, it bespeaks a valued ability of the organism to survive and adapt. These adaptive modes most often do require a large price be paid by the child. His learning regarding himself, other people and inanimate objects is severely limited. The energy of the child is consumed with survival maneuvers and dealing with his anxiety, fear of assault, loss of parent and loss of love from the parent. There is little energy then available to learn about himself and his world.

It is yet to be learned how specific treatment programs interrupt this process and help the child be more available for learning.

References

1. Broadhurst, D.D.: "Project Protection: A school program to detect and prevent child abuse and neglect," *Children Today*, 1975, *4* (3), 22-25.

2. Elmer, E., and Gregg, G.S.: "Developmental characteristics of abused children," *Pediatrics*, 40:596-602, 1967.

3. Gregg, G.S., and Elmer, E.: "Infant Injuries: Accident or Abuse," *Pediatrics* 44:434-439, 1969.

4. Morse, C.W., Sahler, O.J.Z., and Friedman, S.B.: A three-year follow-up study of abused and neglected children, *Am. J. Dis. Child.* 120:439-446, 1970.

5. Martin, H.P.: The Child and His Development, in Kempe, C.H., and Helfer, R.E. (eds.): *Helping the Battered Child and His Family* (Philadelphia: J.B. Lippincott Co., 1972), pp. 93-114.

6. Martin, H.P., Beezley, P., Conway, E.F., and Kempe, C.H.: "The Development of Abused Children," *Advances in Pediatrics*, 1974, *21*, 25-73.

7. Sandgrund, A., Gaines, R.W., and Green, A.H.: "Child Abuse and Mental Retardation: A Problem of Cause and Effect." *Journal of Mental Deficiency*, 1975. Vol. 19, No. 3, 327-330.

8. Gil, D.G.: *Violence Against Children: Physical Child Abuse in the United States*, Cambridge, Mass.: Harvard University Press, 1970.

9. Elkind, D.: "Perceptual Development in Children," *American Scientist*, Sept./Oct. 1975, pp. 533-541.

10. Malone, Charles A.: "Safety First: Comments on the Influence of External Danger in the Lives of Children of Disorganized Families," *Amer. J. Orthopsych. 36:* 6-12, Jan. 1966.

11. *The Neglected-Battered-Child-Syndrome—Role Reversal in Parents* (New York: Child Welfare League of America, 1963).

12. Morris, M.G., and Gould, R.W.: "Role Reversal: A Necessary Concept in Dealing with the 'Battered Child Syndrome,'" *Am. J. Orthopsychiatry* 33:298-299, 1963.

 *Chapter 9*

Personality of Abused Children

Harold P. Martin and **Patricia Beezeley**

Until just recently, very little has been known about the personality of abused children. The authors recently reviewed the literature and found primarily statements of absence or presence of emotional disorder in abused children with only a few authors commenting on specific traits of these children.[1] It is unclear why this area of behavioral research has received so little attention to this point. As pointed out in the first two chapters of this book, we are now at a point where the more general morbidity of this syndrome is beginning to undergo investigation.

Indeed, this entire book emphasizes the psychological trauma to abused children. Various chapters have detailed personality characteristics of the child at the time of abuse, during testing procedures and in various treatment settings. It is our intention in this chapter to pull together much of these scattered data and impressions. We shall furthermore give some specific findings in a follow-up study of 50 abused children with an emphasis on the role of the environment after the incident of physical abuse. Some general maxims concerning the personality of abused children are included, as is a discussion of significant issues in doing developmental research with this patient population.

The authors' follow-up study of 58 abused children included an assessment of neurologic and intellectual outcome[2] and an assessment of the personality of 50 of these children. A detailed report of that latter study has been accepted for publication elsewhere[3] but some highlights need attention here.

Nine characteristics of these children who ranged in age from two years to thirteen years with a mean age of six and one-half years were noted. A child was classified as displaying such a trait only when all three examiners independently so categorized the child and only when there was evidence from teachers, parents or welfare staff that these same traits were noted outside the evaluation interview, that is, at home or school or with peers. While there was no control group, the investigators were impressed not only with the frequency of these characteristics but also by the degree to which these traits seemed prominent in the personality matrix of the children.

Characteristic	Percentage of Children
1. Impaired Capacity to Enjoy Life	66%
2. Psychiatric Symptoms, e.g., eneuresis, tantrums, hyperactivity, bizarre behavior	62%
3. Low Self-Esteem	52%
4. School Learning Problems	38%
5. Withdrawal	24%
6. Opposition	24%
7. Hypervigilance	22%
8. Compulsivity	22%
9. Pseudo-Mature Behavior	20%

We were unable to group these traits statistically into clusters or to correlate them with age, sex or intelligence. However, several trends did show themselves. School learning problems and psychiatric symptoms were frequently seen in the same child. The children with marked hypervigilance or with pseudo-mature behavior had mean intelligence scores above the average while the withdrawn and oppositional children had mean intelligence scores measured at 93 and 86 respectively. None of the seventeen children who were either compulsive or pseudo-mature had recognized learning problems in a school setting.

There was no correlation of behavior with the type of injury nor the age at which abuse had first been recognized, but the correlation between the environment of the child subsequent to the abuse and his present function was striking. The 50 children were placed in one of four groupings on the basis of absence or presence and the severity of psychiatric symptoms at follow-up. The degree of psychiatric symptoms correlated most highly (< 0.001) with the child's present perception of the impermanence of his present home. The stability of the present home, whether biologic, foster or adoptive, was negatively correlated with the degree of pathology at the 0.05 level. The number of changes in home placement was also correlated at this level with present symptomatology.

Less statistically significant, but nonetheless impressive to the investigators, was the trend for those children whose caretakers were emotionally disturbed or who were still in families where rejection and physical punishment were common to have more psychiatric symptoms than those living with less disturbed and less punitive parents.

Perhaps these data are most helpful insofar as they emphasize that events and parental behavior *after the incident of abuse* play an important role in psychopathology and personality development of abused children.

Several overriding maxims or conclusions have been made from various observations of abused children. These points will be emphasized time and again in the other chapters.

1. The child's personality is affected and shaped by the total environment in which he lives. The specific incidents of physical assault *are* a psychic trauma. However, the broader picture, which may include rejection, chaos, deprivation, distorted parental perceptions, unrealistic expectations as well as hospitalization, separation, foster placement and frequent home changes, is in the long run more significant to the child's development.
2. There is no one classical or typical personality profile for abused children. One does repeatedly see certain traits in many abused children which are quite striking, such as hypervigilance, anxiety and diminished self-esteem. But all abused children are not alike. Some are cooperative; some are oppositional. Some are apathetic; some are hyperactive. Some are quite charming; others can be quite unpleasant. Our task is to identify those traits which are over-represented in a population of abused children, those traits which are particularly maladaptive to development, and are so rigidly and deeply ingrained in the child that they restrict the boundaries of continued growth and development.
3. Abusive children are chameleon in their adaptation to various people and settings. In behavioral research, the setting in which the child is observed must be kept in mind, as pointed out by Appleton in Chapter 11. This is particularly true of abused children. A major mechanism of survival for an endangered child is modification of his behavior according to the surroundings. Their behavior at home, at school and in the examining room shows greater fluctuation than does the behavior of other children. One must not generalize about such children from only one data base.
4. The abusive environment does impact and influence the developing child's personality. On this point there really can be no question. While the field of infant study is still primitive and murky, there no longer seems any question that even very early life's experiences on the neonate and infant affect the developing psychic structures. A host of investigators since Spitz's[4,5] landmark work have corroborated this.
5. A most difficult dilemma arises as we try to categorize the effects of the abusive environment on a child's personality. Any particular personality trait can be seen as a symptom, a distortion, a problem, or an adaptation of the child to his environment. When we consider the poor self-concept of the abused child, we tend to think of this as a developmental problem. His hypervigilance may be seen as an adaptation to a dangerous environment. Opposition or acted out anger are viewed as symptoms. His object-relations are considered a distortion or a delay in development. And yet this seems not only too simplistic a categorization but also misleading in its implications.

Each of these personality traits can and should be viewed from several viewpoints. Impaired trust is not only a developmental problem, but also it may be the best and most appropriate adaptation of the infant to inadequate parents. It is surely a delay or distortion of development. And we can clearly see in the adult how impaired development of trust plays out in what we traditionally call "symptoms." Hypervigilance is clearly an adaptive mechanism for the child in a dangerous environment. It also is a distortion in development and is unquestionably a symptom which seriously impedes learning and the development of a sense of self. Thus, any trait can be viewed from multiple perceptives.

This issue touches on a related phenomenon wherein we categorize traits and behaviors as good or bad. Docile behaviors frequently are thought of as good. The authors are reminded of a workshop of a few years past where there was a presentation of common psychological sequellae of the abusive environment. A member of the audience took this opportunity to comment that "maybe children need a touch of abuse. You describe many of these children as polite, obedient, and compliant. What's wrong with that? I could use some of that in my own children." But, at what price to the child is he polite, obedient, and compliant? Why is he unable to risk non-compliance? And how will these traits impede the healthy growth of this young child?

As one observes and works with abused children, there must be more than a categorization of common personality configurations. The above questions must be asked and considered to fully understand the impact of the abusive environment on the child, both now and as he grows older and matures.

Developmental Research

There has not been adequate study of the psychological consequences of abusive environments on children. Our experience with hundreds of abused children has impressed us with the price such children pay in terms of unhappiness, psychiatric symptoms and blocks to normal development. There are many unanswered questions in this area. Considerable thought must be given as to what and how the personalities of abused children should be studied. Mr. Appleton has presented his professional views on this subject in Chapter 11. Some comments from these authors seem appropriate here. Friedman[6] has pointed out the value of studying these children as a way of understanding the development of early object relations.

One of the most common investigative methods of understanding children is to document the effects of childhood experiences in adolescents and adults. Numerous examples come to mind. The effects of sexual molestation of young females has been studied. The impact of a child being reared by a psychotic or schizophrenic parent and the influence of having been adopted have also been investigated. Such investigations tend to study these phenomena by counting and measuring the number of people with such backgrounds who fit into certain categories, such as neurosis, sociopathy or psychosis. Alternately, specific behaviors are noted such as divorce rate, criminal prosecution or delinquent behavior. Such data may have value, but it seems quite limited. In fact, it may obfuscate more important issues. For example, there may be the implication that such childhood experiences have had little or no impact on the developing child because as adults there cannot be demonstrated a statistically significant increase in certain categories of psychopathology.

The real question, it seems to us, is what is it like for a child to live in an abusive home. What price does the child pay for having been so reared? What does the child go through and how does he adapt?

The possibilities for practical developmental research seem unlimited. A number of lines of development might be profitably traced. Anna Freud's[7] breakdown of developmental lines might be one paradigm to use, or the theories of Piaget or Mahler or Erickson. What happens, for example, to the line of development of object-relations in a child who has been abused? The development of separation-individuation[8] and its vicissitudes throughout life would bear study. Superego development or aggression, or the sense of self need explanation in the child raised by assaultive parents.

These developmental issues do not stop with childhood, but are worked over repeatedly in life. One's self concept, for example, while having essential analage in early childhood, is a major issue of adolescence, and is revived for further development in every subsequent stage of life, e.g., maturity, parenthood, middle age. Through such a developmental approach to abused children, we should gain insights which will be applicable and helpful in understanding the aggressive adolescent or the abusive adult. Just as easily, one might profitably take the stages of trust or initiative or autonomy that Erickson[9] describes and see how they are distorted in the abused child—and—how this plays out in adult life in the abusive parent.

The point to be made is the importance of looking at developmental issues in the abused child, not just a counting of labels and categories. This is especially important as developmental issues continue throughout adult life. By studying and understanding the impact on development of the abusive environment, we not only will learn about the child and what therapeutic interventions are possible, but we shall also learn about the adolescent, the adult parent or the grandparent of the abused child and how these developmental distortions or derailments have played out in adult life. We should be primarily interested in the price the child pays for growing up in his abusive environment—for this is so much more crucial and pragmatically helpful—than to determine only the predilection for the abused child to fall into one of several societally cannonized categories.

Summary

It may seem ironic, at first glance, that a book which is primarily emphasizing the psychosocial aspects of the abusive environment and the role they play with the child's subsequent development, should have such a short chapter on the personality features of these children. We again remind the reader that very specific data about these children's personalities are included elsewhere in this book. Drs. Gray and R. Kempe have described what these children are like when they come to an emergency room or are hospitalized. Drs. Rodeheffer and Martin point out various personality traits which impinge upon the testing situation as well as those which inhibit learning. The discussion of various treatment modalities such as crises care, preschool and psychotherapy would have been incomplete without describing the behaviors which determine the goals of such interventions. Indeed, no chapter in this book completely ignores the psychological consequences of abuse.

We have given in very brief fashion some results from a specific study of personality of 50 abused children. Characteristics of these children are noted with an emphasis on the environmental factors after the incident of physical assault. From all of these data the authors have set forth five general maxims or conclusions regarding the abused child's personality. We have pointed out the need to view specific behaviors or traits of the child from a variety of perspectives if we are ever to hope to understand these children. The reader is cautioned, in terms of future investigation, to look more carefully at developmental issues in these children rather than to study the effects of child abuse only by categorizing or counting the numbers of persons with specific labels or diagnoses. We truly feel that insofar as it may be possible to understand how the abusive environment affects children's development, that one may make a major contribution to understanding the development of all children.

References

1. Martin, H., Beezley, P., Conway, E., Kempe, C.H.: The Development of Abused Children I, A Review of the Literature, *Advances Pediat.* 21, 1974, pp. 25-44.

2. Martin, H., Beezley, P., Conway, E., Kempe, C.H.: The Development of Abused Children II, Physical, Neurologic and Intellectual Outcome, *Advances Pediat.* 21, 1974, pp. 44-73.

3. Martin, H.P. and Beezley, P.: The Development of Abused Children: Personality Characteristics, Accepted for Publication, *Devel. Med. Child Neurol.*, 1976.

4. Spitz, R.: Hospitalism: An Inquiry into the Genesis of Psychiatric Conditions in Early Childhood. *Psychoanal. St. Child I*, 53-74, 1945.

5. Spitz, R., Wolf, L.M.: Anaclitic Depression: An Inquiry into the Genesis of Psychiatric Conditions of Early Childhood, *Psychoanal. St. Child II*, 323-342, 1946.

6. Friedman, R.A.: The Battering Parent and His Child: A Study of Early Object Relations. *Intern. Rer. Psychoanal.* 2:189-198, 1975.

7. Freud, A.: Normality on Pathology In Childhood: Assessments of Development, Vol. VI of *The Writings of Anna Freud* New York: Intern. Univ. Press, 1965.

8. Mahler, M.S., Dine, F., Bergman, A.: *The Psychological Birth of the Human Infant: Symbiosis and Individuation*, New York: Basic Books, 1975.

9. Erikson, E.H.: *Childhood and Society*, New York: Norton, 2nd Ed., 1963.

✳ *Chapter 10*

Special Problems in Developmental Assessment of Abused Children

Martha Rodeheffer and **Harold P. Martin**

This chapter takes up the issue of the difficulties in obtaining accurate developmental information on abused children. Given the high incidence of developmental delays and deficits in these children, an assessment of developmental strengths and weaknesses is especially important. Indeed, it is our strong recommendation that developmental assessment be routinely obtained on every abused and neglected child to insure the earliest possible identification of any problems needing intervention. In view of the particular importance of developmental assessment for abused children, those behaviors of the child which make this assessment difficult and problematic are discussed in some detail.

This is not intended to be a primer for those who do developmental testing. Indeed, this chapter is intended to be read by a variety of people interested in abused children, not just developmental testers. As we describe the behavior of abused children in the testing situation, it should be clear that this has meaning in terms of similar behavior of these children in other settings. As we point out how the tester may modify his or her testing behavior to obtain "better" behavior from the child in the testing situation, it should be clear that we are really suggesting techniques of maximizing age-appropriate behavior of these children which should be applicable to a variety of environments, not just the testing environment. As we point out the pitfalls in interpreting developmental test data, the same issues are relevant to anyone who is in contact with the child and who, for similar reasons, may erroneously label the child as incompetent.

Developmental Assessment

There are a number of ways commonly used to obtain behavioral data on children's development, e.g., interview with parents, casual observation, periodic

The work of these two authors has been supported by the Grant Foundation and Maternal Child Health #926 of Dept. of H.E.W.

screening examination and complete detailed evaluation. It is this last method, the complete detailed evaluation, we shall be speaking about in this chapter.

A few pertinent comments on the limitations of the other methods may clarify when complete developmental evaluation is indicated with the abused child. Assessment of development based only on information elicited from parents during *interviews* is often unsatisfactory. It must be pointed out that children's developmental histories provided by abusive parents are notoriously unreliable and are markedly inconsistent with medical records available on these children. The typical abusive parent has a very distorted view of the child and classically describes the child in ways that are not corroborated by others. *Casual observation* is the most common method of developmental assessment. Parents, caseworker, foster families, friends and neighbors of the child may all have impressions of the developmental status of the abused child. The adequacy of this information is dependent upon the skill and knowledge of the observer. These observations may be valuable and accurate, or they may be quite misleading. While *screening* of development is a most valuable procedure, by definition it is not a methodology to understand the developmental status and needs of children. Its value is in determining for which children the screener needs to obtain detailed developmental assessment and consultation from specialists. However, screening *per se* is neither a diagnostic tool nor an instrument for helping with treatment and management. Frankenburg and Camp's recent book on pediatric screening[1] is a valuable reference to those interested in utilizing screening tests.

Complete development assessment on the other hand has three components. For an accurate picture of the child's total development, the assessment should include a developmental history, a physical examination of the child (especially of the neurologic system) and a formal developmental test. The vagaries of obtaining an accurate developmental history from most abusing parents has been mentioned above. In addition, however, it is possible to obtain information concerning past events in the child's life such as newborn nursery records, information regarding the pregnancy, history of medical problems, any pre-school or day care records, etc. This information must be available on every abused child if we are to understand his present developmental status. The physical examination of the child is also essential. This will undoubtedly be done at the time when non-accidental injury is suspected or confirmed. The main point to be stressed is that the physician or nurse who makes that examination needs to attend not only to the primary basis for bringing the child, i.e., a history of injury, but also do a complete physical examination with special attention to the neurologic functions of the child. (See Chapter 6.) It is the formal developmental test, however, that will give us the most meaningful data about the child's developmental status, with the history and examination being important primarily for understanding and interpreting the developmental test data obtained.

It is this aspect, the developmental testing, that we address in this chapter. There are several reasons for choosing to discuss this particular aspect of the abused child. First, our experience in testing several hundred abused children is that their behavior in the testing situation makes developmental assessment much more difficult than it is for other children. It is partially for this reason that most abused children are labeled as less capable than they actually are. Further, formal testing provides a unique opportunity to observe and understand the young abused child. The experienced evaluator assesses not only the end-product of the child's efforts, that is, what he successfully does and does not do, but also attends to the child's style of approaching and attempting to master tasks. The manner in which the child relates to the examiner is also studied, providing an opportunity to observe how the child reacts when expectations to perform are being placed upon him by an adult. The evaluator has the opportunity to assess the child's impulse control, need gratification, response to praise, ability to imitate, investigativeness, ability to use adults and response to controls. There are a host of psychological parameters which are in vivid focus during the developmental testing situation. Insofar as the evaluator of the child is experienced and capable enough to attend to these behaviors of the child, he will reach an understanding of the child which should prove to be valuable information for the adults around the child: parents, teachers and therapists.

The developmental testing situation provides a condensed miniature view of how the child behaves in a variety of other settings. Inasmuch as the formal developmental test is a reliable standardized instrument, the examiner can compare the individual child to hundreds of other children of the same age who have undergone the identical testing procedure. The similarities and differences between the behavior of the child being tested and what one typically sees in other children will then be apparent. The tester is interested in what the child does and does not do. He is interested in what the child can and cannot do. He is interested in the manner in which the child behaves. Finally, he is interested in what might be helpful to the child in terms of enhancing his developmental progress.

No attempt will be made here to discuss the variety of developmental tests which are available—nor to differentiate developmental tests from other types of tests such as those which purport to measure intelligence, perceptual motor ability or speech and language. It should be pointed out to the reader, however, that we are primarily addressing the developmental testing of children under five years of age. Some of the tests which we have used have included the Bayley Scales of Infant Development,[2] the Yale[3] which is a modified Gesell test, and the McCarthy Scales of Children's abilities.[4] For further information on developmental testing, for those interested, we refer you to Illingsworth's book on development of the infant and young child,[5] and Knobloch and Pasamanick's recent revision of *Gesell and Amatruda's Developmental Diagnosis.*[6]

For those completely unacquainted with developmental testing of young children, a few brief comments are in order. The formal assessment is structured in such a way as to provide an estimate of the child's current level of development in such areas as speech, language, personal-social, gross motor, fine motor and adaptive abilities. Some developmental tests, however, provide only overall scores for a few categories such as mental and motor development, leaving to the examiner a teasing out of the various components of the child's performance. The child is presented with a series of tasks, presented in a game-like format, in which the examiner instructs or models for the child how the task is to be accomplished. The performance of the child is then compared with normative performance data of other children. Most children find developmental tests a great deal of fun. In addition to responding to questions, there are games such as puzzles, form boards and block designs to build. Interaction is considerable as the child and examiner play ball, draw together or look at picture books. One of the essentials of developmental testing is that the child should sense that the examiner is interested in playing and interacting with him, rather than sense that he is being evaluated. Yet the developmental test is not identical to a free play interview. Structure is imposed on the child. He may have little, if any, choice of what toys to play with and in what order. He is required to sit, or move about, or try to solve a task or relinquish toys, all at the discretion of the examiner. So while the child is experiencing a situation wherein an adult is making demands and placing expectations upon him, albeit in a relaxed, fun, interactive manner, it is not at all dissimilar to what he normally experiences in his home, in a preschool or in almost any setting with adults; and the child's behavior and response to the testing situation will usually mirror his behavior in a number of other natural settings.

Behaviors of Abused Children During Developmental Assessment

As previously stated, most abused children appear less capable than they actually are. The discrepancy between the abused child's abilities and the way in which he presents himself to adults is apparent in many areas of day-to-day functioning including the formal evaluation setting. The discussion below explores the abused child's behaviors during developmental assessment and some of the factors contributing to these behaviors. We are primarily focusing on those behaviors which interfere with the testing and which, more important, will also interfere with the child's learning. Hence, these are behaviors which potentially are leading to real developmental delays.

Hypervigilance. The dynamics of the formal evaluation setting exacerbate the unusual hypervigilance of the abused child. He arrives in the examining room with a past history of punitive experiences with adults and his learned expectations regarding adult-child interactions affect the way he behaves during the testing. His tendency to perceive threat, whenever under close surveillance by an adult, is in dynamic interplay with the intense scrutiny inherent in the evaluation setting. Preoccupation with the examiner and attempts to reduce the anxiety aroused by the evaluation procedures may have a deleterious effect upon the abused child's ability to focus attention on the materials and may reduce his ability to perform. He is alert to the examiner's every move, often focusing attention on the examiner's face rather than on the materials needed for the task. If the examiner moves his hand to pick up a pencil, he may find the child observing him diligently, completely distracted from the task. It appears to be of utmost importance for the child to "read" the whims of this stranger with whom he finds himself. The child is slow to relax and trust the examiner's good will toward him. He behaves as if he is extremely vulnerable and must be in constant readiness for unexpected events. He is easily distracted from the tasks at hand. Every door nearby being shut, footsteps in the hall, voices, sounds of air conditioners, will be distracting, often bringing inquiry from the abused child, seeking some explanation for events that are not comprehensible to him.

Fear of Failure. The abused child demonstrates an unusual sensitivity to failure. His efforts to avoid failure are intense. The format of the developmental evaluation procedures presents particular difficulties for the abused child. The tasks presented to the child begin with things the child can easily perform. However, in order to test the outer limits of the child's abilities, the tasks are sequenced so that they become progressively more difficult. Adequate testing requires administration of items which are beyond the child's abilities. For the child to be willing to attempt tasks that are difficult for him, he must have developed some tolerance for ambiguity and frustration for failure. He must have realistically accepted limitations appropriate for his age, understanding that many things are rightfully beyond him at this stage of development. To do well on testing, he must not have undue fears of the consequences of being unable to perform a task when asked to do so by an adult. The abused child's observably increasing anxiety over his inability to perform is distinctly different than that of a normal child's, and his effort to flee the possibility of failure takes many forms. He may scan the examiner's face for cues or ask for reassurances that he is on the right track. Indeed, when such reassurances are withheld, some abused children will change correct answers and become quite disoriented, anxious and uncooperative. Failing to elicit approving feedback from the examiner appears to trigger a sense of fear. The child seems to be overwhelmed by anxiety which then stimulates efforts to avoid the tasks.

The abused child typically has received a great deal of punishment for failure to perform up to the abusive parents' standards. Abusive parents are frequently characterized as having unrealistically high expectations for their children. Indeed, abuse often occurs when the child is perceived by the parent as willfully withholding some desired behavior, even when that behavior is actually beyond the child's abilities to perform at his age. Such a parent is quick to point out the deficiencies of the child's approximations to the task. The abused child who is actually precocious in some areas of development of particular significance to the parents, may be evaluated as inadequate by his parents' standard. In the absence of feedback and positive messages about his performance, the child fail to internalize positive feelings about his own efforts and products. At least in the presence of adults the abused child becomes unable to enjoy or evaluate as "good," his own products apart from the adult's standard. This will have considerable importance in his developing concept of self, and ego-ideals.

Difficulty Attending to Instructions. It is often apparent to the examiner that the abused child is not appropriately focused in on the task being presented. He often does not seem to hear or see the task, but rather responds regressively to the materials. Several different things may be occurring. As for all young children, the visual stimulus of the materials presented produces an impulsive desire to touch and manipulate the materials. It is anticipated that with increasing maturity, the normal child will become able to resist immediate gratification of that desire without experiencing undue tension. However, with the abused preschooler, the desire to touch may result in extreme forms of behavior which preclude attending to the specific task required. For example, some of these children give in to the impulse, grabbing the toys from the examiner in a desperate attempt to obtain them. Early in the testing, one more often sees the child as very inhibited, reluctant to play with toys except on demand. But, as he very quickly comes to accept the safety of the situation, his impulsiveness and tremendous neediness come to the fore. Laying out the materials in the prescribed manner becomes next to impossible. For such a child, the examiner finds his suitcase or store of testing materials an irresistible pull to which the child moves insistently and annoyingly throughout the session. This child has difficulty becoming involved in any one toy and seems insatiable in his desire to obtain everything available. He has a great deal of difficulty relinquishing materials but moves away from materials whenever the examiner attempts to structure the task.

On the other hand, some abused children have over-learned the lesson to *not touch* things unless given permission. They exhibit many signs of tension. Inhibition of activity is apparent as these children often tentatively "announce" what they want to do and make darting looks at the examiner, finally reaching for materials only when the examiner gives permission.

In either extreme, it is notable that the preschool-age abused child often does not appear to hear, or at least does not respond to the verbal instructions that accompany the examiner's laying out the test materials. Occasionally the abused child will simply repeat the examiner's exact words in rote fashion while making no attempt to act meaningfully on the words being echoed. The "task" is mistakenly perceived to be a request to imitate the examiner's words or label items in a fashion more typically used to teach very young children to talk. The abused child's limited response to verbal statements and demands of others is unusual. It is as if the child is fixated on an earlier developmental type of response pattern, even while some other aspects of language have progressed.

Perhaps the spoken word has been of much less significance in the child's experience than the non-verbal messages and physical movement of the adult caretaker. In focusing on non-verbal communication, perhaps verbal meaning is less available to the child whose anxiety is raised by the adult's surveillance of him. Perhaps the child's verbal interactions with the adult have largely been in the form of repeating adult demands, rather than talking freely and spontaneously from the babbling stage of language development onward.

Verbal Inhibition. Verbal items are difficult to administer to abused children, but occasionally provide insight into their preoccupations. While labeling items may be responded to readily, more difficult tasks are notable for the paucity of the responses. Projective testing is frequently abandoned with these children because of the limited verbal responses they give and the amount of prompting necessary to obtain them. The abused child has great difficulty with word finding and organization of thoughts in response to questions, even while it may be apparent, by his pointing when pictures are used, that he comprehends key elements of the task. His spontaneous language frequently reveals a much greater language capacity than his responses to structured questions.

It is speculated that the abused child has learned that it is dangerous to talk and consequently has reduced his verbal output. Verbalization is an important step in cognitive development and learning in that it requires an abstracting procedure that primary thinking does not. The specificity of response required in verbalization is an important developmental skill that requires practice and feedback from others. Such experience is often not part of the abused child's history.

Failure to Scan. Many abused children fail to scan adequately in situations requiring discrimination between events. They tend to impulsively embrace the first possible solution and fail to perceive that there is a better one. The failure to entertain the possibility of alternative solutions is rooted in the child's method of coping with anxiety and the accompanying regression. It is also reinforced by standardized examination procedures when direct feedback as to success or failure to the child is not allowed.

Passive-Aggressiveness and Resistance. While the defensive coping mechanisms vary greatly from one abused child to another, the authors have been struck by the amount of passive-aggressiveness exhibited by these children. Most abused children are excessively compliant as this formal assessment session commences. Direct refusals to attempt the tasks presented by the examiner are generally rare. However, the child's efforts may become increasingly half-hearted and oppositional in nature as the tasks become more difficult and he experiences more threat of failure. Superficially, he may continue to give an impression of cooperation and a desire to please the adult. However, the child may be saying "yes" or echoing the instructions but *not* acting in accordance with his own verbalizations. He may attempt to substitute his own activities for the tasks presented. The particular nature of this defensive style of coping with pressures, results in a sense of confusion and frustration on the part of the examiner. Gradually he becomes aware of the dissonance between the child's stated intentions and behavior. The child's seeming denial of his own resistance makes it more difficult to deal with the defensive maneuver head-on. It is difficult to recognize finally that the child is very subtly, cleverly and passively obstructing what the examiner is wanting to get done. At times this seems very much imbedded in a struggle over control of the situation—who will decide, who will call the shots. It can easily be seen as a very important coping mechanism that the child disguise his willfulness so as to avoid anger and abuse. His developing autonomy, initiative and self are taking a somewhat circuitous route, as he is not safe to *openly* disagree, oppose, refuse what adults want of him. And yet he *is* disagreeing, opposing, refusing. The examiner may find himself becoming frustrated and angry with his inability to accomplish the formal developmental assessment. Emotions felt by the examiner toward the child at this point may facilitate some empathy for parents and other caretakers who are involved in the daily management of the child.

Interpretation of Developmental Data

The most difficult task for the authors has been the interpretation of the data, making sense of what the developmental status and potential of the abused child truly is. This difficulty is shared by others who see the child in other settings: at school, at home, at play. Why the difficulty?

We usually are faced with data which show the abused child as unable to perform age-appropriately. If one only looks at what the child does and does not do, he is usually functioning in a delayed or retarded range. Yet there are other data which strongly suggest that this is not a true reflection of the child's ability. For one, the examiner has noted the many behaviors of the child which clearly have interfered with the child's performance. One thinks, "What if the child had been less anxious, less vigilant, less distractable, less afraid of failure?" Unquestionably, the testing did not reveal what the child *might* be capable of doing. On the other hand, perhaps these personality traits of the child have not only interfered with the testing results, but have also interfered with his learning to such a degree that he is truly not capable of any more than he was able to produce on the test.

One also typically finds an unusual amount of unevenness and scatter in the child's performance. Many abused children fail easy items and then pass much more difficult ones. Or they may pass an item and then fail that same item when re-assessed days or months later. Test-retest reliability of abused children is poor, and a confusing profile of abilities results from repeated testing. There is considerable scatter between subtests of the test. The results of developmental testing on the children at the National Center Preschool has been discussed in Chapter 6. There we saw that the mean developmental quotients varied up to sixteen points between different subsets. In some areas of abilities the child may be quite delayed, while above age-level in others. Merely to add up scores and determine a developmental quotient is not only irrelevant, it is truly misleading.

A further compounding of the general confusion results from neurologic findings noted in the testing as well as from formal physical examination. The examiner not only notes inabilities of the child, for example, to perform such gross motor tasks as hopping, negotiating stairs, jumping, etc.; he also notes the poor quality of the motor tasks which are successfully completed. The abused child is often awkward, maladroit, and painstaking with his motor performance. He may additionally have unusual muscle tone, poor reflex development, impaired sensory-motor integration, or any number of other neurologic signs. As discussed in Chapters 6 and 8, we are no longer so ready to assume immediately that those neurologic signs are necessarily secondary to structural or functional organic abnormality of the central nervous system. Experience and/or the lack of appropriate experiences may be the basis for these findings. Anxiety may be reflected in the tremors, hyperactive reflexes, awkwardness, etc. While in some respects the differential diagnosis between brain damage and the effects of negative environmental factors is not helpful, nonetheless, with the abused child this question is frequently being asked. After all, the child has been injured, the chances of traumatic damage to the brain are great. It may be important, as well as of interest, to the court, parents and others, whether the behaviors one sees are secondary to physical trauma, or are attributed to an inadequate environment.

We are frequently left unable to make some of these diagnostic distinctions with any real sense of conviction. More often we are simply able to describe the child as we saw him—commenting and emphasizing the many behaviors which make it clear when the testing performance is *not* a reflection of the child's developmental potential. What we most often need to do in order to make an accurate diagnosis is to provide as optimal an environment as possible for the child and then over time see what changes in behavior are made. Reassessment after a period of optimal environment then may be diagnostic, or at least helpful, in making a more long-term prognosis about the child's development and neurologic state and potential. With an adequate home setting and with appropriate treatment established for the child, over time we can see the capacity of the child to "catch up" in his development. We usually see in post-treatment follow-up quite a different child. There are fewer of the behaviors which interfere both with testing and with learning. There is less scatter and less unevenness in performance. Many of the neurologic signs which were first noted are no longer observable.

In many ways, this is not different than with any child whose development one is asked to assess. The philosophy of looking not only at the child and his developmental status at one point in time, but *also* of observing his *rate* of development was one of the important basic tenets of the pioneers of child development, such as Gesell. Yet with the abused child, its importance becomes ever so much more prominent. The young abused child presents a much more difficult and complex picture to sort out and adequately understand. The abused child has had injury which might have damaged brain tissue. The abused child has been living in an inadequate environment with a deviant parent-child relationship. With the known importance of those factors in influencing development, it then becomes essential to see what developmental progress can be made by the child when his environment is made as supportive and growth-promoting as is possible.

This brings us to the third and final section of this chapter. Part of the task of interpretation of results of developmental testing is for the evaluator to be able to discover ways and means of enhancing the developmental progress of the child. On one level that means a critical look at treatment recommendations such as home environment, school placement or specific treatment modalities— all of which are discussed in the second section of this book. On a more specific level, this requires the evaluator to determine, during the testing situation, what type of approaches and stances of the adult will make it easier for the child to function and perform more successfully in any environment. It is just these approaches and behaviors of the developmental evaluator which have been found to be helpful to the child, that can be transmitted to parents, teachers or therapists of the child, indeed to any adult who is in a position to help in promoting the child's growth and development. So we shall turn to those modifications which are important and valuable in the testing situation to maximize the child's comfort and performance. The recommendations which follow for working with abused children will appear insofar as they can be used by adults in settings other than testing to similarly help the child learn and develop.

Recommended Modification of Developmental Assessment Procedures

Given the dynamic characteristics of abused children, it is apparent that assessment conducted under rigorous standardized conditions will tend to produce inordinate anxiety in these children. This anxiety activates extreme defensive maneuvers which, while possibly serving to reduce the immediate tension the child is experiencing, greatly interfere with his performance on assessment tasks presented to him. If the examiner is determined and presses on, regardless of these defensive maneuvers, it is likely that the child's behavior will further deteriorate and that his coping mechanisms will become increasingly regressive. Such head-on confrontations and ensuing power struggles will result in premature abandonment of efforts to formally assess the abused child. At best, assessments completed under such adverse conditions are likely to produce inaccurate, depressed estimates of the child's capabilities or potential. The only meaningful interpretation of scores obtained in this way on formal measures would be as representative of the child's functional level under conditions of extreme stress.

Evaluation procedures need to be modified in order to maintain cooperation and optimal effort with the abused child. Herein lies a dilemma for the examiner. Using formal methods to assess children allows the examiner to compare the performance of a particular child to that of other children of the same age by utilizing the data available in tables of statistically derived norms. Such norms are meaningful only when the assessment items are presented to the child in the same standardized manner as originally administered to the children in a normative sample. If the task is modified, for example, by allowing more trials or more time, or by giving instructions or demonstrations which provide additional cues as to how to perform the task, then meaningful comparisons of this child's performance cannot be made on the basis of the normative data provided, as the task is not the same in the two cases. If the examiner modifies the formal procedures, the normative data cannot be utilized. If he does *not* modify the procedures, the abused child is unlikely to cooperate and persevere long enough to complete the required tasks. This dilemma cannot be completely resolved in either direction. It is possible, however, to utilize some assessment strategies that will minimize the likelihood that the child will experience incapacitating anxiety. Such strategies can be employed while, by and large, maintaining the standardized procedures required for utilization of normative data. If such strategies are used, it is imperative that the examiner interpret the child's performance cautiously as that which he is capable of producing under optimal conditions, as opposed to how he performs given the more commonly available contingencies of social reinforcement from adults in day to day situations.

If the examiner begins the formal assessment session as he would with any other child, he will have opportunity to observe at what point the child's anxiety begins to interfere with his ability to perform. The limit of the child's frustration tolerance is valuable clinical data. However, the examiner must walk a tight line in determining when the frustration is likely to precipitate defensive tactics in the child which will interfere with his willingness to perform. At such points, the examiner may find some of the following suggestions useful.

Adjusting Strategies to Developmental Level. Abused children are frequently delayed socially and emotionally. The examiner must interact with the child in ways appropriate to his developmental level, regardless of his chronological age. It will sometimes be necessary, especially with abused children, to use techniques that would usually be reserved for younger children. When the child is distressed, distraction may prove a most effective strategy. As with any toddler, it is often wise to present the abused preschooler with the next testing toy before trying to get him to relinquish the one he has in his hands. Toys to be used in the next task are best kept completely out of sight until the moment they are actually presented. The transfer of toys used in the assessment must be made smoothly, moving them quickly in and out of the assessment kit, thus arousing the least possible distress in the child.

Reducing Threat. The supportive atmosphere provided in the evaluation of any child bears special attention here. An offer of candy or other treat may be used as an initial relationship builder that will cause the child to approach the examiner. Sitting down with the child on small chairs, makes the adult a less looming figure. Speaking softly and gently to the child, a kindly demeanor and warm facial expressions are essential components of the evaluation session. Sudden moves are to be avoided as much as possible as the examiner prepares the child for each event, prior to its taking place.

Motivation. The full attention of a kindly adult whose "suitcase" is stocked full of miniature toys and games is sufficient to elicit the curiosity and cooperation necessary for assessing most children. The smiles and pleasure of the examiner in response to the child's efforts are sufficient rewards. The evaluator increases the probability of the child persevering by judicious application of social reinforcers (smiles, touch, positive comments about how hard the child is trying). However, some abused children are not able to draw upon the available support of the examiner, no matter how kindly, and social reinforcers may need to be supplemented with primary reinforcers. For such children the behaviors needed may be elicited and rewarded through the use of food. The evaluator may want to have on hand a store of foods such as raisins, sugar coated cereals, miniature marshmallows, or small tidbits of any food the child likes and for which he will work. In general, the sequence applied is as follows: The child is asked if he would like a tidbit of desirable food, thereby eliciting his interest; then receiving the tidbit is made contingent upon performance of a prior behavior needed for the assessment. Any serious attempt at a response, right or wrong, is rewarded.

Getting and Holding Child's Attention. A major requirement in working with abused children is getting their attention focused in on the task itself, instead of on everything around them. Testing will proceed most smoothly in a room reduced of the distractions of other toys and observers. With toddlers, it is common practice to have a parent in the room, at times holding the child on the lap. However, the abused child may be too concerned and preoccupied with the parent to focus in on the assessment tasks. If the testing is not proceeding well, a parent might be asked to join the examiner, or, as the case may be, to leave the examining room for a "cup of coffee." The manner in which brief separations are discussed and handled by both parent and child is of diagnostic importance regarding their relationship.

Before proceeding with the instructions for a task, the examiner needs to obtain the complete attention of the child. This is sometimes difficult with anxious abused children who are attempting to reduce their anxiety by avoiding the task. If eye contact can be achieved prior to giving the instructions, the examiner will have a better opportunity to assess what is happening to the child. The abused child needs first to comprehend the instructions. The initial problem is to get the child to *"listen* to what the examiner says." Though this may seem simplistic, it appears to be a crucial step with which many abused children have difficulty. Some preschoolers have been noted to perceive the task as repeating the examiner's words by rote; when the materials for the task are subsequently presented, the child may not make any connection with the verbal instructions. If standardized administration permits, the examiner may want to repeat the instructions again, once the child has handled the materials. If the child is failing the items largely because he is not listening, the examiner may even want to ask the child to repeat what the instructions are prior to presenting the materials. This not only informs the examiner of how much the child understood but also provides a cognitive mediation of activity on the child's part. If this improves the child's performance, the examiner will want to make note of that for caretakers who work with the child.

The abused child is overly sensitive to distractions. Often he ceases working on a task to look anxiously at the examiner who begins to record responses or make notes. It is important, in such situations, that the examiner wait until the child has completed the response, before recording it.

Abused children are extremely easily distracted by auditory stimuli. They appear anxious and inquire into the source of the sound, needing to know what is happening at all times. The examiner should explain what the noise is, but might also inquire what the child thought the noise was.

Reducing Sense of Failure. When the child begins to show signs of stress in the face of failure, the examiner may find it helpful to slip in several short, non-test items that the child can pass with ease. Such interspersing of success allows the child to relax and interrupts the defensiveness that grows in the face of the increasing difficulty of items necessary in obtaining the prescribed number of failures on each task. They examiner must carefully select such "breather" items to insure that they provide no cues or extra practice for actual test items.

If the child fails an item, the examiner may point out or comment on any successful approximations to the task that the child made. Even minor problem-solving attempts can be acknowledged. For example, when the child simply fills all the holes with pegs, but makes many errors in color-coding them, the examiner might say with pleasure, "You filled *all* the holes," and smile acceptingly at the child while removing the materials.

With the last failure in the prescribed series the examiner might say, "Let's do it together," and proceed to do the task himself, but leave the very obvious finishing touches for the child so he may achieve a sense of closure. This must not be done in situations where the child's performance on a subsequent task would be benefitted by seeing the task performed correctly.

Emphasizing the Play—Milieu for the Child. It has been commented on above that typically and by design, developmental tasks are imbedded in a "play" situation. And yet this becomes even more crucial to the abused child. Consider for a moment the environment in which the child has been living. The parents have been critical of the child, especially of his inabilities, his inadequacies.

Punishment and abuse have been the result of the child not meeting the parents' expectations and demands. The child is now in a testing situation where a new and strange adult is making demands and placing expectations on him. Furthermore, the older child (perhaps above two years of age) has some awareness of why he is being tested. He may feel the testing has something to do with where he will live—or in some way be scheduled because of his misdeeds. The older child may feel he is being tested to determine if he has something wrong with his brains. All of this adds up to a situation wherein "being tested" is anxiety producing and threatening. From the very beginning, we explain to children and parents that we are wanting to spend some time with the child to talk with him, play with him, and to learn to know him. We may further add we are interested in knowing how his muscles move and work—what kind of things he likes to draw, play with, or do.

During the testing one frequently used task is to see what the child's capacity for remembering a series of numbers is. It may be explained to the child that "We are now going to play a listening game. I am going to say some numbers, and you need to listen very carefully to see how many of them you can remember and say back to me. O.K. now, are you listening really carefully?" Another language task is to have the child respond to action agents—e.g., what sleeps, what burns, what melts, what flies, etc. This may be introduced as a "thinking game" in which the examiner is going to say a word and the child is going to "think of something that *does* what that word means. In point of fact, there are a number of tasks on any developmental test which are really not typical games, but rather are situations wherein the examiner wants and expects the child to solve a problem or perform a task. Yet it is quite possible for these tasks to be enjoyable, fun activities.

Perhaps the most important issue here is for the examiner to truly feel himself that he is not going to be testing a child, but rather that he is going to be using a test to try to understand a child. That subtle step can be accomplished wherein the feeling of being tested, or being evaluated, or being graded, does not need to be what the child is feeling. He instead may feel something more akin to a sense that the evaluator is wanting to relate with him, to play with him, to understand him.

Summary

We started out from a position that some developmental assessment should be made for every abused and neglected child. That may or may not require formal developmental assessment, including development testing. Observations of the child and developmental screening tools may be adequate to assure one that the child's development is normal or clarify that it requires more detailed study. We then pointed out some of the special considerations in testing the abused child. We noted that the child's behavior usually interferes with his performance and confounds our understanding of his capabilities on developmental test items.

Yet, it was emphasized that this very same behavior is important to identify and note, for it may be the most critical area of deviation for which the child needs help. Nonetheless, because of the unusual behaviors of abused children which are obvious in a testing situation, as well as the typical findings on testing and neurologic examination, interpretation of the child's developmental status and prognosis are especially difficult and susceptible to error. We have further pointed out some of the ways in which the developmental evaluator can maximize the ability of the child to learn and to perform.

Perhaps one of the most important issues raised herein is to point out to the reader what he should expect from an adequate, developmental assessment. One should not accept a report which only reports on the child's passes and failures. One cannot simply take a numerical score from testing and make any meaning of it without further data from the evaluator. The evaluator is obligated to try to understand the child, not just to report his performance on a test. Behaviors of the child should be described. Strengths and weaknesses should both be attended to. There are at least two critically important tasks of the evaluator which one should insist upon. First is an explanation of *why* the child performed as he did. A Developmental Quotient of 65 means nothing except that the child obviously did much more poorly than most children his age would. The real question we want addressed is why did he do that poorly. What evidence is there that the performance was reflecting retardation, anxiety, inadequate environmental experience or sensory deficit. The second major task of the evaluator is to supply whomever requested consultation with treatment recommendations. These treatment recommendations will vary in their depth and helpfulness. They will hopefully include consideration of treatment modalities which are essential or which might be helpful to the growth and development of the child. They may further include considerations of the way and manner in which parents and other adults will find success in helping to optimize the growth and development—and the happiness of the abused child.

References
1. Frankenburg, W. and Camp, B.: *Pediatric Screening Tests.* Charles Thomas, Springfield, Ill., 1975.

2. Bayley, Nancy: *Bayley Scales of Infant Development.* New York: Psychological Corporation, 1969.

3. Yale: Composed of selected test items from the Gesell Developmental Schedules (Gesell, A., and Amatruda, C.S.: *Developmental Diagnosis,* New York: Hoeber, 1947); Stanford-Binet Intelligence Test (Terman, L.M. and Merrill, M.A.: *Stanford-Binet Intelligence Scale Manual for the Third Revision,* Form L-M Boston: Houghton Mifflin Co., 1960); Merrill-Palmer Mental Tests (Stutsman, R.: *Guide for Administering the Merrill-Palmer Scale of Mental Tests,* New York: Harcourt, Brace & World, 1948), and the Hetzer-Wolfe-Buhler Baby Tests (Buhler, C.: *The First Year of Life,* New York: John Day Co., 1930, pp. 189-277).

4. McCarthy, D.: *McCarthy Scales of Children's Abilities*, New York: Psychological Corporation, 1972.

5. Illingsworth, R.S.: *The Development of the Infant and Young Child: Normal and Abnormal* (Fifth edition), Baltimore: The Williams and Williams Company, 1972.

6. Knobloch, H., and Pasamanick, B., (eds.): *Gesell and Amatruda's Developmental Diagnosis: The Evaluation and Management of Normal and Abnormal Neuropsychologic Development in Infancy and Early Childhood*, Third edition. New York: Harper and Row Publishers, Inc., 1974.

✳ *Chapter 11*

Ethological Methods Studying the Behavior and Development of Young Children from Abusing Families

Peter L. Appleton

Introduction

Clinically and biologically, we need to know how individual children contribute to, and cope with, insecure relationships with their caretakers.[a] In order for therapists to correct attachment breakdown, and in order to understand the biology of social and cognitive development, we need to know the behavioral details of ongoing social interactions in families. Most significant, we need to know what short-term and long-term adaptive strategies individual children have *naturally* available for dealing with crisis in relationship. Equally, we need to know what *natural* limitations there are on what an individual child can tolerate in crisis during the early years.

Many of the recent advances[1-4] in the understanding of human attachment have been based on ethological methods and theory. This essay is about the relevance of ethology for the understanding of attachment breakdown and its consequences.

Ethology is the biological study of behavior. Methodologically, it is characterized by accurate, non-inferential descriptions of the ongoing behavior of, in this case, children, usually in a naturalistic setting. Descriptions are built up of the behaviors typically shown by individuals of a particular species, how these behaviors are organized, and how their development proceeds during a period of immaturity. In young children, for instance, crying tends to occur on separation from a caretaker.[1,2] But as the child develops, he can usually tolerate separation

[a]Margaret Lynch asked me to write this paper. I am grateful for discussions with both Dr. Lynch and Dr. Christopher Ounsted. The group work with the children, and the observations, could not have been done without the help of Jennie Hart, Sue Kenrick, Aagje Korving, Bridget Leverton, Aiden McFarlane and Barbara Twining. I am happy to thank Dr. Gordon Claridge, Professor Ray Helfer, Theresa O'Hanrahan, Felicity Huntingford, Dr. Harold Martin, and Dr. Lars Smith for their comments on a first draft.

more readily, and he actually explores the environment further and further away from a caretaker.[5] Another example comes from human language development. Towards the end of the first year of life, and on into the second, a child shows active "prespeech," together with pointing, object play and smiling.[6] As the child learns a language, the accompanying behaviors still remain in the same combination or grouping.

For ethologists, these observed regularities in the short-term, and developmental, organization of behavior have the same theoretical significance as species-regularities in anatomical structure, physiology or morphology.[7] They adapt the animal to the environment in which it has evolved. Behaviors have been selected naturally because they increase the probability of survival. This theoretical position originates with the work of Charles Darwin[8-10] and forms the mainstay of Bowlby's recent,[1,2] but already classic, discussion of human attachment or bonding.

Bowlby argues that the primary function of attachment behavior (i.e., that function which had the greatest survival premium) during man's evolution, was protection from predators. Clearly, attachment behavior also functions to keep the youngster near a food source. It is important that it also forms the context for the child's cognitive and social learning.

Ethological Method with Particular Reference to Children

Behavior Categories. An ethological investigation begins with a period of what has been called "creative observation." The individuals one is interested in (whether they be of a particular species, or of a subgroup within a species, such as autistic children or abused children) are watched, with a minimum of intrusion, for a lengthy period of time. The observer soon begins to see behavioral regularities. He then makes explicit, by description, the material basis of these impressions. Behavioral regularities, at the simplest level, which when named we shall call behavior categories, may be functional ('give' or 'take'), or morphological ('cry' or 'smile'). They are not inferential, e.g., there is no such behavior as 'aggressive' behavior.

Behavior Category Groupings. How is behavior organized? Which behavior categories tend to go together regularly? For instance, in young children (run, jump, playface) forms a grouping, as does (smile, talk, point, give, receive). These groupings, which can be established by correlation techniques,[11-13] are the first step toward analyzing context. By using multivariate statistical analysis, one can analyze both the fine structure of groupings and how groupings themselves correlate.

Situations. Behavior groupings take on their meanings further from the interactions in which they are embedded or expressed. How is the expression of behaviors and behavior groupings initiated, maintained and terminated by the partner in the interaction? For instance (approach, arms up, cry, cling) is terminated by certain maternal contact variables.

Several investigators have recently pointed out[14,15] that it is crucial, in the study of social development, to tease out the contributions made in a social relationship, by each partner. Pure frequency measures of behavior, such as crying on separation, carry no such information.

The above procedures then provide a methodology for the description of regularities in sequences of social interaction in the young child. Methods of sampling behavior sequences have been comprehensively reviewed by A. Altmann.[16]

Other important aspects of method are discussed by Hutt and Hutt,[17] Hinde,[18,19] Blurton Jones,[3] and McGrew.[20]

Behavior Groupings in Normal Young Children

Empirical child ethology is a very recent discipline. There have only been a few studies of behavior groupings in children, and still fewer of their development. The details set out below are therefore entirely preliminary and open to dispute.

1. *Child-Mother Interactions*

   a. *(Approach, cry, arms up, cling)*

   This grouping[21] is the essentially proximity-maintaining strategy which tends to be very specific to a familiar caretaker. It is this aspect of the child's relationship with a caretaker which Bowlby pays most attention to.

   b. *(Smile, look at, talk, point, give, show object)*

   This grouping is frequently shown to caretakers but also to other familiar adults. It is the social context in which a language is learned.[6,22] Recently more attention is being paid to this aspect of relationship, and particularly to the growth of what has been called 'intersubjectivity.'[23,24] That is, in a normal, reciprocal relationship, the child and the caretaker build up a shared world of meanings, of reference, such that language learning is a voyage of discovery for both the child and the caretakers. As Newson and Newson put it "the origin of symbolic functioning should be sought, not in the child's activities with inanimate objects, but rather in those idiosyncratic but shared understandings which he first evolves during his earliest social encounters with familiar human beings who are themselves already steeped in human culture" (Newson and Newson, 1975, p. 445).

   c. *(Laughter)*

   A recent study[25] has examined the situations which elicit laughter in infants. As Bruner[22] has indicated, those caretaker behaviors most likely to produce laughter are exactly those that will induce crying and avoidance when performed by a stranger. So the caretaker will, as it were, 'play at' separation, hiding briefly, or make sudden movements, or sudden noises, or pretend to be an animal.

2. *Child-Child Interactions*

   a. *(Smile, talk, point, give, receive)*

     This social play grouping, demonstrated in two-year-olds and four-year olds,[11,13] is clearly developmentally related to the similar grouping expressed to adults.

   b. *(Take-tug-grab, hit, push, frown)*

     This is the familiar object dispute of young children.[11] It frequently arises out of the social play grouping when an object exchange escalates into claim for possession.

   c. *(Laugh, playface, run, jump, wrestle)*

     This is rough-and-tumble play.[11,13] It is ethological investigation which has shown this to be quite independent of social object play in young children, and independent of fighting (take-tug-grab, etc.).

The Behavior of Young Children from
Abusing Families

In this section I shall formulate several hypotheses about the behavior of children from abusing families. These hypotheses will be based on our experience working with these children and their families at the Park Hospital for Children, Oxford.[26-28]

It should be made clear that the hypotheses have not been tested. They may be regarded as research guidelines.

I shall lay out the hypotheses in terms of differential expression of behavior groupings demonstrated in normal young children.

1. *Child-Adult Interactions*

   a. *(Approach, arms up, cling, cry)*

     The hypothesis is put forward that the threshold for elicitation of the above, proximity-maintaining grouping, is lower in abused children, and that the grouping is more intensely expressed.

     Such a condition could arise through—

     (i)   the child being sick[29] and therefore crying with less provocation than is usually necessary. This would normally be an adaptive strategy in terms of Bowlby's theory, because a sick infant is at greater risk for predation;

     (ii)   caretaker unpredictability. The parents may be literally unpredictable, or their behavior might be continually at variance with the child's needs.

     A further hypothesis is that on actual separation, in an unfamiliar environment, the proximity-maintaining grouping may be expressed to one unfamiliar adult, and maintained selectively with that one individual, until the return of the caretaker. This would also be an adaptive move.

   b. *Comfort avoid, arch back when picked up, gaze avoid, hide head in hands, rock, bang head*

     It is hypothesized that the above behaviors can occur on separation, in abused children, even in the presence of familiar adults.

c. *"frozen watchfulness"*[30]

The child is typically stone silent and does not move. He or she may watch, but no other signals are given off, either to the caretaker or to anyone else.

Those children who demonstrate this behavior grouping may have been repeatedly abused.

Presumably "frozen watchfulness" is, adaptively speaking, the last stand. The child has learned, after repeated abuse that gaining attention is followed by punishment.

It would follow from the above set of hypotheses, that abused children, as individuals, spend a great deal of time either scanning for possible separation, or trying to correct actual separation, primarily by crying to attract attention. Presumably, over time, a caretaker would become less and less tolerant, the child more and more suspicious, until communication is paralyzed by "frozen watchfulness."

d. *(Smile, look at, talk, point, give, show object)*

It is hypothesized that abused children spend relatively less time expressing the above, social-language, grouping.

This would arise through—

(i)   the child's attention being frequently occupied in scanning for, and correcting, separation, therefore precluding the social-language grouping.

(ii)   the social-language grouping being less often responded to, or elicited, by caretakers.

One consequence of this would be language or speech retardation in a group of abused children.

As we described in the previous section, it is in the context of the social-language grouping that a shared understanding of symbolic gesture, specific to individual relationships, is built up. Pawlby (cited by Newson and Newson, 1975),[24] in a study of normal mother-infant interactions, found that "some of the (mothers) talked spontaneously about trying to get on the same wavelength (as their infants)" (Newson and Newson, 1975, p. 441). The occurrence of abuse must mark the condition par excellence, of failure to establish communication. A number of authors have remarked on how parents of abused children occupy a fantasy world concerning the needs and behavior of their children. Quite false meanings are attributed to the child's behavior.

e. *(Laughter)*

It is hypothesized that the abused child will have relative difficulty in discriminating 'play' approaches.

2. *Child-Child Interactions*

a. *(Smile, talk, point, give, receive)*—social play

b. *Take-tug-grab, hit, push, frown)*—object disputes

It is hypothesized that, as a consequence of difficulties experienced in the expression of the social-language grouping to caretakers, social play with other children more frequently escalates into object disputes.

Directiveness. It has been our experience that children of all degrees of deprivation show a clear self-regulatory directiveness in their behavioral development when they become temporarily secure. It is as if they are catching up on lost time. This may occur when the abused child is removed from a parent, comes out of 'frozen watchfulness' and begins to explore and to smile and give people objects. Or it may occur when the mother of a previously silent, watchful, passive child, without language, is helped therapeutically to 'tune into' her child's signals. The social-language grouping may then emerge, very quickly and readily, with all its components present, and the child will then actively constrain his caretakers to reciprocate to this grouping and teach him a language.

Again it makes biological sense that the child is not knocked totally out of developmental gear by interactional crises; development is directively organized.[31]

Individual Differences. Children vary enormously in their reaction to insecurity and hostility. Some of the differences in strategy will of course reflect different experiences, e.g., 'frozen watchfulness' probably indicates fairly severe deprivation and abuse. But genetic variance will also predict differences in strategy. Some individuals will be constitutionally more prone to anxiety than others. When this condition interacts with suffering abuse, one would predict that fear of social unpredictability or novelty would inhibit learning continually during development. There are also probably fairly large individual differences in developmental genetic constraints on language development.

A biologically-based taxonomy of individual differences in child behavioral development is urgently required. From a biological vantage point one would be reluctant to begin to make predictions about individual differences in relation to abuse, from dimensional approaches[32,33] to child psychopathology. Such an approach has been based on questionnaire, checklist, interview and rating scale responses concerning child behavior, not direct observation using non-inferential categories.

These studies, then, are of the relation between behavior and the perceptions or meaning systems of those doing the ratings.[34] As it is the infringement of internalized cultural norms which leads to a child being referred for psychiatric help, questionnaire studies beg the very questions we should be asking. A biologically meaningful approach to individual differences would have to begin with biologically meaningful material such as behavior groupings, or psychophysiological characteristics[17] and study how these are differentially realizable in different social settings, during development. Biologically defined autonomic lability in one family might mean 'nervousness,' yet in another family 'sensitivity.'

A developmental taxonomy of individual differences, beginning with biological material, and examining its differential expression, as a function of intersubjective and cultural meanings, would yield information of therapeutic value in the individual case.

Appendix

Observation of abused children, and children at risk for abuse. There are two types of ongoing facility for therapeutic intervention with abusing families at the Park Hospital for Children.

First, there is an in-patient family unit which has specialized in the treatment of families in which a child has already been abused. A detailed description of the unit and the nature of the treatment may be found elsewhere.[26,27]

Second, there is a project aiming to explore one method of intervention in families where there has been a voluntary indication that the child (preschool) might suffer physical abuse. A group of about eight mothers and their children visit us for a one and one-half hour session once a week. The mothers and the children are separated but remain in adjacent rooms.

The observations, which led to this paper, were made in both the above settings. We observed the children away from their mothers, in free play, and in interaction with their children. All the children were preschool, varying from early infancy to four years of age.

References

1. Bowlby, J.: *Attachment and Loss.* Volume 1: Attachment. London, Penguin Books, Ltd., 1969.

2. Bowlby, J.: *Attachment and Loss.* Volume 2: Separation: Anxiety and Anger. London: Penguin Books, Ltd., 1973.

3. Blurton Jones, N. (ed.): *Ethological Studies of Child Behaviour.* London: Cambridge University Press, 1972a.

4. Richards, M.P.M. (ed.): *The Integration of a Child into a Social World.* London: Cambridge University Press, 1974.

5. Rheingold, H.L. and Eckerman, C.O.: The infant separates himself from his mother. *Science*, 1970, 168:78-83.

6. Bruner, J.S.: The ontogenesis of speech acts. *Journal of Child Language,* 1974, 2:1-9.

7. Blurton Jones, N.: Ethology and early socialization. In Richards, M.P.M. (ed.), *The Integration of a Child into a Social World.* London: Cambridge University Press, 1974.

8. Darwin, C.: *The Origin of Species.* London: Murray, 1859.

9. Darwin, C.: *The Expression of the Emotions in Man and Animals.* London: Murray, 1872.

10. Darwin, C.: A biographical sketch of an infant. *Mind*, 1877, 2:286-294.

11. Blurton Jones, N.: Categories of child-child interaction. In Blurton Jones, N. (ed.), *Ethological Studies of Child Behaviour.* London: Cambridge University Press, 1972c.

12. Van Hooff, J.A.R.A.M.: Structural analysis of chimpanzee social behaviour. In Von Cranach, M. and Vine, I. (eds.), *Social Communication and Movement—Studies of Interaction and Expression in Man and Chimpanzee.* London: Academic Press, 1973.

13. Appleton, P.L.: A Social Ethological Study of Young Children and Its

Relevance to Clinical Child Psychology. M. Sc. Thesis. Scotland, U.K.: University of Glasgow, 1975.

14. Blurton Jones, N.: Characteristics of ethological studies of human behaviour. In Blurton Jones, N. (ed.), *Ethological Studies of Child Behaviour*, London: Cambridge University Press, 1972b.

15. Bernal, J.: Attachment—some problems and possibilities. In Richards, M.P.M. (ed.), *The Integration of a Child into a Social World*. London: Cambridge University Press, 1974.

16. Altmann, J.: Observational study of behaviour-sampling methods. *Behaviour*, 1974, 49:227-267.

17. Hutt, J. and Hutt, C.: *Direct Observation and Measurement of Behavior*. Springfield, Ill.: Charles Thomas, 1970.

18. Hinde, R.: Some problems in the study of the development of social behaviour. In Tobach, E., *et al.* (eds.), *The Biopsychology of Development*. London: Academic Press, 1971.

19. Hinde, R.: Aggression. In Pringle, J.W.S. (ed.), *Biology and the Human Sciences*. London: Oxford University Press, 1972.

20. McGrew, W.: *An Ethological Study of Children's Behaviour*. London: Academic Press, 1972.

21. Blurton Jones, N. and Leach, G.: Behaviour of children and their mothers at separation and greeting. In Blurton Jones, N. (ed.), *Ethological Studies of Child Behaviour.*, London: Cambridge University Press, 1972.

22. Bruner, J.S.: Nature and Uses of Immaturity. *American Psychologist*, August 1972, 687-708.

23. Ryan, J.: Early language development—towards a communicational analysis. In Richards, M.P.M. (ed.), *The Integration of a Child into a Social World*, London: Cambridge University Press, 1974.

24. Newson, J. and Newson, E.: Intersubjectivity and the Transmission of Culture: On the Social Origins of Symbolic Functioning. *Bull. British Psychological Society*, 1975, 28:437-446.

25. Stroufe, L.A. and Wunsch, J.P.: The development of laughter in the first year of life. *Child Development*, 1972, 43:1326-1344.

26. Lynch, M., Steinberg, D. and Ounsted, C.: Family Unit in a Children's Psychiatric Hospital. *British Medical Journal*, April 1975, 2:127-129.

27. Ounsted, C. and Lynch, M.: Aspects of Bonding Failure—The Developmental Approach to Child Abuse. (Chapter in preparation for R. Helfer and C.H. Kempe book, 1976.)

28. Kinnaird, D., *et al.*: A children's group, and a mother's group, for families in which there is threatened abuse. Manuscript in preparation. Oxford, England: Park Hospital for Children, 1976.

29. Lynch, M.: Ill Health and Child Abuse. *Lancet*, August 1975, 16:317-319.

30. Ounsted, C.: Biographical Science. An Essay on Developmental Medicine. In Mandelbrote, B. and Gelder, M.G. (eds.), *Psychiatric Aspects of Medical Practice*, London: Staples Press Ltd., 1972.

31. Somerhoff, G.: The abstract characteristics of living systems. In Emery, F.E. (ed.), *Systems Thinking*, London: Penguin Books Ltd., 1969.

32. Quay, H.C. and Werry, J. (eds.): *Psychopathological Disorders of Childhood*, New York: Wiley, 1972.

33. Kolvin, I., *et al.*: Dimensions of behaviour in infant school children. *British Journal of Psychiatry*, 1975, 126:114-126.

34. Peterson, D.R.: The scope and generality of verbally defined personality factors. *Psychological Review*, 1965, 72:48-59.

35. Other reference material germane to this work: Ainsworth, M.D.S., Bell, S.M. and Stayton, D.J.: Infant-mother attachment and social development, 'socialization' as a product of reciprocal responsiveness to signals. In Richards, M.P.M. (ed.), *The Integration of a Child into a Social World*, London: Cambridge University Press, 1974; Bateson, G.: *Steps to an Ecology of Mind*. New York: Ballantine Books Inc., 1972; Blurton Jones, N.: An ethological study of some aspects of social behaviour of children in nursery school. In Morris, D. (ed.), *Primate Ethology*. London: Weidenfield and Nicholson Ltd., 1967; Harre, R. and Secord, P.F.: *The Explanation of Social Behaviour*. London: Blackwell Scientific Publ. Inc., 1972; Tinbergen, N.: Functional ethology and the human sciences. *Proceedings of the Royal Society* (B), 1972, 182:385-410; Tobach, E., Aronson, L.R., and Shaw, E. (eds.): *The Biopsychology of Development*. London: Academic Press, 1971.

2. *Neurologic Damage to the Child.* It has been pointed out in Chapter 6 the very intimate interwoven aspects of the "traditional" neurological approach to children with the intellectual and psychological aspects of his neurological function. Neurologic damage or dysfunction do relate to emotional growth and development. Rutter, Graham and Yule's[10] data from their Isle of Wight studies have greatly clarified this phenomenon. I refer you here to their book, *A Neuropsychiatric Study in Childhood*, Chapter 12. In a study of the rate of psychiatric disorder in the entire population of ten- and eleven-year-old child residents on the Isle of Wight, they found a significant relationship between psychiatric disorder and organic brain disorder. In their study, they found 6.6 percent of the general population (excluding significantly mentally retarded children) to have psychiatric disorders of significance. Psychiatric disorder was nearly twice as common (11.6 percent) among children with chronic physical disorders not involving the brain. When children with brain disorders were evaluated, the rate of psychiatric disorder was 34.4 percent. This difference was noted both in children identified by parents as having psychopathology, as well as when that referral came from the child's teacher. The final diagnosis of psychiatric disorder was based on a judgment by a psychiatrist based on interview with parent, a report from the classroom teacher, and a psychiatric interview with the child himself. Differences in the severity of handicap and in whether the handicap was visible to others were not critical factors in the incidence of psychiatric disorder. While I.Q. was an important feature in those children with lesions above the brain stem, low I.Q. did not solely account for the high rate of psychiatric disorder in epileptic children. The authors came to the conclusion that "it appeared that the most important feature in relation to the much higher rate of psychiatric disorder in the neuro-epileptic children compared with the physically handicapped children, was the presence of dysfunction *specifically* of the brain. That is not to say that other factors were unimportant . . . but rather that the presence of organic brain dysfunction was the main feature associated with the finding . . . "

This association, noted in a study such as this, ostensibly has nothing to do with abused children. But this seems to me an extremely pertinent point when we are dealing with a population of children where one expects from 25 to 50 percent of the children to have varying degrees of damage or dysfunction of the central nervous system. Some of what we see in an abused child over the developmental years then may be accounted for or related to his neurologic damage, rather than to the environment of his family. We sometimes forget that psychic functioning does take place in the nervous system. While the subject was hopefully covered adequately in Chapter 6, it seems worthwhile to reiterate here. Defense mechanisms, impulse control and social behavior are all under the control of the central nervous system. Given defects or disabilities in the biophysiological function of the brain, those psychological processes will be more or less easy to accomplish. We can easily take a page from various medical conditions of the nervous system. In PKU there is emotional lability, as there is purported to be in various types of minimal brain syndromes. Affect is altered in hypothyroidism, one of its effects on the neurologic function of the human. Chess[11] has pointed out the considerably greater risk of autistic behavior in the blind and deaf child, a phenomenon related both to parental and social receptivity to such a child, as well as the limits on the neurologic capabilities of such a child.

Traditional defense mechanisms as described by Anna Freud,[12] and other modes of coping and adaptation are based on neurologic maturation. Inasmuch as these mechanisms of adaptation are for the large part unconscious maneuvers, rather than consciously thought-out mechanisms, we may forget they require a degree of maturation of neurologic function. Consider such mechanisms as denial, reaction formation or sublimation. They are not operative in infants and toddlers because of the immaturity of the central nervous system. If we start from that premise, that even unconscious modes of adaptation are rooted in the nervous system and require a certain degree of maturation to be available to the human, then a logical further step in thinking would be to accept that their development and use may be limited by neurologic damage or dysfunction. Neurological damage may play out in deficits in certain thinking modes or in perceptual awareness, or in the development of specific psycholinguistic abilities. I am further suggesting, then, that damage to the central nervous system may limit the personality development of the child in a variety of ways, including constrictions on modes of adaptations. As we try to understand how abused children grow and develop and why there are considerable differences in the effects of the abusive environment on the child's personality, the neurologic integrity of the child is one factor to be considered. In addition to the inherent biologic-psychological "givens" of the child, and in addition to the environmental stresses, are the effects of neurologic damage on the child's unfolding personality.

3. *Important Others in the Child's Life.* There has been, appropriately enough, primary emphasis on the family in understanding growth and development of children. The nuclear family usually provides the basic and perhaps sole backdrop for the child's development in the first few years of life. I wish to draw attention here to the occasional influence of other significant people in the lives of many children. We can certainly draw on our own personal experiences, as well as from the lives of children with whom we have worked, to appreciate the importance of non-family significant others. This is especially recognized in the older child. Most of us can relate to this in considering that in our own lives there have been important figures who have had considerable influence on our development. They may have been a schoolteacher, a neighbor, a scoutmaster or Sunday school teacher, an aunt or uncle, a dance or piano teacher. And so we recognize in older children that specific people outside the home can have very

important and sometimes monumental influence on the developing child. Unfortunately, most of us have little memory of people or events from our first four years of life. Scholars and investigators in child development tell us that these first years of life are the most important time in the shaping of subsequent personality; and further, that the influence of adults on the infant and young child is most critical during this time. When taking histories of a specific abused child we naturally focus on the relationships of the child to his family members, especially his parents. What I am suggesting is that there may be people outside the nuclear family whose influence on the abused child may have been tremendously important, and in some cases explain the surprising lack of pathology in some children with horrendous family histories.

To examine this source of influence on a child's development, let us take up the concept of separation-individuation once again and its ultimate goal of object constancy as a developmental sequence for exploration.

The newborn baby and his mother are early on psychically fused, a stage of normal symbiosis. What begins very soon for the child is an increasing awareness of separateness from his mother. He truly has to learn that he and his mother are not one—not a unitary symbiotic unit, but two separate persons. Over time then he learns to be separate from his mother—and sustain both physical and intrapsychic separateness with a minimum of attendant anxiety. His autonomy carries him from the mother's lap to an exploration of the world around him. This process of separation continues into the child's growing relationships with people "other than mother." Intertwined with the child's beginnings at separation are his steps towards individuation. By that, Mahler[13] and McDeavitt[14] are referring to those intrapsychic advances that mark the child's development of specific styles and individual characteristics. He becomes an individual. The biologic stamp of the species is modified as he becomes a specific person, an individual different from all other individuals. These attainments which occur over the first three to four years of life require maturation of his motor apparatus as well as of capacities such as memory, anticipation, and control of emotions for the culmination of the attainment of object constancy. This attainment, the development of object constancy, is the foundation for subsequent object relations in later life. To define or describe "object constancy" is a challenging task. A flavor of its meaning may be forthcoming from some occasional descriptions, however. It is with the development of object constancy that the child appreciates people in terms other than how those people relate to himself. People, including parents, are no longer seen solely as need-gratifying objects. There is a recognition that people have parts of their lives which have nothing to do with the child, or the self. It is only after object constancy has been achieved that the child can appreciate qualities in a person which are irrelevant to himself. Even more important, object constancy is essential before empathy or altruism can develop. Before object constancy is developed, the child is incapable of considering what life is like for others, inasmuch as others exist only in terms of their relationship to the child. A mother is a feeder, a comforter, a punisher, a bather, a dresser, etc. After object constancy is developed she becomes more. She then can be viewed as someone who has certain talents unrelated to the child, as a social being who has friends, acquaintances, needs and traits of her own. Earlier, with the development of object permanence,[15,16] the child came to realize that inanimate objects have an existence of their own even when out of the perceptual surroundings of the child. With libidinal object constancy, something similar but considerably more extensive is appreciated in relationship to significant people. The parent exists and is appreciated by the child even when that parent is out of view of the child and even when that parent is not administering to the child. There can be love of the parent for qualities other than need-gratification.

Inasmuch as people can be appreciated for other traits than those related to the needs of the child, this is to say that need-gratification is no longer the entire basis for relationships with people. A further implication of this concept is that there is a hierarchy of importance of adults; and that hierarchy is not entirely based on the degree to which the adult meets the child's needs. When this developmental stage is *not* accomplished, one sees the child who is indiscriminately affectionate. The child's love and attachment will be directed toward whomever he is relating with at the moment. No special place is given to certain people, like parents, because anyone who can and does meet the child's needs is of primary importance at that very moment. Without object constancy, people can be exchanged as easily as toys or as unfeelingly as one changes clothes. Anyone will do as well as anyone else, the only importance of people is the degree to which they are need-gratifying objects. There is no special love or attachment to mother—only love for her administrations, attachments to her motherly functions.

The child without a sense of object constancy is briefly described inasmuch as this is what is usually seen in children who have had a series of mother-surrogates in the first few years of life. In this instance, object constancy has not developed because there literally has never been any constant object for the child to relate to.

For the child to negotiate this developmental sequence, certain conditions must be present in his life. As alluded to above, there must be a maternal figure who is constant—who is there, available, predictable, and who has offered good-enough mothering from the beginning. The child needs help from his mother in gaining the courage and confidence to separate. He needs to be assured that when experimenting with separation, that mother will be there for him to return to. There is a stage of separation-individuation called rapprochement by Mahler.[13] Here we see the child going off on his own—taking forays into another room, or out into the yard. But periodically he must return to make sure that mother is still there. His sense of security is not yet internalized but resides in the existence of the mother. He must periodically touch base, and one literally sees the child become anxious, return to the physical proximity of mother, look at her or frequently come up to her and touch her, and then have the security to leave again for another foray into his own world. The mother must be able to allow the child to leave her—to separate from her. And she must be able to function as that psychic security for the child to return to and leave again and again. If she views the child's beginning separations as desertion of her by the child, her disappointment, anger or depression may play out in sabotaging his separation. Similarly, as the child individuates, becomes his own person, the parent must encourage the dissolution of the early symbiosis of mother and child, must forsake any fantasies of the child being a mirror-image of herself. She must encourage and allow the child to become his own person—to develop his own personality—or the child will not be able to individuate, but will continue to function only as an extension of the parent, a phenomenon not uncommonly seen in the dynamics of the abusing family.

One of the purposes of this apparent diversion is to point out that not infrequently one sees an abused child who has separated and individuated from parents and has a nice sense of object constancy despite a family history which would seem to have made such a developmental step impossible. The mother may have been a very inconstant figure, coming and going from the child's life with erratic frequency. The parent may have been incapable of helping the child to separate and individuate—either resisting the child's attempts, or not being available for the child to return to as a safe haven from the anxieties of growing up. In such instances, one might do well to look more carefully for other important figures in the child's life. Sometimes one finds that a baby sitter, or a friend of the family, or sometimes even an older sibling took on that parental role and supplied good-enough mothering in sufficient quantity for the child's development to continue. Especially in families where the child has been pervasively neglected by the parents, one may find that someone other than the biologic parent functioned as the mother-surrogate to enable separation-individuation to occur.

When studying various types of disadvantaged children, our stance is usually to understand the problems and pathology of children. What may be just as important and rewarding is to try to understand what has been responsible for those few children who turn out quite healthy and normal. It may be just as important to clarify why some children grow up so well adjusted, when coming from substandard homes, as it is to document the injurious effects of that same home environment. I am suggesting that we must not focus entirely on the nuclear family in trying to understand the vicissitudes of development of the abused child, but must broaden our inquiries to seeing how adventitious gratuitous people and events in the child's life have been essential for the child's relative lack of developmental distortions and deviations.

4. Biologic Considerations in Addition to Neurologic Damage from Trauma. It seems unnecessary, other than for the purposes of emphasis, to remind the reader that the effects of poor medical care, undernutrition, family chaos, and poverty may be profound on the development of such autonomous ego functions as memory, learning, perception, language and thinking. Hurley and others[17-20] have pointed this out very nicely.

Even when potentially damaging biologic events are in the child's background, the effect of the economic and social level of the family play a critical role in the degree to which the biological event will effect the child. Drillien[21] demonstrated this phenomenon in her extensive study of prematures. The effect of the prematurity on the subsequent intelligence of the child, for instance, is related to the socioeconomic status (SES) of the family with whom the child grows up. This compounding effect of the socioeconomic environment of the child on the actualization of effects of prenatal and perinatal events has also been quite brilliantly demonstrated in the work of Werner and colleagues.[22] While the ingredients of socioeconomic class are numerous and confounding, it seems clear that nutrition, medical care, housing, and biologic factors such as rate of infection are different in differing SES, and causally related to development of neurologic, cognitive and personality problems.

This is not the point to discuss and debate the question of whether child abuse occurs more frequently in low SES families than in middle or upper class families. That issue has been taken up in Chapter 1. It is this author's very strong belief that child abuse and neglect, while occurring across class lines, is considerably more common in poor and socially disadvantaged families than in more advantaged homes. Regardless of the validity of this impression, it must be recognized that in reports of abused children, nutritional and medical neglect occur in high frequency. In two follow-up studies of abused children from the Denver group,[23,24] failure to thrive accompanied physical abuse in over 30 percent of instances. Elmer[25] and Birrell[26] have similarly found undernutrition alarmingly common in abused children. Indeed, Elmer has gone beyond just nutrition of the child. In her 1969 study she compared abused children to a group of children who had had accidental injuries. She and Gregg[27] were impressed that signs of neglect such as poor hygiene of the child, minimal well-baby care and erratic care for illnesses were all much more common for the abused children; e.g., 76 percent of the abused children and only 13 percent of the "accident" victims showed a lapse in child care. These factual data were even more impressive than their ability to measure differences in mother-baby interaction.

This all suggests then, that abused children have a considerably greater chance of having poor and inadequate child-care, and this aspect of the child's background must be considered in assessing the basis for developmental problems.

Very briefly, it is important to remind the reader that undernutrition, for example, can and does result in both transient and permanent central nervous system damage in the very young child. Several reviews of the relationship of nutrition to child development have been published[28-33] and will not be dealt with in detail here. Essential is the finding of permanent biochemical and anatomical deficits in the brains of children suffering protein and calorie undernutrition during the periods of rapid brain growth.

Apart from this effect of undernutrition during the first two years of life, there are behavioral consequences of undernutrition at older ages, and of less serious nutritional deficiencies. Attention span, activity level and learning ability are affected by nutritional status, general health status, unnoticed and/or untreated infections. One of the most obvious and common examples of this is the consequences of inadequately treated frequent middle ear infections (otitis media)—a conductive type hearing loss secondary to fluid accumulation within the middle ear space. When inadequately treated and recurrent, one is left with a child who has had long episodes of mild to moderate hearing deficiency. When this is the pattern during the first few years of the child's life, speech reception, language production, and articulation all suffer, often considerably. Especially given the concept of critical periods, a concept that seems to be quite germane to language development, the lack of normal speech and language development during the first two or three years of life may result in a child whose language deficits are never entirely remediable. Here then may be an example or prototype of the type of developmental delay or distortion we can see in abused children which is secondary to inadequate child-care practices from the parents. This, then, is a fourth dimension of development of abused children which may account for the variation in outcome of the child.

5. Malevolent Environmental Influences. It has been said over and over again in this book that the abusive environment affects the child—not just the physical trauma alone. I am suggesting that we might analogize abuse to the effect a seizure disorder has on a child. The sequelae of a seizure disorder will vary according to the context in which it is embedded. The seizures may be caused by hypoglycemia (low blood sugar), encephalitis, trauma, tumor, viral respiratory infection, kidney disease, etc. There may be an effect of the seizures *per se* on the child. But more important, the associated condition, with which one finds the seizure occurring, will have the major impact on the child. Similarly, abuse usually occurs in association with other malevolent environmental conditions. Our experience has suggested that it is frequent to find at least one of the following conditions in the abusive home:

A. Medical and nutritional neglect, referred to above.
B. Significant psychiatric disturbance of one or both parents.
C. Sexual abuse.
D. Maternal or parental deprivation and/or neglect, both physical and emotional.
E. Social and/or economic disadvantage—this is referring to the disadvantages of being born into and raised by a family of lower socioeconomic status. It may

also refer to dysfunction of the family regardless of income level; e.g., alcoholism, divorce, high mobility, frequent job changes, inadequate housing, chaotic and inadequate function of the family as a unit. One may find either social or economic disadvantage in the abusive environment.

The child's development will be influenced in a negative way by any one of these conditions, whether or not abuse is present in the home. It seems appropriate then to consider briefly the effects of these associated elements on child development. The consequences of medical and nutritional neglect have been discussed above under the 4th variable affecting the abused child's development. At this point I am addressing inadequate parenting from the psychosocial viewpoint. It should be pointed out, that usually when a child is underfed or is being poorly taken care of, this is usually a sign that maternal inadequacy is present. Emotional deprivation or neglect may be identified or suspected, then by poor child-care practices. Part of the effect of undernutrition or inadequate hygiene or medical care then stems from the associated emotional deprivation the child is suffering.

5B. *Psychiatric Disturbance in Parents.* Kempe and Helfer have suggested that 10 percent of abusive parents are psychotic or seriously disturbed. More recently we have been impressed that a greater percentage of abusing parents are seriously emotionally disturbed. The parent may not be psychotic, or may not demonstrate his psychopathology in many areas of life, but the degree of reality testing and rational thought (*vis-à-vis* the child) are limited. A number of studies have pointed out the effects on children of having mentally ill parents. Rutter[34] feels that behavioral disturbance in the child is particularly likely to exist when the parents' personality disorder is either of long standing or when the child is involved in the symptoms of the parents' illness, the usual case in child abuse. Rice *et al.*[35] studied children of parents who were hospitalized for mental illness. Almost one-half of the children were physically mistreated. Neurotic traits and behavioral difficulties were manifested by almost half of the children. They point out the hazards to children of leaving them in a family where there is constant stress resulting from parents' mental illness. These studies were preceded by earlier reports of the influence on the children of mentally ill parents. The degree to which the parents' emotional disturbance impairs their homemaking and parental roles is more important than whether the parent is psychotic or neurotic, a point especially relevant to the abused child. Insofar as this is true, the issue may not be whether the abusing parent is psychotic or whether some other psychiatric label is more appropriate, but rather, in what ways the parents' emotional disturbance involves the parental role of the mother or father. Much of Anthony and Benedek's recent book on parenthood[36] is applicable here, but especial attention should be given to Spitz's article[37] on the effects of personality disturbances in the mother on the infant. Melitta Sperling's chapter[38] on the clinical effects of parental neurosis on the child, and Giovacchini's[39] observations concerning separation-individuation difficulties and how they play out in adult pathology are pertinent here. Grunebaum's[40] recent book has a nice review of the literature (pp. 180-188).

In summary, not only must psychotic patterns of parenting be of concern to us, with respect to the child's development, but the neurotic or otherwise disturbed parent whose emotional problems involve the child (as by definition they do in child abuse) and whose parenting capability is handicapped must also raise considerable concern to us. Certainly the effects of the abusive environment on the child may lie in the effect the emotional problems of the individual parent has on the child. By inference, to help minimize the damage to the child, one may have to focus on the emotional milieu in which he is growing, i.e., the psychiatric status of his parents.

5C. *Sexual Abuse.* The relationship between physical abuse and sexual abuse has been neither clarified nor documented. The two are rarely discussed together, rather as if they are quite separate entities. Perhaps this is largely because studies of physical abuse have focused on the infant and very young child, while sexual abuse tends to occur in preadolescent and older children. It is this author's contention that the two syndromes frequently coexist and that sexual victimization and physical abuse are often different signals of identical home situations. There are three bases for thinking that the two entities are not so separate as the literature might lead us to believe.

First is the anecdotal data from school personnel and others who are in contact with adolescents. School staff tell us that physical abuse blends into sexual abuse especially in females as preadolescence arrives. The two may be seen in the same children. Unpublished studies (Steele) in a population of acting-out adolescent girls further tended to corroborate the frequent finding of physical abuse and sexual molestation in these girls.

We have furthermore been impressed with considerable sexual overtones in the physical abuse of younger children. In a number of instances, especially where the man of the family had left or deserted, sexual provocation by the mother of the abused child was striking. Even when both parents were in the home, the competitiveness of the parents for the attention of the three to six year old was more than we normally see during this Oedipal period. In one family, the mother of a rather severely abused five-year-old girl described her daughter as a Jezebel, being flirtatious and seductive with men. In fact she described instances where the five year old daughter would invite strange men home for dinner, a behavior mother saw as sexually seductive in nature. Another abusing mother would go to her seven year old son's bed when she was afraid or upset and cuddle up to him for comfort. This same mother defended her modern attitude towards sexuality, such as her habit of walking about the house unclad, and bathing with her son. At any rate, in our psychotherapy study of twelve

Oedipal aged children, we were quite impressed with the sexuality of the parent-child relationship.

Finally, one must be impressed with studies of sexual victimization such as DeFrancis' report[41] of 1000 children wherein the sexual offender was a member of the household in 27 percent of the instances and 37 percent were friends or acquaintances of the family. In 11 percent of the families, physical abuse other than sexual was directed toward the victim or other family members. Child neglect was noted in 79 percent of the families. In a study of a small sample of incest cases,[42] it was noted that in 65 percent of the families, violent abusive behavior by the father was directed toward family members. The prevalence of violent behavior in the families of children who have been sexually assaulted by family suggests that abused children may be at higher risk of sexual abuse at an older age when the sexuality of adolescence may prompt such a response from parents.

Short and long term follow-up studies of sexually abused victims show surprisingly few adjustment problems in these victims. MacDonald[43] states that personality problems in the child frequently precede the assault and even contribute to it. However, although follow-up studies fail to show *severe* deviation in mental health following sexual abuse, more subtle effects would be expected, including deviation in personality structure, ambivalence regarding sexuality, feelings of guilt and other conflicts. At this stage of knowledge one can only say that the sexually abused child will perhaps be no more disturbed or neurotic than the general population, but he may have different types of conflicts and personal scars. This is, however, another factor to be considered in assessing the long-term effects of the abusive environment on the child and adult who has been physically abused and also sexually provoked and mistreated.

5D. *Maternal Deprivation and/or Neglect.* I am choosing the term *Maternal,* realizing full-well that emotional deprivation or neglect is not limited to an insufficiency of care by mothers. However, historically this term has been used. I am truly referring to a child who is emotionally neglected by the important figures in his life (mother and father) and who is deprived of the "good-enough mothering" (which can unquestionably be supplied by a mother or a father). The concept of maternal deprivation itself is too ambiguous for scientific study as pointed out by Yarrow.[44] He suggested that deviant maternal care might fruitfully be subdivided into four different types: (1) Institutionalization; (2) Maternal Separation; (3) Multiple Mothering; and (4) Distortions in the Mother-Child Relationship. In the case of the abused child, by definition almost, the fourth subtype of maternal deprivation is existent. As one looks at the immense literature concerning the effects of maternal deprivation, rarely is the exact nature of the deprivation delineated.

While maternal deprivation (i.e., distortions in the mother-child relationship) might seem to always exist in the child abuse syndrome, I have chosen not to equate the two situations for a number of reasons.

First, striking a child is not considered pathologic behavior in our society. The only differentiation of "normal" assault (i.e., corporal punishment of children) from child abuse is the extent and nature of the assault or its consequences to the child. If you happen to spank a child with just a bit more force than usual and hence leave a bruise, "normal" parenting behavior suddenly may become child abuse. In our society we have determined that it is quite proper for very big and large people (parents) to strike very small and weaker people (their children) in the interests of the smaller person learning how to behave properly. We may admit that the motivation could be catharsis of anger, or might feel that frustration from not knowing other ways to control or teach the child is the basis for corporal punishment. And, of course, there is a time-honored tradition that withholding the rod will result in a spoiled child. One needs only consider what one sees in any grocery store or department store. The amount of hitting and striking of children for what appears to be rather normal behavior is remarkable. Hence, it seems grandiose to consider maternal deprivation to be present every time a child is physically abused.

The second basis for not equating deprivation or neglect with abuse comes from our clinical experience. There is considerable variation in the mothering behaviors of abusive parents. In many instances, neglect, rejection, anger, dislike or strong ambivalence predominate. In other instances, normal loving maternal behaviors and feelings predominate with occasional outbursts of impulsive anger directed toward the child. In this latter instance, the child is not deprived of normal maternal behavior except during the brief outbursts of uncontrolled anger.

We turn to the effects of maternal deprivation or neglect on children. The literature is immense and cannot be adequately surveyed here. In brief, however, it is worth mentioning the very early reports of Brenneman,[45] Bakwin[46] and Ribble.[47] They delineated the need for maternal stimulation in the developing child, described the loneliness of children deprived of their mothers and speculated that some of the effects of hospitalization were related to a lack of mothering behaviors.

Spitz,[48] Bakwin,[49] Spitz and Wolf[50] and Goldfarb[51] related deprivation of mothering in institutions to very dire consequences including death, permanent mental retardation, neurologic dysfunction and behavioral deviation. Bowlby[52] in 1951 went so far as to suggest that a bad home with a mother was superior to almost any institution, a stance he later modified.

Prugh and Harlow[53] and Coleman and Provence[54] later pointed out that significant maternal deprivation could occur when children are living with their parents. This "masked deprivation" has serious consequence to the child's development, albeit in less severe form, than complete absence of mothering.

Still later, investigators have attempted to correlate *specific* parental behaviors with specific behaviors of the child. For example, Talbot[55] reported a significant (p. 0.001) correlation between certain symptoms in children (truancy, destructiveness, stealing and school failure) and specific parental behaviors (high index of authority and low index of approval of their children). This increasing sophistication in the study of the effects of parental attitudes and behavior is sorely needed and still limited in scope.

Any serious student of child development cannot help being impressed by the exhaustive data pointing out the effects of maternal deprivation and neglect on the developing child. But what of the abused child? Here too, the personality of the child may be more related to the adequacy of mothering than to the phenomenon of physical abuse *per se*. I have been struck with the fact that abused children who are also emotionally neglected do much worse than those where more adequate parenting is present. In fact, I am suggesting that this may be a most important parameter of the abusive home in terms of making prognostic statements and planning treatment.

There are a large number of abused children for whom their parents have very little affection and/or investment. These are the children who are apt to be kept in their rooms and their cribs as infants. These are the children who are apt to be poorly fed, have poor hygiene, and present as unhealthy dirty unkempt infants and children. There is, however, another group of abused children where this is not the case, but rather where they present as clean well-dressed children who have been cared for both physically and emotionally. This type of parent very often will staunchly defend his physical punishment of the child. One not infrequently sees this situation where the father is either in the military service or is steeped in a very fundamentalist religious background. This parent is apt to have a considerable investment in the child—being very concerned that his child grows up to be compliant, to follow the rules, to know how to "make out in a very tough hard world." In this type of home, the child is wanted, tended to, and certainly not neglected. Rather, the high investment the parents have in the child is a distorted rigid type of upbringing where any means to "teach the kid to obey" seem indicated. This is not to suggest that this same dynamic is always present in the home where the abused child is highly cathected. Nonetheless, the point to be attended to here is that abused children may be neglected and deprived of good-enough mothering—and alternately that the abused child may be in a home where considerable love and attention (even though it may be quite distorted in nature) are provided him. It is my contention that the children from these two types of homes vary considerably, that the more potent malevolent feature of the home is maternal neglect—maternal deprivation. I would further suggest that the prognosis for keeping the child in the home is much worse in the former situation, even with considerable treatment provided for the parent.

When one considers the effects of the abusive environment on the child, perhaps the most important feature to be attended to is the adequacy of mothering behaviors in the parents, rather than the type or severity of the physical assault. Insofar as the child is unloved, uncared for, and inadequately mothered, his developmental prognosis is grim. In the abusive home where this is not the case, but parents care about the child and his happiness and future, the psychological scars of being physically assaulted will be much less prominent.

5E. *Social and/or Economic Disadvantage.* This issue has been touched upon in the previous section on the Biologic Considerations in the Abused Child. I raise the issue again that while child abuse does occur in all social classes, there is a predominance of low socioeconomic status (SES) families *reported.* There are at least three explanations for this. First, most medical centers and agencies who report child abuse studies in the literature primarily serve low income families, so that there is a considerable bias in their total patient population. Second, middle and upper class families are much less likely to arouse the suspicion of abuse in their private physicians. Even when suspected, these families are often not reported to public agencies, so do not come to the attention of child-abuse agencies. Third, it is the author's contention that one would expect to find a higher prevalence of abuse in families of lower SES. The data of Gil[56] tend to substantiate this. If one considers that one of the ingredients of child abuse is stress on the family, one would necessarily assume that in the lower economic status families the increased stresses of daily living would augur for more abusive behavior. Poverty, poor housing, job instability, poor education and few salable skills are but a few of the common denominators found in high frequency in the lowest SES families, along with crowded conditions for larger families. The opportunity to be away from one's child in times of stress is less available to low income mothers or fathers.

Whether child abuse is more common in low income families or not, when an abused child comes from such a home, the effects of the social and economic disadvantage must be taken into consideration when trying to sort out the factors responsible for the child's developmental problems. I have previously referred to the work of Drillien[21] and Werner[22] in pointing out the additive factor of social disadvantage in children with biologic high risk events. Other authors have emphasized, in addition to the lack of cognitive modeling and stimulation, the effects of minimal prenatal care, crowding, poor medical care, marginal nutrition and an overall suboptimal physical environment on the child's development. I further point to the study of the ecology of abuse in a military community. Sattin and Miller[57] found that abusive families, as compared to non-abusive controls of similar SES and military rank, tended to live in specific target areas of the civilian community where housing and physical environment were markedly inferior. At the National Center in Denver, we have similarly been impressed with the tendency for many abusive families to cluster in specific geographic parts of the community and to be clearly impaired in their ability to manage their homes.

Whether the social and economic disadvantage of many abusing parents is merely an additive factor in the etiology of abuse, or whether the social disadvantage is a reflection of inadequate personality function of many abusing parents, the effect of the poor living conditions is visited upon the child, abused or not. This then, is but another environmental factor which must be considered in explaining the variation in the effects of the abusive home on the development of the child.

6. *Effects of Treatment.* The effects of our therapeutic intervention for the abused child and his family should, and certainly can, have considerable impact on the subsequent development of the child. The effects of treatment might be divided into two categories. The first would be those effects which we deliberately plan and hope for. These effects are extensively discussed in the second section of this book which is devoted entirely to treatment for the abused child. Therein we consider the effects of psychotherapy, educational therapy, specific treatment of developmental delays, the possible therapeutic effects of foster placement, and how treatment for the parents may benefit the child.

There is another facet of treatment for the abused child—and here I am referring to the iatrogenic effects of treatment—that is the unintended harm and trauma which result from our treatment planning. This was briefly alluded to in the introduction to this book. It is a maxim in medicine that there are risks and dangers attendant to every treatment procedure we prescribe—indeed, even the giving of counsel or advice can have far-reaching effects we never imagined or dreamt of. One learns early in training, for instance, that every chemical in the world is a potential poison—the entire issue is to determine a dosage which has a great chance of helping the patient with a minimal risk of causing unwanted harmful side effects. Even plain water can be fatal to a patient if the dosage is too high. Aspirin can be fatal. A certain percentage of people who receive any drug, any inoculation, any surgical procedure, will have harmful side effects. This awareness of the potential for our helpful administrations to make the patient worse should be applied to our social manipulations of patients also. Especially true when our treatment is based on unproved data, social biases, and unthought-out advice from social planners or ideas we incorporated at our parent's knee. I am specifically referring to such generalizations as "keep the family together" or "a bad home is better than a good institution," or the accusatory labeling of abusing parents as people unfit to raise children.

Such maxims may look beautiful when crocheted on a wall hanging and hung beside such other old saws as "there's no place like home"—but they have no place in the reasonable deliberations of a child abuse team. When our recommendations are built on such emotionally laden underpinnings, we lose any awareness of the effects of our treatment on the *specific* child and family in question. Early in the course of studying child abuse, the proposition was put forward that all abused children should be hospitalized when diagnosed, even if no medical basis for hospitalization was necessary. This seemed a reasonable plan with considerable merit. What was overlooked in most instances, was the effect of the hospitalization on the child—and perhaps on the family.

In the course of most child abuse cases, the repertoire of treatment recommendations has included putting the child in a hospital, separating the child from his parents regardless of the attachment or the age of the child, placement of the child in a substitute home with new and strange parent surrogates. Rarely included when such social emollients were prescribed were deliberations as to the effects such plans would have on the personality of the child.

What I am truly wanting to impress the reader with is that inevitably our well intentioned, reasonable and necessary treatment will also cause some mischief with the children we are attempting to help. Many abused children must be hospitalized. What is necessary is that we are aware of the effects of hospitalization on children and make attempts to minimize or modify the trauma of such institutionalization. Many abused children will need to be separated from parents. The effects of that parent loss must be acknowledged and to our best ability dealt with. Foster placement is often required. In addition to making foster homes more therapeutic (a subject taken up in Chapter 15), the effects upon the child can be anticipated and modified by appropriate thoughtful intervention.

I am further suggesting that in many instances our inadequate treatment may cause more harm to the child than the physical assault did, or even than the abusive environment. For example, I refer the reader to the large number of children wherein parental rights are either never severed, or that decision is stretched out over many years—all the time during which the child is in a legal state of limbo—in the custody of the state (a very poor parent indeed)—unavailable for adoption or for any meaningful commitment and attachment from parents. A second common plight for the abused child is to have a series of foster home placements while we know that the ability of the child to grow psychologically strong is dependent on a stable home during the early years. In our follow-up study of 58 abused children,[24] we found that 20 of the children had had from three to eight home changes in a mean period of 4.5 years. It is not uncommon to find children as described in the introduction who have had over ten home changes in the first four or five years of life. When evaluating such children, it becomes apparent that these events which occurred *after* the state took custody of the child are the primary etiology of considerable and significant emotional disturbance.

The usual hospital setting is probably one of the very worst homes for a child which we could construct. Separation from parents is a form of parent loss which we usually look upon as a very significant trauma in the life of any child. Our own research with abused children[58-60] has shown that a sense of impermanence in one's home is significantly correlated with emotional disturbance in the abused child.

Like the lemmings in their fatalistic march to the sea, we find child abuse teams sentencing children to new traumas which may cause more emotional havoc and scars than the abusive environment from which they came. If we recognize the potential trauma in such recommendations, then, and only then, will it be possible to provide systems to minimize or prevent those deleterious effects. We know how to provide crises intervention to children at times of trauma. We know how to modify hospital routine to minimize the effects of an institutional setting. We know how to help children who have suffered parent loss. We can break the pattern of repeated foster-home changes. We do not need to keep children in limbo while years pass with us unwilling either to return the child to his biologic parents or determine that for the child's best interests parental rights must be permanently dissolved.

I am proposing that since we consider these phenomenon as *treatment,* we are blinded to their impact on the child. For, when a normal child loses his parent, through death, divorce or desertion, we usually are attuned to the impact on this child and provide help for him. But in the child abuse case, since we are *prescribing* parent loss as a valuable treatment modality, we may not consider our helpful administrations as harmful. With other children we are aware of the tremendous importance of attachment of the child to a mother-figure, and when attachment is tenuous, we become concerned and step in to try to help. But in the child abuse case, it is our treatment system that moves the child from foster home to foster home when foster parents find the child too difficult to deal with. We normally might agree with Goldstein, Freud and Solnit[61] that "each child (shall have) a chance to be a member of a family where he feels wanted . . . ," yet in the child abuse case we often let years pass before we are willing to recommend to a judicial official that the child should or should not be part of his biologic family.

In the developmental evaluation of hundreds of abused and neglected children over the past 9 years, it has become painfully obvious that our treatment interventions are one of the most significant factors which must be considered in understanding the developmental delays, emotional disturbances, and the miseries of the child.

Summary

There is no one profile of abused children. Some are retarded, some are quite bright. They may or may not have delays in motor or speech or perceptual development. They may be withdrawn or oppositional or gregarious social children. We know that certain types of problems and certain personality traits are overrepresented in any population of abused children, but also know that any two abused children may vary considerably in terms of the ravages of their past on their present functioning.

In this chapter I have looked at six different factors to be considered in understanding the variation in the effects of the abusive environment on the child. Much of what has been discussed is not peculiar to the abused child, but is just as valid for any child, and hence is an overview of general child development principles. It seemed to me important to at least superficially cover these parameters of influences on children's development, as they are particularly important when trying to understand children with developmental distortions. Further, many of us who work with abused children are not child development experts, yet are called on to understand and plan for children whose developmental progress is in jeopardy. Three biologic facets of the abused child have been pointed out as affecting the course of the abused child: the inherent biologic equipment of the child; the nature and severity of the neurologic damage from the abuse; and other medical problems of the child such as poor health, undernutrition or unattended illnesses. Three psycho-social facets of the abused child's life have also been addressed: the possibility of people other than nuclear family who may have had a salutary effect; the untoward effects of our treatment regimes; and the various components of the abusive environment with especial attention to neglect and deprivation.

At times I have deliberately and knowingly taken short excursions from our primary destination. At times I have felt pedantic in style. It is anticipated that for some readers much of this chapter is redundant and at best an unnecessary review. For other readers, it must seem but an appetizer and hopefully will stimulate more extensive reading and thought. Perhaps the major underlying basis for this chapter being included is to emphasize that the abuse—the physical assault *per se*—is but one of many factors which will affect and influence the child's subsequent growth and development. It is hoped that by broadening our horizons of considerations, that a better understanding of abused children may be possible.

References

1. Goddard, H.H.: *The Kallikak Family "Classics in Psychology"* New York: Arno Press, 1973.

2. Jensen, A.R.: *Educability and Group Differences* New York: Harper and Row, 1973.

3. Brazelton, T.B.: *Infants and Mothers: Differences in Development* New York: Delacorte, 1969.

4. Brazelton, T.B.: *Toddlers and Parents: A Declaration of Independence* New York: Delacorte, 1974.

5. Brazelton, T.B., Koslowski, B., Main, M.: "The Origins of Reciprocity: The Early Mother-Infant Interaction" in M. Lewis and L. Rosenblum (eds.) *The Effect of the Infant on Its Care Given* New York: John Wiley, 1974.

6. Brazelton, T.B.: *Neonatal Behavioral Assessment Scale* Philadelphia: Lippincott, 1973.

7. Alexander, T., Chess, S., Birch, H.G.: *Temperament and Behavior Disorders in Children* New York: New York University Press, 1968.

8. Freud, S.: "Analysis Terminable and Interminable 1937" in *The Standard Edition of the Complete Psychological Works of Sigmund Freud*, James Strachey (ed.), London: Hogarth Press, 1964, Vol. 23, pp. 240-246.

9. Anthony, E. James: Presentation at Seminar of Depts. of Psychiatry and Pediatrics, Univ. Mo. Med. Center, Columbia, Mo., Nov., 1974.

10. Rutter, M., Graham, P., Yule, W.: *A Neuropsychiatric Study in Childhood* Philadelphia: Lippincott, 1970.

11. Chess, S.: *Psychiatric Disturbances of Children with Congenital Rubella* New York: Brunner/Mazel, 1971.

12. Freud, A.: *The Ego and the Mechanisms of Defense* New York: International University Press, 1966.

13. Mahler, M.S. *et al.*: *The Psychological Birth of the Infant: Symbiosis and Individuation* New York: Basic Books, 1975.

14. McDevitt, J.B.: "Separation—Individuation and Object Constancy," *Journal Amer. Psychoanal. Assn.*, 23:713-742, 1975.

15. Burgner, M., Edgcumbe, R.: "Some Problems in the Conceptualization of Early Object Relationships Part II: The Concept of Object Constancy," *Psychoanal. St. Child*, 27:315-333, 1972.

16. Fraiberg, S.: "Libidinal Object Constancy and Mental Representation," *Psychoanal. St. Child*, 24:9-47, 1969.

17. Hurley, R.: *Poverty and Mental Retardation, A Causal Relationship* New York: Random House, Inc., 1969.

18. Wortis, H.: Poverty and Retardation: Social Aspects, in Wortis, J. (ed.) *Mental Retardation* New York: Grune and Stratton, 1970, pp. 262-270.

19. Wortis, J.: Poverty and Retardation: Biosocial Factors, in Wortis, J. (ed.): *Mental Retardation* New York: Grune and Stratton, 1970, pp. 271-279.

20. Birch, H.G., and Gussow, J.D.: *Disadvantaged Children—Health, Nutrition and School Failure* New York: Grune and Stratton, 1970.

21. Drillien, C.M.: *The Growth and Development of the Prematurely Born Infant* Edinburgh: Livingstone, 1964.

22. Werner, E., Simonian, K., Bierman, J.M., and French, F.E.: "Cumulative Effect of Perinatal Complications and Deprived Environment on Physical, Intellectual, and Social Development of Preschool Children," *Pediatrics* 30:490-505, 1967.

23. Martin, Harold P. in Kempe & Helfer (eds.) *Helping the Battered Child and His Family* Philadelphia: J.B. Lippincott Co., 1972, 93-114.

24. Martin, H.P., Beezley, P., Conway, E.F., and Kempe, C.H.: "The Development of Abused Children," *Advances in Pediatrics*, 1974, *21*, 25-73.

25. Elmer, E.: *Children in Jeopardy* Pittsburgh: University of Pittsburgh Press, 1967.

26. Birrell, R.G., and Birrell, J.H.W.: "The Maltreatment Syndrome in Children: A Hospital Survey," *Med. J. Aust.* 2:1023-1029, 1968.

27. Gregg, G.S. and Elmer, E.: "Infant Injuries: Accident or Abuse," *Pediatrics*, 44:434-439, 1969.

28. Martin, H.P.: Nutrition: Its relationship to children's physical, mental and emotional development, *Am. J. Clin. Nutr.* 26:766-775, 1973.

29. Scrimshaw, N.S., and Gordon, J.E.: *Malnutrition, Learning and Behavior* Cambridge, Mass.: M.I.T. Press, 1968.

30. Birch, H.G.: Malnutrition, learning and intelligence, *Am. J. Public Health* 62:773-784, 1972.

31. Manocha, S.L.: *Malnutrition and Retarded Human Development* Springfield, Ill.: Charles C. Thomas, 1972.

32. Dodge, P.R., Prensky, A.L., Feign, R.D.: *Nutrition: And the Developing Nervous System* St. Louis: Mosby, 1975.

33. Cipriano, A. Canosa (ed.): "Nutrition, Growth and Development," *Modern Problems in Pediatrics*, Vol. 14, 1975.

34. Rutter, M.: Children of Sick Parents: An Environment and Psychiatric Study, *Maudsley Monog. No. 16* London: Oxford University Press, 1966.

35. Rice, E.P., Ekdahl, M.C., and Miller, L.: *Children of Mentally Ill Parents* New York: Behavior Publications, 1971.

36. Anthony, E.J. and Benedec, T. (eds.) *Parenthood: Its Psychology and Psychopathology* Boston: Little, Brown and Co., 1970.

37. Spitz, R.A.: "The Effect of Personality Disturbances in the Mother on the Well-being of Her Infant," chapt. 24, pp. 501-524, in Anthony, E.J. and Benedek, T. (eds.) *Parenthood: Its Psychology and Psychopathology* Boston: Little, Brown and Co., 1970.

38. Sperling, M.: "The Clinical Effects of Parental Neurosis on the Child," chapt. 26, pp. 539-570 in Anthony, E.J. and Benedek, T. (eds.) *Parenthood: Its Psychology and Psychopathology* Boston: Little, Brown and Co., 1970.

39. Giovacchini, P.L.: "Effects of Adaptive and Disruptive Aspects of Early Object Relationships Upon Later Parental Functioning," chapt. 25, pp. 525-538, in Anthony, E.J. and Benedek, T. (eds.) *Parenthood: Its Psychology and Psychopathology* Boston: Little, Brown and Co., 1970.

40. Grunebaum, H., Weiss, J.L., Cohler, B.J., Hartman, C.R., Gallant, D.H.: *Mentally Ill Mothers and Their Children* Chicago: University of Chicago Press, 1975.

41. DeFrancis, V.: *Protecting the Child Victim of Sex Crimes Committed by Adults* Denver: American Humane Association, Children's Division, 1969.

42. Thomas, W.: *Child Victims of Incest* Denver: American Humane Association, Children's Division, 1968.

43. MacDonald, J.M.: *Rape: Offenders and Their Victims* Springfield, Ill.: Chas. Thomas, 1971.

44. Yarrow, L.J.: Maternal deprivation—toward an empirical and conceptual reevaluation, *Psychol. Bull.* 58:459-490, 1961.

45. Brenneman, J.: The infant ward, *Am. J. Dis. Child.* 43:577-584, 1932.

46. Bakwin, H.: Loneliness in infants, *Am. J. Dis. Child.* 63:30-40, 1942.

47. Ribble, M.A.: *Rights of Infants: Early Psychological Needs and Their Satisfaction* New York: Columbia University Press, 1943.

48. Spitz, R.A.: Hospitalism: An Inquiry into the Genesis of Psychiatric Conditions in Early Childhood, in *The Psychoanalytic Study of the Child* New York: International University Press, 1945, Vol. I, pp. 53-74.

49. Bakwin, H.: Emotional deprivation in infants, *J. Pediatr.* 35:512-521, 1949.

50. Spitz, R.A., and Wolf, L.M.: Anaclitic Depression: An Inquiry into the Genesis of Psychiatric Conditions in Early Childhood, in *The Psychoanalytic Study of the Child* New York: International University Press, 1946, Vol. II, pp. 323-342.

51. Goldfarb, W.: Effects of Psychological Deprivation in Infancy and Subsequent Stimulation, *Am. J. Psychiatry* 102:18-33, 1945.

52. Bowlby, J.: Maternal care and mental health, *Bull. WHO* 3:355-533, 1951.

53. Prugh, D.C., and Harlow, R.G.: Masked Deprivation in Infants and Young Children, in *Deprivation of Maternal Care: A Reassessment of Its Effects* (Public Health Papers, No. 14) Geneva: World Health Organization, 1962, pp. 9-30.

54. Coleman, R., and Provence, S.A.: Developmental retardation (hospitalism) in infants living in families, *Pediatrics* 19:285-292, 1957.

55. Talbot, N.B.: Has psychological malnutrition taken the place of rickets in contemporary pediatric practice? *Pediatrics* 31:909-918, June 1963.

56. Gil, D.G.: *Violence Against Children: Physical Child Abuse in the United States,* Cambridge, Massachusetts: Harvard University Press, 1970.

57. Sattin, D.B., and Miller, J.K.: The ecology of child abuse within a military community, *Am. J. Orthopsychiatry* 41:675-678, 1971.

58. Martin, H.P., Beezley, P.: Personality Characteristics of the Abused Child, accepted for publ. *Devel. Med. Child Neurol.* 1976.

59. Martin, H.P., Rodeheffer, M.: Psychologic Impact of Child Abuse, accepted for publ. *Journ. Pediat. Psychol.* 1976.

60. Martin, H.P., Beezley, P.: Prevention and the Consequences of Child Abuse, *Journ. Operational Psychiat.* VI:68-77, Fall Winter, 1974.

61. Goldstein, J., Freud, A., Solnit, A.J.: *Beyond the Best Interests of the Child* New York: Free Press, 1973.

✳ *Section 2*

**Treatment for the
Abused Child**

Chapter 13

An Advocate for the Abused Child

Brian Fraser and **Harold P. Martin**

This book is about abused children. The first section has discussed what the abused child is like and the second deals with the treatment modalities which are available to help the abused child. It has been repeatedly pointed out that the most important priority in any child abuse case is to protect the child from physical injury. It has also been repeatedly pointed out that this goal by itself is not enough. There must be a developmental approach to the child in any case of child abuse.

It was the editor's decision to begin this section with a chapter indicating the need of an abused child for independent representation. And for good reason— for any of our understanding of the child to have any meaning in the real world, an independent advocate for the child is essential. There must be some vehicle to assure that the child and his problems are identified, and that some form of therapeutic intervention follows. Without independent representation and without an independent advocate for the child, there is every reason to believe that the developmental and psychological needs of the abused child will remain unidentified and untreated. This chapter will discuss the need for independent advocacy, will note the different forms of advocacy, and will suggest how that advocacy might best be established.

It is axiomatic to state that there can be no intervention or no treatment until there is some form of identification. But in many cases of child abuse, the rather simple process of identification remains a difficult problem. The majority of children who are abused, neglected or deprived by their parents, are young children. And young children simply do not have the ability to articulate their needs, their hurts and their desires. Identification of child abuse rests largely with the discretion of some third party. But the identification by third parties rests upon two assumptions:

1. That the third party has the ability to identify the symptoms of child abuse, and
2. That the third party, even when he has the ability to identify the symptoms, is willing to act affirmatively.

Both of these assumptions have historically proven to be erroneous.

The simplest but schematically the most basic form of child advocacy in cases of child abuse is the identification of the symptoms and the reporting to some social service agency. While it is difficult to draw the line of demarcation between a lack of knowledge and a lack of willingness to become involved, the results are exactly the same. A failure to identify prohibits by definition the ability to intervene and to offer treatment.

In an effort to compensate for this failure to identify and to report, every state has adopted some form of mandatory reporting by statute.[1] Although definitions of abuse and other provisions may differ, the purpose of all mandatory reporting statutes is exactly the same. There is a group of professions, of disciplines or others in each who are mandated to report those cases in which they have reasonable cause to believe or *suspect* that a child may have been abused.[a] No mandatory reporting statute requires that a person mandated to report develop a definitive diagnosis of child abuse. The reporter's obligation is simply to report those cases in which he believes or suspects that a child may have been abused. Every state requires that some designated state agency receive the report, investigate the report and, once the investigation is completed, determine whether or not this child has been abused. Hypothetically then, every state provides a vehicle for identification, investigation and intervention. The value of any statute, however, is how well it articulates responsibilities and duties and, conversely, how well those persons who are mandated to act are aware of their responsibilities and duties and are willing to fulfill them. For a variety of reasons, professionals have been unwilling to identify and to report cases of child abuse. Comments that "the system doesn't work; I don't want to destroy my therapeutic relationship; intervention is worse than identification; it is something I've been trained to deal with," or "It is an infringement on parental rights," are one-way streets. The proclamation that something doesn't work or can't work becomes nothing more than a self-fulfilling prophecy for those professionals who refuse to act affirmatively on behalf of the child. The first form of child advocacy in cases of child abuse is simply the professional who knows the symptoms of child abuse, who is willing to identify them and who is willing to report.[3]

The abused child does not enter into a child developmental system. He usually enters into a medical system—a social service system or a legal system.

---

[a]Some states have gone further and require that not only cases of suspected child abuse (fait accompli) be reported, but require that circumstances and conditions which would reasonably result in abuse be reported also.[2]

The social service system and the legal system will be considered for the purposes of this chapter as one unit. Neither the social, nor the legal system is oriented toward the identification nor the provision of therapy for the developmental and psychological problems of the child. Medical personnel are concerned primarily with the diagnosis of injury and the delivery of medical services for the inflicted physical trauma or injury which has resulted from parental malfeasance or parental nonfeasance. It is possible that within the medical system, someone *may* take cognizance of the non-medical problems of the child, but this is virtually fortuitous and piecemeal to say the least. Personality aberrations, developmental deficiencies and psycho-social development are usually not areas of expertise for medical personnel.

The social and legal systems are even less likely than the medical system to have any child development orientation. Law enforcement officials, probation personnel, judges, lawyers and social service workers are not trained nor do they possess expertise in the normal development of children or conversely, in developmental disabilities. As is true in the medical profession, there may be personnel in the social or legal systems who do have such expertise, but that is the exception not the rule. Emphasis has been given, in the past, to the areas of investigation, diagnosis of non-accidental physical trauma and the feasibility of filing a proceeding in either the criminal court or the juvenile court. These skills may assure that the child is not again the victim of parental misfeasance, parental nonfeasance or parental malfeasance, but they do not provide the expertise which is necessary to focus on the child's developmental problems. Like the computer, the focus of any system, its values and its results, depend to a large extent upon the expertise, the focus and the philosophy of the personnel who are responsible for the system. The value of any result depends upon the information that is collected and the expertise that is used to evaluate such data. In simple terms, the value of the end result is directly proportionate to the information that is available and the expertise that is used to evaluate it. The court in itself is not an information-gathering vehicle. The court measures and weighs the information that is supplied to it.[4]

The concept of child advocacy can serve not only to identify the child in peril (primary advocacy), it can serve as an excellent vehicle to insure that all relevant information is gathered and utilized for an informal disposition (non-legal) or a formal disposition (utilization of the court). For the purposes of discussion, it may be prudent to explore and consider three further forms of advocacy for children who have been abused, neglected or deprived. These include individual advocacy, the child protection team and the guardian *ad litem*.

Formal Advocacy

1. *Individual Advocacy.*

The authors of this chapter propose that any professional who is involved, has an ethical and a professional obligation to act as an advocate for the child in cases of child abuse, neglect and deprivation. Effective child advocacy in any form must include:

a. Professional education and training. The ability to identify symptoms of child abuse, neglect and deprivation and the willingness to report them (referred to previously as primary advocacy).

b. The ability to evaluate the special needs and problems of the abused, neglected and deprived child (in addition to protection from further physical injury).

c. The ability to distinguish between and clearly delineate, during the development of the treatment plan, the child's own perspectives and interests. A child's concept of time (or frame of reference for time) is considerably different from an adult's.[5] A forced separation of the child from his parents must balance two competing interests. There is the possibility that the child's health and physical safety may be jeopardized by a continuation of his presence in the family home and there is the known psychological damage to a child caused by a forced separation. Similarly, although the best treatment plan may include a continuation of the family unit, any advocate for the child must realize that there is a point at which the child-parent relationship must be terminated. It is ludicrous to continue treatment for the parents, dangling the child before their eyes, after the passage of long periods of time. Children are on one time schedule and parents may be on quite another. If treatment has been unsuccessful and if the prognosis is poor, the parent-child relationship should be terminated.

d. The need to raise two very real questions in regard to the development of any treatment program exists. They are: What effect will the treatment have on a child and what can be done to minimize any possible harmful effects?

e. The need to raise the question of what the salutary effect of treatment for the parents may have on the child. Intervention is quite legitimate as a direct aid for the parents, but it must be kept in mind that this legitimate intervention may provide absolutely no benefit to the child. (See Chapter 20) It is a patent mistake to assume that because the parents are receiving treatment, some of that treatment will filter down to the child and benefit him. Not so. Treatment that is developed or delivered specifically for the parents may have absolutely no benefit for the child.

f. The necessity of insuring that the abused, neglected and deprived child will receive continuing treatment. The medical profession may withdraw once the child's physical injuries are treated. Social service workers often withdraw from the case once it seems that the home environment has been stabilized and there is no longer a danger of future physical harm to the child. Courts, acting on the requests of departments of social services, have only sporadic contact with the child and they, too, have a tendency to focus exclusively on the possibility of future physical harm to the child. External indications of trauma to a child disappear with surprising speed. Superficial stabilization of the home environment may be occasioned by periodic home visits at irregular intervals. The medical profession, the social work profession and the legal profession have an unfortunate habit of all focusing on exhibited injuries and the stability of the home. What is often forgotten is the fact that while trauma is treated and while the home is stabilized, the child's psychological and developmental problems may still be present. An effective child advocate should insure that treatment and support are geared equally to the parents and to the child. Treatment and support should only be terminated when (1) the home is stabilized and the child will be safe; (2) the trauma has been successfully treated; (3) the parents' problems have been successfully treated; (4) and equally important, the child's psychological and developmental problems have been successfully treated.

This individual advocacy role can be adopted by any number of persons after the initial report of child abuse has been filed. The physician who examines and treats the child believed to have been abused, neglected or deprived, can be a natural advocate for the child. If the case has not been incorporated into the legal system, the physician may determine the child's needs and transmit them to the state agency which is handling the case, to the local child protection team if one exists, and of course, directly to the child's parents.

The social service worker or the child protection worker may also become an effective advocate for the child. In the vast majority of states, it is the local department of social services that has been given the mandate to receive reports, complete the intake and make the investigation. If the social worker has been trained in some developmental screening, then she may be the ideal person to identify the child's needs and insure that proper treatment is available. It should be noted, however, that:

a. Most case workers do not have any training in developmental screening (see Chapter 15).
b. As the number of reported cases increase, and the number of agency personnel remains stable, the caseload increases. And, as the caseload increases, the opportunity to screen the child and his siblings for developmental lags, is simply not available.
c. In many cases, the worker envisions (wrongly) a conflict of interests. The agency worker may be the primary therapist for the parents once a case of abuse has been documented. He may feel that to actively advocate for the child, while at the same time, acting as a therapist and a friend for the

parents is an ethical and professional conflict. It is not. If the caseworker is the parents' primary therapist, it would seem to be axiomatic that a child's needs and interests are of primary concern to the parents and to the parents' therapist as well.

The same individual advocacy role can be played by the mental health worker, the public health worker and the educational specialist. In addition, there are often other persons such as lay persons who can play an active role in the advocacy for a child. Unlike the physician and agency personnel, however, they are at a disadvantage. In almost all cases, lay persons function outside the system and look in. From a practical point of view it is simply easier to manipulate or intervene in a system when you understand how that system works and when you work within that system. Nevertheless, reality aside, it is the authors' belief and recommendation that all professionals, paraprofessionals and lay persons involve themselves as advocates for the child. Some persons will have neither the knowledge nor the clout to make a system recognize and treat the child's needs, but they can make their concerns known to others who can. Social and legal systems may be "closed systems," but there is no reason why they should remain so. The philosophy that "this is not my business; I'm not too sure," and "They won't listen to me," are self-fulfilling prophecies. They won't and they can't, unless you do.

There are two other forms of advocacy which the authors have classified under the designation of "formal advocacy." The first is the child protection team and the second is the appointment of a guardian ad litem to represent the child's interests in any judicial proceedings. These three forms of advocacy, although procedurally and functionally different, are not mutually exclusive. To the contrary, all three forms of advocacy are needed to assure appropriate assistance for the child.

2. *The Child Protection Team.*

In the summer of 1975, Colorado enacted into law, a child protection act which legislatively recognized the existence of multidisciplinary child protection teams.[6] Although "teams" have been functioning successfully in numerous counties throughout the country for a number of years, Colorado is the first state to incorporate the concept into statutory framework. Every county in Colorado which receives 50 or more reports of child abuse each year is mandated by law to create a child protection team for that county the following year. Contiguous counties with small rural populations are encouraged to combine and form their own teams. It is the authors' belief that statutory recognition of child protection teams will eventually prove to be the rule and not the exception in most states. The definition of a child protection team[7] is more than two persons from more than one agency. Ideally, the team should include at least one representative from the department of social services (or other agency mandated to receive and investigate reports), the local law enforcement agency, a physician, a psychiatrist, a lawyer and a representative of the local court with juvenile jurisdiction. There is little doubt that a knowledgeable social worker, a lawyer or a physician can make a valuable contribution to the rather complex problems of child abuse. At the same time, however, there is no doubt that all involved disciplines and agencies working together can have a far greater contribution. By bringing together diverse disciplines and professionals, present weaknesses are minimized and present and potential strengths are maximized. Even with the most benevolent of all motives, the doctrines of territorial imperative and professional elitism can only hurt those they profess to be an advocate for—the child. Utilized properly, the child protection team itself can be an active advocate for the child.[8]

If a child abuse investigation has been conducted properly and thoroughly, the collective expertise of the child protection team can be used to analyze the investigatory data. The child protection team should be used to integrate the investigatory data and, utilizing the expertise of different disciplines, reach the proper diagnosis, develop the proper prognosis and develop a viable treatment plan for the abused child and his parents. The child protection team would seem to be the logical unit to evaluate not only the parents' prognosis, but the child's as well. It is axiomatic, to say the least, that a treatment plan for the child cannot be developed until his physical, psychological and developmental needs have been assessed. The development of a viable treatment plan is a process which must weigh not only the collective needs of the total family unit, but the needs of the parents and the child individually. The recommendations of the child protection team must take into consideration and must address the child's own needs. Appendix A, following the text of this book, details an exhaustive listing of questions which must be routinely asked and answered by the child protection team in cases of child abuse.

3. *The Guardian Ad Litem.*

The authors of this chapter recommend another type of child advocate—the appointment of a guardian ad litem for every case of child abuse that terminates in the juvenile court or the district court with juvenile jurisdiction. The concept of a guardian ad litem to represent a child's interests which are independent from his caretaker's is not a new development. The utilization of a guardian ad litem to represent the child's interests in the *child abuse case* is, however, a recent innovation. It is a concept which is beginning to be accepted in more and more jurisdictions throughout the country.[b]

In an effort to fully protect an abused child's interests, a number of states now require that a guardian ad litem be appointed to represent the child's

---

[b]Public Law 93-247 in fact requires that there be provision for the appointment of a guardian ad litem in cases of child abuse as a condition precedent to a state receiving federal funds.

interests. The guardian ad litem is a "special guardian" appointed by the court to represent the child. As a special guardian, the guardian ad litem is not an advocate for the petitioner[c] (usually the Department of Social Services) and he is not an advocate for the respondant,[d] although he may assume one or both of these roles as the proceedings go forward. In legal jargon, he is an amicus curiae, a friend of the court; he is charged with fully protecting the child's interests, and he is ultimately responsible to the court that appointed him.[e]

In the majority of cases which proceed to court, there are usually three attorneys present: the judge, the city or county attorney and the parents' attorney. Once a petition has been filed in the juvenile court, the child, for all practical purposes, becomes a ward of the court, and it is the court's responsibility to insure that the child's safety and interests are fully protected. The judge is then placed in the rather awkward position of not only protecting the child's interests, but also weighing both sides of the argument and rendering an equitable decision. Impartiality is lost if the judge becomes an active advocate for the child. To resolve the dilemma, the judge may transfer his obligation of protecting the child's interests to a third party—the guardian ad litem. It should be noted, however, that the transfer of functions does not negate the court's responsibility to the child. It simply transfers it. The transfer to the guardian ad litem, in simple terms, designates the guardian ad litem as an officer of the court, responsible not only to the child but to the court as well.

The parents' attorney obviously cannot independently represent the interests of the child. In a majority of cases, it is the parents who are accused of inflicting the injuries. And it is the responsibility of the parents' attorney to represent his clients' interests—the parents, not the child.

The petitioner in a child abuse case is usually the local department of social services, and it is usually the city attorney or the county attorney who presents the petition to the court and introduces the evidence. In an increasing number of jurisdictions around the country, the county or the city attorney is simply regarded as a conduit into the courts. It is the local department of social services which receives the report, completes the intake, completes the investigation, analyzes the data for the proper diagnosis, prognosis and treatment plan, decides whether or not to proceed to court or prepares the petition and subpoenas the witnesses. If the city or county

[c]The petitioner is the person who brings the action in the juvenile court. He presents the petition and he has the burden of going forward with the case.

[d]The respondent is the person who is alleged to have abused the child. He responds to the allegations contained within the petition. The respondent is analogous to the defendant in a criminal court proceeding.

[e]For a more technical and legally oriented discussion of the guardian ad litem, see: Fraser, B., "Independent Representation in the Child Abuse Case: The Guardian Ad Litem."

attorney has no part in the investigation and the analysis of data, the only information that he receives is that prepared by the local department of social services. Once a petition has been filed in the court, the city or county attorney assumes a quasi-prosecutorial role. His primary emphasis is not an independent representation of the child's interests, it is an attempt to prove the perpetrator's culpability. The establishment of culpability and the protection of the child victim's interests are not the same.

To fully insure that a child's interests will be protected at all proceedings, the guardian ad litem has four very basic functions. He is:

1. An investigator whose task it is to ferret out all of the relevant information.
2. An advocate whose task it is to insure that all relevant data are presented to the court.
3. A counsel whose task it is to insure that the court has before it all of the viable dispositions.
4. A guardian, in the simplest sense of the word, whose task it is to insure that the child's present and long-range interests are fully protected.

Obviously, the guardian ad litem's ability to function as an advocate, a counsel and a guardian, depend to a large extent upon his ability to function as an investigator. Until a thorough investigation has been completed, there is not enough available data to reach the proper diagnosis, the proper prognosis, and to develop a treatment plan which will adequately reflect the child's needs and interests. If the function of investigation is not adequately pursued, the guardian ad litem has little chance to function adequately and independently as an advocate, as a counsel and as a guardian. The guardian ad litem as the representative of the child may make recommendations to the court. But the court is under no obligation to accept those recommendations as its own. The degree to which it does will no doubt depend upon the guardian ad litem's investigation, his knowledge of the complex factors involved in child abuse and his ability to effectively articulate the options available to the court.

It is the authors' belief that a guardian ad litem should be appointed to represent every child that has been abused in those cases that proceed into the juvenile court. Furthermore, it is the authors' belief that a guardian ad litem should be appointed and should be present at every proceeding in which a child's interests may be adversely affected. Juvenile court hearings may involve as many as five or more separate proceedings. The first is the advisory hearing. At the advisory hearing, the parents are formally informed of the allegations contained within the petition and are informed of their rights. The second is the setting. The hearing for setting is simply the agreement between all parties of a mutually convenient time to debate the allegations. The third is the adjudicatory hearing. At the adjudicatory hearing, there is only one issue to be resolved. Do the parents' behavior or the child's injuries fall within the legal definition of child abuse for that state? At the conclusion of the adjudicatory hearing, if the court declares that the child has not been abused (neglected, or deprived), all legal proceedings cease. If, however, it is resolved that the child has been abused, the juvenile court will order a fourth hearing, the dispositional hearing. At the dispositional hearing, there is only one issue to be resolved. To whom should custody be awarded and what treatment should be offered to the child and his parents?[f] The fifth possible hearing is a hearing for temporary custody. The temporary custody proceeding may be initiated at any point. The purpose of this fifth hearing is to determine whether or not a child's safety is presently in jeopardy and if so to remove the child and place him in a more secure environment until a legal disposition has been reached. For all practical purposes, the issue of temporary custody, usually arises immediately upon receipt of a report of suspected child abuse and before any other legal proceedings have been initiated. In the early stages of a child abuse case, a child is usually taken into temporary custody unilaterally and without a court order by a law enforcement official, a physician or a caseworker. If the assumption of temporary custody is unilateral, most states require within a fixed period of time, a formal hearing on the issues. The guardian ad litem, as an advocate for the child's interests, should be appointed before and should be present at any hearing for temporary custody. The issue in simple terms is a balancing of two very real interests of the child. Is the known psychological harm that results from a forced separation less than the possibility of future physical harm if the child is left with the parents?

Although by definition, a guardian ad litem does not have to be a lawyer, the authors of this chapter strongly urge that any such appointment be made to someone with legal training. As the juvenile court becomes more formalized, as procedures and rules become more structured, an active advocate for the child must have the ability to understand and to manipulate the legal system and this, in turn, would seem to dictate the need for a lawyer serving in this role. Functioning properly, the guardian ad litem is a non-adversarial party whose duty it is to protect the child's short-range legal interests and the child's short-range and long-range interests. A guardian ad litem should have the ability to help the court focus on the child's physical, psychological and developmental needs and interests and help the court address these needs accordingly. If the guardian ad litem has performed his investigatory function properly, the court should have before it all the facts that it needs to equitably determine whether or not this child has been abused. If the

---

[f]At the dispositional hearing the court has three options:

a. Terminate child-parent relationship.
b. Place child in protective custody.
c. Return child to his parents under court supervision.

guardian ad litem is properly prepared, all reports and all evaluations will be available for the dispositional hearing. If utilized properly, the concept of a guardian ad litem should be the most effective advocate for a child in cases of child abuse.

Unfortunately, many lawyers who are appointed as guardians ad litem have little knowledge of the complex problems of child abuse and neglect, have had little experience in the juvenile court and have little knowledge of the physical, psychological and developmental aspects of children. The guardian ad litem does have the option and should utilize the expertise of other professionals who have this knowledge. If a child protection team is currently functioning within the community, the guardian ad litem is free to make full use of their expertise.[g]

As a basic rule of thumb, anyone who is appointed as a guardian ad litem should remember that

1. Every case of child abuse is a potential capital case. The guardian ad litem should exert as much effort in preparing for these proceedings as he would in a capital case.
2. Very few persons have expertise in all areas (medical pathology, psychiatry, social work and law) of child abuse. Never assume that someone else is an expert and be very wary of advice from self-proclaimed experts.
3. To conduct a proper investigation and to insure that specific questions, problems and issues are answered, it is necessary to know what you are looking for. In short, it is necessary to develop at least some superficial expertise.
4. It is the guardian ad litem's obligation to insure that the court is fully aware of the child's needs and to insure that any treatment plan adopted by the court addresses those needs. The role of the guardian ad litem is not a passive one. To fully protect the child's interests, it is necessary to know what you want, how to get it, where to get it, and then to actively pursue it.

Summary

In 1967, almost one decade ago, the Supreme Court said in the case of In Re Gault,[9] that a child's liberty could not be denied without certain substantive safeguards. One of the rights accorded a child facing the possibility of incarceration, was the right of independent representation. It is the author's belief that representation for children who have been abused, neglected or deprived is just as compelling as it is in juvenile delinquency cases. In fact, it

---

[g]In fact, under Colorado's new Child Protection Act, the local child protection team is mandated to notify the guardian ad litem of:

a. Reasons for initiating the petition.
b. Suggestions for optimal disposition.
c. Suggested treatment.

would seem to be ludicrous to suggest that a child is entitled to and needs independent representation in cases in which his liberty is endangered, but is not entitled to and does not need representation in cases in which his life and mental health are endangered. Advocacy and independent representation for children who have been abused, neglected or deprived is an integral part of any good child abuse system.

Advocacy and representation of children can take a number of forms, some formal, some informal, some simplistic and some rather sophisticated and technical. Schematically, child abuse may be broken into three rather broad chronological steps: identification, investigation and intervention. Child advocacy or independent representation is a necessary element at all three steps. The simplest form of child advocacy in cases of child abuse is the ability to identify the symptoms of abuse (or neglect or deprivation) and a willingness to report the case to the appropriate state agency. Until there is some form of identification, there can be no investigation and no intervention.

The second form of advocacy suggested in this chapter goes beyond the simple act of identification and reporting. It involves the ability (usually by those persons who are conducting the investigation) to identify specific physical, psychological and developmental problems. Furthermore, it assumes that the person who identifies the specific physical, psychological and developmental deficiencies will act affirmatively, attempting to offer or arrange for some form of intervention and treatment which will specifically address those problems.

The first two forms of advocacy can be provided by any person who is involved in a case of child abuse. As a practical matter, however, there are a few problems which diminish the practical value of this type of advocacy. The first is that many persons who come into daily contact with young children simply do not have the ability to identify the symptoms of child abuse, much less identify the more specific issues of psychological and developmental lags. Second many persons who do have the ability to identify physical, psychological and developmental problems in young children, simply do not want to become involved. Third, many persons who do wish to act as an advocate for the child's needs lack the clout that is often necessary to influence agency personnel who will make pivotal decisions concerning the child's safety. To a large extent, the social service and the legal systems are "closed systems," and they do not easily lend themselves to this form of advocacy. And, fourth, advocacy of this sort is piecemeal. It is left to the discretion and the ability of the individual citizen. It does not insure that all children who have specific problems and needs will be represented. It simply leaves large gaps in an area in which there should be no gaps.

There are two other more formal and more structured forms of advocacy which are beginning to gain wide recognition and acceptance. The first, is the creation of a multidisciplinary child protection team to evaluate *all* reported cases of child abuse. Unlike the first two forms of advocacy, the child protection team sees all cases of child abuse. It effectively throws a net over all reported cases. Unlike the first two forms of advocacy, the child protection team must have enough expertise to identify specific physical, psychological and developmental problems of abused children, is a part of the system and can manipulate it to the child's benefit and can address the child's specific problems in a treatment plan. Functioning properly, the child protection team should be able to isolate the child's own problems, devise specific solutions and insure that they are an integral part of any treatment plan.

Finally, the concept of a guardian ad litem to represent the child's interests in a court of law is beginning to gain wide acceptance. Usually incorporated into the statutory framework of a state, the guardian ad litem offers the most structured and the most widely accepted form of advocacy for children who have been abused, neglected or deprived. This form of advocacy can have the most definitive effect in matters concerning a child's safety. The guardian ad litem has the opportunity to deliver in person to the final arbitrator, the child's needs and problems, indicate what services and treatment would be most beneficial from the child's point of view and recommend that such services and treatment be incorporated by court order into any treatment plan. Conversely, guardians ad litem do not necessarily have the expertise that is necessary to specifically identify a child's physical, psychological or developmental problems. The guardian ad litem does, however, have the option of consulting with others (i.e., the child protection team or other professional individuals) who do have such expertise.

Traditionally, the child abuse case has been handled as if it were a problem of the parents. The parents' needs were identified and treated and it was assumed that this was adequate treatment for the child. Today, we know that this is not the case. Children have their own needs which exist quite independently from those of their parents'. Treatment should pivot solely on the basis of need—the parents' needs and the child's needs. Adequate treatment should focus equally on the child's own physical, psychological and developmental needs. It is no longer acceptable to assume that help for the parents is synonymous with help for the child. One way to assure that the child's own needs are adequately addressed is to provide that child with an advocate or independent representative.

References

1. Fraser, "A Pragmatic Alternative to Current Legislative Approaches to Child Abuse," *American Criminal Law Review*, 12:103 (1974).

2. Colorado Rev. Stats. Ann. 19-10-104(1) (1973 as amended).

3. Polier, Hon. J.W.: "Professional Abuse of Children: Responsibility for the Delivery of Services," *American Journal of Orthopsychiatry*, 45(3):357 (1975).

4. Delaney, Hon. James J. "The Battered Child and the Law," *Helping the Battered Child and His Family*, Kempe and Helfer, eds., Philadelphia: J.B. Lippincott Co., 1972.

5. Goldstein, J., Freud, A., Solnit, A.J.: *Beyond the Best Interests of the Child* New York: Free Press, 1973.

6. H.B. #1192, now cited as Colorado Rev. Stats. Ann. 19-10-101 to 19-10-115 (1973 as amended).

7. Colorado Rev. Stats. Ann. 19-10-103(2) (1973 as amended).

8. Fraser, B.: *Colorado: Child Abuse and the Child Protection Act,* The National Center for the Prevention and Treatment of Child Abuse and Neglect, Denver, Colorado, 1976.

9. *In Re Gault,* 387 U.S. 1 (1967).

Chapter 14

Treatment of Specific
Delays and Deficits

Harold P. Martin and **Tobie Miller**

The first section of this book has detailed what abused children are like. Apart from the intellectual and psychological problems of these children, a large number are found to have deficits and delays in learning, perceptual discrimination, motor skills, and in speech and language. Chapter 12 has pointed out some of the variables which may account for the effect of the abusive environment of the child's personality and central nervous system functions. To underscore the need for treatment of specific developmental problems of these children, a bit of reiteration seems in order.

In one of our follow-up studies of abused children, 53 percent of the children, at a mean of five years after abuse, had some neurologic findings, with 31 percent of the total group having moderate to severe handicaps which were truly functional handicaps. Forty of 49 abused children were scoring below their age level on a test of visual-motor integration. Other investigators have in general found greater prevalence of neurologic deficits than in our studies, perhaps because the Denver studies have included less seriously traumatized children. In a separate study of 42 abused children reported in 1972, the author noted that 42 percent of the children with normal intelligence scores had significant language delays.

Even more impressive to us are our studies of three to five year olds in the Preschool for Abused Children at the National Center. As noted before, eleven of the thirteen children tested with revised Gesell Schedules had considerably more deficiencies in gross motor and language development than in the other three areas assessed (fine motor, adaptive, personal-social). Our experience with large groups of young children and infants continues to corroborate the perceptual-motor delays and language deficits of these children. More specifically, those children evidencing delays in their gross motor development do not present a consistent profile, either in the degree of severity or the nature of specific neurological deficits. The majority of these youngsters, however, are mildly to moderately depressed in their gross and fine motor skill acquisition, perform tasks with poor quality, and generally have some type of abnormal muscle tone with decreased joint stability. Other neurological findings, such as the presence of residual primitive reflexes, delayed balance and equilibrium responses, and poor protective reactions are commonly elicited.

Given the fact that developmental delays and deficits are found in large numbers in almost any group of abused children, let us turn now to the issue of treatment. The question may well be raised, why should a book on abused children have a section on developmental delays? For after all, the questioner may continue, the management or treatment of children with such deficits is no more germane to abused children than to any child with such problems regardless of the cause. In a sense there is some apparent validity to such a query. The wounds of an abused child, it may be argued, need the same type of intervention as identical wounds in a child wherein the cause was not physical abuse. A fractured leg is treated identically regardless of how the fracture occurred, it may be argued. It then might be stated that developmental delays are treated in specific manners regardless of the cause of those delays. It is at this point that we disagree with our hypothetical critic. There are a number of special issues regarding the abused child with developmental problems. First is the factor that abused children enter into the helping system circuitously—i.e., through the portals of the child abuse professionals. And in point of fact, most professionals working in the area of child abuse are not child development experts. As has been stated repeatedly throughout this book, the primary and often the only orientation to the abused child is toward protecting him from physical assault. Developmental issues are often unrecognized or ignored where the more critical issue of protection of the child from injury preempts developmental assessment and possible remediation for his delays. A second issue with the abused child is the considerably more complex intertwining of environmental and organic factors in the genesis of the developmental delays. Perhaps the treatment of perceptual delays or language deficits should *not* be the same for abused children as it would be for a child where the basis for his developmental problem was quite different. And finally a third issue seems pertinent: the behavior and attitudes of the professionals as well as the approaches utilized to treat abused children may be much more important aspects of the therapeutic intervention than with other children. Let us look at each of these three issues in greater detail.

A knowledge of child development and a developmental orientation to children is not shared by most professionals working in the area of child abuse. The social worker, nurse, pediatrician, lawyer and judge each have their own areas of expertise, their own spheres of interest regarding the abused child. The medical and legal systems which come to bear on the abused child are designed to address the physical consequences of the abuse and the protection of the child from physical harm. The major and oftentimes only concern of these professionals is one of survival of the child, rather than his optimal growth and development. Most mental health professionals involved with abused children seem to be primarily oriented to the same issues, as well as to addressing the psychiatric problems of the parent. In a number of instances where child psychiatrists have been asked for consultation in regards to specific children, their reports have only included an evaluation of the parents, with no psychiatric evaluation of the child in question. A developmental assessment of the abused child is rarely obtained by social service agencies, or by medical facilities. And this is despite the enormous preponderance of developmental problems in these children. For example, a one-year-old child recently abused is placed into foster care. The child protection worker, foster parents or public health nurse may note that the child is delayed in his development. However, there is little consideration of either the cause of the delay or what type of intervention might be helpful in accelerating the child's development. At most, many professionals take the stance of waiting to see how the child progresses in his development in a different setting, the foster home. And yet even when this position is taken, and it is often a reasonable treatment approach, there is little monitoring of the developmental progress of the child and no consultation to determine if some intervention more specific than adequate parenting might be indicated for the child.

This is not meant to be a catharsis for our distress at present policy and function of child abuse teams. Indeed, without a survey of child abuse teams around the country, we cannot be sure of the generalizability of our limited observations. Rather, this point is made to bolster two specific recommendations.

Given the extremely high percentage of abused children with developmental delays and deficits, the first recommendation seems to follow logically. That is that child developmental consultation should be available to every agency which deals in more than a very limited way with abused children. The exact manner of incorporating these services into existing programs would depend upon the idiosyncratic details of each agency in question. Surely any child welfare or child protection agency which deals with more than a handful of abused children per year might well consider having a child developmentalist on the staff—either part time or full time. The courts or guardians ad litem should have available to them consultation regarding the developmental problems and needs of the children for whom they are legally responsible. Medical facilities, child abuse teams, visiting nurse services, and units set up to help these children such as a preschool for abused children all should have developmental consultation readily available to any of the children whom they serve.

The second suggestion refers to the use of such consultation. In different communities there are critical times when a review of a child abuse case takes place—and increasingly this takes place through a multidisciplinary team. Dr. Schmitt and colleagues are in the process of developing a manual of suggested procedures for such child abuse teams. At the time of the review, data are shared and specific questions must be addressed. These questions commonly include: where should the child live; what type of legal action should be undertaken; what are the psychological problems of the parents? We are suggesting that *routinely* a whole set of questions should be raised with regard to the developmental status of the abused child. Many of these questions can be found in appendix A. We have attempted in the appendix to outline the questions that should be considered in every case of child abuse or neglect. Summarily, they can be condensed into asking: What is the developmental status of the child presently; what treatment options should be considered to help the child grow and develop more normally; and third, what will the developmental and psychological effects of our treatment be on the child? These three questions must be addressed early in the course of case management. They may be asked by the child abuse team or by some individual who is formally or informally responsible for the child's welfare, e.g., a guardian ad litem, a physician, a child welfare worker. They may be asked by the judge or his representative at time of legal proceedings. They should probably be asked by all of these people. If and when the answers are not available, perhaps then developmental consultation be requested. The mere use of these questions by professionals on a consistent basis will begin to have the effect of altering their whole orientation and stance toward child abuse. It will be a catalyst in broadening our concern and area of interest in the abused child.

The second issue especially pertinent to the developmental problems of abused children has been briefly discussed in Chapter 6—that is the intimate intertwining of organic and environmental issues in the occurrence and remediation of developmental neurologic problems. This surely is part of the belabored question of nature versus nurture.

Throughout various chapters in Section 1 of this book the point has repeatedly been made that many of the neurologic and other developmental problems of these children may be as much a part and result of inadequate parenting as being secondary to structural damage to the brain. The purpose of bringing this *old chestnut* to your attention here is because it may well relate to the type of treatment procedures we recommend.

Insofar as language delays, learning disorders, motor incoordination or perceptual handicaps are partially or even completely secondary to inadequate interpersonal relationships with the child, this suggests that traditional treatment approaches may not be enough to help the child improve or recover. Language therapy alone may not be enough. Physical or occupational therapy may have severe limitations to their efficiency. And so forth.

On the other hand, just providing a loving stimulating environment may similarly be dooming the child to failure. "Love is not enough" refers to the need for expert help which is required for many delayed or disturbed children. The chapter on Preschools for Abused Children, Chapter 17 points out this need quite well. Given a child with motor disability or speech delay, the stimulating and psychologically attuned atmosphere of a preschool can be most helpful in remediation. Yet, regardless of the basis or cause for the child's developmental problem, there often is a need for specific treatment procedures to implement and supplement the milieu therapy of the school, or for that matter the foster home.

Our point is that treatment procedures for these children are not clear and simple. The delays and deficits of many children are remarkably and often completely remediated with only the institution of a stimulating environment—a good family and home—and a good peer-group educational experience. Repeatedly, we see abused children who, having functioned quite delayed and retarded, completely catch up with no specific treatment other than environmental manipulation. And yet, this is not always the case. Some of the developmental problems do not disappear—some continue to handicap the child's function. In these instances, special therapeutic intervention, in addition to environmental stimulation, is a necessary part of total child care. Treatment should include, if it is to touch on both the organic and environmental components of the abused child's delays, both specific techniques to remediate the neurologic deficits, as well as exposure to activities geared to stimulate normal growth and development. What is most important and critical to the success of the intervention is that these two aspects of treatment be geared to the levels of development at which the child is presently functioning. Presenting activities which require a higher skill level than yet achieved by the child will assuredly impede his progress. Specific help from a therapist who is experienced not only in working with such delays but who also has a broad knowledge of child development is required.

Treatment techniques used with abused children are often the same ones employed with children experiencing delays and deficits for other reasons. It is the therapist's approach to these children which may differ more frequently than the actual techniques. The importance of the professional's attitude and behavior toward the abused child is explained in greater detail later. The activities presented should follow a normal developmental sequence; that is, they should progress in difficulty from low to higher level tasks just as a baby learns to roll, sit, crawl, stand, and finally walk. Basic to all therapeutic endeavors is the introduction of sensory input, referred to earlier as tactile-kinesthetic stimulation, to improve the child's awareness of his body in space and to increase joint stability. Resistance applied to the child's body in the quadripedal and later in the bipedal positions also improves body awareness and stability, as well as helping the child develop protective and balance reactions. Later, upon achieving these basic skills, the child is ready to improve his ability to integrate the two sides of his body, arms and legs together, and to perform higher level gross and fine motor skills. Again, the progression of difficulty is the same for integrative tasks as it is for the more basic skills, from an all-fours position, to kneeling, to standing. The child's bilateral integrative skills should be accomplished at one level before proceeding to the next. This same developmental approach can be valuable to a therapist in treating abused children with fine motor and perceptual-motor deficits as well. A knowledge of normal development and how one integrates information from his sensory, motor and visual perceptual systems is a prerequisite to working with these special children.

Treatment often takes the form of consultation from the therapist where the parent, child worker or preschool staff member may be given the instruction and support to work specifically with the child on the developmental problem in question. We have found this alternative to direct intervention, that of the therapist acting as consultant, to be quite satisfactory at the National Center's Preschool.

Upon evaluating the child in question over an extended period of time, the therapist presents her findings and recommendations to the preschool staff, including explicit instructions and demonstration for direct implementation by the staff, teacher and aides. The therapy is in most instances given in the group setting where the child has been allowed adequate time to adjust to the familiarity of his peers and teachers. In this milieu, therapy becomes routine to the child, an expected and often anticipated part of his daily schedule, a time when he receives special individualized attention from his teacher. Direct intervention by the preschool staff is important for yet another reason. Many of the treatment procedures used to remediate neurologic dysfunction require physical contact, which the child may perceive as threatening. However, involvement with an adult whom the youngster has learned to trust generally relieves his fears and anxieties, resulting in greater cooperation and motivation to work. By receiving therapy at his preschool, the abused child escapes the social stigma of being "different," a label generally attached to other children having to leave school, home, or friends to go to therapy. Treatment provided by the preschool staff also has its practical and economic advantages. The specific treatment techniques, whenever possible, are incorporated into the already existing activity program, minimizing disruptions to the other children and overall scheduling. Second, problems of transportation arrangement and financial payments to cover cost of therapy are virtually nonexistent for the parent, guardian or professionals.

It may be necessary for the abused child with a specific developmental problem to be placed into a treatment program with a therapist. This method of intervention is generally necessary for those children evidencing more moderate to severe developmental or neurologic dysfunction, and in those instances where there is no other individual available to implement the treatment. However, with no other changes in the parenting, home or educational environment in which he lives, the efficacy of treatment is greatly limited. It is as if there is a surrealistic barrier to obtaining the kind of therapeutic results one is used to finding.

The complexity of the interplay between structural damage and environmental factors as they relate to treatment needs attention. This issue comes up more cogently in treatment with abused children than with children with most other developmental problems. While not necessarily the most exhaustive, we refer the reader to some current research of Dr. Ruth Rice. Her data were presented at the Fall 1975 American Psychological Association meetings and are abstracted in the November 1975 APA Monitor. Perhaps her data may serve as an example of this very issue.

Dr. Rice took a group of 30 premature infants and divided them randomly into an experimental group and a control group. In the experimental group the mothers were taught and supported to carry out a specific treatment plan. It consisted of tactile-kinesthetic treatment for fifteen minutes, four times daily, for a period of one month after discharge from the hospital. The two groups of infants were compared at four months of age. There were rather striking differences in the babies. The one area most critically looked at was whether certain neuro-physiological reflexes which should have disappeared by four months of age had in actuality done so. And further whether other reflexive development which should start at around this age had begun to appear. The reflex development of the experimental group of babies was considerably more mature than in the other group. Rice is interpreting this difference as indicating a true difference in neurological maturation, actually reflecting differences in neurophysiology such as myelination of the nervous system, cortical spacing, increasing control by the cerebral cortex of more primitive brain stem functions. A significantly better weight gain in the experimental group is seen by her as evidence of an increase in enzymatic and endocrine functioning. It is also important to note that there was a statistically significant superiority in functioning on the Bayley Scales of Infant Development. The experimental group of babies were more socially adaptive and aggressive.

These babies had more than tactile-kinesthetic treatment. In actuality this scientific language refers to having mothers touch, stroke, hold, rock, and cuddle their babies. So in actuality there were two phenomena occurring. First was the tactile-kinesthetic stimulation which has been shown in a number of studies, even when the affect of a mothering figure is controlled for, to aid in the maturation of the nervous system. This was shown by differences in reflex development, as well as superior developmental progress in these babies. In Rice's study a second phenomenon was evident. Although garbed in the jargon of science, the mothers and babies in the experimental group were spending structured, pleasant times together—four times a day. Rice does not ignore this factor, although she emphasizes the implied neurophysiologic differences, and speaks less to the effect on attachment and bonding. Nonetheless, the babies who were handled this way by their mothers were more socially adaptive. They noted more responsiveness of the mothers and babies to each other. Mothers related their belief that the "baby likes being stroked and held by me."

Perhaps one point to be taken from this fascinating research is that both phenomena were advantageous to the baby. The development, both neurologic and social, of the baby was enhanced by a close, loving mother-child interaction. But further, there is evidence that the specific tactile-kinesthetic stimulation *per se* had an effect on the neurologic integrity of the infant. And perhaps one further step would be to hypothesize that when the two are combined, that the additive strength of such a treatment program is greater than the sum of the individual contributions of loving care and neurologic stimulation.

This, then, is exactly the point regarding the abused child with neurologic delays and deficits. This is a child who has been in an environment where adequate mothering has usually not been available to him. Part of that picture includes an absence of the neurologic stimulation which is required for adequate neurophysiological development and maturation. Given the older child with delays and deficits then, the treatment planning should include both components—should include the availability of a loving caring parental figure—and should include specific developmental treatment approaches to help in the habilitation of the specific developmental deficits in question. This may be done in the child's own home, in a day care setting, a foster home or a preschool, as in the example we previously cited. Either one without the other may well be quite limited in the therapeutic goals one may hope to achieve.

The third issue regarding the treatment of specific delays and deficits in the abused child concerns the understanding and behavior of the therapist who may be working with such a child. The primary point to be made is that the therapist working with such a child will be most effective if she is aware of both the common reactions of abused children to their environments, and can be aware of the specific psychological issues operating with the specific child with whom she is working. Without such knowledge, the behavior of the child may interfere with effective treatment. Further, the child's therapist has the opportunity not only to offer specific treatment for a discrete disability, but also to be a significant psychological therapeutic change agent. Let us consider an example to underscore this issue.

A child's therapist may understandably have a great investment in the child performing and progressing in this therapy. The physical, occupational or language therapist has her own professional and personal needs for improvement in her patients. However, she will often be dealing with a child who has come from a home where performance, progress and being good are the only ways by which he can get approval or keep from getting abused by his parents. The child may well react to his therapist's demands for performance and progress as he does to his parents' demands for performance and progress. This may take several forms in the child's adaptation. He may take the path of total acquiescence out of fear (fear of rejection, fear of pain, fear of the therapist not liking or loving him). It may take the form of overt opposition to the therapist's requests. It may take the form of fairly subtle passive-aggressive behavior which can be confounding to the therapist. The child's reaction may impede the therapeutic goals, or it may just reinforce to the abused child that all adults (including the therapist) are like his parents.

Suppose, however, that the therapist was able to convey and communicate to the child some of the following attitudes:

1. That she, the therapist, likes the child whether or not he can do things she asks of him.
2. That she is not primarily interested in performance and progress, but is really interested in helping the child with problems which are bothering him.
3. That she will hang in there with him—and not desert him by discharging him from treatment because he doesn't "act right."
4. That she is not going to be upset or overwhelmed if the child wants to talk about the injuries he has suffered from his parents—or if he wants to talk about his feelings about past injuries, his handicaps, his parents or whatever. That she will not only not be overwhelmed but will listen and participate in such an exchange.

Insofar as the physical therapist or speech therapist or occupational therapist or educational therapist is able to take such a stance with the abused child, she has the opportunity not only to pursue her traditional therapeutic role, but also to be tremendously effective in helping the child psychologically. In our experience, most children's therapists are important psychological figures to children in treatment. The therapist who works with handicapped children is almost forced to deal with a host of very sensitive issues to the child and to his parents. Such a role, however, is usually not openly discussed or conceptualized by the therapist. She does, however, have the opportunity to help a child learn to enter into a working therapeutic alliance with an adult. She is working with children who must expose and deal with their imperfections and handicaps—about which they have considerable feeling. It is her attitude which may influence the child to view himself as quite different, abnormal and worthless; or may influence the child to view himself as a lovable nice kid with some special problems which can be worked on and become less handicapping.

So again, we are speaking of an issue that is not necessarily peculiar to the abused child. We are speaking to the importance of a handicapped child being understood by his therapist—and how her attitudes and behavior can affect the child's self-concept and interpersonal relationships. It is briefly spoken to here because of the greater need for such understanding and therapeutic stance by the therapist with an abused child with developmental delays and deficits. The professionals we have been speaking of may not have had much training or current support for viewing themselves this way and may have their own personal hang-ups in dealing with child abuse, especially in dealing with the parents of such a child. The implications then are dual. First is the advantage of therapists who are working with abused children to have some understanding of the dynamics of the abused child as well as of the parents. The second implication is that armed with this general knowledge, they can then be better able to understand and relate in an appropriate and psychologically helpful manner with the abused children in their care.

Summary

Neuro-developmental delays and deficits are common in abused children. They may stem from undernutrition, physical injury to the brain or from a variety of environmental factors such as minimal stimulation, distorted mother-child interactions. The types of developmental problems seen in quite high frequency in abused children include: motor incoordination, delays in speech and language; impairment in motor planning (dyspraxia); poor sensory-motor processing; learning disorders; perceptual handicaps. These are apart from, yet very intimately interwoven with the cognitive and psychological delays and deficits of the abused child.

In treatment planning for the abused child, the developmental status and needs of the child should be routinely considered and investigated. The first priority of the child abuse team will be to deal with medical wounds of the child and assure that repeated physical injury does not recur. The second priority in management involves providing as optimal a home environment for the child as is possible. The third priority should be to attend to the developmental problems and needs of the child.

It is recommended that child development consultation be available to agencies who deal with abused children, considering the alarmingly high rate of disability in these children.

The necessity for both emotional and neurophysically sound treatment is stressed. This also underlines the advantage in having consultation from a variety of developmental professionals to preschools, day care centers, foster parents and other units who are undertaking the care of abused children.

Finally, the ability of a therapist who is working with the abused child's neuro-developmental handicaps to function as a very important psychotherapeutic agent is underscored. In point of fact this would not truly be a different or novel role for the child's therapist, but it may be more demanding and stressful. This role needs to be more clearly acknowledged and conceptualized by all therapists working with abused children.

We have been impressed with the improvement in perceptual-motor development of the abused children in the National Center's Preschool. The advantages have been pointed out in having specific and sound remediation procedures while noting that with most abused children this habilitation program can be provided by preschool or day-care staff with routine consultation and monitoring by the professional therapist.

The underlying basis of this chapter has been to stress the need for a developmental approach with abused children. The abused child with developmental delays is, first and foremost, a child. He needs what all children need—a good home and a stimulating environment. He also needs specific help with the neuro-developmental handicaps he endures.

※ *Chapter 15*

Foster Placement:
Therapy or Trauma

Harold P. Martin and **Patricia Beezley**

Foster placement is the most frequently recommended "treatment" for abused children. At least one-half of abused children require some period of temporary foster home placement. While foster care may be considered as a therapeutic intervention by public agencies, this is rarely the case. Not only is foster placement usually not therapeutic, it is probably one of the very most traumatic and potentially harmful things that professionals prescribe for the abused child. Yet, it is possible for foster placement to be a therapeutic experience for children. This chapter will consider some of the uses of foster care and some of the ways that foster care can be made more therapeutic.

Reasons for Foster Care

Foster placement for abused children is usually not even intended as treatment. Rather, it provides the child a safe home environment at a time of crisis and emotional turmoil within the biologic family. With abused and neglected children, foster care provides the necessary protection and physical care for the child.

Using foster care on a short-term crisis basis to provide the child with a stable environment and parental supervision when his parents are in turmoil is a legitimate use of foster care. For abused and neglected children it may be considered an adjunct to treatment where it literally buys time for child protection workers to determine what the biologic home is like. When a child comes to a medical facility with injuries which are thought to be non-accidental, the first and most important thing the professional team needs to do is to assess the entire family situation. If a child is not in need of medical care, it seems ludicrous to hospitalize the child at a cost of $100 or more per day. Instead, the child may go directly from a medical facility or his biologic home to a foster placement. He will remain there until child protection workers make some assessment as to what the parents are like, what the parent-child relationship has been, and how safe the biologic home is for the child. This investigative stage may take only a few hours or it may require several days. The purpose of this type of foster placement then is to assure that the child is in what is assumed to be a safe, known, predictable home until an investigation can be made as to whether the child can be safely reunited with his parents. This home will not be particularly beneficial to the child because it is intended to be short-term and because it is used in the midst of a family crisis that the child will be experiencing to various degrees. The foster parents should not be expected to become psychological parents of the children during these brief holding actions. Rather, foster care provides shelter and food for the child within a family situation which has obvious advantages over institutions like hospitals or receiving institutions.

The legitimate use of foster care on a short-term, crisis basis becomes more questionable as the placement stretches into weeks, months and even years. When an injury has been established as non-accidental, the courts, with advice and counsel from a variety of sources, are left with the responsibility of deciding if and when the child can be reunited with his biologic family. The parents of the child frequently verbalize their relief at no longer having to care for the child on a daily basis; they are frequently reassured that the child's absence is in his best interests. At this point the placement is still being viewed as temporary, as being necessary only until enough changes have taken place with the parents for the child to return. Here again the foster placement is not truly being utilized as treatment or as a specifically helpful maneuver, but rather as a necessary interlude for the child. At this point, predictions as to the length of foster care are usually absent or unavailable. The courts are reluctant to make any final decisions regarding permanent dissolution of parental rights. Therefore, even though abusing parents may be making few social and psychological gains, and even though the home remains an unsafe environment for the child, the usual response by the court is to continue the case for another six to twelve months. Thus, months and years go by with the child still in "temporary" custody of foster parents. Treatment is directed towards the parents and the child is considered to be in a safe environment—albeit not a healthy environment. Because of the tenuous nature of the temporary custody, foster parents are naturally reluctant to become truly psychological parents to the child. Under such conditions, it is understandable that they will be discouraged from making much of a commitment or investment. Thus, the child lives with parent surrogates who remain somewhat aloof and whose parenting role is incomplete and transient in quality. One of the manifestations of this incomplete commitment to the child is the frequent changing of foster placements for so many abused children. It is acknowledged that many abused children are difficult to care for. Yet, it seems to be a common pattern that when the presence of an abused child in foster care becomes somewhat irksome or troublesome, the usual solution is to change foster home placements. A rather discouraged welfare worker described a two-and-one-half-year-old abused girl who, in the course of four months, had been transferred from three different foster homes. In frustration, the worker finally decided to return the child to her parents, as she was beginning to feel that the child was probably going to be better off with poor parenting, where there was now only minimal risk of recurrent physical abuse, than to continue this pattern of parent loss after parent loss and change after change in home placement. In summary, the use of foster care for an extended period of time without the necessary change in orientation from crisis care to therapeutic intervention is most questionable.

Foster care may be legitimately used on a diagnostic basis for the child. This is especially common in cases of suspected neglect, in particular, failure to thrive. This parallels the accepted medical model for diagnosis of failure to thrive. When a malnourished, poorly-grown infant is brought to a hospital, one diagnostic possibility is that the child is not growing because his home does not provide him with either adequate nutrition or an adequate emotional milieu to utilize his nutrient intake. When a diagnosis of failure to thrive or deprivation dwarfism seems likely, the recommended medical course is diagnostic treatment. That is, no tests for organic disease are performed, but rather the child is just fed and treated as all other children in the hospital are fed and treated. No special diet, no medication, and no special treatments are given. If after ten to fourteen days, one sees the child impressively gaining weight, the conclusion can be made that the basis for the child's failure to thrive was a malevolent or an inadequate home environment. This same diagnostic paradigm can also be used with neglected children in foster care. If a child continually gains weight in foster care, but loses weight whenever he returns to his biologic home for extended period of time, then the diagnosis of inadequate parenting has been established.

Foster placement may also be used diagnostically with child abuse cases. If a child is placed in foster care without any special therapy and his development accelerates and moves toward normalcy, then again, the diagnosis of inadequate parenting has been established. This was true with John, three years old, who was brought to the Pediatric Clinic with several bruises by a belt buckle. His parents admitted to beating him, but indicated that this was the first time that they had seriously hurt the boy. Further, they pointed out that John was not a normal child. They gave a history of delayed development, and, in fact, on developmental testing, he was functioning at an eighteen to twenty month level. He was not toilet trained, had tantrums, was aggressive and demanding, and showed little capacity for normal interpersonal relationships. His parents felt he was retarded, brain-damaged and "strange." The judge ordered that the child be placed in foster care and that the parents have therapy to help them sort out their feelings toward John. The decision was made to review the case in six months. However, the hidden agenda was to see how John would develop in his foster home during those six months. The primary question was whether John's development would progress and accelerate in a more "normal" home. In this instance, the foster home placement did coincide with significant developmental progress. Within two months, John was toilet trained. His temper tantrums abated and disappeared within three months. He seemed to understand language and very shortly started using two- and three-word phrases while his word repertoire quickly increased to at least 50 recognizable words. He seemed to be a very different little boy who was now enjoying initiating play with adults. His oppositional behavior had greatly diminished and more often took a passive form. The developmental testing was repeated after six months and showed that his developmental age was now at the thirty to thirty-two month level. While he was still delayed, he had progressed from ten to fourteen months in his development in a time period of only six months. What do we make of this change in John? We must assume that his prior development had been inhibited by his home environment and that his accelerated developmental progress in foster care was diagnostic of inadequate parenting being responsible for his developmental delays. John's developmental course was unusual. Many times the picture with a child such as John is complicated by neurologic delays or brain damage or dysfunction. Also, it is important to note that test scores on repeated developmental testing usually do not show such impressive gains. Rather, when improvement occurs in foster care, it frequently first shows up in pre-social behaviors that are not measured on formal developmental test scores, such as attention span, interest, imitativeness and perseverance. However, the important point is that foster care is often used (sometimes with covert acknowledgement) for diagnostic purposes.

Another legitimate use of foster care is that of a therapeutic experience for the child over an extended period of time. The effects of foster care—the impermanence, the attendant parent loss, the artificial move into a home where foster parents are rarely psychological parents—are disruptive to any child, even on a short-term basis. These issues can be devastating to children who must spend months and years with substitute parents. These issues, however, can be recognized and dealt with. The issues of attachment and therapeutic relationships between foster parents and foster children are impressively presented by Goldstein, Freud and Solnit in their book, *Beyond the Best Interests of the Child*.[1] Determining whether a foster home is therapeutic requires some definitions and realistic appraisals of the purposes of foster care. We must not delude ourselves as to the therapeutic value of a foster home when its only purpose is protection of the child on a short-term basis or a maneuver to buy time to assess the biologic home environment or use as a diagnostic tool. To be therapeutic, foster care must do more than prevent injuries from recurring and more than merely minimize the stresses to the abused child. A therapeutic experience implies that there is something positive and beneficial in the placement that enhances and brings out the strengths and potentialities for growth within the child. Foster care, to be truly helpful, must simulate or provide good parenting.

Good, normal, loving parenting is a force for positive growth and development of children. Foster parents should be capable of offering "good enough" parenting to foster children. This means providing something that is better than the typical quality of parenting that is usually found in our society. To be a good parent one does not need to know elaborate theories about the unconscious or Piaget's theory of development or how to deal with psychological resistances. A good parent operates largely from "instinct," but is also open to information and materials from educators and pediatricians. A good parent allows a child to develop his own interests and strengths regardless of the parent's particular wishes for a child. He balances his love for the child with discipline and allows the child to develop meaningful relationships outside of the biologic family. These are merely examples of the kinds of things that make up good parenting which can be very therapeutic experiences for abused children.

Making Foster Care More Therapeutic

I. Improved Screening. If foster care is to be a therapeutic experience for the child, the couples chosen to function as surrogate parents must be capable of providing good, normal parenting to children. Our experience has been that many abused children are placed with foster parents who are not providing "good enough" parenting. We have seen children physically abused by foster parents. We see foster parents threatening children with deportation to another foster home as a means of controlling a child's behavior. Mostly, however, we see foster parents whose own needs are so interfering with their parenting abilities that the children are getting far less nurturance and adequate help than they need.

The motivations are many and varied for becoming a foster parent!

The choice of foster parenthood is usually an expression of varying degrees of mature capacity for parenthood, the capacity and need to give love to a child, to realize one's own maturity; this in turn may be accentuated by a variety of neurotic motives of varying degrees of severity. In some intances, the choice may be determined almost entirely by narcissistic or neurotic needs, or defensive measures of maintaining psychic equilibrium. It is the crucial balance between the healthy and the neurotic motivations in the parental functioning that we strive to evaluate in our selection and use of foster parents. It is unrealistic to expect to find many foster parents entirely free from neurotic motivations and needs, since the seeking of a foster child is usually, to some degree, the family's way of solving a conscious or unconscious problem.[2]

One type of foster parent that is most concerning with abused and neglected children is the parent who is using foster parenting as a means of proving his own value and worth as an individual and as a parent. An extreme example of this is seen by the number of abusive parents who have applied to become foster parents. When this is a motivation for taking children, then the dynamic of the foster home becomes very similar to that of the abusing home, that is, the child exists in the home to be the source of gratification to the parents. In such a foster home, there is a high investment in having the newly arrived foster child "shape up." Insofar as a child learns to behave, becomes toilet trained, starts acting his age, or accelerates in his development, the parent has evidence to prove that he or she is a "good" parent. The self-esteem of the foster parent rests on the child making progress. This is often the same environmental climate from where the child came. There is a push or pressure for the child to demonstrate the results of good parenting. There is little tolerance of the regression most children exhibit in foster care. The child may be safe from physical harm in the new foster home, but he continues to be in a home where his existence and behavior can only be justified by his meeting the demands and needs of the parents.

To improve the quality of foster care so foster parents are capable of offering "good enough" parenting to the foster children, the criteria of child welfare agencies must shift from predominate concern over square footage of play space in the home to a more critical assessment of parenting abilities. Some of those abilities that must be assessed include:[3] sufficiency of time, availability at critical moments, experience with and insight into parent role, concern with child care practices and information, confidence in the parent role, perception of children and the particular abused child, quality of physical and social interaction with children, tolerance of developmental problems in children, handling of negativism, emphasis on independence and self-reliance versus dependence of the child, expectations and standards set for the child, quality of authority used, types of discipline used, acceptance of responsibility as social arbiter, tolerance of possible shortcomings and deviances of biologic parents, ability to share parenting role with spouse, energy level and resourcefulness, and conscious motivation. (*Selecting Foster Parents* by Martin Wolins, p. 56.) We have outlined in Chapter 20 specific criteria to be used to judge the ability of the biologic parent to provide adequate parenting for their child. These same criteria might well be used to assess foster parents' capacity to provide an adequate home for an abused child.

Motivations for foster parents that might have a negative effect on the welfare of the child include planning the foster child as treatment for their marriage or for their own child, exploitation of the child, extension of maternal control and seeing the child as an object, substitution of foster child for desire adoption or death of biologic child and a mother's wish to re-live her own maternal life.[3] The *very best* foster parents should be utilized for abused and neglected children as such children have suffered the most deprivation and will have some of the most serious psychological injuries. If there are not enough foster homes available and placement of a child is totally dependent upon what family has space, an agency must look critically at its recruitment policies.

II. Team Approach. There is a basic difference of opinion in professional circles as to whether foster parents should be considered as part of a multidisciplinary team working towards helping children, or whether they should just be a substitute home for children in need of placement. The people who feel foster homes should be the latter may argue that the parents should be uncontaminated by knowing anything special. They argue that foster parents should just provide warmth, love, care and concern. In fact, they believe that foster parents are in need of casework services just as abusive parents need casework services. *Casework with Foster Parents*, published by the Child Welfare League of America in 1956, was in its fifth printing in 1973.[2] This piece of literature, still being used in child welfare departments today, stresses the final authority vested in the caseworker to continue or terminate placements of children in foster homes. It explains that such final authority causes foster parents to unconsciously see the social worker as the original parent. The unrealistic attitudes that belong to the early childhood experiences of the foster parent are not to be brought to the attention of that parent, but rather, the caseworker is to help the foster parents to make "corrections" in their feelings through casework services. It is incredible that casework for foster parents continues to be an accepted practice, while in more recent years, the use of paraprofessionals, such as lay therapists, has developed through consultative and team efforts with no mention of casework services being needed or required. As long as foster parents continue to be seen as clients or patients, it is no wonder the recruitment of stable and well-adjusted families continues to be difficult.

Our premise is that foster parents should be considered as part of a multidisciplinary, therapeutic team with consultative services provided and information shared freely. Most abused children are emotionally upset and have special problems and special needs. Some are very difficult to live with, but others may be too easy to live with, that is, the withdrawn, quiet, obsequious, "good" children who are often overlooked as having special problems. It is our premise that foster parents can be better parents to these children if they do have special help in understanding abused children in general and the special problems of abused children within the foster home. Foster parents can also benefit from guidance and counseling in dealing with these children. Such help and support will not make them "professional parents" or child therapists. They can continue to be spontaneous but also be better parents with a program of support, education and counseling. We have seen these efforts be extremely useful with other para-professional groups such as lay therapists. Perhaps the most important quality of work with foster parents is respecting their dignity and being willing to see them as co-workers in the field of protective services.

III. In-Service Education. If the premise is accepted that foster parents need education, support, and consultation in dealing with abused children, the next step is to provide that help on some routine basis, rather than only having it be available when problems arise. When consultation is not available as a routine service of a child protection agency, the foster parents are put into an unfortunate bind of risking a great deal by asking for help. They run the risk of being considered inadequate and incompetent if they ask for assistance in understanding a foster child's behavior. When child welfare agencies do not have established programs in counseling and education for their foster parents, they are clearly giving the message that such services are not needed for "normal" foster parents.

Foster parents need general information about the dynamics of abuse and some understanding of the treatment programs available. If we place a child with asthma, hemophilia or cystic fibrosis with foster parents, we assume those parents need to know about the special condition of the child. The parent of such a foster child needs to know something about the special disease, how it affects the child, and how they as surrogate parents can help manage the manifestations of this special condition. Similarly, we should take this attitude toward child abuse and provide the surrogate parents with information and counseling about the special problems of the child, the effects of the abusive home on the child and how they as surrogate parents might help deal with the manifestations of this syndrome in the child. Also, specific information about a child needs to be shared with the foster parents. Early significant developmental history and some understanding of why the child's parents have abused him would help the foster parent not only be better able to deal with the child but also be more accepting of the parents. Most abused children are very difficult children to deal with and live with. The very high turn-over rate in foster home placements for abused children attests to the difficulties the parents have in relating to these children. In addition to the personality characteristics of the youngsters, the foster placement itself provokes considerable testing-out behavior for many of these children. They tax the patience and understanding of the best of parents. In summary, help to foster parents should be a planned part of the program and not merely provided on a crisis basis with the implication that the foster parents are inadequate surrogate parents.

The means of providing such a program of support for foster parents might be quite varied. It is our bias that group meetings for foster parents should be routinely provided. The purpose of such meetings could be multiple in nature; that is, they could provide in-service education as well as providing an opportunity for foster parents to discuss disturbing behavior of the children in their care. Providing an opportunity for parents to discuss their children so as to identify and alleviate problems as soon as possible is good preventive pediatrics. The group meetings would not be a mechanism for teaching "professional" parenting, but rather a means of providing supportive counseling for surrogate parents of a nature which, in actuality, should be provided to all parents.

For such group meetings to run most effectively, there should be co-leaders who have expertise in child development, child rearing, and perhaps, in group dynamics. It is essential that the professionals not be viewed as judgmental or punitive by the foster parents. This raises the question of the training and the professional role of the child protection worker. Even social workers at the masters degree level have had little training in child development, either in their formal schooling or in their in-service training in welfare agencies. And yet, these are the people to whom foster parents are supposed to turn for help and advice regarding child development. The very title of the child protection agency bespeaks the orientation, that is, protection of the child. But, child welfare workers should be responsible not only for physical protection but also for the welfare and development of the child. The workers should either be in a position to understand the children in their care or be able to know when and where outside consultation is available for that understanding. Therefore, more adequate training for the social workers needs to be done prior to their attempting to provide in-service for the foster parents. It may be extremely useful to utilize co-leaders of different professional backgrounds, for example, a pediatrician and a social worker.

IV. Improving Relationships Between Biologic Parents, Foster Parents and the Children. The relationships between foster parents and the biologic parents of the children who are in foster care are frequently strained and unproductive. In order for the child not to be caught between two sets of parents and in order for him to benefit in the best possible way, these relationships have to be improved. The basic guidelines should always be: What, in the long run, is in the best interests of the child? If foster parents have been screened adequately, their role is validated, and they have been provided with in-service education, then we can begin on the premise that they have a great deal to offer the abused child's biologic parents. Therefore, the following guidelines could be used:

1. The foster parent must not undermine the child's affection for the biologic parent. Phone calls, birthday cards and presents should be allowed if the child is desiring them.
2. The foster parent should attempt to keep the biologic parent informed of what is going on with the child. This may be through weekly postcards or an occasional phone call or a visit with the parents. This information should include not only the positive aspects but also problematic ones.
3. The biologic parent should be allowed to begin visiting with the child within the foster home. This can be much more comfortable for the child, as he is familiar with the home and it can be more comfortable for the biologic parent than a small office in a welfare department. This will be possible only if the foster parent is truly able to welcome the biologic parent into the home and is comfortable in leaving the parent and child alone together.
4. The foster parent must be careful not to give orders to the biologic parent

regarding his care of the child. For example, warnings such as "Be back on time" and "Be sure not to give him any milk" only come across as criticism to the biologic parent.
5. With older children, it is sometimes useful to explain their role as foster parents. This helps the child understand that while the foster parent has interest and love for the child, that payment for foster care removes the onus of charity. This reality data can obviate less helpful fantasies of the child as to the relationship of himself to the foster parent.

As the weeks and months lengthen for children in foster care, they form attachments and lasting friendships with foster parents and other children in the foster home. It is most important to the children that they be allowed to maintain these relationships even after return to the biologic home. This will be much easier for the biologic parents to permit if the relationship with the foster parents has been a good one over the preceding months. If these goals can be accomplished, then foster care can be seen as truly therapeutic.

Summary

Foster care is essential for many abused children. It should provide a stable, safe home environment for a child at the time of crisis and emotional turmoil within the biologic family. It may be necessary to buy the professionals the time to adequately assess the home of a child after suspected abuse has occurred. It may be used diagnostically to determine if the child's developmental problems are the result of an inadequate home environment. Finally, it can be used as a therapeutic, growth-promoting experience for the child, especially the child who remains in foster care for months and even years.

Foster care, as it presently exists in the United States, is usually not designed to be of help to the child other than to provide shelter and alternative living arrangements. To make foster care more therapeutic requires:

1. Better screening of potential foster parents and understanding of their motivations.
2. A team approach rather than a casework orientation towards foster parents.
3. In-service education on a regular on-going basis with foster parents coupled with better training in child development with case workers.
4. Improvement in relationships between biologic parents and foster parents.

A. Browder[4] has recently completed a study which found that "success relates directly to careful selection of parents, to educating the parents and to adequate staff support." Moss[5] and Tizard[6] have recently added to our perspective on adequate foster care.

Foster care has a long history. It stemmed from altruistic and conscientious concerns of neighbors, friends and relatives for children whose parents could not care for them. However, such noble beginnings have developed into the institutionalization of this behavior. And as so often happens, the institutionalization of altruistic behavior has distorted and mechanized foster care, regailing it with rules, regulations and procedures.

Somehow we must revive the heart and meaning of foster care. Somehow we must provide help and support to foster parents of whom we ask so much. Somehow we must make foster care a therapeutic experience for the many abused children who cannot stay with their own family.

References

1. Goldstein, J., Freud, A., Solnit, A.J.: *Beyond the Best Interests of the Child.* New York: Free Press, 1973.

2. Kline, Draza and Overstreet, Helen Mary: *Casework With Foster Parents.* Published by Child Welfare League of America, Inc., N.Y. 5th Printing, 1973, pp. 9-10.

3. Wolins, Martin: *Selecting Foster Parents.* New York: Columbia University Press, 1963, pp. 55-57.

4. Browder, J.A.: Adoption and Foster Care of Handicapped Children in the U.S. *Devel. Med. Child. Neurol.* 16:614-619, Oct. 75.

5. Moss, S.Z. and Moss, M.S.: Surrogate Mother-Child Relationships. *Amer. J. Orthopsychiatry* 45:382-390, April 75.

6. Tizard, J.: The Upbringing of Other People's Children. *Jour. Child. Psychol. & Psychiat.* 15:161-173, 1974.

General

Stone, H.D. (ed.): *Foster Care in Question,* Child Welfare League, N.Y., 1972.

Phillips, M.H., Shyne, A.W., Sherman, E.A. and Haring, B.L.: *Factors Associated with Placement Decisions in Child Welfare.* Child Welfare League, N.Y., 1973.

Sherman, E.H., Neuman, R., Shyne, A.W.: *Children Adrift in Foster Care: A Study of Alternative Approaches.* Child Welfare League, N.Y., 1973, #F46.

✳ *Chapter 16*

Psychotherapy

Patricia Beezley, Harold P. Martin and **Ruth Kempe**

Abused children not only must deal with the effects of physical attacks and injuries, but they must also deal psychologically with parents and a home environment in which the abuse occurred. This means dealing with rejection, neglect, emotional disturbance in parents and other distorted and disturbed parent-child interactions. The child not only has physical injuries and wounds but also he has psychological injuries and wounds. When medical personnel get called in to attend to the physical injuries, there is rarely attention and treatment for the psychological damage of the child. The primary paradigm under which child abuse teams have operated is to provide psychological treatment for the parents and nothing other than foster care for the child. The child is left, then, with no one who can help him understand his fears, conflicts, rage, and depression.

The authors have completed two retrospective studies on abused children and have noted personality disturbances.[1,2] With an interest in further pursuing the effects of the abusive environment on children, the authors began a pilot study which provided psychotherapy for abused children. This chapter will report on the characteristics of these children, the issues dealt with in therapy and the results of the psychotherapy. Other types of psychotherapeutic help for abused children will also be discussed.

Method of Study
The names of twelve physically-abused children between three years eight months and eight years of age were obtained from case records at the National Center for the Prevention and Treatment of Child Abuse and Neglect in Denver. All of the children had had non-accidental injuries and, with only two

exceptions, their parents had had contact with a social worker or lay-therapist at the National Center for a minimum of one year.

Eight of the children seen in psychotherapy were boys and four were girls. Eight were in their biologic homes, two were in foster care, and two were in adoptive homes. The last two had been injured by their adoptive parents.

It was explained to each parent that we were interested in knowing more about their child and their child's personality because we assumed that the hospitalizations, changes in homes, and perhaps the abuse the child had suffered, must be affecting their child in some way. We were interested in finding out how their child was coping with these traumatic events. We deliberately excluded children who were identified as being emotionally disturbed and children for whom psychotherapy had been recommended by professionals in the community. Rather, we were interested in "normal" abused children who had not been identified by society as psychiatrically disturbed.

A thorough evaluation of each child was made prior to, and at the completion of, twelve to fifteen months of psychotherapy. The evaluation included cognitive, speech-language and neurologic testing. The following tests were utilized: Welchsler Intelligence Scale for Children (WISC),[3] Intelligence Scale, Form L-M (Stanford-Binet),[4] Illinois Test of Psycholinguistic Abilities (ITPA),[5] Peabody Picture Vocabulary Test (Peabody),[6] Developmental Test of Visual-Motor Integration (Berry).[7] The parents were invited to observe the testing with the child's therapist through a one-way mirror. However, only three of the twelve mothers observed and no fathers did. The child's therapist offered to meet with the parents and share the material from the evaluations and from the child's treatment. All of the mothers participated in this at some point and four of the fathers did.

All of the children were seen once or twice a week for play therapy sessions in the playroom at the National Center. Ten of the children were transported to and from their therapy sessions by either the therapist or a volunteer; three of these children were transported by their mothers at some point during their year of therapy. Two of the children were transported by their mothers throughout their treatment. The sessions were 50 minutes long and were non-directive and supportive. The children were encouraged to express their feelings and conflicts through play and verbalizations. The primary focus of the play therapy sessions was to find out as much as possible about these children. However, additional treatment goals were formulated as follows:

1. Help the child understand and experience that there can be other and more satisfactory relationships with adults than what his experience had been with his own parents. That is, that adults can be trusted and adults can like the child and find pleasure in being with him.
2. Help the child identify, acknowledge, and share his feelings.
3. Help the child enjoy play, have fun, and find pleasure in age-appropriate behavior.

4. Increase the child's self-esteem and self-confidence.
5. Encourage the child to develop satisfactory relationships with teachers, relatives and friends outside of therapy. Encourage him to look for other sources of need-gratification than his parents or his therapist. Help him maintain at home and at school, the gains that he makes in therapy.

Four therapists provided the treatment for the twelve children: a child psychiatrist, a developmental pediatrician, a clinical psychologist and a psychiatric social worker. The therapists met weekly for supervision and consultation with two child psychiatrists. The evaluations were completed by the pediatrician, the psychologist and a speech-language pathologist.[a]

Evaluation of the Children
The testing and evaluation of the twelve children prior to, and at the completion of therapy was done for two purposes. The primary purpose was to have information as to the cognitive, speech-language and neurologic status of the children prior to therapy. For that reason, results from only the pre-therapy testing will be presented below. The other purpose was to determine if there were changes in pre- and post-testing data, that is, would therapy affect cognitive, speech-language and neurologic performance? The major area of change was in the speech and language function of the children and is addressed in more detail in Chapter 7.

Eleven of the twelve children were given the Weschler Intelligence Scales; the twelfth child was given the Stanford-Binet. This child had an I.Q. of 128 on the Binet. The results of the other eleven children are as follows:

Mean Verbal I.Q.	102.4
Mean Performance I.Q.	100.0
Full Scale I.Q.	
Mean	102.2
Range	78-117
Median	109

Results on the Peabody Picture Vocabulary Test showed similar scores with a mean derived I.Q. of 101.7.

While the results on the ITPA are covered in some detail in Chapter 7, it seems relevant to summarize some of the findings:

Five children had psycholinguistic ages slightly below their chronological age.
Five children had psycholinguistic ages slightly above their chronological age.
Two children had identical psycholinguistic and chronologic ages.
The mean psycholinguistic age of the group was 67.5 months, while the mean chronological age at testing was 66 months.

[a]The authors wish to acknowledge Harriet Stern, M.D., Esther Conway PhD. and Florence Blager PhD. for their contributions to this study.

The children all had neurologic examinations and on that basis were assigned a score of 0 through 3. Category 0 designated those children with completely normal neurologic examinations. Category 1 designated those children with minimal neurologic findings which were not judged to be handicaps in terms of the child's function in school or play. Category 2 was used to describe those children with mild neurologic delays or deficits which were seen as handicapping, especially in learning situations. They included such findings as impairments or delays in perceptual ability, poor motor planning (dyspraxia), mild abnormalities in muscle tone, and a variety of "soft" neurologic findings. (See Chapter 6.) A designation of class 3 described children with moderate to severe neurologic abnormalities, usually quite gross, including paresis (weakness), focal signs, sensory impairment of vision or hearing, seizure disorder and paralysis. The neurologic findings are as follows:

Eight children were in category 0.
Three children were in category 1.
One child was in category 2.
There were no children in category 3.

Eleven of the children were given the Berry Test of Visual Motor Integration. The mean Visual Motor Integration (VMI) age level was 5.7 months below the mean chronologic age of the children. Nine of the children had VMI scores below their expected age level, and only two had VMI scores at or above their chronologic age level.

On physical examination the children appeared healthy, with none having significant medical problems. Four of the twelve had heights which were more than two standard deviations below the mean for age. One child had a weight which was similarly substandard. None of the children had microcephaly.

In summary, these children appeared fairly normal, at least in gross measurements. Their intelligence fell within normal limits, as did their receptive language and their psycholinguistic ages. Their health was good, with only one of the twelve children having significant neurologic problems.

And yet, it must be remembered that these are fairly gross measurements of the neurologic and cognitive status of the children. More subtle and refined measurements might well have identified some less obvious difficulties. It should be noted that one-third of the group were small for age in height. Eighty percent of the children had difficulties in visual-motor integration. In Chapter 7, Dr. Blager has pointed out some of the interesting features of the profiles taken from the ten different subtests on the ITPA. Perhaps part of the implication of this is that these children appeared to be normal and were in many respects, at least to the degree that they were not mentally retarded or brain-damaged. And yet, on closer and more detailed examination, areas of difficulty on profiles of strengths and weaknesses may indicate subtle handicaps of abused children.

Observations During Psychotherapy

There was no single personality profile for these abused children. However, a number of themes emerged repeatedly during the course of therapy with almost all of these children. Each of the significant and common issues is briefly discussed below.

1. *Trust-Mistrust.* Very quick acceptance of therapy, eagerness to come and to have more frequent appointments, reluctance to leave the play room, and obvious pleasure in the play situation were characteristic of all the children throughout most of their treatment. However, it soon seemed apparent that this did not mean a real trust of the therapist or the development of a working alliance with him. For a few children, treatment was broken off prematurely by their parents, but for the others the beginnings of trust seemed to be developing before the end of therapy. Age may have been a factor to some extent; younger children were readier to trust than older children who tested the therapist longer but then were able to use him in more of a working alliance. There was considerable testing out of the therapist, especially around the issue of whether the therapist would punish them physically. Some children seemed to believe they only had to find the therapist's "breaking point" and then they would be hit. Early on, most of the children were reluctant to be touched, even when playing games. Eye contact was slow in developing. The strength and duration of the distrust was striking in several of the patients. One six-year-old boy had been in therapy twice a week for six months. He had seemed, gradually, to build a positive alliance with the therapist, demonstrating affection for her and enjoyment of the play sessions. Nonetheless, at Christmas time when the therapist gave the child a present of some Christmas cookies during the therapy hour, the child refused to eat them until the therapist first had one. The child sheepishly admitted that he was afraid that poison had been put in the cookies.

2. *Need for Nurturance.* Intense need for nurturance, both physical and emotional, seemed an outstanding feature of the children's behavior. Early evidence of this was their marked orality. They would overeat from the candy jar, sometimes eating steadily until it was empty before they turned to play activities, or eating some and stuffing their pockets with the rest. Even with full pockets they might often dip into the candy jar of one of the secretaries on the way out. Some demanded to have more and better toys to play with, more time with the therapist, more trips to the park or to the store for food. They kept close track of what the therapist gave them, requesting elaborate and expensive presents, such as bicycles and tree houses from the therapist for Christmas or birthday. While some of the younger children could not easily verbalize such requests, the wishes came through in their play. Most of the children were demanding and draining of

the therapist; the insatiable quality of their neediness was considerably more noticeable than with non-abused children.

3. *Regression.* In addition to oral preoccupation, regression was also particularly noticeable in the intensity and tenacity of interest in water play. Some children who are compulsively neat and clean spent most of their hour in water play, gradually becoming more and more messy. As might be expected, these children had difficulty with toilet training, chiefly because of the very high standards for early performance set by their parents. Regression to messiness in other play was delighted in by these children who gradually lost their anxiety about messing but were careful to keep their own hands and clothes clean for the end of the hour. It was our impression that for some children the route to acceptance of these impulses was only possible through the use of water play in which they could, at first, pretend to wash everything and, thereby, be very clean.

4. *Object Relations.* Age-appropriate object relations were difficult for these children. Often a child seemed to relate to the therapist only in terms of the therapist meeting his or her needs. Just as their self-concept was poorly developed, some children had great difficulty in reacting openly and spontaneously with the therapist. Few showed any curiosity about the therapist or treated him as an individual or a person. Again, the younger children seemed better able to do so but rarely did express direct liking for, or anger toward, the therapist. One patient, even after six months of twice a week therapy, could not remember the name of the therapist outside the therapy room. While heavily involved and seemingly attached to the therapist in the play room, the relationship changed quite abruptly at the end of the hour. The children often left the room quite nonchalantly, ignoring the therapist, as if the treatment had meant nothing to them. Although, as stated above, this may have related, in part, to the necessity to readjust themselves so totally outside of the treatment hour, it also seemed to indicate a difficulty in maintaining object constancy. This problem was also very apparent at times of separation such as vacations or cancellations. These children almost uniformly denied the importance of object loss in their lives—a problem which for some of them was quite overwhelming in its frequency. Many of them had had many separations, or the constant threat of separation to cope with, and they seemed unable to do so except by denial. The importance of loss of the therapist at times of vacation was also denied, and only very gradually could some of these children admit that separation did matter to them and did cause them pain and anger.

5. *Capacity for Pleasure.* Perhaps the most striking characteristics of these children was their inability to let loose and have fun. Many did not laugh for months, coming into the play room as somber "little adults" with sadness or depression not verbally expressed but very much evident. What play they engaged in and enjoyed seemed more to please the therapist than

to please themselves. Toys and games were put into the context of work, or competition or meeting the expectations of the therapist. Many of the children seemed to have had little experience with toys or play, especially with an adult. It sometimes seemed as though the children had never been influenced by the pleasure principle or that it had taken a very distorted pathway in influencing their lives. They seemed surprised that the therapist demonstrated pleasure and enjoyment from games and play. As modeling and identification did develop, they were able to begin to uninhibitantly experience joy in their play.

6. *Self-Concept and Self-Esteem.* Most all of the children viewed themselves in a very negative light. They described themselves as "stupid," "liked by no one," "can't do anything well," and "bad." They were unable to admit to or take pride in things that they obviously could do well. They were quite hesitant to try new activities, obviously fearful of failure. Shame and humiliation were quick responses.

A few seemed to lack any real sense of self. Perhaps this was related to their parents' concept of them as not individuals but need-fulfilling objects. It might also have been related to erratic home placements and frequent separations. It was most strikingly seen in a little girl who had been in ten foster homes. She could not comprehend, at age six, that she had a name that she carried with her, regardless of whose home she was living in. The children's drawings of people were primitive in almost every case. Some children were totally unable to draw pictures of themselves although other non-person drawings were age-appropriate in quality. Others would try, but the resultant product was often primitive with missing body parts and distorted relationships.

7. *Conscience.* The superegos of abused children, or at least their value systems were quite rigid and punitive. They were surprisingly judgmental and critical of themselves, as well as of others. They reacted very strictly to the dress and behavior of adults. They were very upset when other children transgressed their absolute rules of right and wrong. These rigid and critical attitudes seemed to interfere with their ability to develop relationships with other children. "Being bad" themselves or observing this in other children, filled them with righteous indignation and, at times, alarm.

In actuality, it was hard to know whether or not these children had really developed an internalized super-ego structure. If they had, it seemed to us to be a rigid, primitive super-ego with punitive tendencies probably derived from identification with aggressive, punitive parents. The children did seem to be parroting their parents' values and seemed to have accepted their parents' inappropriate assessment of them quite completely. This led to their lack of self-esteem and fears of being "bad," as well as to the prohibition of pleasure and the ability to enjoy themselves. Shame and humiliation, as well as fear of reprisal, were common, but we felt less certain about the presence of guilt. It might be that these children do have specific variations in super-ego values similar to the lacunae described by Johnson and Szurek[8,9] representing the distorted values of their parents in particular areas. Even in the older children, their perfectionistic adult-like preachings about right and wrong were primarily attached to the consequences of being bad. The whole issue of super-ego development in abused children needs extensive exploration, as it surely is a most complicated and important aspect of adults who were abused as children.

8. *Anxiety and Fears.* Like all children, abused children have worries about loss of parents and loss of love of parents. We had anticipated that these children would all be preoccupied with the physical abuse they had suffered. And, while this was played out in some fashion with all of the children, the most pressing anxieties of the children were usually not fear of physical attack. We were tremendously impressed with the amount and degree of chaos and threatening events occurring in these children's lives. At first, in fact, we had trouble differentiating whether much of what the children talked of was fantasy or reality, as there was such a constant barrage of psychological stresses in their lives. One child's mother made two suicide attempts during the year of therapy. Parents left the home, neighbors got injured in accidents or shootings, families were in trouble with the law or landlords, fathers lost jobs and so forth. The significance of these events were surely colored by the past experience of these children, but nonetheless, they were often bombarded by frightening, chaotic, aggressive real-life events which were of more worry to them than an episode of a beating some months ago. We must not assume that the child is primarily reacting to events which we, the therapist, react to, such as episodes of physical abuse. Rather, the children were reacting and trying to cope with an environment where the physical abuse was but one of many stresses and often not the most prominent or worrisome to them.

9. *Aggression.* Abused children have been described as being docile, compliant, and almost obsequeious with adults. Indeed, the direct expression of aggression toward adults was a difficult area for these children. However, the children's stories and play in treatment were filled with aggression and brutality. Dolls and fictional characters were forever getting hit, maimed and killed. Some of the children repeated in play the traumas they had experienced. One child who had had three skull fractures on three separate occasions as an infant filled his play with stories of humans and animals having head injuries. Another child whose mother had attempted to drown him when he was a baby, began his treatment by drowning the young boy doll in the bathtub and then having the mother doll taken by the police to jail. It almost seemed eerie that some of the children seemed to have such memories of their traumas even from infancy.

Given what was said above in the section on fears and anxieties, one must assume that these children were reacting to the physical attacks they had had, but more often on an unconscious level. They rarely, if ever, could verbalize these concerns directly. Their rage was deep-seated and intense, and their wishes for retaliation against their parents were coupled with their fears of what might happen to them should their wishes come true. Sometimes as transference reactions developed, we saw the children's anger and aggression turn towards the therapist, but almost always in a very indirect, subtle or passive-aggressive form. Accidents abounded resulting in the therapist being hit by a ball, equipment broken, and so forth. Direct expression of aggression, either in behavior or verbalizations, were almost non-existent.

10. *Thought Disorder.* Two of the children seemed unable to distinguish between fantasy and reality much of the time. However, their verbalizations were not free-flowing, bizarre free associations. Hence, they did not superficially appear as disturbed, perhaps explaining the fact that neither parents nor school teachers considered them disturbed. Nonetheless, the distinction between reality and fantasy was quite tenuous and often blurred. These two children were difficult to treat because of the degree of the pathology. It was of concern that they might later, in adulthood, develop paranoid qualities.

11. *Sexuality.* It must be recognized that most of these children were of an appropriate age to be in the midst of their Oedipal stage of development and that we, as therapists, had limited contact with their parents. And yet, despite this, we were impressed with the seductiveness and sexualization of the parents' relationships with their children. One mother, whose husband had abandoned the family three years earlier, climbed into bed with her seven-year-old son whenever she was upset or lonely. She, like many of the mothers, went about the house in a seductive state of undress. There were often open, competitive bids for affection from the two parents towards the young child. One mother described her four-year-old daughter as a "sexy, flirtatious girl who would obviously get into trouble with men." Some of the parents had sexual relations with their children present in the room. Abusing parents frequently look to their children for need-gratification and it should not be surprising that sexual needs of the parents are not immune from that dynamic. While often disguised and unconscious, the degree to which the child was turned to for non-genital, sexual gratification was impressive and concerning.

In addition to these twelve children who were seen in a pilot study, primarily to learn more about abused children, the authors have also seen ten to fifteen other abused children in psychotherapy for other purposes. These additional children were placed in therapy because of someone's concern about their emotional status, so they represent a more obviously disturbed segment of the abused population. Findings similar to the above eleven points have been noted in these other abused children. However, included in this latter group were children whose parents referred them because of worries regarding their children's hyperactivity and aggression. These children were sometimes inappropriately seen by their parents as dangerous, violent and innately bad. Certainly their behavior was difficult to control and their capacity to modulate their behavior and control impulses was minimal. However, it was our impression that many of these children were acutely anxious and, given an environment with benevolent control, recognition of their needs and fears, and a good deal of structured activity, they responded very well. The questions of an underlying neurologic basis for their hyperactivity was often present, and at least a minimal degree of neurological involvement was present with some of these children. However, their good therapeutic response came not in relation to drug treatment, but after reappraisal of the parents' concept of the child and the environmental changes described above. The most difficult change to effect and maintain was in the parents' concept of their child; their need to see the child as uncontrollable became a major therapeutic focus.

One group of abused children not seen either in the pilot study or in the additional group was that of the very disturbed, psychotic or borderline children. It is assumed that they would not be referred to such a facility as the National Center because their behavior would require more complete professional intervention such as hospitalization. It is known that some children diagnosed as autistic or schizophrenic do have a history of being abused. But this history is often submerged in the concern over the child's severe symptoms. Its relevance to the development of illness is not clear as yet. Certainly, it has seemed surprising to us, at times, that some children have withstood alarming degrees of physical and psychological trauma with delays in ego-development but with otherwise relatively intact ego-functions. Much research remains to be done in this area.

Results of Psychotherapy

Results of treatment varied considerably with each child. The most improvement was seen: (1) if the parents were willing to let the child make changes and were willing to make changes themselves, and (2) if the therapist could influence the environment, such as the school setting, relationships with others and help the child within the playroom. For those children who remained in therapy for one year, the following gains were generally seen:

1. Increased ability to trust adults. Many of the children maintained contact with the therapist following termination of treatment. They called when their goldfish died or when the family moved and they had a new address or when family members were ill; in other words, they had learned how to use life-lines.

2. Increased ability to delay gratification. As the months passed, the children gradually came to eat and hoard less food. Their insatiable demands developed into age-appropriate requests and wishes.
3. Increased self-esteem. Many of the children began to feel better about themselves within the playroom and the school setting, but this is very difficult to maintain unless the parent is making significant progress in his or her own therapy.
4. Increased ability to verbalize feelings. Most of the children learned that it could be safe in certain settings to express conflicts and feelings. Generally this did not get the children into danger at home, for the children seemed to have an astute awareness of when they could verbalize feelings and when they could not. If their parents were making changes, they began to do this at home as well as in therapy.
5. Increased capacity for pleasure. As the children began to work through some of their conflicts and through regressive stages began to have some of their needs met that had not been met by their parents at the age-appropriate time, the children began to free up. They began to actively pursue particular games with excitement. Role playing became more comfortable, and even fun, for them.

Abused children have the capacity to make changes. The younger they are, the more resiliancy they have. Children between the ages of two and four in the therapeutic day care setting, will make more changes and at a faster rate, than children between the ages of four and eight seen in play therapy once or twice a week. This pilot study has demonstrated that it takes quite some time to establish a trusting alliance with an abused child. For that reason, short term therapy has significant limitations. However, other modalities such as intensive, short-term, daily contact might result in quicker progress.

Summary and Discussion

Two years ago we began seeing a number of "normal" abused children in psychotherapy, motivated by our wish to learn more about the types of psychological injuries these children suffered, how they adapted and coped with their environment, and what might be helpful to them. Along the way we have worked with other abused children in psychotherapy because they needed therapy. We feel we have learned a great deal about these children. In our pilot study we quickly became impressed with the fact that while these children had not been identified as having emotional problems, they, indeed, had very serious psychiatric difficulties. Some of our observations are discussed above.

However, despite the title of this chapter, we are not trying to sell the idea of formal psychotherapy for most abused children. There are, of course, many abused children who need moderately long, traditional types of psychotherapy. But we are trying to convey our deeply felt conviction that almost all abused children have psychological injuries and that some type of intervention needs to be made available to these children. For many years now we have recognized that at times of special stress children need and can greatly benefit from an understanding psychotherapeutic agent. This often is the child's physician, nurse, welfare worker, concerned teacher or friend. We recognize that when the child is facing the death of an important person, divorce or separation of the family, the onset of illness in a sibling, illness or hospitalization for himself, or even a geographical move, it is then that the child needs someone to whom to turn for understanding and help. Often in such circumstances the child's parent is not emotionally available to help the child through such a stressful time. Someone else is needed to help the child deal with his fears, frustrations, sadness, and threats to integrity. The literature suggests that this type of preventive psychotherapy, which often would not take place in a therapist's office, may be critical in terms of a child's subsequent emotional development. Chamberlin[10] and Zager[11] point out how the child's physician can offer such help to children.

Periods of stress in the lives of abused children are often obvious. Apart from the incidences of physical trauma, there are the separations, hospitalizations, court hearings, foster placements and changes in visiting rights with the biologic parents. Who is available to help the child sort out his feelings and reactions to these stresses? Again, it can be almost anyone who can be sensitive to what the child is going through and help in that process. The long range effects will be minimized if someone is able and willing to offer support. Perhaps short term but more intensive intervention in times of stress is the most valuable therapy[11] needed by abused children.

There are a number of other types of psychotherapeutic options that should be considered. Day care or pre-school placement can be extremely valuable especially if there is a staff member there who has some psychological interest and sophistication and is able to leave her "education" tasks to relate to the child's psychological concerns. Group therapy, especially with latency age children, is being investigated at the National Center as a mode of help. We have been impressed with the very valuable help abused children have realized from the few child welfare workers who have made the time to spend regular sessions with the abused child—whether in foster care or with biologic parents. In Chapter 15 we have taken up the issue of how foster care can be a very therapeutic experience for the child.

We have further just begun to think of developing some cadre of non-professional therapists for abused children modeled somewhat after the lay-therapy program developed at the National Center for abusing parents. While this potential is yet to be explored, at first examination it seems a viable therapeutic option. However, there is ambivalence about such an endeavor, for it truly seems that the manpower is available to offer psychological help to abused children. There are teachers, physicians, nurses, child welfare workers, mental health professionals, as well as psychiatrists, psychologists and social workers. The consideration of developing a new group of people to help abused children with their psychological needs is, in some way, an acknowledgement that those people who are around and available are not providing what is needed to the abused child. Perhaps we should not so quickly give up and circumvent those already available, but strive toward motivating them to provide the necessary help and support needed by the child. More sophisticated psychological expertise may be needed in the form of consultation for many of the non-traditional professionals for them to be comfortable in viewing themselves as psychotherapeutic agents. But it seems to us that the various options available and to be considered to provide help and treatment to the psychological injuries of abused children will not be successful until some basic, underlying premises are accepted. First and foremost is the acknowledgement that abused children have psychological injuries which need attention. Once that is really believed and felt, then we have the impression that the logical implications can be worked out. There must be some conviction that therapeutic intervention can be helpful and that it is the right of the abused child. Once over these two philosophical hurdles, we can expand our exploration of by whom and how this help should be provided.

We look forward to the day when the typical child abuse team will have routinely, as part of its agenda, the questions: What are the psychological problems this child is facing and how can we best help the child?

References

1. Martin, Harold P. (M.D.): "The Child and His Development," in *Helping the Battered Child and His Family*, edited by C. Henry Kempe, M.D. and Ray E. Helfer, M.D., Philadelphia: J.B. Lippincott Co., 1972.

2. Martin, Harold P. (M.D.), Beezley, Matricia MSW, Conway, Esther F. PhD., and Kempe, C. Henry (M.D.): "The Development of Abused Children," in *Advances in Pediatrics*, edited by Irving Schulman, Vol. 21, Year Book Medical Publishers, Inc., 1974.

3. Wechsler, D.: *Weschler Intelligence Scale for Children* New York: The Psychological Corporation, 1949.

4. Terman, L.M., and Merrill, M.A.: *Stanford-Binet Intelligence Scale Manual for the Third Revision, Form L-M* Boston: Houghton Mifflin Co., 1960.

5. Kirk, S.A., McCarthy, J.J. and Kirk, W.A.: *Illinois Test of Psycholinguistic Abilities* Urbana: Univ. of Illinois, 1968.

6. Dunn, L.M.: *Peabody Picture Vocabulary Test* Minneapolis: American Guidance Service, Inc., 1965.

7. Berry, K.E.: *Developmental Test of Visual-Motor Integration, Administration and Scoring Manual* Chicago: Follett Educational Corporation, 1967.

8. Johnson, Adelaide M.: "Sanctions for Super-ego Lacunae of Adolescents," in *Searchlights on Delinquency*, edited by K.R. Eissler New York: International University Press, 1949, pp. 225-245.

9. Johnson, Adelaide M. and Szurek, Stanislaus: "The Genesis of Antisocial

Acting Out in Children and Adults," in *Psychoanalytic Quarterly*, 21 (1952): 323-43.

10. Chamberlin, R.W.: Management of Preschool Behavior Problems, *Pediat. Cl. N. Amer.* 21:33-48, Feb. 1974.

11. Zager, Ruth: The Pediatrician and Preventive Child Psychiatry, *Clin. Pediat.* 14:1161-1167, Dec. 1975.

 *Chapter 17*

Preschool for Abused Children

Joan Mirandy

This chapter concerns the therapeutic value of a group education setting for abused children. The primary focus is on the utilization of a preschool setting as primary therapy for children between the ages of two and one half and five. Similar goals of therapy for younger or older children can be met by day-care or public schools respectively. The term "preschool" is used synonymously with head start and day care programs, as all have the potential to provide a therapeutic environment for the abused child. We attach great importance to the therapeutic value of preschool for abused children, and, happily, preschools are available in most communities, although they have rarely been recognized as therapeutic settings for special children.

Advantages of a Preschool Setting
It is our hypothesis that preschool can and should be viewed as group therapy for abused children. There are several advantages and goals of such a preschool experience all of which can be possible in any good preschool.

1. *Respite for the Parents*—Enrollment in a preschool, in essence, removes the child from his parents for several hours a day. This has advantages both for the parents and for the child. The usual abusive parent finds the presence of his child a stress. Low-income families especially have little opportunity to be away from their children because of the cost of baby sitters or school settings. Absence may or may not make the heart grow fonder, but it certainly serves the purpose of giving the abusive parent some relief from the stress of parenting a child 24 hours a day. The child also benefits from having a few hours a day away from an abusive environment.
2. *Developmental Stimulation*—There is minimal developmental stimulation in

most abusive homes; when one does find the parent attempting to stimulate the child in the home setting, it usually provokes considerable emotionality in both parent and child. Most abusive families have little energy for trying to help the child grow and develop. The parents tend to view the child as a source of their own need fulfillment and are consequently not able to try to meet the needs of the child. Parents place unrealistic demands and rigid expectations on their child and become angry when the child is not able to measure up. The stimulation of learning in a school setting, then, provides perhaps the only healthy motivation for growth and development of these children.

3. *Remediation of Developmental Lags and Deficits*—This has been taken up in Chapter 14. In that chapter it was pointed out that a preschool setting is an ideal place for children to get specific help with delays and deficits they may have in speech and language, motor coordination, perception and learning skills. The high incidence of developmental lags in abused children has been pointed out repeatedly in Section 1 of this book. A preschool staff with consultation from appropriate professionals in other fields is an optimal use of manpower for providing treatment for these developmental deficits.

4. *Socialization*—The abused child has had very poor models of interpersonal interactions. The preschool setting provides the opportunity for the child to learn how to relate to his peers and to the adult preschool staff. He can learn not only how to get along with others but how to obtain pleasure and gratification from relating with other children and adults who are quite different from his only other adult models, his parents. The modeling of peers and the adult staff make it possible for the abused child to relook and reconsider his whole personal social relationships.

5. *Help with Personality Traits*—Chapters 5, 8, and 9 have pointed out how a number of personality traits and behaviors in abused children are handicapping. They handicap the child in learning, in socialization and in being happy. A sensitive psychologically-oriented preschool staff can be a very effective psychotherapeutic team in helping the child understand and modify his feelings and behaviors so as to make his life less narrow and disturbed.

Purposes and Program of Circle House Therapeutic Playschool

The National Center for Prevention and Treatment of Child Abuse and Neglect established a therapeutic playschool in order to offer daily treatment to a group of ten to fifteen abused children between the ages of two and one half and five. The term "playschool" was chosen because the school did not want parents to feel the stress of having their child in a "cognitive" environment, yet it wanted an awareness that this was not "babysitting" but a valuable, individualized service for the child. Circle House Therapeutic Playschool charges no fees and serves a four-county area. All children who attend have been physically abused, and a protective court order had been filed not more than six months prior to admittance. Thus most of the families are still in some turmoil. The school operates from 8:30 to 2:30 four days a week and provides lunch, nap, and snacks in its daily program. Transportation is coordinated with local welfare departments. The staff is comprised of two teachers trained in early childhood education and one paraprofessional; professionals in the fields of medicine, psychiatry, psychology, speech and language, social work and sensory motor development are available to the staff for consultation. Each child receives a thorough evaluation assessment upon enrollment. The program provides a warm, nurturing environment wherein the child can feel safe with adults and be freed up to develop a healthy personality. In addition to providing peer socialization and group skills, the program is individualized for each child in order to meet his emotional needs and to develop an intensive stimulation program for developmental lags.

While the following pages shall be addressing the author's own experience in what is perhaps a model program, understandably not yet available in most communities, we shall be emphasizing what might be of value for a staff at any "regular" preschool which is willing to take up the exciting challenge of working with an abused child within a normal preschool setting.

Characteristics of an Abused Child in a Preschool

Over the past year we have had nineteen children in the preschool for abused children. The most striking observation is that the abused child usually has no "middle ground" but operates at one or the other end of a spectrum. He is a child of extremes. For instance, he may be very very passive, or very very aggressive. Most of the child in the Circle House Playschool entered as very passive, inhibited children.

During the first few months of the school experience, the children were overtly compliant, anxious to please, seeking out permission before initiating any new action. They were quite hypervigilant to the total environment of the preschool. None of the children demonstrated any separation anxiety in leaving mother, and they were indiscriminately and often physically affectionate with adult strangers. They were oblivious to peer interaction. There was often a hollow smile on a child's face and a complete void of emotions. All lacked true joy. The children rarely expressed anger or pain, and they had a poor sense of safety, frequently injuring themselves. Crying was either *highly* infrequent or continual with or without apparent provocation. Most abused children appeared compulsively neat and orderly in the classroom, often cleaning up after peers; they shied away from dirty or messy activities. Play was often non-creative and use of materials was highly repetitive, the majority of such children appear to be lacking basic play skills. A child might compulsively sit at a table and play with the same toy all morning or might be very scattered, active and highly distractable, with no real involvement with any activity or toy. It is important to note that because of performance anxiety, many abused children look less competent than they really are and can easily be mislabeled a "slow-learner," or as mentally retarded. Many abused children do have legitimate delays, especially in the areas of speech and gross motor development, which may warrant outside consultation for the teacher. Most of the children have poor expressive language skills and respond to voice tone and not verbal content of others.

It is crucial to stress that most of these traits, such as neatness, perseverance, quietness, compliance and politeness are valued in the "normal" child and that if the teacher is not aware of the abused child's special needs, these traits may be further reinforced. An abused child has the ability to initially blend in *too* well and slip by unnoticed.

Treatment Goals

Given that abused children often display the above behaviors, any treatment program should incorporate the following goals for each child: (1) to form a positive self-image; (2) to establish trust in other people; (3) to acknowledge his emotions; (4) to vent aggressions and receive support in dealing with them; (5) to experience positive adult and peer interactions; (6) to learn how to communicate needs and feelings verbally; (7) to develop alternative and more acceptable means of coping behavior; and (8) to improve developmental lags.

Teaching Methodology Used to Achieve Treatment Goals

A methodology that has been successfully used at Circle House Therapeutic Playschool focuses around the need for consistency among the total staff with limits and routines. The value of consistent people and consistent adult behavior for the abused child who has lived in a highly unpredictable world cannot be overstressed. It is crucial that the teaching staff be gentle, patient and warm. If the child is in a large school, it would be wise to choose one teacher to be a "special person" for the abused child. The use of volunteers and of many new faces sharing a day should be avoided, if possible, for the child may initially lapse back into his "safe" compliant routine each time he encounters a new person. Good staff communication and reevaluation of the child and his program is critical so that there is consistency among staff members in the child's treatment.

The classroom environment should encourage choice and success for the child. The child will require a great many positive interactions before he himself feels he has succeeded and is valued. There is little immediate reward in working with an abused child, and because of his many provocative behaviors, he can be difficult to like at times. Teachers need to encourage each other and realize they are not alone in their feelings about the child. Also, it is legitimate and healthy to show anger at an unreasonable behavior of the child. When there is anger, it should be expressed so that the child may see that other adults get angry at unacceptable behaviors but do not respond with physical violence, or with verbal condemnation of the child.

A safe environment should be maintained for the child at all times; he should not be permitted to hurt anyone, including himself, nor should he be hurt by others. Destruction of school materials should not be permitted, though appropriate aggressive outlets such as pillows, wood-working, a punching bag and clay should be available at all times. Also, sensory stimulation and "messy" activities that the child does not receive at home should be available daily. This includes water play, finger paint and play-dough. Initial participation in such activities requires a great deal of patience and teacher encouragement.

Children who have been abused often reenact their home environment in play. Thus, it is not uncommon to see a child throw a doll, whip it, hit its head and threaten it verbally. The child should not be stopped or reprimanded, but the teacher should model through play and verbalization more appropriate ways to care for the baby and meet its needs. Perhaps here it is important to mention that initially, throughout all play, the teacher should play with the child and model play for him. Over time, peers will begin to serve the same function. Although the abused child initially ignores peers, they are the most valuable resource in the classroom. The teacher will need to play a major and active role in the encouragement of friendships.

Since the abused child is accustomed to irrational limits at home, it is important that the teacher provide him with a reason each time she says "no." Also, if possible, the teacher should redirect the child to a more acceptable activity, still retaining the child's original intention. For example, if the child wanted to jump off a table, the teacher should stop him, explain the danger and lead him to a place from which it is safe to jump. In that way the child learns you do not disapprove of him and his ideas but rather of the particular behavior.

It is necessary to verbalize a great deal with abused children in order to provide communication skills, labeling information and overall stimulation. It is particularly valuable to label emotions and pain to the child so that he may begin to acknowledge his own feelings.

Many abused children seek constant physical comfort and cuddling while others do not like to be touched at all. It is important to respect the child's wishes for touch/no touch as much as possible. His reactions may stem from fearfulness or indicate his tenuous capacity to trust adults.

Results of a Preschool Experience

Subjective data kept daily by the teaching staff at Circle House Playschool are the basis from which the statements that follow have been made. After a period of "testing out" the environment, abused children begin to establish trust in adults, form positive adult and peer relationships and achieve overall gains in self-confidence which in turn cuts down on their avoidance, anxiety, and manipulative behaviors. Generally within three months newly developed inner controls permit them to listen better and to control frustrations and wait confidently for a toy, their turn, etc. They are openly pleased with themselves, develop play skills, independently approach new activities and show gains in learning. Language becomes a tool used to express needs and emotions; children cry and smile appropriately and have more overall affect. The time span for such changes, of course, will vary with individual children, the severity of their home environment and the composure of the classroom environment. It has been our experience that the healthier the peer group, the more rapidly the child is able to assimilate the above changes. The child may not show any gains for the first few weeks. It is important for the teacher to remember that the child is initiating a long, slow process of change and that he must back up in his development and establish the basic trust that he did not receive as an infant.

David is a case in point. He entered the preschool at 45 months of age. He was a nice, neat, orderly little boy. He worked hard and persevered on tasks. He avoided touch by any of the staff. He talked little and had minimal interactive play with peers. His immature articulation added to a picture of a child who seemed like a bright child of a younger age. Visitors might view him, for example, as a very nice precious child of two and one half to three years of age. He would leave the nursery school easily to go with different consultants for testing procedures. Within six weeks his behavior started to change. He resisted leaving the preschool. He started playing more with other little boys and started enjoying very aggressive rough-and-tumble play. He started to tolerate messy play with water, finger-paints and play-dough. His quantity and quality of speech increased. In one sense he was no longer such a "nice" little boy. His changes were seen by the staff as real developmental advances as he became less inhibited, less fearful and more interested in age-appropriate relationships with peers and adult staff.

This is in contrast to Elmo, a 55-month-old boy. Elmo entered the preschool as a very aggressive highly verbal little boy with many mannerisms and adult-like phrases from the ghetto. In contrast to David, Elmo was in no danger of being overlooked by staff. He sought their attention and approval and often engendered their laughter by his antics. His learning was interfered with by his preoccupation with being observed, approved and applauded. His play with peers was aggressive and often hostile. It took at least two months before his adultomorphic behavior started to subside, more given-and-take play was possible and before he could start enjoying tasks without an audience. After six months in the preschool, it was obvious that he was ready for graduation to a normal preschool or a regular kindergarten class. He was no longer a disruptive boy in a group and could play and work without constant one-to-one attention from adults or peers.

It has been our experience that the child's new "personality" usually does not cause trouble at home, for the child appears to be selective about what he shows his parents. It is hypothesized that the abused child has learned survival techniques and will not endanger himself at home with new provocative behaviors; rather, he appears to be quite capable of managing two separate environments. Various parents have reported to teachers at Circle House Playschool that their child listens better, behaves more acceptably at meals and bedtime, and is not as hyperactive at home. The parent's changing perception of the child is an important issue and is taken up later in this chapter.

Special Concerns

Documentation: The school should maintain good contact and rapport with the case worker and the courts. All schools should be notified by social services that the child has a history of past abuse, so that the teacher is alerted to the child's special behaviors and needs, possible signs of reinjury, and how to relate to the parent. The teacher should keep a daily written record on any child who has been abused. This should include comments on the child's health, appropriateness of dress for current weather conditions, any questionable bruises, the child's school behavior and emotional status. Although it is hoped that the parent is able to maintain impulse control, this is not always the case and written documentation with specific dates by the teacher is often crucial evidence in a court case.

In the Circle House Playschool the abused child is casually checked during daily routine toileting for bruises or other signs of non-accidental trauma. In any preschool the teaching staff must not ignore injuries to the child. If and when there are injuries which makes the teacher suspect non-accidental trauma, the child should be examined by a pediatrician or family physician.

Teachers do have a special obligation, by law in most communities, to report suspected abuse and neglect. The teacher in any school setting is not required or expected to *diagnose* abuse, but she is obligated to communicate any concerns about abuse that she notes. Here is another reason for a recommendation that the school staff and the child welfare worker have regular and ongoing communication from the very start of the child's entry into preschool. The welfare worker can be helpful in expediting investigation of concerns around abuse and can help the school in establishing clear-cut procedures on how to file a suspicion of child abuse report.

Transportation: It seems perhaps mundane and unnecessary to speak of the importance of arranging transportation for the abused child. However, our experience has taught us that the parents have considerable ambivalence toward their child going off to play and have fun and learn things from others. Family crises are common with abusing parents, and the priority of getting the child to a preschool is quite low in the order of importance to these families. From the very beginning, then, the preschool staff should try to assure, working with the parents or welfare agencies, that a plan of transportation for the child is established which will not be easily interfered with at the whim of the parents. It is also pertinent to note that many times these children are sent off to school inadequately dressed for the weather and with no breakfast. The school, to be optimally helpful to the child, must have contingency plans for providing adequate clothing for the child, and to offer the much-needed nutrition when the children's needs have not been met by their families.

Parents: Probably the most difficult issue for preschool staff to deal with is the parents of the abused child. Abusive parents have enormous needs of their own, and it is impractical and impossible for the preschool staff to provide much for these parents. Ideally, the parents of the abused child should be involved with a variety of other helping people: case workers, lay-therapists, parents anonymous or treatment groups. The preschool staff cannot be expected to be therapists to the parents, but they can serve as friends and make appropriate referrals to other professionals who might better help the parent. If there are more than two or three abusive parents in a school, the teacher should consider someone else to be supportive in the "friend" role as it can be considerably draining in time and energy.

And yet any preschool program is severely limited if there is no involvement with parents, whether abusive or average normal parents. It is the author's recommendation that parents, especially abusive parents, be invited to join a mothers' group, come to frequent family nights at the school or be involved in other school functions established for the parents. The parent, jealous of the attention and "goodies" the child is receiving, will feel better if she is also being given to in some manner. If this is not done well, the child may be withdrawn from the school by the jealous parents.

A very difficult and sensitive area centers around routine parent-teacher conferences. It is especially important to keep in mind the great need the parent has for his child to "be good." Hence, it is important that the teacher not speak of the child's inadequacies, difficulties, weaknesses. Comments which might be taken by other parents as helpful suggestions will more often be taken by the abusive parents as evidence of bad behavior for which the child must be punished. And yet the teacher is often in the same bind concerning talking to the abusive parents about the strengths and abilities of the abused child. The parent often does not want to hear the good either. The mother may wonder why the child is so good for the teacher and yet so bad at home. Insofar as the abusive parent has an investment in seeing her child as a "bad" child, she will not be pleased at the positive comments of the teacher. The best way for the teacher to start the conference is to attend to the parent, not the child. Most abusive parents do not really want to talk about their children anyway, and will quickly turn the conversation to their own concerns and interests. Insofar as the mother is interested in discussing the child, the teacher should remain relatively neutral in terms of any sort of good or bad behavior of the child and try to elicit from the parent what her concerns and views are, so as to know and anticipate the parents' reactions to the child's progress at school.

It is admittedly an unsatisfactory answer to the involvement of the parents. Ideally one would like to see the school staff and the parents working together as a team. Yet we need to point out that this working alliance between school and home is often not possible. It would be ideal if there could be carry-over from school to home. We would like to see rapid changes in the parent-child interaction, but this is difficult to achieve unless simultaneous home-based efforts occur. Given the multiple problems of the abusing parent, it is not realistic to expect the average preschool teacher to have the expertise to work with these parents in depth. Subsequent chapters take up the issue of affecting change in the parenting abilities of abusive families. In a special program for abused children, some professional staff such as a psychiatric social worker may take on this role. In an average "normal" preschool our experience suggests that a good preschool setting can offer more to an abused child than any other mode of therapy. Group interaction, developmental stimulation, modeling of interpersonal relationships, improvement of developmental delays and psychological help with feelings and behaviors can all be part of a good preschool program.

Summary

A model program such as the National Center Preschool for abused children might be seen as an elaborate and expensive unit which cannot easily be duplicated in many communities. Three responses should be noted. For one, a specialized preschool program for abused children has limited goals, the ultimate one being to prepare each child to enter and benefit from a regular school program, preschool or day-care center. Children in a special preschool for abused children are graduated when the point comes where they will be tolerated and will be able to benefit from a regular community program. Most of the children in our preschool have reached that point in from six to twelve months.

The second point to be stressed is that a special preschool program for abused children is in reality offering multiple services to the child and family. In addition to the usual educational goals, a special preschool for abused children offers much that is usually only obtained through psychotherapy, speech and language therapy, and neuro-developmental rehabilitation. In the end, the expense of a special preschool program, such as we have described, makes it unnecessary for the child to be *separately* enrolled in a variety of treatment modalities. Occasional consultation from different professionals is in fact much less expensive than the children being treated separately by each of these therapists. The cost of special education for these children is another savings to be considered. Early preschool intervention should be able to prevent the need for such special help at later ages for most abused children.

Finally, it is important to note that most abused children *can* from the outset be easily placed in a regular preschool, head-start, or day care program. Such programs can meet these children's needs with minor adjustments in their regular routines. They must be careful to not overlook or to reinforce the "good" behavior of the inhibited, frightened abused child. More than the usual amount of one to one attention will be required with these children. Consultation from professionals outside the discipline of education may be required. Cooperative efforts with the caseworker or lay-therapist of the parent will be required.

This chapter has attempted to point out some of the special behaviors of the abused child and how a preschool program can address the special needs of abused children. All children who have been abused or neglected need and can benefit from a preschool experience. While there are few facilities especially designed for abused children, there are preschools, head starts and day care programs in every community. There is no question that the most important needs of the child relate to having a secure, loving home environment. The importance of parents is no less relevant when that home environment is suboptimal. However, the abusive family cannot meet many of the needs of their children. Abusive parents would not be able to meet the needs of normal, average children, and this inability is even more significant in the abused child. For the abused child is a wounded child—a damaged child in many respects. He has developmental lags and delays, immature socialization skills and psychological wounds. We need to consider how best to help the abused child with his special problems and needs. We are suggesting here that a preschool setting should be a basic treatment modality for such a child.

✳ *Chapter 18*

Crisis Nurseries

Mary McQuiston

Child abuse occurs at a time of stress; usually there are numerous ingredients playing their respective roles in adding to the overall predicament of the parent. The child is but one of the crucial factors which plays into the moment of crisis. Unfortunately, the child is available for attack. The child may play some role in the production of stress for the parent, but he is also the target for frustration, disappointment and anger. He becomes the target for displaced anger—anger which arises from a number of sources.

We have seen that parents who have the potential to attack their children need critical relief support systems available to them; and they must learn to make use of these systems when pressures and circumstances build to a boiling point. And yet, these are the very parents who find it very difficult, if not impossible, to use community resources, babysitters or relatives for child care. Indeed, they rarely have any life-lines for themselves or for their children.

Helping agencies often are viewed as threats by these isolated parents. Experience and community opinion suggest that social service agencies are often accusatory and punitive. Agencies that provide and encourage intermittent or continuous child care are especially suspect. Many questions arise in the mind of the battering parent: "Will they think I'm a bad parent?" "Will they take my kids away?" "What if they find a mark on my child?" "Will they think that I'm a bad person?" This distrust makes it difficult to provide relief in the form of child care for such parents.

Experience at the National Center for the Prevention and Treatment of Child Abuse and Neglect has shown that operating a crisis nursery for abused children is feasible and profitable to the children and their parents. Before describing how such a facility can be most helpful, it seems appropriate to outline some of the bases on which the Crisis Nursery at the National Center was established. Certain needs of the parent and child require some attention; goals to meet these needs are as follows:

1. These parents need prompt relief from their children when under stress. This time of stress precipitates abuse. If, at such a time of crisis and duress, the child can easily be placed in such a 24-hour, seven-day-a-week nursery, not only is the child in a safe place, but the parent has one less stress to deal with.
2. Abusive parents need to learn how to use help. They are notoriously distrustful of so-called helping agencies as well as of neighbors, relatives and especially of professionals. Much has been written about the need to help the parent utilize life-lines. One such type of life-line for them to learn to use is a facility that offers prompt and short-term care for their children.
3. Abusive parents need to learn to recognize when there is increasing risk of harm to their children. One of the goals of any treatment program for abusive parents is to help them learn to anticipate stress and act accordingly. Most parents can learn very quickly when life's circumstances are building up to a boiling point. It is at this time that they should know to put their children in a safe place until the emotional storm has passed.

   Abusive families need a place where they can leave their children in such times of stress. Such a facility, however, *must* be a non-judgmental setting where there is a minimum of red tape involved in order to place the child at any time. Because of frequent distrust of social agencies such as child welfare, families often find it easier to utilize a facility which is not too closely identified with such agencies.
4. One of the goals of treatment (mentioned in Chapter 16) is to help these parents allow their children to obtain nurturance from people outside the nuclear family. To allow this requires a stage of altruism in regard to one's own child; a level that is minimally available to most abusive parents. This involves an ability to allow one's child to develop good feelings for other people, a difficult and threatening phenomenon for parents who tend to view their child as a principal source of their own need gratification.

Our crisis nursery has helped abusive parents with each of these treatment goals. The facility provides relief for parents by being willing to care for their children temporarily when life is particularly stressful and difficult. The staff of the nursery helps the parents learn when such crisis care is needed; how to anticipate when troubles are mounting; and when to recognize the need for the child's placement in a safe setting. Staff not only provides this respite care for the child, but is also available to talk with self-referring parents and to help them learn to use helping people. This requires an empathetic, non-judgmental staff which is attuned to the predicament of the parent as well as of the child. At the point when parents are able to use such a facility, they have obviously become capable of allowing others to give to their child; they have then begun to deal with the fondness and attachment that their children may develop towards the staff of such a nursery.

What then are some of the roles a crisis nursery can play with the child who is placed there? When a crisis nursery was established at the National Center for the Prevention and Treatment of Child Abuse and Neglect, the primary goal for children was to provide a safe place for children when parents are under stress. Throughout the past year, a number of other services to these children have been identified and deemed to be necessary.

1. First, as mentioned, is the need to provide a safe place for children at times when they are at great risk of physical assault in their own homes. This goal alone seems to us to justify the expense of such a facility. This is truly a means of prevention of physical abuse of children. Data from parents confirm that placement of their children has kept the children safe from physical assault.
2. When children are brought to a crisis nursery, the parents are in a state of crisis. This state of crisis has usually been building over some hours or days with increasing anger, frustration and disorganization of personal and family function. At the time of admission, the child is reacting to the events and emotional milieu of the family and should be considered in a state of crisis also. One of the most important goals of our staff is to help the child deal with his own anxiety and fearfulness, as well as his reaction to separation from parents.
3. As will be discussed below, a crisis nursery must be more than just a place for room and board for a child. Placement in a crisis nursery provides an opportunity to identify the child's problems so that appropriate intervention can be planned and implemented. We use the crisis stays for identification of medical and developmental problems of the child. Common medical problems encountered are undernutrition, anemia, infections, sensory deficits, seizure disorder and lack of immunizations. Developmental delays and deficits are identified in a large percentage of such children. A complete physical examination and series of developmental screening tests can be given to any child admitted. This is the first step—*identification*—towards aiding the parents to obtain the additional help which the child needs.
4. The high frequency of developmental problems of abused children has been documented and discussed elsewhere. Developmental stimulation may be provided directly or indirectly through a crisis nursery. If the duration and frequency of placement in a crisis nursery is high, the staff will begin to make a difference in the developmental progress of the child. As the developmental needs of the child are identified, the staff can help parents find appropriate local resources for the child such as day-care setting or preschool; they may work directly with the parents by making suggestions for stimulation of the child; or a referral may be made for a visiting nurse service or a developmental

clinic. A crisis nursery should optimally be run conjointly with a day-care setting for children who are not in crisis. In this latter instance, the child in a crisis nursery who is identified as having developmental problems will be channeled into a day-care setting within the same facility.

The American Academy of Pediatrics[1] has insisted that day-care facilities must provide all four of the following: (a) a rich environment for the child; (b) an environment wherein the child can explore and learn; (c) help for families to secure medical, dental and mental health services; and (d) social and emotional support for the family. A crisis nursery or a preschool must also provide *all* of these to serve abused children adequately.

A crisis nursery must be able to offer care for children for at least 24-72 hours. It must operate 24 hours a day and seven days a week and be available to accept children at any hour if it is truly to provide a safe alternative to the child at risk of abuse. Licensing of such facilities is often quite difficult. Our nursery is fortunate not to have had such administrative problems as we are licensed as an extended care unit of the Colorado Medical Center Teaching Hospital. Other attempts in the Denver area to establish such facilities have faced difficulties with licensure, especially to provide around-the-clock care for children under three years of age. Many states have no provisions for licensure of such facilities. The solution to this dilemma will vary from community to community.

Guidelines must be established as to which children will be accepted into such crisis care and by what means they are to be referred. One may limit the facility to abused children or may more broadly take children who are neglected but at no risk of physical abuse. We have chosen the former path. Children are accepted when there is a previous history of abuse. The nursery was established to offer care for children when there is a crisis. That determination—whether or not the parents are in a state of crisis—must be the *parents'* judgment, not that of the staff of the nursery. The nursery must be willing to accept a child for care when the parents feel there is such a need. Most of the referrals to our nursery come from social service agencies and from our own lay therapists and social workers. However, not uncommonly parents call and refer themselves. Occasionally parents take advantage of the service when they are basically looking for a facility to baby-sit for their child so they may go out for the evening, take a short trip or attend to their own medical needs. However, despite this, the staff must *not* be in the position of forcing the referring parents to prove that they need such a facility at the time of referral. The staff must always err on the side of accepting the child, and when inappropriate referrals are made, they can be dealt with at a later time.

It is of extreme importance to minimize the administrative headaches for the parents; such obstacles will decrease the prompt use of a crisis nursery. A minimum of questions are asked. The parent will need to sign a few release forms to allow medical intervention, if needed. Brief information cards are filled out requiring such basic information as: child's name, parents' name, address, phone, emergency contact. We discuss our program with the parents and ask basic questions around eating and sleeping routines, focusing on the parents' special knowledge of the child's behavior. We support their need to get away and may suggest available help to the parents. We have learned that many parents bring their child to our facility as a disguised way of obtaining help for themselves. Hence, the staff must be sensitive to the veiled cry for help from the parents upon admission of the child.

The parents are encouraged to call at any time to inquire about their child, allowing the child to speak directly or by phone to the parent. We remind the parents to give us an approximate time for their return and further remind them that we are normally available to care for their child only for a maximum of 72 hours. Most parents at the time of their child's admission are distraught and not concerned with the specific program of the nursery. Either verbal or written information should be given them as to what will happen to their child. If a nursery regularly obtains developmental screening and/or medical examination of the child, the parents must be so informed.

A crisis nursery is basically a treatment center for the child, and the first priority of such a facility must be the protection of the child's interests. Hence, we are not willing to accept a child with any promise of collusion with the parents regarding the child. For example, if the child has evidence of suspected non-accidental injuries at the time of admission, we will file a report on such a child to the appropriate social agency. We will not keep the admission of the child secret from welfare agencies if they have custody of the child. If a parent requests information around these policy issues, we are very direct and honest with them. Protection of the child is foremost in the design of a crisis nursery facility.

The Nursery Setting

After the parent and child have been introduced to the facility and the parent leaves, our attention turns to the child. We are particularly attuned to what the child has been going through over the past few days and what the immediate needs of the child are. The adaptation of the child to his particular stress may vary. Three common behaviors of the child are overt anxiety and fearfulness, frozen inhibited watchfulness or extreme compliance with staff.

The obviously anxious, fearful child may require hours of soothing to dampen their crying and raging. The compliant or inhibited child may exhibit no overt reactions to his new situation. We have found that soothing talk and a nice warm lap are often the most the child can tolerate initially. Every child loosens up and becomes less inhibited or fearful; however, the amount of time varies considerably. Usually within about 24 hours, we see the child beginning to explore his new environment, checking out play materials as well as the adults and other children. This beginning investigation of the environment may then expand into a realization that, "Yes, indeed, these are safe people. Maybe I can play a bit; it's okay." This point takes a while in coming. It may never develop or may only develop when the child is returned again.

A variety of play materials is available. However, only a limited choice of materials is visually accessible; overstimulation is to be avoided. We have found that these children can move in their play more appropriately when the setting is free of too much stimulation. The physical setting of our facility has two rooms available to the children so that smaller groups by age or interest can be available to the child.

The most important component of any crisis nursery is its staff, and its staff policies. The National Center Crisis Nursery was established to serve a maximum of six to eight children at any one time. Two child-care workers are on duty at all times. Even when the census is low, we have found that two workers are required. Additionally, an on-call or backup system must be established for those times when the census is exceeded or circumstances require more than two staff members. The unit is coordinated by an early childhood specialist serving as head teacher in the Crisis Nursery. The child care staff have varying backgrounds. We require experience with toddlers and preschool-age children, either through work experience, or through the experience gained by being a parent. We are looking for child-oriented staff who can serve and remain the child's advocate while still being able to be empathetic with the parent. The personal characteristics of the staff are primary over any more objective experiential requisites. While this is not the place to describe our in-service training programs or regular weekly staffings, it must be mentioned that the work in a crisis nursery is difficult and stressful for staff. Planned efforts must be made to recognize and obviate some of the emotional stress of any staff member who works day in and day out with abused children and their parents.

In addition, we expect staff members to help in the recognition of medical and developmental problems of the children; thus, regular, ongoing in-service programs are essential.

Medical consultation to such a facility is necessary. Children who need continual medical attention are brought to a crisis nursery. We have had outbreaks of salmonella, shigella, chicken pox and other infections in addition to pneumonia, otitis media and seizure disorders. Medical consultation must be available on a 24-hour-a-day basis. We have referred to the high incidence of chronic medical problems of such children, as well as developmental and emotional concerns. We have needed to utilize developmental, psychological and neurological consultation on many of our children. The data can be helpful for treatment recommendations to parents and/or social service agencies who are involved with the family.

Effectiveness of Program

We are convinced that a properly run crisis center for abused children can prevent abuse to children. Several parents have reported to us that if they had not been able to place their children easily and quickly in a facility such as ours, they know that they would have physically attacked them.

We have identified a large number of medical and developmental problems in children which were then attended to by family or social service agencies. John came to the child unit at ten months of age. Protective services had had custody of him since he was one month of age, at which time his mother had dropped him on his head, with a resultant concussion. On the first day in our unit, he was discovered to have a right hemiparesis (partial paralysis of the right side of his body), a neurological problem which had gone unnoticed by parents, caseworker and medical personnel in a child care clinic. It was also noted that this boy might have been having seizures. An EEG was obtained which showed a highly abnormal pattern. Indeed, within ten days the child started having obvious frank seizures. An overall developmental delay was also noted which prompted the nursery staff to obtain consultation for developmental stimulation for this little boy. The staff has identified hearing losses, infections, neurologic problems and developmental delays in a number of children, even when the family had had regular contacts with lay-therapists or caseworkers in their homes. In each instance, it was clear that neither the lay-therapist nor caseworker had identified these problems.

The children who have entered at times of crisis have benefited from the staff's attention to their anxiety and fearfulness. In infants and younger children there is a gradual diminution in their obvious distress. The withdrawn frozen child gradually is able to come out of his shell and interact with staff and peers. In the somewhat older child, his ability to master his anxiety through verbalizing his fears to the staff is noted.

We have been able to help parents utilize other helping agencies and to trust and allow others to help in the care of their children. For the very first time, some mothers have been able to use nurseries or baby-sitting services for their children after one or two contacts with the crisis nursery. When specific treatment services are indicated for the child or the staff has felt that a preschool experience for the child is required, we have seen parents who never before used such services be able to enroll their child in such programs.

Parents have learned to anticipate those times when the stresses of their lives are building to a crisis and to call us or bring the child to our unit as a healthy preventive measure. We have offered much support and nurturance to the parents who have brought their children here. We have often become the focal point in a child abuse case—with parents who have come to trust us then coming to us for help when they feared that repeat abuse might occur. We have found it is possible to focus primarily on the child and his protection and interests without a polarized stance that excludes the parents from our concern.

Summary of Basic Needs

1. Space must be adequate for the children to be admitted. Licensing regulation

in each state will recommend or require certain square footage per child. Further regulations may stipulate staff-child ratios, usually one to four. Even the smallest of facilities will optimally have three rooms: one for infants and young toddlers, one for the older preschool children, and a third room for sleeping. The facilities should look and feel like a home, with adequate storage space for toys and equipment which, if not stored, would provide too stimulating and chaotic an environment for the child.

2. Crisis care requires at least two staff members, even if there are only two children present. An illness, an emergency, or a child who critically needs one-to-one attention are common. The staff must have had the experience in living or working with young children. They must be emotionally relatively healthy to sustain the stress of such work. The children in such a facility are under stress, and many are delayed, poorly treated and emotionally disturbed. The staff must be willing to let the children go back home after a few hours or a few days. Open communication and on-going staff development are paramount.

3. Referrals can be made from social agencies, hospitals, schools, friends, neighbors or from the parents. A 24-hour-a-day hotline can be advertised and circulated within the community.

4. A maximum census must be established. Plans must be made for those times when an influx of children exceeds the capacity of the facility, for no child whose parents are in crisis can be turned away. A number of means of planning for such an instance can be developed, such as cooperative efforts with receiving homes of a child welfare agency or emergency hospitalization.

5. A back-up system for medical consultation and for psychological and developmental consultation should be provided. The medical backup may come from a child-care clinic, private physician or a team of medical specialists. Such consultations are often utilized.

Perhaps the most essential clue as to whether a crisis center for abused children is adequate is whether or not it is used by potentially abusive parents and if reinjuries fail to occur. If the facility offers adequate services to the child, to his parents and to responsible agencies concerned with the family, the facility will be quickly utilized and become part of all protective services.

Expanded Services

A good crisis nursery will experience pressure to expand its services in a number of directions. One of the goals of a crisis nursery is to help abusive parents learn to use friends and professionals and agencies in an appropriate manner. We have also wished to help abusive parents allow their children to form relationships with adults from outside the nuclear family. As these families have come to trust the staff, requests have come for the crisis nursery to care for their children in non-crisis situations. These requests have come from the parents as well as from therapists working with parents. Families who plan to attend group treatment or individual psychotherapy sessions have asked the crisis nursery to "take" their children on a regularly scheduled basis certain hours each week. The therapists have at times suggested that such a service is essential to enable the parents to attend regular, scheduled therapy. A crisis nursery may opt to provide this service. Alternately, it may extend its services to help the parents find other baby-sitting services. In either case, the staff of a crisis nursery will be asked to extend their original services, either to provide regular child-care or to help parents and professionals to find this child-care elsewhere. Therapists of the families have often suggested that the family should not have to be in a state of crisis for child care to be provided. They have made the point that it would be quite therapeutic for the family to be able to learn to leave their children with responsible caretakers on a regular basis to have some time for themselves in social activities, such as going to a movie or eating dinner out. Indeed, for the parents to be able to leave their children and enjoy themselves is often an impressive therapeutic success. There will be requests for the crisis nursery to provide routine child-care particularly since abusive parents may have developed a uniquely trusting relationship with the crisis nursery staff that has not yet extended to other adults. However, the provision of such added services, if not planned for, can compromise the primary purpose of such a facility to provide child care at times of crisis. The attachment of the staff of a crisis nursery to the child and parents coupled with a wish to be more helpful to them also plays into the temptation to provide non-crisis services.

A crisis nursery staff will often be able to provide some type of developmental stimulation program for the children under care. When children are only kept in the facility for two or three days, the staff just begins to see the potential of the children and the helpful effects of developmental stimulation for the children. In a number of instances, where community resources were limited, the staff at this nursery will want to bring certain children into the facility several times a week on a regulary scheduled basis to provide a basic stimulation program for them.

The role of a crisis nursery in providing a safe source of respite care for a child when the parents are in a state of crisis is, in and of itself, a worthy service to provide. Just as important, however, is the ability of the staff at the crisis center to see to it that important and significant problems of the child are going to be attended to after the child is discharged. Without such a service, a crisis center has only done half of its job in trying to help abused children.

Summary

Through such a program a number of valuable therapeutic goals for the abusive parents may be met or encouraged.

1. The crisis center provides a safe environment for the child at a time when the chances of physical abuse are great if he were to remain with his parents.

2. Abusive parents can learn to accept and use help from an outside agency and can learn to anticipate those stressful times when it is in the child's best interests to be briefly separated.
3. Parents can begin to develop some trust in adults and allow their child to receive nurturance and care from adults outside the nuclear family.
4. The psychological stresses of the child at time of crisis can be dealt with.
5. The staff has the opportunity and the obligation to recognize and identify medical and developmental problems of the child. Once identified these problems can be treated by other community resources after the child is discharged from the crisis center.
6. Crisis nursery programs can be set up in homes, churches, community centers or schools. Businesses or service organizations can offer such services. The opportunities are limitless and the need extremely great.

References

1. *Pediatrics*, Vol. 51, No. 5, May 1973, p. 947.

✳ *Chapter 19*

Residential Family Therapy

Helen Alexander, Mary McQuiston and **Martha Rodeheffer**

A residential treatment program for abusive families was started at the National Center in 1974. It was conceptualized by C. Henry Kempe as an alternative to separation of the abused child from his family. In truth, it arose from a dissatisfaction from traditional therapy models. As late as 1974 we were still being told that ". . . successful treatment includes psychotherapy for parents and temporary removal of the children from the homes."[1] Our interest in residential treatment also arose from a desire to significantly improve the parent-child interaction. It was felt that through short-term but intensive residential treatment specific needs of the child, his siblings and the parents could be provided. Finally this treatment program was established to identify more clearly what approaches could be most helpful to these families so that they could be developed and implemented in out-patient settings. Our experience to date has shown that through residential short-term therapy these goals can be accomplished.

There have been a few other residential treatment programs for abusing families. Each varies somewhat in content and form and will be only briefly described here.

For the past eight years, Park Hospital in Oxford, England has been admitting mothers with their children for the purpose of assessment and management of problems that have arisen between parent and child.[2,3] The unit was first conceived as providing intensive psychotherapy for families with children having psychiatric abnormalities. However, over the last few years there has been a dramatic increase in the number of referrals for both actual and threatened abuse; currently abusive families account for 80 percent of the admissions to the unit. Lynch reports that 80 percent of the families have returned home with their children from this short-term crisis intervention program.

Since 1972, the Triangle in Amsterdam has admitted parents along with their children who are in danger because of existing or impending problems in their family situation.[4] Initial focus of treatment is upon resolving problems of living in terms of budgeting, financing, housing and work. The second thrust is toward disentangling relations within the family through "therapeutic conversation," child-management sessions and actual practice of new ways of interacting with the children.

The Hospital for Sick Children in Toronto admits mothers and sometimes fathers to its in-patient ward along with the child.[5] Parenting skills are taught by modelling by the staff, and a decision is reached as to whether it is advisable to return the child to its home. Treatment programs developed and initiated in the hospital are then carried out by the original referring agency.

In the United States, residential treatment programs for abusive parents have materialized in New York, Denver, St. Louis and Los Angeles. The Center for Parent and Child Development at the New York Foundling Hospital admits up to eight mothers and ten children into residence at any one time.[6] Fathers or paramours participate in the treatment services but do not live in. The three to four month residential period is followed by up to a year of "after care" and supportive services. The mothers and infants being treated at this center come primarily from "hard core" poverty and ghetto living.

In 1973 federal funding was provided to two projects designed to develop and explore the residential treatment modality for abusive parents.[7] The Family Care Center located in the Watts area of Los Angeles is affiliated with the Martin Luther King Medical Center. The Family Resource Center is affiliated with the St. Louis Children's Hospital.

Each of these programs vary in content and form. The important point is that several different groups have felt that residential treatment for abusive families is an alternative to traditional modes of therapy. Each has as its basic premise the wish to keep children and their abusive parents from separation and to have impact upon the parent-child interaction.

Circle House in Denver is a family treatment center which provides twenty-four-hour services to abusive families. Up to four families are in residence at any one time. It is composed of two separate units that are closely coordinated and share the same building: the Family Unit and the Child Care Unit. The Family Unit is geared toward the parents and those children who are under their parents' supervision and care at any given time. The Child Care Unit is child-oriented and provides child care as needed and is available around the clock for both the particular child who is under court-ordered protection and, also, for the child's siblings.

A family is accepted in residence for a period of from four weeks to several months. The optimal length of residence is yet to be determined. A family is presently accepted in residence for three months, followed by a subsequent three months of an outpatient treatment program. When a protective services caseworker or other therapist from a community agency has been involved with the family, he or she becomes part of the treatment team and must continue to maintain frequent contact with the family throughout their stay. Prior to admission, initial psychiatric evaluations are made of each parent to determine treatability and appropriateness of this treatment choice. Initial treatment plans are developed from this pre-admission evaluation.

Before describing the program in more detail, it would be helpful to consider the status of the family upon admission, for we must deal from the very beginning with the stressful events through which all the family members have just passed.

The Family before Admission

Once a report of abuse or neglect is made, a series of crises are experienced by both the child and his parents. The child has suffered physical trauma (and significant lack of nurturing) at the hand of parental figures upon whom he is dependent for his most basic needs. The child is then faced with an abrupt and often dramatic separation from these parents at a time when he is especially in need of comforting and assurance. Though the parental care may have been meager, it is still the major source of any nurturance the child has experienced. It has usually been the only source of security he has known, and he is understandably frightened by losing his parents. The child typically faces several more uprootings. If a petition is sustained and protective custody ordered, the receiving home to which he was originally brought is replaced with a foster home within sixty days in accordance with the law. Periodic visits with natural parents allowed under the supervision of child protective caseworkers cannot quell the storm of confusion and anxiety that rages within the child, who is too young to comprehend and deal with the complexities of the situation that evolved out of his parents' wrath toward him. In the course of hospitalization and foster care placements, the child must somehow cope with multiple parental figures and the different expectations and limitations of each relationship.

Meanwhile, the parents experience a traumatic series of events. Whatever the parents are already feeling regarding the injury or neglect they have inflicted upon their child, they must now deal with the additional pressure of disapproval of their parental behavior from a wide network of people. Authorities descend upon them in the form of police, social service workers and a guardian ad litem. These strangers intrude into the sanctity of their home, asking embarrassing questions, inquiring into their lives directly and through neighbors, friends and relatives, forcing them to surrender their child to unknown individuals, and ordering them to appear in court within twenty-four hours to rebut the charges and show cause as to why the temporary police hold for protective custody should not be continued. In court the parents listen to a series of charges emanating from the data gathered by these strangers about their stability, their behavior and their attitudes. On the basis of evidence presented, the court may order temporary custody of their child until a more complete hearing can be held. A social services caseworker demands access into their lives, trying to be helpful but also gathering information to be presented at the adjudicatory hearing which the parents face some weeks or months later. If, at that adjudicatory hearing, abuse or neglect is legally established to have occurred, then a number of expectations and repeated court hearings will be set in motion at the dispositional hearing.

At this time of crisis, stress and chaos the parents may be directed to a social service caseworker, a psychotherapist, a parents group or a lay therapist. It is clear that despite whatever gains may be possible from such services for the parents, that this traditional therapeutic model is largely ineffectual in meeting the *child's* needs or in effecting significant changes in the parent-child relationship.

It is at this time, then that the family enters Circle House.

Treatment of the Parents

Phases of the Program. For most families there are several phases through which they pass. During the three months of residential treatment, there are roughly three phases—the intial acclimation; the working phase; and the final time of in-residence work to prepare the family for discharge.

Initially, the family is frightened and overwhelmed by all that has occurred and in need of a safe, supportive, nurturing home. The parents need relief from the pressures of child care and the children need protection from parental attack. Yet both have intense needs for contact with one another in the aftermath of the forced separation that occurred. In the beginning days of treatment little is required of the parents beyond keeping of their therapy appointments. A temporary regression is accepted as a legitimate need in the parents' attempt to gather strength and sustenance from others. The focus of the treatment plan at this point is primarily supportive, with staff reaching out to the parents with concrete expressions of help and interest. Time is allowed for bonding to occur with the personnel at Circle House. The loosening of pathological ties within the immediate and extended family is facilitated by providing the parents with a new extended family in the form of the Circle House staff and other families in residence. The early days in residence are a time of testing and establishing trust, a chance for parents to discover relationships in which they are valued, accepted, and even liked. The lay therapist makes a speical effort to bond with the parents during this time. He or she accompanies the parents on outings, invites them to engage in activities, transports them to appointments about town and helps them learn to utilize the public services available to them.

Much to the surprise of the abusive parents who have usually learned to view any type of play or self-indulgence as "bad," the staff gives approval for participation in activities that provide the parent real pleasure. Activities that provide a chance of success and a pride in accomplishment are facilitated by the paraprofessional staff and group therapists. Individual initiative in a group setting is reinforced as parents actively participate in the selection and planning of weekly group events for parents.

In the second phase of residential treatment, increased expectations are made of the parents in terms of therapy, contributions to daily living routines in the family unit, and involvement in the care and management of their children. These expectations create considerable anxiety in the parents and lead to increased confrontations with the paraprofessional staff and treatment team. It is an important stage of active conflict and resolution, occurring with the continued support of the therapeutic milieu. This is a crucial phase in determining the parents' strengths and ability to continue to meet their own needs and still adequately care for their young children. During this time critical decisions are faced by both the parents and the treatment staff regarding the parents' desire *and* ability to bond with and provide for the needs of each of their children.

In the final phase of residence, there is often a period of panic related to discharge; to the loss of the constant availability, attention and support of the Circle House staff. During the transition phase of treatment the parents receive important reassurances of continued caring and friendships in their return visits to the Circle House. The repeated separations and reunions during the parents' outpatient program facilitate repeated verbal expressions of welcome and continued involvement in their lives. Both staff and parents are engaged in a separation-individuation process that requires time and some grieving of the loss of closeness. The increased attention of the lay-therapist and the continued interest and concern of the staff for the parents' well-being provides support for the adjustment to being home again.

As families prepare to leave, a heightened expression of neediness is seen, e.g., wishes to take items with them, requests to take food to the apartment, a renewed "grabbiness" that was seen early in the program. This can precipitate both genuine concern for how the family is going to handle the loss of the 24-hour care and it can also provoke anger from staff. That this is a symptom of separation and the sense of impending loss must be understood and some preparation be made for this recurrence of neediness. A farewell party that is a very special event for the family is a way of responding to this as well as providing a celebration of their growth and readiness to move out. A small token gift comes from all the staff as another response to the loss that is felt on both sides. Often humor can be useful in recognizing the wish to take some of the "goodies" they have been experiencing. One family frequently mentioned how much they needed a washing machine, and slowly we developed a game of joking about taking a piece at a time, gaining recognition of the wish as well as the reality. When the family returns for visits, snacks or meals are important as continued expression of our willingness to share with them.

It is during this third phase of in-residence treatment, as well as during the next three months of out-patient therapy, that one of the most important goals of the treatment must be faced head-on. That is the need to help these families obtain and accept help from others in the community. In such a short treatment program it is clear that much therapeutic work will need to be done after discharge from the program. The family is involved with a case-worker and has a lay-therapist. They may need to continue in psychotherapy with some other professionals apart from Circle House. Marital counseling may be indicated. Their children will need to be in treatment programs also, such as a preschool setting. It is during this final phase of residential therapy that the families come to realize that once the umbilical cord to Circle House is cut, that they must engage with other people and agencies to obtain what they want and need for themselves and their children.

There are two primary aspects of the residential programs for parents which one might look at separately, the milieu of the setting, and the more formal therapy sessions.

The Therapeutic Milieu. Nurturing and facilitative roles with the parents are filled by paraprofessionals working under the direction of an experienced social worker in the Family Unit. The parents are provided human warmth, friendships, and emotional support. The therapeutic milieu undergirds the more formal treatment process by providing a setting in which, with the help of the staff, interpersonal conflicts can be played out and brought to resolution; new skills can be learned and integrated through practice over time, and insights can be translated into behavior.

The facility is as "homelike" as possible with private sitting-bedrooms for each couple and a separate bedroom for the children of each family. A central kitchen, a common dining room, family room, laundry facilities and craft areas are shared by all the families in residence. Housekeeping responsibilities are shared with the help and guidance of the staff. Preparation and eating of meals are also shared experiences under the supervision of the cook. Food is provided and parents participate in the planning and preparation of meals. Breakfast is managed by each family for itself. Lunch is prepared by the cook. Dinner preparation and clean-up are negotiated between the cook, the families and other staff. A variety of recreational activities, hobbies and crafts are available to the parents.

Daily routines of the family continue as normally as possible while in Circle House. One parent continues to work. The other parent, whose role includes the major caretaking of the children for the family, does not work while participating in the treatment program. This regulation makes possible full utilization of the uniqueness of the residential treatment program. The parents are free to come and go, except that their participation is expected in therapy, planned activities, scheduled visits with their children and negotiated child care responsibilities. The child under court order leaves the Circle House only with prior arrangement between the county social services caseworker, the treatment team and the staff of the Child Care Unit. From the first day in residence parents have multiple contacts with their children every day within the Circle House setting.

Formal Treatment Plan. This includes once a week individual psychotherapy and weekly marital therapy. All parents participate in an evening therapy group led by male and female co-therapists. Intervention in parenting attitudes and skills takes place through parents' observations of the staff and through formal parent-child interaction sessions described in some detail later. The parents are seen regularly (at least twice a month) by their social service caseworker and are additionally seen regularly by their lay-therapist who will be working with them for an extended time after discharge.

It seems obvious that there is extensive interaction between the staff of Circle House and the parents as well as at least six different therapy modalities occurring during their brief residential stay. These formal therapies will be discontinued within three months after discharge—although the lay-therapist and caseworker will continue to work with the family. As mentioned above, it is not uncommon to recommend continued formal therapy for the parents from some source other than Circle House after the six months of treatment is completed.

Treatment for Abused Children and Their Siblings

In most cases the abused child comes to Circle House from a stay in a receiving home or foster care home. During the week preceding his admission, the child makes short visits to the Circle House for assessment of his development. During this series of visits he sees his family and becomes familiar with his new home. Developmental tests are administered, speech and language is evaluated, a structure play interview takes place, and medical evaluation includes a physical examination, assessment of neurological development, and bringing medical records up to date. The early childhood specialist in charge of the Child Care Unit at the Circle House then integrates the findings and recommendations of the professionals who have evaluated the child. From this interdisciplinary data she develops an individualized therapeutic stimulation program to be utilized when the child moves into Circle House. Siblings of the abused child receive the same type of evaluation and individualized programming. When the abused child first enters residential treatment, he or she is under twenty-four-hour care of the Child Care Unit, as are the siblings.

The development of the Child Care Unit as a separate entity within Circle House evolved as the staff discovered how much the parents needed respite from the care of their child in order to break the destructive cycle of parent-child difficulties. As families came into residence at Circle House the pervasiveness of negative and harsh patterns of parental behavior and the disturbed behavior in the child became apparent. The staff was unsure whom they should comfort and nurture as both parent and child were in obvious need. To turn to the child was a cruel "set up" for both parent and child, yet ignoring the child's needs was impossible. Consequently, parents and staff had a difficult time forming an alliance because of the negative feelings both were experiencing. Parents sensed the critical attitude developing around their parenting. Each time the workers intervened with the child, the parents responded with increased anger toward the child and toward the staff. The need for the child to be assured of adequate care and therapeutic intervention while the parents' needs were also being attended to was accomplished by providing separate units to care for each while allowing daily contact between them. The Child Care Unit was established with a plan for a more gradual parental assumption of child care responsibilities when both parent and child had responded to the therapeutic regime and were in a less disturbed state.

The Therapeutic Milieu. The Child Care Unit provides the child with a nurturing, homelike atmosphere in which he is well cared for, protected and presented with warm, supportive interactions with adults in a *predictable* environment. It provides the child with a haven of his own where he can play and explore his world without the number of limits that would be set upon him if he was with his parents.

An average day in the residential Child Care Unit is comprised of normal routines (such as bath time, nap and meals) free play, therapeutic stimulation sessions, and visits from the parents. The major portion of the time is allotted for free play within the planned environment which is filled with toys and materials appropriate to the child's level of development.

An effective day-care program for abused children has many characteristics in common with any *good* day-care program. That is, there is frequent opportunity for free choice, experimentation with materials and exploration of relationships. However, the abused child is not accustomed to such freedom and tends to become over-stimulated or anxious when presented with choices he is not used to making. Initially, therefore, a calming environment is provided by offering limited choices and by helping the child stay with the choices he makes. These children need special help in learning how to play.

Consistency and predictability are essential to the child. Consistency in a twenty-four-hour setting is difficult because of the number of different workers involved. Consistency, however, is extremely important as abused children display disturbances that are magnified by changes and unpredictable settings. The staff works diligently to provide a basic sameness upon which the children can depend. While there are individual differences in dealing with the children, the basic limits and guidelines are adhered to by all staff. A daily routine with the child is established and a schedule is planned with the parents who will gradually assume more responsibility for the child's care. The same worker greets the child in the morning, dresses and feeds him, and brings him to the Child Care Unit until this responsibility is transferred to the parents. Similarly, the evening bath and bedtime routines are provided consistently by one worker for the child.

Formal Treatment Plan. Intensive therapeutic services are planned for the abused child and his or her siblings. If the child falls in the age range of between two and one half and five years of age, he attends the Therapeutic Preschool at the National Center. Infants and toddlers who are too young for the play-school receive special "therapeutic stimulation sessions" during specific times which are scheduled to provide one-to-one help and attention to the child. A paraprofessional assigned to take a special daily interest in the child spends these half-hour sessions in planned activities designed to promote socialization, develop skills and correct developmental lags. Activities for these individualized sessions are planned in conjunction with the early childhood specialist who directs the unit. Most toddlers can benefit from this type of focused attention for only one or two hours a day. If a child continues to demonstrate extremely disturbed behaviors after the initial adjustment period upon moving into Circle House, intensive play therapy with a professional child therapist is also initiated, in addition to the provision of therapeutic playschool or therapeutic stimulation sessions.

Treatment Focused on the
Parent-Child Relationship

It is the inadequacy of parenting skills and the extreme use of punishment in the management of their children that brought these parents to Circle House. All parents in residence have assaulted one of their children themselves, or have failed to protect their child from the assault of another person. Therapeutic interventions focused directly upon changing the nature of the child-rearing attitudes and patterns are a vital part of the treatment process. While in residence the parents are exposed to good methods of child care and introduced to new ways of thinking about children. They are encouraged to try new ways of interacting with their children. They experiment with new techniques of managing their children and establishing consistent daily routines.

The parents' contact with their children while in Circle House is carefully planned and considers the problems and needs of both the parent and the child. The treatment team prescribes how frequently contact between each parent and the child will take place, the timing and location of the contact, whether or not a staff person will be present, and the amount of childrearing duties the parent will assume at each phase of the treatment process. These daily contacts are monitored and reevaluated each week the family is in residence. In the early weeks of treatment, when emphasis is upon nurturance of the parents and establishment of a working relationship with them, few expectations are placed upon them in terms of daily care and management of the child. However, by the end of the three months in residence, parents are expected to have assumed full care of their children in preparation for taking them back into their family home.

Visiting with Children. Initial visits between parent and child take place in the Child Care Unit where they can be monitored by the staff and where the parents can observe the child care workers interacting with children other than their own. These parent visits are scheduled at times during the day when the child tends to be in a good mood and when demands for child management skills are at a minimum. In the beginning daily routines of dressing, feeding, bathing and putting children to bed, activities that are likely to precipitate parental stress if the child exhibits even normal willfulness and resistance are all handled by the staff of the Child Care Unit. Instead, parents are invited to do fun things with their children, e.g., to play with them, to read to them, to give them treats and snacks. The parents are encouraged to "get down and play," exploring the child's world along side of him without assuming responsibility for his care. The Child Care staff delights in the child's play with the parent and in his growing ability to become involved in play materials in the parent's presence. The parents quickly learn that they receive approval for encouraging their child's age-appropriate behavior, rather than the previously valued unrealistic adult-like behavior. The worker reinforces positive parenting behaviors by paying attention to the parent and by verbalizing about the pleasure the child is showing with the parent at such times. Thus, the parent begins to hear and internalize a new set of values regarding what a good parent does with children and what normal children do in the course of their development. Particular attention is paid to the parents' attempts to engage their children in positive ways. Out of the growing sense of themselves as good and successful persons arises the basis for their seeing their child as good also.

Observing Good Models. From the first week of treatment onward each parent is scheduled to observe early childhood specialists in the Child Care Unit several times a week as the worker plays with and cares for children other than the observing parent's children. This casual observation over time, with no pressure to perform or compete in a specific manner themselves, is a crucial step in the process of learning new approaches to parenting. When parents are observing, the child care worker "thinks aloud" about the activity she is engaged in with the children. For example, when the activities of preschoolers in the unit become overwhelming to a barely crawling infant, the worker might restructure the environment so that the infant has a safe, secluded corner of the room in which to pursue his own exploration of materials. However, when setting about to arrange some natural barriers with cushions, furniture, boxes, etc., the worker "thinks aloud" expressing empathy for the infant's anxiety, an intention to protect him, and what she is doing so the child will be able to relax and play. Thus the worker indirectly focuses the attention of the parent upon the crucial aspects of planning involved in providing nurturance, protection, and age-appropriate activities to stimulate the child's growth and development. The worker's verbalizations assist the parent to cognitively mediate what he or she is experiencing without demanding a response from the parent. These observation sessions stimulate discussion with parents regarding normal child development and management of children at different ages. The normalcy of the child is constantly stressed as Child Care workers respond to abusive parents unusual perceptions of their children and the extreme concerns they have about their children's everyday behavior. The workers empathize with the parents' exasperation with the child's growing willfulness even while verbalizing excitement about the importance of the child's efforts to act on his own. Parents are encouraged to allow the child to assert himself, but also to channel those assertions and to maintain reasonable, consistent limits on his behavior.

Exploring New Ways of Interacting with Children. The casual discussions growing out of the observations in the Child Care Unit supplement the more formal therapeutic sessions focused on parent-child interaction which follow. Formal "parent-child interaction sessions" are introduced by the child psychologist or early childhood specialist after the parents have been in residence for one month. In these sessions videotaping is utilized extensively to capture vignettes of the parents interacting and playing with their children. These videotapes are then played back to the parents with the therapist eliciting from them their goals and concerns, focusing on important aspects of the interaction and reinforcing positive parenting behaviors demonstrated. The behavior of the child on the videotape is studied in terms of the behaviors of the parents that elicited or reinforced that behavior. Empathy for what the child experienced during the interaction is elicited by asking parents to talk about what it probably feels like to be a child in that situation.

Child management techniques are modeled, discussed and practiced during the sessions, and problem areas receive specific attention. For example, if mealtimes are creating difficulties between parent and child, sessions are arranged so that a meal can be videotaped. The therapist may model an appropriate way of handling the routine with the child, and the parent may then be invited to practice that one or try out a method of his own. Such enactments are followed by playbacks of the videotapes with discussions of the parent's goals and the probable outcome of doing things in certain ways. If the parent is dissatisfied with the outcome of the interaction on tape, he or she has the opportunity to erase it and try again. Positive parenting behaviors elicited and reinforced during these sessions tend to increase the interactions between the parent and child in the daily living in Circle House. It is assumed that those behaviors that work for the parent and make his interactions with the child easier will be maintained by self-reinforcement after he returns to his own home.

Information about normal child development is introduced in the sessions by the psychologist doing a formal development assessment of the child in the presence of the parents. The assessment is performed with the therapist explaining the meaning and significance of what the child can do. Discussing the implications of the child's developmental level is utilized as a means of explaining the child's everyday functioning, correcting misperceptions and helping the parents set more realistic expectations for their child. Specific "games for parents and children" are demonstrated by the therapist and practiced by the parent in the sessions. Toys which are appropriate to the child's developmental level are discussed and shown to the parent, with encouragement for them to build or purchase similar toys and bring them to subsequent sessions to try them out with the child. These procedures facilitate the parents taking some initiative in helping the child achieve the next level of development and doing so in a "playful" manner.

Practicing Good Child Management. As treatment progresses the child begins to visit his parents in the Family Unit and the frequency and length of the contacts are increased. The parents are encouraged to take their child on brief outings during the day. In this latter phase of treatment parents join the worker during daily child care routines. Gradually, the parent and the staff worker begin to switch positions, with the worker becoming the observer and the parent assuming more and more of the responsibilities for child care. Those routines with which the parent seems most likely to succeed are transferred over first. For example, if the child loves his bath and the parent is likely to experience a happy exchange with the child, this would be the parent's first major responsibility. The agreement with the parent is that he or she will carry out a routine activity during a specific time period. If the parent is not able to accomplish the routine, as might be the case with an ill or overly-tired child, the parent is relieved of his duties by the Child Care worker at a predetermined time. If failure is experienced by the parents in carrying out the routine, renegotiation of child care is initiated with the parents temporarily abdicating some of the responsibilities back to the staff. The parent is never allowed to fail repeatedly with the child. Rather, the failure experience is analyzed with the staff, problems identified, solutions posed and modeled before the parent attempts to "practice" again. If the parent is unable to succeed, the task is reduced in scope until success is within reach. As each routine is mastered, another is added until the parents have full responsibility to care for the child, and the worker fades comfortably into the background. At this point the Child Care Unit is used only for prearranged babysitting and relief from child care during crises. Both parents and child then begin to prepare to go home.

Results, Findings, Advantages

In the preceding pages we have described what we are trying to accomplish and how we are working towards those ends in a residential setting for abusive families. Very briefly we should now point out some of the key findings and accomplishments of this residential treatment. We have particularly wanted to emphasize that much of what we have accomplished and learned should have relevance for non-residential, out-patient settings. It is hoped that the reader will consider how our findings and therapeutic successes might be utilized in his own community.

1. The most important advantage of this program has been the ability to keep the family together while relieving the parents of most child-care responsibilities during a time of crisis. This has meant that the bonds and attachment of parent

and child have not been disrupted, and yet the child and parents have had the safety and security from relieving parents of 24-hour care for the child and his siblings. This might well be accomplished by other means, such as having the abused child placed in a therapeutic day care setting or in a family learning center while either the child is returned to the parents in the evening or the parents join the child for evenings and nights.

2. Residential care has provided the opportunity to include the father and the siblings in the treatment regime. The father is seen as an important part of the family and is also involved in the care of the children. It is felt that this is an important and essential aspect of successful intervention with abusive families. Perhaps the working hours of professionals in out-patient settings need to be altered so that they are available to provide help to the working father during evenings or on weekends.

3. The parents' ability to observe healthy models of interaction has been a much more important component of this program than was anticipated. This is especially true of the parents ability to observe children other than their own and to observe adults dealing with their own children as well as with other children. We have seen this same therapeutic effect in "co-op" nurseries wherein mothers must come into the nursery or preschool on a regular basis. In this format, they see the normal behavior of other children and ways in which other parents and staff deal with children's behavior.

A second component of this modeling is the observation of the adult staff in the Family Unit. Here the families see how other adults deal with the stresses and the pleasures of everyday life as well as the interpersonal exchanges of staff. It is as if many of these families have had no models of interpersonal interactions other than the pathological relationships of their own parents.

4. The residential setting has provided the opportunity to provide in great quantity the friendship, help and nurturance which abusive parents so desperately need, indeed which seems a necessary precursor to any true therapeutic work being accomplished. This, too, should be possible in an out-patient or day-program from paraprofessionals as well as professionals.

5. Critical to this program has been the opportunity to seriously and systematically intervene and help in building a more healthy parent-child relationship. The parent-child interaction sessions are still in the developmental stage and are carried out by either a child psychiatrist or psychologist. However, it would seem feasible to utilize a number of other people in this treatment modality in other settings. It might be possible for a staff member of a preschool or a day care center, if adequately trained, to provide this parenting therapy. It is possible that foster parents, if adequately selected and trained, could provide this help. A very interesting program based on education and behavior modifications has been utilized by Margaret Jeffrey in Australia in the homes of abusive parents.[8] Her very exciting accounting of this program is appropriately subtitled, *Practical Ways to Change Parent-Child Interaction in Families of Children at Risk.*

6. The residential treatment program deliberately addressed the parents and children separately—and then again as a unit. This is essential to any treatment program for abusive parents. A model for this has been the formal psychotherapy for the two parents. One therapist sees the father in therapy weekly, a second therapist sees the mother, and once weekly the two therapists work with the two parents as a couple. In this model, it is acknowledged that each parent has problems and needs of his or her own quite apart from his or her spouse. It is also acknowledged that the two parents *as a couple* need to deal with their marital relationship.

So with the child. The parents have needs and problems of their own. And so does the child. And yet beyond, or in addition to that, the *parent-child relationship* needs attention and treatment. The parents have responded very positively to this approach without artificial compartmentalization. They learn how their own personal strength and weaknesses affect their attitudes and relationships to their spouse and their children.

7. Twenty-four hour residential care of these families has provided a great deal of diagnostic and prognostic information. For one, the child not only has the extensive developmental evaluation as described above, but under the observation of the child care staff he is more fully understood than is possible in brief traditional evaluation sessions. A comprehensive treatment plan can be established which takes into account his developmental and psychological profiles.

The same is true of the parents. The staff of Circle House have been particularly impressed with the very inadequate parenting of these parents. This is also noted in their interaction with the non-abused siblings of the child. Indeed, it has been quite distressing to the staff to fully realize the depth and breadth of the parents' inadequacies in terms of their children. These data are usually not discovered in out-patient settings. It speaks to the tremendous need these parents have for learning how to adequately parent all of their children.

This diagnostic capability of a residential treatment setting makes it possible to more quickly come to prognosis regarding the ability of the parents to respond to treatment and to be able to care for their children adequately. This seems a most important need which must be duplicated in other settings. We have spoken in other sections of this book about the inordinate periods of time that abusive children remain in foster care, their parents in treatment, before a final decision as to placement of the child is accomplished. Ms. Chase's book[9] poignantly details this common phenomenon which leaves both child and parents in emotional limbo.

8. The staff who are working with abusive families need a format to discuss their findings—and their feelings. Staff must be able to accept limited goals for the families, or frustration and a sense of failure will set in. Complete rehabilitation of these families is not possible. Not only is it unrealistic given the short time of six months with which to work, but it is probably unrealistic given

the life-long history of deprivation and abuse the parents have. This is a critically important point for any worker involved with these families in whatever kind of setting. The goals for therapy might well be to accomplish those changes in parents and children which are outlined in Chapter 16. When one considers the background of these parents, it is actually astonishing to see the gains in self-concept, in the marital relationship, and in the child-parent interactions which we have been able to see and document.

Summary

We have pointed out the goals of a residential treatment setting for abusive parents and given some details regarding the program at the National Center in Denver. We have been able to see considerable progress in the families through such a program. Just as important, we have begun to understand many aspects of treatment which are required by these families which we feel can be instituted in non-residential settings. The previous section of this book outlines the most important of those treatment issues.

To help these abusive families, we must find ways of offering treatment without the extended separation of the abused child from the rest of the family. We must involve the father in treatment and in the parenting therapy. The siblings are also involved in this dysfunctional family unit and require our help. Whatever the specific treatment package for abusive families is, it must include a plan to intervene therapeutically in the parent-child interaction. It is suggested that quicker means of making a prognosis regarding the parents' ability to care for their children be established. And finally, the professionals and paraprofessionals working with these very depleted and deprived families must learn to establish realistic and limited treatment goals with which we can all be satisfied and pleased.

The role of residential therapy in most communities is unclear as yet. It remains in an investigative phase. It clearly offers much that is difficult to provide in present agency policies and practices. It is an expensive treatment modality although the long-term costs of alternative treatment approaches may be even higher in dollars and in human suffering. Short-term residential therapy might well be a treatment modality to be considered by communities. An alternative would be to alter and augment present resources so as to accomplish the same therapeutic goals.

References

1. Blumberg, Marvin: Psychopathology of the Abusing Parent. *American Journal of Psychotherapy*, January 1974, 21.

2. Lynch, M.: A place of safety: An in-patient facility for abusive families. Paper presented at the Ad Hoc International Conference on Child Abuse, Bellagio, Italy, October 1975.

3. Lynch, M., Steinberg, D., and Ounsted, C.: Family unit in a children's psychiatric hospital. *British Medical Journal*, 1975, 2:127-129.

4. van Rees, R.: The Triangle: A Therapeutic Social Center. Amsterdam, Holland, Manuscript, 1975.

5. Pakes, E.H.: Child and Family In-Patient Unit. The Hospital for Sick Children, Toronto, Canada. Private correspondence, 1974.

6. Fontana, V.J. and Robison, E.: A multi-disciplinary approach to the treatment of child abuse. Prepublication draft, 1975. (Submitted to *Pediatrics*, May 1975.)

7. Cohn, A.H., Ridge, S.S., and Collignon, F.C.: Evaluating innovative treatment programs in child abuse and neglect. *Children Today*, 1975, 4(3):10-12.

8. Jeffrey, M.: Therapeutic Intervention for Children at Risk and Their Families. In *First Australian National Conference on the Battered Child*, Sandy Williams (ed.), pp. 103-111, Western Australia: Department Community Welfare, 1975.

9. Chase, N.F.: *A Child is Being Beaten*. New York: Holt, Rinehart and Winston, 1975.

Chapter 20

Therapy for Abusive Parents:
Its Effect on the Child

Harold P. Martin and **Patricia Beezley**

The whole issue of psychotherapy for abusive parents might, at first glance, seem out of place in a book which is focused on abused children. And yet there are good reasons for including this subject in such a book. The parents of an abused child constitute the most critically important part of the environment in which that child lives. (See Chapter 2.) The abused child has a part of his environment, the parents, which is not functioning optimally for the child's developmental growth. From an orientation towards the abused child, then, one might consider therapy for the parents as a type of environmental therapy or manipulation which can benefit the child. The child-oriented professional cannot be oblivious to the abusive parents, just as he cannot ignore the physical or educational environment of the child.

There are three different ways in which one might consider psychotherapy for abusive parents. They are not mutually exclusive and each has validity and relevance separately and conjointly.

First is the acknowledgement that abusive parents have a need for and a right to help, even if the child does not indirectly benefit. Abusive parents are unhappy, troubled, disturbed people. Even if we ignore for the moment the abused child, the troubled parent needs and deserves help. The act of child abuse is usually a dramatic indicator of a more pervasive troubled personality. A number of authors, most notably Steele and Pollock,[1] have detailed the typical and various forms of personality constellations of such people. Others, most notably Gil[2] and Polansky,[3] have pointed out the social circumstances of many of these parents. It is part of our medical and social responsibility to provide help to these adults, even if there is no benefit to the child. It must be kept in mind, for example, that the goal of reuniting the family is not necessarily in the child's or parents' best interests. It may be therapeutic success for the parent to be able to comfortably relinquish the child. Kempe[4] has especially spoken to this point.

A second consideration of therapy, for the parents, is the advantage to the child of the parents' improved state of mental health. This is true even if the therapy has in no way focused on the parent-child interaction. It is both theoretically and pragmatically true that any child is in a better environment if his parents are emotionally healthy than if his parents are troubled or disturbed. Insofar as the parent has a better self-concept, has improved object-relations, and can more readily utilize a variety of people for "life-lines," the child is in a better environment. If, as repeatedly pointed out in various chapters of this book, the child is reacting to the emotional climate of his environment, then an improvement in that environment should be to his advantage. This is true even though, as shall be pointed out below, we may be able to measure very little difference in the parent-child interaction even after considerable therapy for the parent.

A third way of considering therapy for the abusing parent is to focus primarily on the changes in the attitudes and behaviors of the parent towards the child. In our experience, therapy for abusive parents usually does not have such a focus. Hence we see parents who have benefited from therapy and yet continue to be rejecting, harsh and quite punitive with their previously abused child. This issue and the manner in which therapy can intervene in this child-parent relationship will be addressed.

Given these three purposes or views of psychotherapy, three other therapeutic issues with parents will be considered in this chapter. First will be some discussion of the components of effective therapy for abusive parents and how such therapy varies from the therapy mental health professionals usually and traditionally provide for their patients. Second will be an exploration of how therapy can impinge upon the parents' attitudes and behaviors towards the child. And third, given therapeutic gains in the parents, we shall address the question of how one can assess the readiness and ability of the parents to provide adequate parenting for the abused child.

Components of effective therapy for abusive parents. There have been a number of valuable and helpful treatises on providing therapy for abusive parents.[5-11] It would be redundant to review this work. Various types of therapy have been utilized including traditional psychotherapy, lay therapy, case work, group therapy, marital counselling, and residential therapy. Each has some distinct advantages and some clear limitations. What might be more valuable would be to consider *how* therapy for abusive adults might be different from what usually occurs in therapy with other types of patients. There seem to be special problems and issues with most abusive parents which are less commonly seen with other types of patients served by mental health professionals. There are five of these special considerations to note.

1. *It is essential to involve more than one person in the treatment process.* For one thing, treatment with abusive parents is usually a two-part process. There is first a need for a nurturing or reparenting experience. This is the role typically taken by lay-therapists and occasionally by public health nurses or caseworkers. It seems essential that this type of help be provided initially. Without this service (actually it is a type of therapy), little else will be accomplished. The second part of the process is the more traditional attempt to resolve internal conflicts with psychological insight and understanding. These two different processes of therapy can be provided by a single therapist, but it is our experience that this is very difficult for the therapist and is extremely draining. Indeed, the needs of most abusive parents are so great that it is unrealistic to expect any one individual to meet those therapeutic needs. The most successful experiences patients at the National Center have had has been when multiple therapies have been utilized. This might take any number of combinations such as involvement in Parents Anonymous and individual psychotherapy; or a lay therapist for the mother, group therapy for the parents and casework. Experience with the lay-therapy program at the National Center has reinforced our beliefs that most abusive parents need an intensity and degree of "mothering" and friendship which is rarely available from more traditional sources of therapy.

   It should also be noted that abusive parents commonly have developmental conflicts which include the splitting of objects into good and bad. It takes some time for the parent to incorporate both the good and bad aspects into the same person. Alternative significant figures in their lives may be essential for the parent to stay in treatment.

2. *Treatment of abusive families requires much more outreach than is normally done in traditional psychotherapy.* Abusive parents are suspicious, distrustful and extremely needy, with minimal ability to delay gratification. If put on a waiting list, they will probably never be seen at a local mental health clinic. The parents may require evidence of concrete giving in order to believe that the therapist really cares about them. This may take various forms, visiting the parents in their home, calling on the phone periodically to see how they are doing, and concrete suggestions for problem solving. These patients are frequently labeled as resistant or unmotivated. They do considerable testing out, and to use an analytic model of discussing why the patient shows up at the wrong time or on the wrong day will be met with the patient's exodus from therapy. This outreach also means that the secretary's role is critical. It is imperative that the parents be made to feel welcome. Friendly comments, offering refreshments while waiting and a genuine pleasure in seeing the parents by the receptionist or secretary may initially be much more important to the patients than what goes on in the formal therapy. These parameters of therapy may make the therapist somewhat uncomfortable depending on his philosophical background.

The need for this type of outreach was first identified by the pioneer work of Brandt Steele.[1,12] It was striking and impressive to see this erudite psychoanalyst altering his usual treatment stance with these patients, going to their homes to have dinner, calling them to just see how life was going between sessions, and being available to talk with them at any time about the vicissitudes of their lives. Such therapeutic measures stemmed from an early recognition of the need for the development of a working alliance and the patient's belief that the therapist really does care for and about him. There is also a need for some re-parenting if any insight-oriented work is to be possible.

3. *Treatment for abusive parents is not as short or time-limited as with other patients.* The period of treatment will vary from patient to patient. The initial intense treatment frequently needs to continue from eight to 24 months. Certainly any mental health clinic which limits therapy to a few weeks or is only crisis-oriented will not be able to be helpful to these patients. While there should be a gradual diminution in the frequency and intensity of therapy sessions, most of these families will need some contact from important therapeutic figures for many years. In essence, the therapists have offered themselves as parental transference figures—and just as good parents, the therapists must be available for periodic contact. This often takes the form of occasional phone calls, letters or requests for a few therapy sessions. In fact, this should be seen as a sign of therapeutic growth. One of the important goals of therapy is to help the parents to be able to develop trusting and important relationships with other people. A further critical goal of therapy is to help the patients to be able to reach out and develop life-lines which they will utilize in times of stress. It would be an indication of success, therefore, if one's patients would be able to call the therapist even after many months or years when the patients are dealing with some stressful event in their lives. It is an indication that they have truly developed a sense of trust in their new "psychological parent." The more common expectations of self-sufficiency and dissolution of transference reactions to the therapist are neither optimal nor possible with most of these patients.

4. *Court ordered therapy or involvement with representatives of the courts provides some special problems in therapy just as it does with other patients where the legal system is either requiring the therapy or requesting and requiring periodic feedback from the therapist.* Therapists in general do not like to work with patients who come to them out of coercion, for it does not coincide with theoretical models for motivation. Some of these patients indeed do not want or are not willing to make changes in their lives. And yet, most of the abusive parents who have come into treatment out of legal or social coercion rather quickly demonstrate their need and wish for a better life both external to themselves and intra-psychically. Their anger and hostility towards the court or social agency, as well as their anger and

hostility towards the therapist, can and must be dealt with early in the treatment. The issue frequently comes up where the court requires the therapist to provide some written document of the patients' progress in therapy. This can be an opportunity to allay distrust and increase the working alliance, depending on how it is handled by the therapist. One method is for the therapist to prepare this document jointly with the patient. Certainly the patient should have the opportunity to read and discuss the document before it is sent to the court or social agency. Such sharing of information provides an opportunity to acknowledge the reality that the patient is coming to the therapist partly because he has abused his child. It offers the therapist and patient an opportunity to work together towards an objective assessment of the patients' psychological status, and, especially important, to look at the gains and strengths of the patient as well as the areas where more work and change are needed. It gives the patient the chance to have realistic feedback from a therapist, which is all too often not available in more traditional psychotherapy. If this seems uncomfortable to many therapists, it may be because it is a departure from their usual mode of working with patients. It nonetheless can be used as a very helpful therapeutic process for the patient and for the therapist.

5. *The reactions and counter-transferences of the therapist are especially common and important when working with an abusive parent.* The abusive parent is often such a very needy and depleted person that there is great pressure towards the therapist "adopting" the patient with inappropriate counter-transference implications. While the patient needs much nurturing, giving and caring, it is essential that the clinician provide this as part of a rational therapeutic program, rather than out of his own need to parent the patient. The limitations on therapeutic goals, the slowness of change and the testing out by the patient can easily engender rage or disappointment in the clinician who is too heavily invested in his own ability to "cure" his patients.

Often the whole issue of child abuse may be ignored by the therapist. This denial on the part of the therapist happens often enough to comment upon it as a special reaction to be alerted. This is especially true when the patient has not come to the therapist officially labeled as a child abuser—but in a more traditional manner. The parent may describe feelings of loss of impulse control, and the therapist may not attend to it. Threats of violence towards children may be viewed as fantasies, wishes, and fears, but the therapist must have enough sense of reality to realize that the child may be in danger.

This relates to the fact that the subject matter in therapy with abusive parents is in and of itself threatening to many therapists. We have all, at times, been furious with our own children and have perhaps spanked, slapped or hit them. The content may stir up in the therapist his own past with memories of being physically punished. The qualitative differences between these phenomena and what abusive parents may do on a continuous daily basis must be kept in mind. Blind spots or discomfort of the therapist may be seen when he has unresolved reactions to his own childhood or to his relationship with his own children. Sometimes this content is dealt with by rescue fantasies on the part of the therapist who wishes to save the poor helpless child from all cruel adults. This is especially apt to occur if the therapist has had deprivation in his own background. Competition with the parent-patient may result in a critical judgmental stance by the therapist.

Unresolved problems within a therapist are not peculiar to working with abusive parents; counter-transference reactions must always be a concern of any conscientious clinician. However, such reactions seem to be evoked more easily in the treatment of child abuse. The therapist is dealing with the issue of parental physical punishment of a child. This content itself is ubiquitous to the childhoods of all therapists. The abusive parent is a very dependent needy patient who is apt to appeal to the need all therapists have to take care of and "parent" their patients. The cruelty and socially unacceptable behavior of the patient towards his child can easily evoke anger and revulsion from the therapist. Denial or rage may be the resultant reaction from the therapist. Child abuse is an emotionally potent behavior with high valence for eliciting unresolved conflict with therapists.

Therapy and its relationship to the attitudes and behaviors of the parent towards the child. A distressing finding to those who are concerned about the abused child is the frequency with which therapy for the parent results in no detectable changes in the parent-child interaction. Detailed measurements of parent-child interaction are extremely difficult to make. It may be possible that some improvements in the care of the child have accrued, but nonetheless the home often remains an inadequate environmental milieu for the child.

In our follow-up study of 58 abused children done by the authors a short while ago,[13] the children were evaluated at a mean of 4.5 years after abuse had first been documented. It was disheartening to note the current behavior of the parents towards the previously abused child. Parents of 21 of the children had had psychotherapy as part of their treatment program; 90 percent of the children of these parents were still in the biologic home. Even though the children were no longer being battered in the technical or legal sense, 68 percent of them at follow-up were still experiencing hostile rejection and/or excessive physical punishment. It should be noted that these children were faring much better than those whose parents had received no formal treatment. Of those parents who had received only case-work or services from a public health nurse, only 43 percent of the children were living with them at follow-up. Thirty-six percent were still in foster care and 21 percent had been adopted. The families where no formal treatment had been instituted for the parents were even less satisfactory. In this group of children only 40 percent were living with the parents, and of those, 83 percent were the objects of rejection and excessive physical punishment. In all three groups of parents there remained considerable chaos in the family function. This is pragmatically significant, inasmuch as it was found that the degree of psychiatric symptoms of the children correlated at the 0.05 level with unstable family function. Repeatedly we have seen the situation develop where the abusive parent is accurately seen as making personal improvements through a variety of treatment modalities, and yet there is little ostensible change in the parents' distorted views of the child or in the aberrent child-rearing practices.

One must wonder how this seeming paradox can be explained. A number of reasons have been suggested above. That is, the therapist working with the parent may all too willingly exclude from the content of the treatment the parents' behavior towards their child. In actuality this may be essential in the early weeks and months of treatment. Early on, most abusing parents are not able to focus on their child and his needs. The parent has conflicts, problems and distress of his own which are pressing for relief. The parent is typically a deprived needy person who cannot tolerate the therapist showing primary interest in the child. Repeated experience in working with abusing parents has prompted Steele to comment:

> Although protection of the infant is a main goal, direct interest in the infant should be avoided by the therapist, paradoxical as this may seem. Attention should be focused almost exclusively on the parent. (Steele and Pollock,[1] p. 126)

It has been pointed out above that the treatment of abusive families may require a two process procedure. The first process is that of nurturance and caring for the parent, a procedure of re-parenting, if you will. The second process includes dealing with the psychic conflicts and pathology of the adult patient. We are suggesting here that there needs to be a *third* part of the treatment of abusing parents—where treatment deals directly with the abnormal and distorted parent-child relationship.

There are a number of ways that this third part of treatment for the parents can be provided. It is possible for the same therapist to deal with all three phases of treatment, although this is difficult and requires an expertise which many therapists who deal exclusively with adults may not have.

The beginning of this third phase of treatment may indeed be instituted from early on in the treatment regime. This can most optimally start through modeling of appropriate adult-child interactions for the abusing parent. Indeed, the best place to start with abusing parents is *not* to try to change their behavior with their child, but for them to see how others behave with their and other children. We have found it helpful to have the parent view the various testing procedures carried out on their child, whether in the room or behind a one-way mirror. While one does not expect changes in the parents' subsequent behavior so soon, it is helpful for the parent to observe how someone may deal with their child's behavior in a more appropriate manner than they. Whether the child is hyperactive, inhibited or oppositional, the parent has the chance to see modeled for him alternative ways to deal with such behavior.

The benefits of this modeling have been noted in Chapter 19 where this is described as an important aspect of residential treatment for the whole family. We have also found that the crisis nursery, day-care or preschool also provide the opportunity for the parents to see how adults can deal with normal and problematic child behavior. These latter settings also provide the opportunity for the abusive parent to see how other children behave. This often has been most helpful as the parents come to realize that their own child's behavior is not all that unusual as compared to that of other children of the same age. Foster-care homes could also be used in much the same manner. Modeling of appropriate adult-child interactions could be provided as well as more direct help to the parent in learning how to deal with his child.

A number of other approaches to intervening in the parent-child interaction should be considered. Insofar as the behavior of the parent towards the child is based on internal conflicts, an insight-oriented therapy is incomplete if these conflicts are not made part of the treatment contract. Even the therapist who deals exclusively with adults should be able to deal with these conflicts in the therapy sessions. To avoid them is to deny one of the important concerns of the adult and the basic symptom for which the parent was referred for treatment.

We have not found a didactic-oriented approach to child rearing very helpful for most abusing parents, but others have not had the same experience. Classes or courses in parent effectiveness training, for example, have been used with some success by others. We have found most abusive parents not ready for this until many months after identified abuse. Even then, we have found many parents able to grasp the intellectual rationale for what is offered with less ability to change their behavior.

Group work such as Parents Anonymous can be helpful to parents in changing their ideas and behavior towards their child. The support and the confrontation of other abusing parents in such a group is the important ingredient of such therapy.

Perhaps the most exciting and promising approach to this phase of therapy is the direct approach towards modifying behavior of abusing parents with their children. This has been described in some detail in the chapter on residential therapy (Chapter 19). It should be stressed, however, that such attention to the parent-child interaction need not be done in a residential setting. It can be done not only in out-patient settings, but also in the homes of the parents through the efforts of child welfare staff.

Another format for addressing the interpersonal relationships of the family is family therapy. This mode of treatment has received too little attention with abusive families. Timing is again the critical key to success. Both parents and child usually will require some individual therapy before it will be possible to see them as a family group with safety and some assurance of possible success. Family therapy has the advantage that there is no one person identified as the patient. In such a treatment setting, it is readily seen that all members of the family play some part in the family dysfunction.[14] Direct work can be done with the family regarding verbal and non-verbal communications.

In summary, the relationship between the parent and child is the primary symptom in the child abuse situation. While all members of the family may need a variety of types of treatment, it is essential that this primary symptom of the family dysfunction be addressed. The parents' expectations, fantasies and conflicts around the child must be dealt with in therapy. The behavior of the parent in child-care practices must be modified and improved. If the inadequate parenting for the child is not addressed directly and improved, then we have done less than a complete job in offering treatment.

When is the parent ready to provide adequate parenting to the abused child? This question almost always arises at some point in the therapeutic management of child abuse. The most common situation is where the abused child has been placed in foster care while the parents have received a variety of types of treatment. At various points the question arises as to whether the return of the child to the parents is indicated. Even when the child has continued to live with his biologic parents, the courts or social welfare agencies may have legal custody of the child until there is evidence that the parents can provide adequate parenting for the child without supervision. The above question might well be asked when considering foster care for the child, e.g., can these foster parents provide adequate parenting for the child.

All too often very inappropriate measures of parenting ability are used. For example, agencies frequently expect the parents to take certain advice, such as getting a job, keeping therapy appointments, obtaining better housing and so forth. If and when these requirements are met, the agency may be inclined to return the child to the family, and conversely may advise against return of the child if these criteria have not been met. Clearly, these criteria have nothing to do with the parents' ability to provide an adequate home for the child. Meeting these criteria may only be a measure of the parents' cooperativeness with the social agency or may only be a measure of the parents' improvement in areas other than in childcare. It is our position that criteria must be used which are *directly* related to positive changes in the interaction with the child. To see psychological growth in the parent is gratifying and valuable; it may or may not reflect an ability to adequately parent the abused child.

Indications that the parents can provide an adequate environment for the child rest in two separate areas. The parent must evidence improvements in his own psychological status; and the parent must evidence certain attitudes and behaviors towards his child.

1. *Psychological improvement in the parent.* Every therapist has his own guidelines for improvement in patients' psychological status. They will be valuable guidelines for assessing the parent's capacity for change. However, given the types of psychological issues which augur poorly for the children, certain additional guidelines might be added. Some of these will overlap with the usual criteria of therapeutic success.

   a. Decreased isolation. One would want to see the abusive parent begin to become involved outside the nuclear family with other people and with activities such as work, hobbies and play.

   b. Increased pleasure in life. This relates to the above. The parent's life is typically austere and barren. One would want to see the parent taking pleasure out of his or her life in a variety of settings. If the parent remains sad, depressed and unable to enjoy his life, he will not be able to provide an adequate home for the child.

   c. Increased self-esteem. This may take the form of the parents being pleased about how they have handled a situation. It may manifest as the parents acknowledge their strengths and abilities no matter how mundane they might seem. It should be reflected in the parents' unwillingness to acquiesce to the inappropriate demands and expectations of others, that is an ability to say "no."

   d. An ability to use life-lines. Kempe and others have repeatedly drawn attention to the inability of abusive parents to turn to others for help and sustenance. With change in this dynamic, the parent will turn to friends, loved ones, therapists or agencies for help and assistance when appropriate. Once he is able to do this, there is less likelihood the parent will become overwhelmed and turn to the child for concrete or emotional help and support.

   e. Improved handling of stresses and crises. One expects the parent to begin to recognize stresses and the potential for crises in an anticipatory fashion. Further, one expects the parent to learn ways to solve or adapt to stresses or crises such as medical problems, unemployment and emotional stress. The adaptation will take the form of utilizing "life-lines" and any number of other solutions which will mean that the child, when returned, will not be in danger of being the target for the parents' frustration.

   f. More realistic self-expectations. As the parent develops more realistic expectations of himself, he not only will stop being so self-critical but also will have more realistic expectations of his child.

   g. Alternative ways of dealing with anger. More appropriate ways of discharging anger would be expected as the parent learns to anticipate stress and crises, to deal with frustrations, and to utilize other people for help. The acting out of anxiety and anger must be curbed for the professional to feel comfortable about returning the child to the home.

h. Fewer pathological interpersonal relationships. Abusive parents commonly have inappropriate and unhealthy relationships with their parents, spouses and significant others. One would expect to see the development of more normal and healthy relationships and the development of more appropriate object choices in the future. It is common for an abusive parent to repeatedly choose a mate who is sadistic and physically abusive to the spouse and child. One would want to see the parent interrupt this pattern of masochistic object-choice as an improved self-concept would dictate that he deserves a better friend or mate.

i. Utilization of therapy and treatment. Perhaps it is a summary statement to suggest that the abusive parent is showing real gains if he is able to utilize the treatment resources and therapy which heretofore had been viewed with hopelessness or distrust. When the parent is able to utilize treatment, it suggests that he has hope of a better life, an ability to trust others and the capacity to use others for help and sustenance.

These guidelines suggest that there have been significant changes in the abusive parent which, if coupled with changes in the relationship to the child, suggest that an adequate home for the child is possible.

2. *Improvement between parent and child.* This issue is the most essential and critical area to determine if the parents can provide an adequate home for the child. Psychological improvement in the parent may not coincide with improvement between parent and child. In fact, some parents experience personal gain only because they do not have the child care responsibilities. It is no easy task to describe or define in detail what constitutes good parenting. We are more often able to identify inadequate parenting. Nonetheless, whatever therapy the parents have received, it has been incomplete if the treatment has not dealt with the role of the adult as a parent. We should have some confidence that good-enough parenting will be provided when we can see the following:

a. The parent sees the child as an individual. This is a shift from seeing the child primarily as a need-satisfying object for the parents. It further involves a respect for the individuality of the child rather than the view of him as an extension of the parent.

b. The parent enjoys the child. When the parent is able to experience pleasure with the child and enjoy his presence and behavior, then we have some assurance that adequate attachment and bonding are present.

c. The parents' expectations of the child are age-appropriate. This marks a shift from the highly unrealistic expectations of most abusive parents.

d. The parent is able to tolerate the child's negative behavior. This involves allowing the child to have anger and express it in some manner. It means that the parent can appreciate the child even though the child may misbehave or give negative feedback to the parent. It requires enough of a sense of self and self-confidence by the parent that absence of positive reinforcement does not threaten the ego integrity of the parent.

e. The parent can allow the child to receive emotional "goodies" from people outside the family. This has wide implications. It means that the family is not so isolated that need gratification must come from within the nuclear family. It implies that the parent has loosened his unhealthy symbiotic-like interdependency with the child. It further means that the parent will be able to allow the child to receive treatment and therapies which are recommended. It reflects an altruistic love for the child which can endure the pain and struggle of allowing the child to grow up.

f. The parent is comfortable with expressing positive affect directly to the child. He praises the child and experiences genuine love for him. He is able to hug, hold and know the child without expecting that these affections will be returned.

These are but a few of the types of guidelines we might well use in determining whether a parent is capable of providing a growth-promoting family life for the child. They might be applied to parents when deciding when the child might return to the biologic home. They might be applied to foster parents. They might be applied to any proposed parent surrogate for the child.

In a sense, this third goal of therapy for the child—the provision of an adequate family life—is the real crux of all treatment for the child. For when the child is in such a home, the parents will see to it that his medical needs are met. Such parents will also want the developmental and psychological needs of the child to be met. While it is undoubtedly true that "love is not enough," nonetheless, it is equally true that it is the foundation upon which other needs for the child can be built.

Summary

Abusive parents are unhappy, troubled and disturbed persons. They have a need for and a right to help even if the child does not benefit. However, the child pays much of the price of the parents' psychological problems. He may benefit from the treatment of his parents via an improved home environment. That is, if his parents make personal gains in therapy, such gains will be reflected in the climate of the home. However, to insure that the parents' attitudes and behaviors towards the abused child change, the distorted parent-child interaction requires direct intervention.

This chapter reviews the components of effective therapy for abusive parents, including some of the special problems. Also, it introduces a number of approaches for altering parent-child interaction. Finally, it suggests specific guidelines to be used to determine if and when parents are able to provide an adequate home for their child.

Despite the variety of psychological problems that the parents must work through in therapy, we must not forget the preexisting symptom. The parents were unable to provide a safe and adequate family environment for their child. This symptom must be dealt with directly. Resolution may take various forms. The parents may acknowledge that they are unable or unwilling to provide adequate parenting for the child in question. Hopefully this will be identified quickly so that alternate, more satisfactory relationships can be provided for the child. The resolution of the preexisting symptom more often will take the form of changes in the parents' attitudes and behaviors towards the child so that good-enough parenting will be provided.

References
1. Steele, B.F., Pollock, C.B.: A Psychiatric Study of Parents Who Abuse Infants and Small Children in Kempe and Helfer (eds.) *The Battered Child, 2nd Edition.* Chicago: University of Chicago Press, 1974, pp. 89-134.

2. Gil, D.G.: *Violence Against Children: Physical Child Abuse in the United States* Cambridge, Mass.: Harvard University Press, 1970.

3. Polansky, N.A., DeSaix, C., Sharlin, S.A.: *Child Neglect: Understanding and Reaching the Parent,* New York: Child Welfare League, 1973, #G-18.

4. Kempe, C.H., Personal communication.

5. Helfer, R.E., Kempe, C.H. (eds.) *The Battered Child, 2nd Ed.* Chicago: University of Chicago Press, 1974.

6. Kempe, C.H., Helfer, R.E. (eds.) *Helping the Battered Child and His Family* Philadelphia: Lippincott, 1972.

7. Franklin, A.W. (ed.) *Concerning Child Abuse* New York: Churchill Livingstone, 1975.

8. Leavitt, J.E. (ed.) *The Battered Child: Selected Readings* General Learning Corp, 1974.

9. *Children Today,* Vol. 4, May-June 1975, pp. 2-12.

10. Ebeling, N.B., Hill, D.A.: *Child Abuse: Intervention and Treatment* Acton, Mass.: Publishing Sciences Group, 1975.

11. Schmitt, B. *et al.: Child Abuse Primer for Multidisciplinary Teams,* to be published in 1976.

12. Steele, B.: *Working with Abusive Parents: From a Psychiatric Point of View* United States Dept. of Health, Education and Welfare–Office Child Development #OHO75-70, 1975.

13. Martin, H.P., Beezley, P., Conway, E., Kempe, C.H.: "The Development of Abused Children" *Advances Pediat.* 21:25-73, 1974.

14. Rosenthal, P.A., Mosteller, S., Wells, J.L., Rolland, R.S.: "Family Therapy with Multiproblem Multichildren Families in a Court Clinic Setting." *Journal Amer. Acad. Child Psychiat.* 13:126-142, 1974.

※ *Chapter 21*

Resistances and Obstacles
to Therapy for the Child

Harold P. Martin and **Patricia Beezley**

Introduction

With every treatment modality that can be offered for abused children, there are difficulties and obstacles. Parents are often poorly motivated to obtain needed services for their children. But apathy is not the only problem. Many abusive parents are openly resistant to their children receiving help in psychotherapy, preschool, speech therapy or whatever. The dynamics involved in this resistance are complicated and extremely difficult for the professional who must attempt to deal with them. Because of the special circumstances of the abused child and a conflict of loyalties, he, too, may be resistant to therapy.

Mandatory reporting of injuries and court-ordered treatment further complicate any therapy offered for the abused child. To establish and maintain an alliance with the child's parents despite these issues requires considerable expertise.

Also, the reactions of the child's therapist, including countertransference feelings are a special difficulty. The therapist must constantly be attuned to his feelings and behaviors.

Finally, resistance of professionals and agencies prevents many children from receiving the treatment they need.

This chapter will discuss the above issues in some detail. Hopefully, as more professionals become aware of these obstacles and difficulties, increased efforts will be made to assure that abused children receive therapy.

Parents' Resistances

Abusive parents frequently make it difficult for professionals to provide any type of treatment for abused children. They may refuse any services for their child unless it is court-ordered. Even if they superficially agree, they may not fully cooperate. They may fail to bring their child for therapy sessions and feel no need to offer an explanation or excuse. If home-programs are being conducted by speech or perceptual-motor therapists, parents may be minimally responsive. If the child is to be picked up by the therapist or teacher at home, the parent may not have awakened the child or dressed and fed him. With older children, the parent may not have reminded them of their appointment and may have encouraged them to be not available.

The basic issues underlying the resistance of abusive parents to getting help for their children are complex. On the surface there are often relatively simple explanations. For one, the abusive parent may not be invested in making sure the child is well cared for. In 1969, Elmer and Gregg compared young children who had been abused with a group of children with accidental injuries. They found poorer hygiene, minimal well-baby care and erratic care for illnesses in the former group even though their data suggested that the children who had been abused had been *easier children to care for.* The basis of this relative neglect is not always clear. In some instances it seems to stem from overwhelming social pressures with poverty, instability and large families all sapping the physical and psychic energies of both parents. In other instances, this is not the case, and the relative neglect is rooted more clearly in a lack of investment or cathexis in the child. Abusive adults frequently have significant distortions or gaps in their object relations development, with deficiencies in the area of object constancy. They view other adults and children primarily in terms of what these people can give to them. They have little ability to empathize with others and care about them. Friendships are lacking, and even spouses are seen primarily in terms of need gratification for the other parent. The child is not seen as an individual with interests, needs, abilities which are to be valued except insofar as they coincide with the parents' needs. With such a deficit in normal object-relations, it is no wonder that abusive parents are poorly motivated to expend time, energy or monies to assure that their child gets something which is needed, be it well-baby care, a preschool experience or therapy.

In addition to this relative apathy toward getting help for their abused child, there are some other dynamic issues underlying the resistance of parents to therapy for the child. We have primarily seen these more active resistances surfacing in the parents who had their children enrolled in the pilot study of psychotherapy for abused children (see Chapter 16). We not only saw active resistance to the children being brought for therapy but also saw a wide range of maneuvers on the parents' part to sabotage the effects of the therapy. Because these more dynamic resistances were first noted in the psychotherapy study with abused children and inasmuch as they are most glaringly obvious there, we shall discuss parents' resistance to therapy for their children in terms of our observations with psychotherapy. The reader is reminded that these same issues can and often will be operating in the resistance of parents to any type of therapy, such as physical therapy, school experience and language therapy.

Psychotherapy with abused children leads to resistances and obstacles that may be a part of any attempt to do psychotherapy with children. With abusive families, however, the frequency and intensity of the resistances are very much increased, sometimes leading to the parents breaking off the treatment for their children prematurely. Because it seems that some of these failures might be avoided with adequate recognition of their occurrence and the use of preventive measures, the complications of play therapy will be enumerated.

In the pilot study of twelve children, no coercion was brought to bear on the parents to agree to participate. Naturally, one must assume that some of the parents reacted as though their participation would be a sign of good parenting. More difficult, of course, is a situation where court-ordered therapy for the child is undertaken against the wishes of the parents. In the latter case, increased problems of non-cooperation and resistance are encountered.

Any therapist of children can attest to the resistances encountered in dealing with parents. With the parents of these abused children, however, more frequent, more intensive and more special types of resistances arose. First was the reluctance of the parents to their children developing attachments to the therapist. Sometimes this developed in the context of the therapist being seen as a competitor either for the child's attention or as being a "better parent" than the biologic parent. This issue did not seem to be related primarily to the person of the therapist, inasmuch as most of these parents also objected to and attempted to sabotage the good feelings the child developed towards school teachers, neighbors, friends and other therapists. One mother, after having worked hard for over two years to get a big brother for her son, quickly became intensely jealous, expressed concerns that the big brother must be a homosexual and demanded that he be dismissed. This dynamic occurred because of the parent's wish for the child to meet the parent's own emotional needs and, as the child's world included more people of importance outside the family, the ability of that child to love and care for that parent exclusively was compromised.

A second striking phenomenon was the parents' jealousy of the attention their child was getting. Abusive parents are very dependent, needy adults who have never been adequately parented themselves. For this reason, the psychotherapy pilot study was deliberately set up so that no child was accepted in therapy unless the parent was regularly seeing a therapist, either a traditional psychotherapist or a lay-therapist. Most of the parents were also involved in some group therapy, and many had case workers from social service departments. It was our intent that the parents would already have someone or several therapeutic people to whom they could turn for sustenance. However, it quickly became apparent that this was not adequate. The jealousy of the parent was often quite obvious. When the therapist came to pick up the child at his home, the child was frequently not there or not dressed and ready to go; the parents took that opportunity to talk to the therapist about their own problems. When the therapist stayed in the car waiting for the child, the parent might come out to sit in the car to talk. There were many slips of tongue wherein the parent referred to the child's therapist as his or her own therapist. Parents would call to talk about issues completely unrelated to the child. A few parents even asked to come into the play room and spend some time there with the therapist. One mother, when her son's therapy was terminating, asked if now it was "her turn to begin play therapy." At times this neediness of the parent took the form of the parent making up problems concerning the child to motivate the child's therapist to sit and talk with the parent. This same phenomenon was seen, although less strikingly, with other professionals working with the child. When the parent did come to talk with the child's preschool teacher or other therapist, the interviews quickly turned from the child to the parents' personal concerns.

Both of these forms of resistance required the child's therapists to have some regularly scheduled contact with the parents either through periodic vists or phone conversations. It was necessary for the therapist to attempt to lessen the feelings of preemption of the parent and take careful pains never to unwittingly play into the competitiveness felt by the parents. Also, it was very helpful if the parent could have his or her own therapy hour the same hour that the child was in treatment. This seemed to decrease the competitiveness between parent and child.

A further type of resistance relates to the parents' displeasure with changes in their children. These parents were impressively ambivalent toward behaviors of their children of which they openly complained. The investment parents have in their children remaining "problem children" is often seen in any child guidance population. This took on special significance as we saw parents using forceful, physical punishment and emotional rejection in reaction to behaviors of the child which they were alternately reinforcing. Perhaps this should not have surprised us, as many of the parents seemed to need a scapegoat in their homes. In their identification with their children they had a need to see in the children the bad qualities in themselves. Further, there seemed to be a resentment when the child was seen as increasingly able to deal with problems which the parent, him or herself, could not deal with.

The authors were concerned from the first that the children might make changes in behavior during the course of therapy which might place them at more risk of physical abuse. It was hoped that by having a lay-therapist, public health nurse or case-worker involved such a danger could quickly be identified and averted. However, we did not see the risk of physical abuse occur. The children seemed to quickly learn what was acceptable only outside the home and which new behaviors could be exposed at home. Problems arose when the parents visited preschool or observed various therapies such as speech therapy. The child was confused and ambivalent as to how to behave.

If the parents noted any behavior changes, they usually objected to the therapist or else reinforced the old behavior patterns in the child. Early warnings by the parents were heeded very quickly by the child. Nonetheless, it was a serious barrier to the psychotherapy unless the therapist was willing to get involved with the parents and try to work through their ambivalence. Some examples might clarify this phenomenon. Parents complained about their children's lack of response to controls or limits, and yet many parents were seen as encouraging and reinforcing such misbehavior. One parent objected to her child's unwillingness to verbalize his feelings. As he started making tentative attempts to express his feelings, the mother would ridicule him. She would be angry at the therapist because her son would not talk to the therapist about the things that upset him, but then she constantly implied to her son that the therapist was telling her everything that he said in therapy. Another six-year-old boy was dealing with his therapist around the issues of modesty, privacy and seductiveness. When he confided to his mother his discomfort at her habits of walking about the home in sheer underclothing or in a robe with nothing on underneath, she quickly dismissed his concern. She further became quite angry with the "old fashioned" therapist, justifying her bathing with the boy and her liberated views towards nudity.

For the child, too, the difficulties in accepting and using therapy seem greater than for the usual child patient. Many abused children have never been exposed to a different set of values than those of their parents; the acceptance of behavior in the play room, which would never be allowed in the home, brought clearly into focus the possibility that previously accepted beliefs or rules might be wrong. For children to whom pleasing adults is a major priority and often the only way to stay out of danger, any uncertainty about how to behave might lead to anxiety and conflict. Sometimes spelling out clearly the difference between playing freely in the play room and conforming elsewhere helps clarify to the child how to resolve this dilemma and lessens his fear of not pleasing the therapist. A conflict of loyalties is frequent in psychotherapy with children, but the abused child's fear of criticizing his parents is much more intense because he is so vulnerable and has so little experience that would encourage him to trust the therapist to protect him. The stress of trying to please adults with obviously different expectations of him can be great and probably does lead to much of the testing behavior with therapists. As his feelings are expressed more directly and he becomes more clearly aware of some of the frustrations he feels at home, a child often finds himself in conflict and may wish to avoid this pain by resisting therapy himself, or by denying the problems that exist for him. It may well be that some of the apparent indifference to the therapist outside of the play room is related to his difficulty in reconciling such different relationships and the necessity for coping with his personal world at home which is so different from that of the play room.

In summary, the obstacles to effective psychotherapy with abusive families were more intense and pervasive than our experience has been with most other families in therapy. The special dynamics of abusing parents make many of these difficulties understandable. The abusing parent may barely tolerate the child forming allegiances and affection for others, even peers. The abusing parent also wants to be "parented," played with, and cared for, even at the expense of his child's therapy. He may need a bad child to be a scapegoat or may be able only to identify with a child he perceives as evil and worthless, as he was brought up to feel so about himself. For the child, a conflict in values and loyalties makes it difficult for him to use therapy. For treatment to be effective all of these factors must be considered and dealt with by the child's therapist and by the therapist involved with the parent.

Reporting and Court-Ordered Treatment

Whether treatment of the abused child is voluntary or not, there is a need for the child's therapist to develop some type of alliance with the parents if the treatment is not to be sabotaged. One difficulty which arises is the dilemma of the therapist when the child patient comes in with bruises, pinch or bite marks, or other evidence of non-accidental injury. By law the professional is required to report any suspicions of this sort. There is considerable reluctance to report injuries in many instances, especially when the injuries are not of medical significance. When the child's therapist has been helping the parent with his or her angry impulses toward the child, he may feel that reporting a medically insignificant non-accidental injury will result in a disrupture of whatever trust and alliance has been built with the parent. Parenthetically, this same issue is especially difficult for the therapist of the parent.

Difficult though it is, we eventually came to realize that such injuries cannot be ignored just because we had the child in psychotherapy, preschool, physical or speech therapy. In many instances we came to realize that this was a non-verbal communication from the parent that he or she was wanting some help at that time, that is, the parent was informing us that impulse control was tenuous and help was needed. At other times it was seen as a testing out of the therapist, testing where the allegiances of the child's therapist lie and at other times testing whether the therapist would excuse, ignore or condone the punishment. If handled with concern and empathy for the parent, it need not interrupt therapy. When reporting was done, the parent was called or talked to *prior* to calling child protection services. The need and the legal obligation to report such injuries was thoroughly explained to the parent. When the relationship between the child's therapist and the parent was fairly good and the home was not considered medically unsafe, almost without exception we were able to communicate to the child protection agency information to help them perform their protective role in a sensitive and helping manner. When the therapist was encountering counter-transference feelings and unconsciously feeling competitive or critical of the child's parents, there could develop a wish to be punitive and judgmental towards the parents. The therapist of the child must be especially careful not to fall into the common polarization of professionals in child abuse who take either the side of the child or the side of the parent. The therapist knows that the child patient has been physically abused in the past, perhaps on repeated occasions. Bruises and minor abrasions which would go unnoticed in another therapy suddenly can take on fearful and unrealistic alarming proportions to the therapist who is not clear about his role. Inasmuch as the therapist is seeing himself as a helping person to both the child and parent, he will be unwilling to report many instances if he feels that reporting such injuries is not a helpful thing to do. The public agencies charged with responsibility for abused children must somehow avoid increasing mistrust and assure the clinician that the child abuse report will not result in a punitive, counter-productive attack on the family.

Court-ordered treatment presents special difficulties for the therapist. Although it initially increases the resentment and the resistance of the parents, such treatment can be successful. Initially, the parents' fear and resentment must be recognized by their own psychotherapist and the child's therapist. An opportunity for the expression of such feelings must be provided. It may then be very helpful to move quickly on to a more positive focus with the child's therapist indicating his beliefs that whatever has happened, the parents really do want to do the best for their child. He should also indicate his readiness to work with them to promote the family welfare. Parents who deny all problems and state that they only need to be left alone are especially difficult; a matter of fact discussion of necessary arrangements may avoid confrontation until a more positive relationship and some trust can be established. Recognition of the parents' own authority and provision of some choice for them in the management of their child in the treatment plans can help to encourage them in seeing some possible benefit for them in treatment for their child. It is essential to avoid criticism of the parents and their child-rearing practices, even while they invite it, for they, like their children, will test the therapist's capacity to accept them as they are long before they can begin to face the possibility of change.

In summary, court-ordered therapy places an extra burden on the therapists of both the parent and child to be more sensitive than usual to subtle resistance and to work harder to overcome it by trying to relieve the parents' anxiety and feelings of helplessness.

Reactions of the Therapist

Every child therapist, if open and honest with himself, is attuned to the development of rescue fantasies, competitive feelings with the child's parents, and other counter-transference phenomena with child or parent. When doing therapy with abused children, such reactions are even more apt to develop than with other types of child patients. The child has been mistreated and inadequate parenting is the underlying basis for the child being referred for therapy in the first place. Insofar as the therapist has unresolved feelings of not being well-nurtured himself as a child, identification with the abused child is a real danger. Perhaps some elements of rescue fantasies reside in most helping professionals, but given the abused child as one's patient, it is even easier to want neurotically to "save" the child from his inadequate parents. Self-scrutiny regarding unrealistic rescue fantasies, such as conscious thoughts of adoption of abused patients, is essential throughout the treatment process. Concern and altruism which are essential to good therapy must not be confused with unconscious counter-transference reactions which are inimical to the therapeutic process. Inasmuch as the abused child has been mistreated, it is easy for the therapist to self-righteously condemn the parents and develop feelings that he or she could do better than the child's abusing parents. The sensitivity of abusing parents to criticism, coupled with their unusually great need for approval and affection, make such counter-transference feelings of the therapist especially damaging to any type of working alliance between parent and therapist.

A second type of reaction of the therapist is the frequent sense of frustration and disappointment felt, especially near termination. The therapist experiences unrealistic, unconscious feelings of inadequacy. The children with whom we work are very needy children whose orality has been alluded to in Chapter 16. Because most of them came from homes where the capacity of the parents to give to the children was severely limited, the children seemed to never be able to get enough. One can easily feel that he is just not able to give enough; this engenders a sense of inadequacy which, while not realistic, is supported by the dynamics of child and family. One therapist likened the therapy to trying to feed a marasmic, starved child by giving him an ice cream cone once a week. The reality is that a play therapy hour is an intensive, pleasurable, but time-limited experience in sharp contrast to the child's usual life. It cannot make up for what happens the rest of the week.

Obviously, the therapist had to work out such feelings and reactions in consultation, in talking with other therapists and in being attuned to his own personality idiosyncrasies. We are aware that it is not always considered in professional good taste to share and expose one's own painful struggles with being a therapist. We chose to share some of our own personal reactions because we feel they are likely to develop in others working with abused children. Everyone who has worked with abusing parents has had similar reactions to work through and has had to recognize the limitations of what he can offer.

Professional Neglect

We have spoken so far of the resistances of parents to allowing their children to get help. The special problems of reporting and court-ordered treatment have also been addressed. We have touched on the reactions of the professional to the abused child and to the parent and how those reactions may unwittingly play out in such a fashion as to interfere with good therapy. It would be a serious omission not to comment on the frequency with which professionals and agencies overlook the treatment needs of these children.

We were struck with the resistance on the part of child welfare staff to implement various treatment modalities for those abused children under their legal care. In the children studied and reported on in Chapter 9, we recommended psychotherapy for seventeen and preschool for thirteen of the 50 children. These recommendations were rarely carried through. The resistance we encountered from welfare agencies was different than the resistance we saw with parents. The professional resistance was more passive in nature. Child welfare or child protection staff frequently request consultation around a child for whom they have some concern. After an evaluation, the treatment plan is discussed. There is no open resistance to recommendations for therapy for the child, but nothing is implemented. When confronted, the child welfare staff say that there are not enough funds to pay for the treatment or that treatment resources cannot be found or finally that the department has reservations about the real need for such treatment.

It is difficult to know what the underlying basis for such resistance to treatment for abused children really is. In large part it seems to stem from the general stance of child welfare and child protection agencies; that is, the protection of the child is not only the primary but perhaps the only responsibility that the agencies truly feel towards the child.

This very question has recently been examined by Polier in the April 1975 issue of *American Journal of Orthopsychiatry*. Perhaps the overwhelming case-loads of individual workers in such agencies requires a prioritization of concerns for children which leaves treatment of psychological and developmental problems quite low in the scheme of things. At least it seems pertinent to point out to professionals who see abused children that this is an issue which, if not anticipated and dealt with, may make much of their work with abused children go for naught.

Child welfare staff are no more likely to neglect the psychological and developmental needs of the abused child than any other professional. In the introductory chapter of this book, a number of issues were raised as to why there has been so little attention paid to the plight of the abused child by physicians, mental health professionals and others over the years. Chapter 13 details the need for a child's advocate so that his therapeutic needs will not go overlooked by a variety of agencies and professionals. A review of those two chapters will provide the reader with a number of explanations for this professional neglect of the abused child.

Summary
This entire book deals with the consequences of the abusive environment to the child and the various treatment approaches that should be considered to alleviate those consequences. This particular chapter has attempted to explore some of the obstacles to providing help to the abused child by looking at the resistances of parents, the special circumstances of reporting, and court-ordered treatment, the reactions of therapists to their patients, and the factor of professional neglect of the abused child. These issues must be examined and dealt with for the abused child to receive the types of help he needs.

Chapter 22

Summing Up and Moving On

Harold P. Martin

This chapter is being written after all the preceding pages were conceived, written, edited and re-edited. It is the end of a journey for the author, as it is for the reader. From my memory of public speaking, I can recall that there are three things to accomplish in a speech. First is to let the audience know what you are going to say. Second is to say it. And finally, tell the audience what you have just said. And so this book—and so this chapter. Perhaps the most succinct summation would be to stress that abused children not only have medical wounds, but also have psychological and developmental wounds which need identification and treatment. The authors have attempted to detail what some of those wounds are and to suggest specific treatment modalities which have proven helpful. There have been a number of related issues which we have felt it necessary to explicate and expound upon. For those whose time has not allowed detailed reading of all chapters, and for those who may have found that the text of this book has at times obfuscated the primary message, a reiteration of the primary important points seems in order.

1. Well over half of abused children will have significant neuro-developmental or psychological problems which need attention. Mental retardation, learning disorders, perceptual-motor dysfunction, cerebral palsy and impaired speech and language are among the most common developmental delays and deficits to be found. Personality distortions are also found in the majority of abused children. While there can be no one uniform personality profile, the abused child pays a large psychological price including unhappiness, inability to act and feel like a child his age, anxiety and fear and poor and tenuous interpersonal relationships.

2. The consequences to the child must be seen not primarily as secondary to the physical abuse *per se*, but as being secondary to the entire abusive environment in which he lives. He is not only exposed to physical assault, but

may also be exposed to emotional neglect or deprivation, emotionally disturbed parents and medical and nutritional neglect or indifference. He lives in a home where the parent-child relationship is disturbed and distorted. Physical abuse is but one critical sign of that disturbed relationship.

3. There are factors within the child which can place him at greater risk of being abused, given parents with a greater than average propensity to physically assault their children. Especially important are those factors in the child, or during pregnancy, labor or delivery which interfere with normal bonding and attachment between parent and child. A mismatch between the parents' expectations and the actual child may reside in a child's innate deficiencies. The child does not cause abuse, but he *does* play a role in the abnormal child-parent relationship.

4. Developmental, neurologic and psychological consultation should be available to any agency dealing with abused children. Some assessment of the child's developmental and psychological status should be obtained on every abused child, either informally or through consultation from subspecialists. The neurological function of the child deserves special attention during the medical examination.

5. Entry of the abused child into the medical system can provide the opportunity to identify and deal with the child's developmental and psychological wounds as well as attending to his medical problems. We have suggested how hospital staff can make hospitalizations a therapeutic experience for the child and mobilize a number of people to make appropriate treatment plans for the child.

6. We have pointed out how developmental testing can be used not only for the purpose of diagnostically assessing the child's developmental status, but also how it can be used to note behavior and coping mechanisms of the child which should have important treatment significance for parents, teacher or other adults in contact with the child. In truth, this same concept is apropos of any professional contact with the child. The case-worker on a home visit, the physician or nurse seeing the child for routine medical care, or a therapist or preschool teacher who is seeing the child can, in addition to carrying out his primary professional goals, observe and monitor the traits of the child with a view as to how the child can best be understood and helped.

7. Because of our interest in offering treatment and habilitation to the perpetrators of child abuse—the parents—there is always some risk that the broad needs of the child may go overlooked. There needs, then, to be a spirit of child advocacy to maximize the chance that the child's problems and needs will be identified and attended to. This advocacy for the child may come from any involved professional. It may take the form of a more formal advocacy such as a guardian ad litem or the child-protection worker. And finally, it should be part of the routine operations of all child-abuse teams. Appendix A includes a list of some questions which should be asked, and hopefully answered, by a child abuse team on every abused or neglected child in the community.

8. A variety of treatment approaches to the abused child have been described. We have especially focused on treatment for developmental delays and deficits, crisis care, psychotherapy and preschool or day care. We have not spoken much in this book about the role of the public schools in providing help to the abused child. I refer the reader to Chapter 17 wherein the goals of a preschool for abused children are listed. These might also be goals for the public school. Public schools have the resources to be a major therapeutic force for the child, and for the family.

These various treatment modalities for the child have worked. They have made possible considerable growth and development in the abused child. They should be considered as treatment options for all abused children.

9. The whole issue of foster care has been addressed. It was pointed out how foster care with its attendant separation of child and family is an additional stress to the child and to the child-parent relationship. A number of suggestions have been made as to how foster care, when it is needed, can be a therapeutic experience for the child, and for his parents. This requires a revamping of the foster-care system so that it does not isolate the child from his family. It should provide a healthy, therapeutic, parenting experience for the child, and be available to help improve the relationship between biologic parents and their abused child.

10. We have stressed that there is no one victim of the child abuse syndrome. Everyone in the family is caught up in a disturbed and dysfunctional family unit. While we have stressed the needs of the abused child, it should be noted again that the siblings of the abused child, and the father of the child have been relatively neglected in our treatment planning.

11. Psychotherapy for the parents is discussed, particularly in terms of how that therapy *can* impact on the emotional milieu of the child. The parents' attitudes, feelings and behaviors toward the child must be dealt with as a major goal of therapy. This can take place in a variety of settings and in a number of different ways. It can be accomplished in a residential setting for abusive families, or in a family-learning center. It can be part of the goals of traditional therapy from case-worker, psychotherapist, group therapy or home maker.

12. This was not intended to be a book about abusive parents, but about abused children. And yet, the importance of the parents to the abused child is so paramount that we have necessarily included data about the parents in terms of their influence on the child. We have described the environment of the abused child, trying to see characteristics of the parents from the child's viewpoint. Resistances and barriers that abusive parents may raise to preclude therapy for the child have been discussed. One cannot treat the abused child in a vacuum, nor the parents apart from the child. To do so will preclude the opportunity to improve the parent-child relationship which is the primary pathology in the child abuse syndrome.

13. The effects of our treatment planning for the abusive family will often provide new problems and stresses for the child and the parents to deal with. We

have pointed out many of these iatrogenic effects and suggested that we pay particular importance when our treatment plans will weaken rather than strengthen the bond of attachment between parent and child.

There is a great deal yet to be done. I am particularly stressing the need to learn more about various developmental lines of abused children. One must wonder what happens to aggression in abused children as they grow older. The development of the child's self-concept and his conscience are areas for considerable research. The relationship of abuse or neglect to later learning disorders of children is not clear. I have referred a number of times to the need to study the development of object-relations in the abused child. These and many other developmental issues need study and explication. In addition to being fruitful areas of research to enable us to be of more help to the abused child, a secondary goal of such studies would be the light which could be shed upon the development of normal children. Furthermore, as we study these developmental issues, we will learn more about the abusive parent. The parent (abused himself as a child) is still dealing with these same developmental issues, e.g., self-concept, conscience, interpersonal relationships, trust and aggression. In studying the vicissitudes of developmental issues—in children—we inevitably learn about these same problems in adults, thus providing us new insights into understanding and treating the abusive adult.

The syndrome of child abuse raises a number of ethical, social and political questions. I have assiduously tried to avoid most of these more far-reaching implications. In closing, however, I wish to raise very briefly one very natural subsidiary issue. Children do not belong to their parents. Nor do children belong to society. They belong to themselves. They are not owned or possessed by anyone. Many people have an investment in the child. And various people have different responsibilities to the child. Up until age 6, most of the responsibilities for any child reside with his parents. The parents are responsible to feed the child, to teach the child, to love and nurture the child. The child's health, medical care, well-being, personality development and developing knowledge and skills are all in the hands of the parents. The increasing frequency and recognition of child abuse and neglect suggests that this may be too great of a burden for an increasing number of parents. In cases of child neglect or child abuse, we are only seeing the *extremes* of failure in parenting. We are truly viewing the failure of a parent, or of two parents, to assume all of those responsibilities for their child. This suggests to me that we should rethink the whole issue of placing all of those responsibilities for the raising of children solely with the parents.

After age six, it is clear that society takes a larger and larger role in assuming some of the responsibilities of caring for children. The development of knowledge and skills is now taken over primarily by the school system. Indeed, society says that the child can no longer remain at home with his parents exclusively, but must be exposed to an outside learning environment for several hours daily for several months of every year. We insist that the child have certain immunizations at this time, and for the first time in the child's life we require periodic medical examination and often provide such services as visual or hearing screening by our public schools. The child's learning, medical care, and to some degree his personality are no longer the exclusive responsibility of the parents, but are shared by others in the society.

I am suggesting that we might well provide more support to families for sharing in the responsibilities of childrearing *before* the child reaches six years of age. I am not suggesting that children become the wards of the state—but rather, that society provide considerably more support and help to families with infants and young children. There is increasing evidence that many parents cannot adequately meet their many responsibilities to their children, at least not completely by themselves. A number of suggestions for providing this support have been made. Dr. C. Henry Kempe has repeatedly suggested that we should consider the establishment of a health-visitor for every child in this country. This would be a nurse or some other medically trained professional who would visit the child and parent periodically in infancy and early childhood. This could be a resource for the parent in helping with medical care of the child, as well as helping with routine child-care practices. Day care centers should be available, not only for children of working mothers, but for any mother who finds the press of 24 hour care for her children more than she can comfortably handle. There are very few resources for parents who need or want help in management of their children. Some turn to pediatricians as they once turned to extended family. I am suggesting that there needs to be a cadre of childhood specialists available to families when discipline problems or child-care practices need discussion or counsel.

I have intentionally not attempted to draw a blueprint for the provision of such services to families. I am only trying to outline a problem as I see it. I am struck with the tremendous isolation of most young parents today. There is less support and help in raising families in urban America than in a more rural and less mobile country. In the syndromes of child abuse and neglect, we see parents who are unable to meet their responsibilities to their children. In less graphic form, I am impressed that this is increasingly true for non-abusive parents also. The complete responsibility for the welfare and development of children is too great for many parents to shoulder all by themselves. All of us in society have some interest and investment in our children growing up as strong and healthy as possible. There is no logical reason why society should wait until a child reaches six years of age before offering support to a family in the tasks of helping a child learn, grow and develop. I have no special programs to advocate. Others have suggested day care, preschool programs, health visitors or any number of other programs all aimed at providing alternative support to parents in raising their children. Parents should not have to admit to "failure" to have help in raising their children. In today's society, all parents should have help and support available to them in understanding and providing for their children.

There has been an emphasis in this book in shifting from an exclusive preoccupation with the physical injuries of the abused child, to the more chronic neurologic, developmental and psychological injuries. One takes a calculated risk in such a shift in emphasis. Society—citizens, professionals, legislators—has been so impressed with this form of cruelty to children that considerable progress has been made possible. State laws have been revamped to better protect children. The federal government, with the urging of Senator Mondale, has invested considerable money in studying and preventing child abuse. Child abuse teams are being developed across the country. Professionals in a variety of disciplines are getting involved. We have been shocked and frightened by the tales of death, torture and maiming of children at the hands of their parents. Our attention has been captured, and our consciences pricked. I would hope that there will be sustained interest and concern in the psychologic price that children pay for suboptimal parenting. I can only hope that sustained interest will be maintained in the agonizing consequences of children being unloved, deprived and neglected. I hope that our interest will not stop at the boundaries of child abuse but will more broadly encompass concern for man's inhumanity to children.

Appendices

Child Protection
Team Format

Below is a listing of questions to be addressed by whatever person(s), agency(ies) or team is responsible for the abused child. It is recommended that each of these questions be considered by the child protection team at the time of referral and at every point thereafter when treatment planning is being considered or reviewed.

1. *What is the developmental status of the child?* Consider:
   a. General intelligence and learning
   b. Motor skills and coordination
   c. Speech and language
   d. Socialization with peers, siblings, adults
   e. Personality: coping styles, interests

   Gather material through:
   f. Observations of the child
   g. History from adults who know the child
   h. Developmental screening
   i. Consultation from child development specialists

2. *What are the child's reaction to recent events in his life?* Consider:
   a. Injuries
   b. Medical evaluation and treatment of injuries
   c. Separation from parents, siblings, families, surroundings
   d. Hospitalization
   e. Foster home placement

3. *What other factors in the child's home, besides physical abuse, are deleteriously affecting his growth and development?* Consider:
   a. Poverty
   b. Neglect/deprivation/understimulation
   c. Undernutrition
   d. Serious emotional disturbances in parent
   e. Sexual abuse
   f. Family instability: unemployment, numerous moves

4. *What are the treatment needs of the child?* Consider:
   a. Consistent pediatric care
   b. Speech therapy
   c. Physical and/or occupational therapy
   d. Educational therapy: day care, preschool, special educational help in primary school
   e. Psychiatric therapy: play therapy, group therapy, supportive therapy from a paraprofessional
   f. Continuation of previous meaningful relationships with relatives, neighbors, peers, teachers
   g. Crisis help for immediate stresses, i.e., preventive psychological help

5. *What effects will the treatment recommendations for the whole family have on the child?* Consider the effects of:
   a. Long-term foster care
   b. Court hearings
   c. Visiting privileges of parents
   d. Evaluations of family
   e. Treatment for the parents
   f. Home visits by professionals

6. *Who will be assigned to monitor the child's subsequent course and progress?* Consider roles of:
   a. Guardian ad litem
   b. Protective service worker
   c. Child's therapist

7. *Has parent-child interaction changed?* Consider:
   a. Parents' attitudes toward child
   b. Parents' behavior toward child
   c. Child's reactions to parents

All of these questions must also be addressed to all of the abused child's siblings. When these questions are built into the routine evaluation by each child protection team, the team will inevitably become more child oriented in their deliberations.

The rights and needs of the parents must not be overlooked or sacrificed, but the attention to these questions should assure a more optimal balance of the divergent interests of parents, child, and society.

✳ *Appendix B*

Reference Index

Ainsworth, M.D.S., Bell, S.M., Stayton, D.J.: Infant-mother attachment and social development, 'socialization' as a product of reciprocal responsiveness to signals. In Richards, M.P.M. (ed.), *The Integration of a Child into a Social World.* London: Cambridge University Press, 1974. *Page 137.*

Alexander, T., Chess, S., Birch, H.G.: *Temperament and Behavior Disorders in Children.* New York: New York University Press, 1968. *Pages 31, 141.*

Altmann, J.: Observational study of behavior-sampling methods. *Behaviour,* 1974, 49:227-267. *Page 131.*

Anthony, E.J., Benedek, T.: *Parenthood: Its Psychology and Psychopathology.* Boston: Little, Brown & Co., 1970. *Pages 34, 150.*

Anthony, E.J.: The Reactions of the Parent to the Oedipal Child, chapter 12, pp. 275-288 in *Parenthood: Its Psychology and Psychopathology.* Anthony and Benedek editors. *Page 35.*

Anthony, E.J.: The Reactions of Parents to Adolescents and to Their Behavior, chapter 14, pp. 307-324 in *Parenthood: Its Psychology and Psychopathology,* Anthony and Benedek editors. *Page 35.*

Anthony, E. James: Presentation at Seminar of Departments of Psychiatry and Pediatrics, Univ. Mo. Med. Center, Columbia, Mo., November 1974. *Page 142.*

Appleton, P.L.: A Social Ethological Study of Young Children and Its Relevance to Clinical Child Psychology. M. Sc. Thesis. Scotland: University of Glasgow, 1975. *Pages 130, 132.*

Bakwin, H.: Loneliness in Infants, *Am. J. Dis. Child.* 63:30-40, 1942. *Page 153.*

Bakwin, H.: Emotional Deprivation in Infants, *J. Pediatr.* 35:512-521, 1949. *Page 153.*

Barnett, C.R., Leiderman, P.H., Grobstein, R., Klaus, M.: Neonatal Separation: The Maternal Side of Interactional Deprivation. *Pediatrics,* 1970, 54:197. *Page 32.*

Baron, M.A., Bejar, R.L., Sheaff, P.J.: Neurologic Manifestations of the Battered Child Syndrome. *Pediat.,* 1970, 45:1003-1007. *Page 76.*

Bateson, G.: *Steps to an Ecology of Mind.* New York: Ballantine Books Inc., 1972. *Page 137.*

Bayley, Nancy: *Bayley Scales of Infant Development.* New York: Psychological Corporation, 1969. *Page 115.*

Benedek, T.: The Psychobiology of Pregnancy, chapter 5, pp. 137-152 in *Parenthood: Its Psychology and Psychopathology,* Anthony and Benedek editors. *Page 34.*

Bernal, J.: Attachment—Some Problems and Possibilities. In Richards, M.P.M. (ed.), *The Integration of a Child into a Social World.* London: Cambridge University Press, 1974. *Page 131.*

Berry, K.E.: *Developmental Test of Visual-Motor Integration, Administration and Scoring Manual.* Chicago: Follett Educational Corporation, 1967. *Pages 75, 202.*

Birch, H.G.: Malnutrition, Learning and Intelligence, *Am. J. Public Health,* 62:773-784, 1972. *Page 149.*

Birch, H.G., Gussow, J.D.: *Disadvantaged Children—Health, Nutrition and School Failure.* New York: Grune and Stratton, 1970. *Page 148.*

Birrell, R.G., Birrell, J.H.W.: "The Maltreatment Syndrome in Children: A Hospital Survey," *Med. J. Aust.* 2:1023-1029, 1968. *Pages 49, 148.*

Blumberg, Marvin: Psychopathology of the Abusing Parent. *American Journal of Psychotherapy,* January 1974, 21. *Page 235.*

Blurton Jones, N.: An Ethological Study of Some Aspects of Social Behaviour of Children in Nursery School. In Morris, D. (ed.), *Primate Ethology.* London: Weidenfield and Nicholson Ltd., 1967. *Page 137.*

Blurton Jones, N. (ed.): *Ethological Studies of Child Behaviour.* London: Cambridge University Press, 1972a. *Pages 129, 131.*

Blurton Jones, N.: Characteristics of Ethological Studies of Human Behaviour. In Blurton Jones, N. (ed.), *Ethological Studies of Child Behaviour,* London: Cambridge University Press, 1972b. *Page 131.*

Blurton Jones, N.: Categories of Child-Child Interaction. In Blurton Jones, N. (ed.), *Ethological Studies of Child Behaviour.* London: Cambridge University Press, 1972c. *Pages 130, 132.*

Blurton Jones, N.: Ethology and Early Socialization. In Richards, M.P.M. (ed.), *The Integration of a Child into a Social World.* London: Cambridge University Press, 1974. *Page 130.*

Blurton Jones, N., Leach, G.: Behaviour of Children and Their Mothers at Separation and Greeting. In Blurton Jones, N. (ed.), *Ethological Studies of Child Behaviour.* London: Cambridge University Press, 1972. *Page 131.*

Bowlby, J.: Maternal Care and Mental Health. *Bull. WHO* 3:355-533, 1951. *Page 153.*

Bowlby, J.: *Attachment and Loss.* Volume 1: Attachment. London: Penguin Books, Ltd., 1969. *Pages 32, 73, 129, 130.*

Bowlby, J.: *Attachment and Loss.* Volume 2: Separation: Anxiety and Anger. London: Penguin Books, Ltd., 1973. *Pages 129, 130.*

Brazelton, T.B.: *Infants and Mothers: Differences in Development.* New York: Delacorte, 1969. *Page 140.*

Brazelton, T.B.: Neonatal Behavioral Assessment Scale. *Clinics in Devel. Med. #50,* Philadelphia: J.B. Lippincott, Col, 1973. *Pages 31, 140.*

Brazelton, T.B.: *Toddlers and Parents: A Declaration of Independence.* New York: Delacorte, 1974. *Page 140.*

Brazelton, T.B., Koslowski, B., Main, M.: The Origins of Reciprocity: The Early Mother-Infant Interaction. In M. Lewis and L.A. Rosenblum (eds.), *The Effect of the Infant on Its Caregiver.* New York: John Wiley and Sons, 1974. *Pages 33, 140.*

Brenneman, J.: The Infant Ward. *Am. J. Dis. Child.* 43:577-584, 1932. *Page 153.*

Broadhurst, D.D.: Project Protection: A School Program to Detect and Prevent Child Abuse and Neglect. *Children Today,* 1975, 4 (3), 22-25. *Page 94.*

Bronfenbrenner, U.: The Origins of Alienation. *Scientific Amer.,* August 1974, 53-61. *Page 20.*

Browder, J.A.: Adoption and Foster Care of Handicapped Children in the U.S. *Devel. Med. Child. Neurol.* 16:614-619, October 1975. *Page 198.*

Brown, R., Billings, V.: *Three Processes in the Child's Acquisition of Syntax.* Harvard Educ. Review, 35:133-152, 1964. *Page 90.*

Bruner, J.S.: Nature and Uses of Immaturity. *American Psychologist,* August 1972, 687-708. *Page 131.*

Bruner, J.S.: The Ontogenesis of Speech Acts. *Journal of Child Language,* 1974, 2:1-19. *Page 130.*

Burgner, M., Edgcumbe, R.: Some Problems in the Conceptualization of Early Object Relationships. II: The Concept of Object Constancy. *Psychoanal. St. Child,* 1972, 27:315-331. *Pages 72, 146.*

Caffey, J.: On the Theory and Practice of Shaking Infants: Its Potential Residual Affects of Permanent Brain Damage and Mental Retardation. *Am. J. Dis. Child,* 1972, 24:161-169. *Pages 67, 76.*

Chamberlin, R.W.: Management of Preschool Behavior Problems. *Pediat. Cl. N. Amer.* 21:33-48, February 1974. *Page 212.*

Chase, H.P., Martin, H.P.: Undernutrition and Child Development. *N. Engl. J. Med.,* 1970, 282:933-939. *Page 32.*

Chase, N.F.: *A Child Is Being Beaten.* New York: Holt, Rinehart and Winston, 1975. *Page 248.*

Chess, S.: *Psychiatric Disturbances of Children with Congenital Rubella* New York: Brunner/Mazel, 1971. *Page 144.*

Children Today, Vol. 4, May-June 1975, pp. 2-12. *Page 252.*

Cipriano, A., Canosa (ed.): "Nutrition, Growth and Development," *Modern Problems in Pediatrics,* Vol. 14, 1975. *Page 149.*

Cohn, A.H., Ridge, S.S., Collignon, F.C.: Evaluating Innovative Treatment Programs in Child Abuse and Neglect. *Children Today,* 1975, 4(3):10-12. *Page 236.*

Coleman, R., Provence, S.A.: Developmental Retardation (Hospitalism) in Infants Living in Families. *Pediat.,* 1957, 19:285-292. *Pages 79, 153.*

Colorado Rev. Stats. Ann. 19-10-103(2) (1973 as amended). *Pages 166, 170.*

Crabtree, M., *The Houston Test for Language Development, Part I and Part II.* 10133 Bassoon, Houston, Texas, 1963. *Page 84.*

Darwin, C.: *The Origin of Species.* London: Murray, 1859. *Page 130.*

Darwin, C.: *The Expression of the Emotions in Man and Animals.* London: Murray, 1872. *Page 130.*

Darwin, C.: A Biographical Sketch of an Infant. *Mind*, 1877, 2:286-294. *Page 130.*

DeFrancis, V.: *Protecting the Child Victim of Sex Crimes Committed by Adults* Denver: American Humane Association, Children's Division, 1969. *Page 152.*

Delaney, Hon. James J.: "The Battered Child and the Law," *Helping the Battered Child and His Family*, Kempe and Helfer, (eds.), Philadelphia: J.B. Lippincott Co., 1972. *Page 167.*

Dodge, P.R., Prensky, A.L., Feign, R.D.: *Nutrition: and the Developing Nervous System* St. Louis: C.V. Mosby, 1975. *Page 149.*

Drillien, C.M.: *The Growth and Development of the Prematurely Born Infant* Edinburgh: Livingstone, 1964. *Pages 148, 155.*

Dunn, L.M.: *Peabody Picture Vocabulary Test.* Minneapolis: American Guidance Service, Inc., 1965. *Pages 75, 84, 202.*

Ebeling, N.B., Hill, D.A.: *Child Abuse: Intervention and Treatment*, Acton, Mass.: Publishing Sciences Group, 1975. *Pages 2, 252.*

Elkind, D.: Perceptual Development in Children. American Scientist, September/October 1975, pp. 533-541. *Page 98.*

Elmer, E.: *Children In Jeopardy.* Pittsburgh: University of Pittsburgh Press, 1967. *Pages 1, 148.*

Elmer, E., and Colleagues: *Report of a Study of Abused Children*, presented at American Psychiatric Assn. meeting, Anaheim, California, spring, 1975. *Pages 2, 83.*

Elmer, E., Gregg, G.S., Developmental Characteristics of Abused Children. *Pediatrics*, 1967, 40:596-602. *Pages 1, 48, 65, 94.*

Erikson, E.H.: *Childhood and Society.* New York: Norton, 1963. *Pages 74, 109.*

Fontana, V.J.: *The Maltreated Child.* Springfield, Ill.: Charles Thomas Publisher, 1974. *Page 2.*

Fontana, V.J., Robison, E.: A Multi-disciplinary Approach to the Treatment of Child Abuse. Prepublication draft, 1975. *Page 236.*

Fraiberg, S.: Libidinal Object Constancy and Mental Representation. *Psychoanal. St. Child*, 24:9-47, 1969. *Page 146.*

Frankenburg, W., Camp, B.: *Pediatric Screening Tests.* Springfield, Ill.: Charles Thomas, 1975. *Page 114.*

Franklin, A.W., (ed.) *Concerning Child Abuse* New York: Churchill Livingstone, 1975. *Pages 2, 252.*

Fraser, B.: Legislative Approaches to Child Abuse. A compilation (loose-leaf), The National Center for the Prevention and Treatment of Child Abuse and Neglect, Denver, Colorado, 1973. *Page 3.*

Fraser, B., Fine, A.: The Battered Child. *The Colorado Lawyer*, 3(6):33, April 1974. *Page 3.*

Fraser, B.: A Pragmatic Alternative to Current Legislative Approaches to Child Abuse. *American Criminal Law Review*, 12:103, 1974. *Page 166.*

Fraser, B.: A Pragmatic Approach to Child Abuse. *American Criminal Law Review*, 12:103, 1974. *Page 3.*

Fraser, B.: Child Abuse and Neglect: Alternatives for State Legislation. ducation Commission of the States, *Report No. 44*, December 1974. *Page 3.*

Fraser, B.: Toward a More Practical Central Registry. *Denver Law Journal,* 51(4):509, 1974. *Page 3.*

Fraser, B.: Legislative Status of Child Abuse Legislation. In Kempe, C.H., Helfer, R. (eds.), *The Battered Child.* Chicago: University of Chicago Press, 2nd ed., 1974. *Page 3.*

Fraser, B., Besharov, D.: Child Abuse and Neglect, Model Legislation. Education Commission of the States, September 1975. *Page 3.*

Fraser, B.: Pediatric Bill of Rights. *South Texas Law Review,* 16(3):245, 1975. *Page 3.*

Fraser, B.: *Colorado: Child Abuse and the Child Protection Act,* The National Center for the Prevention and Treatment of Child Abuse and Neglect, Denver, Colorado, 1976. *Page 171.*

Freud, Anna: The Role of Bodily Illness in the Mental Eye of Children. *Psychoanalytic Study of the Child,* 1952, 7:69-81. *Page 65.*

Freud, A.: Normality and Pathology In Childhood: Assessments of Development, Vol. VI of *The Writings of Anna Freud* New York: International University Press, 1965. *Page 109.*

Freud, A.: The Ego and Mechanisms of Defense. In Anna Freud, *The Writings of Anna Freud.* Vol. II. New York: International University Press, 1966. *Pages 42, 80, 144.*

Freud, S.: *Heredity and the Aetiology of the Neuroses,* from *The Standard Edition of the Complete Psychological Works of Sigmund Freud,* Vol. 3, pp. 141-161, James Strackey, (ed.), London: Hogarth Press, 1962. *Page 31.*

Freud, S.: *Analysis Terminable and Interminable 1937,* from *The Standard Edition of the Complete Psychological Works of Sigmund Freud,* James Strachey (ed.). London: Hogarth Press, 1964, Vol. 23, pp. 240-246. *Page 142.*

Friedman, R.A.: The Battering Parent and His Child: A Study of Early Object Relations. *Intern. Rer. Psychoanal.* 2:189-198, 1975. *Page 108.*

Galdston, R.: Observations on Children Who Have Been Physically Abused and Their Parents. In Leavitt, J.E. (ed.), *The Battered Child—Selected Readings.* New York: General Learning Corporation, 1974. *Page 2.*

Gesell, A., Amatruda, C.W.: *Developmental Diagnosis.* New York: Hoeber, 1947. *Page 77.*

Gil, D.G.: Incidence of Child Abuse and Demographic Characteristics of Persons Involved. *The Battered Child.* R.E. Helfer, C.H. Kempe (eds.), Chicago: University of Chicago Press, 1968 (first edition), pp. 19-40. *Page 46.*

Gil, D.G.: *Violence Against Children: Physical Child Abuse in the United States.* Cambridge, Mass., Harvard University Press, 1970. *Pages 2, 14, 27, 96, 155, 251.*

Gil, D.G.: Unraveling Child Abuse. *Amer. J. Orthopsychiat.,* April 1975, 45:346-356. *Pages 14, 77.*

Giovacchini, P.L.: Effects of Adaptive and Disruptive Aspects of Early Object Relationships upon Later Parental Functioning. chapter 25, pp. 525-538, in Anthony, E.J., Benedek, T. (eds.), *Parenthood: Its Psychology and Psychopathology.* Boston: Little, Brown & Co., 1970. *Page 151.*

Goddard, H.H.: *The Kallikak Family "Classics in Psychology."* New York: Arno Press, 1973. *Page 140.*

Goldstein, J., Freud, A., Solnit, A.J.: *Beyond the Best Interests of the Child.* New York: Free Press, 1973. *Pages 6, 158, 168, 192.*

Goldston, Richard: Observations of Children Who Have Been Physically Abused and Their Parents. *American Journal of Psychiatry*, 122:440-443, 1965. *Page 57.*

Gray, G.W., Wise, C.M.: *The Bases of Speech.* New York: Harper & Brothers, 1959. *Page 90.*

Gray, J., Cutler, C., Dean, J.: Studies in progress. *Page 27.*

Green, A.H.: Self-Destruction in Physically Abused Schizophrenic Children: Report of Cases. *Arch. Gen. Psychiatr.*, 1968, 19:171-197. *Page 36.*

Gregg, G.S., Elmer, E.: Infant Injuries: Accident or Abuse. *Pediatrics* 44:434-439, 1969. *Pages 95, 148.*

Grunebaum, H., Weiss, J.L., Cohler, B.J., Hartman, C.R., Gallant, D.H.: *Mentally Ill Mothers and Their Children* Chicago: University of Chicago Press, 1975. *Page 151.*

Harre, R., Secord, P.F.: *The Explanation of Social Behaviour.* London: Blackwell Scientific Publ. Inc., 1972. *Page 137.*

Heiskanen, O., Kaste, M.: Late Prognosis of Severe Brain Injury to Children. *Dev. Med. Child Neurol.*, February 1974, 16:11-14. *Page 67.*

Helfer, R., Kempe, C.H.: *The Battered Child, 2nd edition.* Chicago: University of Chicago Press, 1974. *Pages 13, 252.*

Hinde, R.: Some Problems in the Study of the Development of Social Behaviour. In Tobach, E., *et al.* (eds.), *The Biopsychology of Development.* London: Academic Press, 1971. *Page 131.*

Hinde, R.: Aggression. In Pringle, J.W.S. (ed.), *Biology and the Human Sciences.* London: Oxford University Press, 1972. *Page 131.*

Holman, R.R., Kanwar, S.: Early Life of the Battered Child. *Archs. Dis. Childh.*, 1975, (50)1:78-80. *Pages 47, 48.*

Howell, S.E.: Psychiatric Aspects of Habilitation. *Pediat. Cl. North Amer.*, 1973, 20:203. *Page 30.*

Hurley, R.: *Poverty and Mental Retardation, A Casual Relationship* New York: Random House, Inc., 1969. *Page 148.*

Hutt, J., Hutt, C.: *Direct Observation and Measurement of Behavior.* Springfield, Ill.: Charles Thomas, 1970. *Pages 131, 134.*

Illingworth, R.S.: *The Development of the Infant and Young Child: Normal and Abnormal, Fifth Edition.* Baltimore: The Williams and Williams Company, 1972. *Pages 11, 115.*

In Re Gault, 387 U.S. 1 (1967). *Page 175.*

Jeffrey, M.: Therapeutic Intervention for Children at Risk and Their Families. In *First Australian National Conference on the Battered Child.* Sandy Williams (ed.), pp. 103-111, Western Australia: Department of Community Welfare, 1975. *Page 247.*

Jensen, A.R.: *Educability and Group Differences* New York: Harper and Row, 1973. *Page 140.*

Johnson, Adelaide M.: Sanctions for Super-ego Lacunnae of Adolescents. In *Searchlights on Delinquency*, K.R. Eissler (ed.), pp. 225-245, New York: International University Press, 1949. *Page 208.*

Johnson, Adelaide M., Szurek, Stanislaus: The Genesis of Antisocial Acting Out in Children and Adults. *Psychoanalytic Quarterly*, 21 (1952): 323-343. *Page 208.*

Kalverboer, A.F.: *A Neurobehavioral Study in Preschool Children.* Suffolk, England: Lavenham Press, 1975. *Page 71.*

Kempe, C.H.: Paediatric Implications of the Battered Baby Syndrome. *Archives of Diseases of Childhood*, 46:28, 1971. *Page 1.*

Kempe, C.H.: A Practical Approach to the Protection of the Abused. *Pediatrics*, Vol. 51:804, April 1973. *Page 1.*

Kempe, C.H., Helfer, R. (eds.), *The Battered Child.* Chicago: University of Chicago Press, 1968, 1974. *Page 1.*

Kempe, C.H. *et al.*: Predictive Studies of Child Abuse. In progress. *Page 27.*

Kempe, C.H., Helfer, R. (eds.), *Helping the Battered Child and His Family.* Philadelphia: J.B. Lippincott Co., 1972. *Pages 1, 27, 252.*

Kempe, C.H., Helfer, R.E.: Innovative Therapeutic Approaches. *Helping the Battered Child and His Family.* C.H. Kempe and R.E. Helfer, (eds.), Philadelphia: J.B. Lippincott Co., 1972. *Page 51.*

Kempe, C.H., Silverman, F., Steele, B., Droegmueller, W., Silver, H.: The Battered Child Syndrome. *Journal of American Medical Association*, 181:17-24, July 1962. *Page 1.*

Kennell, J.H., Jerauld, R., Wolfe, H., Chesler, D., Kreger, N.C., McAlpine, W., Steffa, M., and Klaus, M.H.: Maternal Behavior One Year after Early and Extended Post-Partum Contact. *Dev. Med. Child Neurol.*, 1974, 16:172. *Pages 32, 73, 89.*

Kestenberg, J.S.: The Effect on Parents of the Child's Transition into and out of Latency, chapter 13, pp. 289-306 in *Parenthood: Psychology and Psychopathology*, Anthony and Benedek, (eds.). *Page 35.*

Kinnaird, D., *et al.*: A Children's Group and a Mother's Group for Families in Which There Is Threatened Abuse. Manuscript in preparation—Park Hospital for Children, Oxford, 1976. *Pages 51, 132.*

Kirk, S.A., McCarthy, J.J., Kirk, W.A.: *Illinois Test of Psycholinguistic Abilities.* Urbana: University of Illinois, 1968. *Pages 84, 202.*

Kirk, S.A., Kirk, W.A.: *Psycholinguistic Learning Disabilities: Diagnosis and Remediation.* Urbana: University of Illinois Press, 1971. *Page 86.*

Klaus, M.H., Jerauld, R., Kreger, N.C., McAlpine, W., Steffa, M., Kennell, J.H.: Maternal Attachment: Importance of the First Post-Partum Days. *N. Engl. J. Med.*, 1972, 286-460. *Pages 32, 73, 89.*

Klaus, M., Kennell, J.: Mothers Separated from Their Newborn Infants. *Ped. Clinics. N. Amer.*, 1970, 17:1016. *Pages 32, 43, 48, 73, 89.*

Klein, M., Stern, L.: Low Birthweight and the Battered Child Syndrome. *Amer. J. Dis. Child*, July 1971, 122:15-18. *Pages 33, 48.*

Kline, Draza, Overstreet, Helen Mary: *Casework with Foster Parents.* New York: Child Welfare League of America, Inc., 1973. *Pages 193, 195.*

Kolvin, I., *et al.*: Dimensions of Behaviour in Infant School Children. *British Journal of Psychiatry*, 1975, 126:114-126. *Page 134.*

Knobloch, H., Pasamanick, B.: *Gesell and Amatruda's Developmental Diagnosis—The Evaluation and Management of Normal and Abnormal Neuropsycho-*

logic Development in Infancy and Young Children. New York: Harper and Row, 1974. *Pages 11, 115.*

Leavitt, J.E.: *The Battered Child–Selected Readings*. New York: General Learning Corporation, 1974. *Page 2, 252.*

Lee, L.L.: *Developmental Sentence Analysis*. Evanston, Ill.: Northwestern University Press, 1974. *Page 85.*

Lenoski, E.F.: Paper presented at Seminar on Child Abuse, Denver, Colorado, September 30, 1974. *Page 58.*

Lewis, M., Rosenblum, L.A.: *The Effect of the Infant on Its Caretaker*. New York: John Wiley and Sons, 1974. *Page 28.*

Lewis, M.: *Clinical Aspects of Child Development,* Philadelphia: Lea and Febinger, 1971. *Page 11.*

Lynch, M.: Ill Health and Child Abuse. *Lancet*, August 1975, 16:317-319. *Pages 46, 132.*

Lynch, M.: A Place of Safety: An In-Patient Facility for Abusive Families. Paper presented at the Ad Hoc International Conference on Child Abuse, Bellagio, Italy, October 1975. *Page 235.*

Lynch, M., Ounsted, C.: A Place of Safety. *Child Abuse and Neglect–The Family and the Community.* R.E. Helfer and C.H. Kempe, (eds.), Cambridge, Mass.: Ballinger Publ. Co., 1976. *Page 45.*

Lynch, M., Steinberg, D., Ounsted, C.: Family Unit in a Children's Psychiatric Hospital. *British Medical Journal*, 1975, 2:127-129. *Pages 43, 132, 135, 235.*

Lystad, M.H.: Violence at Home: A Review of the Literature, *Amer. J. Orthopsychiat.*, April 1975, 45:328-345. *Page 14.*

MacDonald, J.M.: *Rape: Offenders and Their Victims* Springfield, Ill.: Chas. Thomas, 1971. *Page 152.*

MacKeith, R.: The Feelings and Behavior of Parents of Handicapped Children. *Devel. Med. Child Neurol.*, 1973, 15:524-527. *Page 30.*

Mahler, M.S., Pine, F., Bergman, A.: The Mother's Reaction to Her Toddler's Drive for Individuation. Chapter 11, pp. 257-274 in *Parenthood: Psychology and Psychopathology*, Anthony and Benedek, eds. *Page 35.*

Mahler, M.S., *et al.*: *The Psychological Birth of the Infant: Symbiosis and Individuation.* New York: Basic Books, 1975. *Pages 21, 72, 109, 145, 146.*

Malone, Charles A.: Safety First: Comments on the Influence of External Danger in the Lives of Children of Disorganized Families. Amer. J. Orthopsych. *36*: 6-12, January 1966. *Page 100.*

Mandelbaum, A., Wheeler, M.E.: The Meaning of a Defective Child to His Parents. *Social Casework*, 1960, 41:360. *Page 30.*

Manocha, S.L.: *Malnutrition and Retarded Human Development.* Springfield, Ill.: Charles C. Thomas, 1972. *Page 149.*

Martin, Harold P.: The Child and His Development. In *Helping the Battered Child and His Family*, C. Henry Kempe and Ray E. Helfer (eds.). Philadelphia: J.B. Lippincott Co., 1972. *Pages 76, 83, 95, 148, 201.*

Martin, H.P.: Nutrition: Its Relationship to Children's Physical, Mental, and Emotional Development. *Amer. J. Clin. Nutrit.*, 1973, 26:766-775. *Pages 76, 149.*

Martin, H.P.: Parental Response to Handicapped Children. *Devel. Med. Child Neurol.*, 1975, 17:251-2. *Page 30.*

Martin, H., Beezley, P., Conway, E., Kempe, C.H.: The Development of Abused Children, Part I: A Review of the Literature; Part II: Physical, Neurologic and Intellectual Outcome. *Advances in Pediatrics*, Vol. 21:25-73, 1974. *Pages 1, 28, 33, 48, 74, 95, 101, 105, 148, 201, 256.*

Martin, H.P., Beezley, P.: Prevention and the Consequences of Child Abuse. *Journal of Operational Psychiatry*, 1974, 1:68-72. *Pages 33, 48, 157.*

Martin, H.P., Beezley, P.: The Personality of Abused Children. *Developmental Medicine and Child Neurology*, Accepted for Publication, 1976. *Pages 1, 105, 157.*

Martin, H.P., Rodeheffer, M.: Psychologic Impact of Child Abuse. Accepted for publication, *Journ. Pediat. Psychol.*, 1976. *Page 157.*

Martin, P.: Marital Breakdown in Families of Patients with Spina Bifida Cystica. *Devel. Med. Child Neurol.*, December 1975, 17:757-763. *Page 30.*

McCarthy, D.: *McCarthy Scales of Children's Abilities.* New York: Psychological Corporation, 1972. *Page 115.*

McDevitt, J.B.: Separation—Individuation and Object Constancy. *Journal Amer. Psychoanal. Assn.*, 23:713-742, 1975. *Page 145.*

McGrew, W.: *An Ethological Study of Children's Behaviour.* London: Academic Press, 1972. *Page 131.*

McRae, K.N., Ferguson, C.A., Lederman, R.S.: The Battered Child Syndrome. *C.M.A. Journal*, 1973, 108:859-866. *Page 48.*

Merrill, E.J.: Physical Abuse of Children: An Agency Study. In V. DeFrancis (ed.), *Protecting the Battered Child*, Denver: Amer. Humane Assoc., 1962. *Page 17.*

Miller, J.F., Yoder, D.E.: A Syntax Teaching Program. *Language Intervention with the Retarded.* J.E. McLisn, D.E. Yoder, and R.L. Schiefelbusch, (eds.). Baltimore: University Park Press, 1972. *Page 90.*

Milowe, I.D., Louri, R.B.: The Child's Role in the Battered Child Syndrome. *J. Pediatr.*, December 1964, 65:1079-1081. *Page 36.*

Morris, M.G., and Gould, R.W.: "Role Reversal: A Necessary Concept in Dealing with the 'Battered Child Syndrome,' " *Am. J. Orthopsychiatry* 33:298-299, 1963. *Pages 14, 100.*

Morris, M.G., Gould, R.W., Mathews, P.J., "Toward Prevention of Child Abuse," *Children*, 11:55-60 (March-April 1964). *Pages 1, 57.*

Morse, C.W., Sahler, O.J.Z., and Friedman, S.B.: A three-year follow-up study of abused and neglected children, *Am. J. Dis. Child.* 120:439-446, 1970. *Page 95.*

Moss, S.Z. and Moss, M.S.: Surrogate Mother-Child Relationships. *Amer. J. Orthopsychiatry* 45:382-390, April 75. *Page 198.*

Mussen, P.H., Conger, J.J., Kagan, J.: *Child Development and Personality*, New York: Harper and Row, 1974. *Page 11.*

Mysak, E.D., *Speech Pathology and Feedback Theory.* Charles C. Thomas, Publisher; Springfield, Illinois, 1966. *Page 90.*

The Neglected-Battered-Child Syndrome—Role Reversal in Parents. New York: Child Welfare League of America, 1963. *Page 100.*

Newberger, E.H., Hyde, J.N.: Child Abuse: Principles and Implications of Current Pediatric Practice. *Ped. Clinics of North America*, Vol. 22, 695-715, Philadelphia: W.B. Saunders Co., August 1975. *Pages 2, 15.*

Newson, J., Newson, E.: Intersubjectivity and the Transmission of Culture: On the Social Origins of Symbolic Functioning. *Bull. British Psychological Society*, 1975, 28:437-446. *Pages 131, 133.*

Olshansky, S.: Chronic Sorrow: A response to Having a Mentally Defective Child. *Social Casework*, 1962, 43:190. *Page 30.*

Ounsted, C.: Biographical Science. An Essay on Developmental Medicine. *Psychiatric Aspects of Medical Practice.* Mandelbrote, B. and Gelder, M.G. (eds.). London: Staples Press, Ltd., 1972. *Pages 52, 133.*

Ounsted, C., Lynch, M.: Family Pathology as Seen in England. *Child Abuse and Neglect—The Family and the Community.* R.E. Helfer and C.H. Kempe, (eds.). Cambridge, Mass.: Ballinger Publ. Co., 1976. *Pages 43, 45.*

Ounsted, C., Lynch, M.: Aspects of Bonding Failure—The Developmental Approach to Child Abuse. (Chapter in preparation for R. Helfer and C.H. Kempe book, 1976.) *Pages 132, 135.*

Ounsted, C., Oppenheimer, R., Lindsay, J.: Aspects of Bonding Failure: The Psychopathology and Psychotherapeutic Treatment of Families of Battered Children. *Dev. Med. and Child Neurol.*, 1974, 16:447-456. *Pages 31, 43, 51.*

Pakes, E.H.: Child and Family In-Patient Unit. The Hospital for Sick Children, Toronto. Private correspondence, 1974. *Page 236.*

Paraskwopoulos, J.N., Kirk, S.A.: *The Development and Psychometric Characteristics of the Revised Illinois Test of Psycholinguistic Abilities.* Urbana: University of Illinois Press, 1969. *Page 86.*

Pediatrics, Vol. 51, No. 5, May 1973, p. 947. *Page 228.*

Peterson, D.R.: The Scope and Generality of Verbally Defined Personality Factors. *Psychological Review*, 1965, 72:48-59. *Page 134.*

Phillips, M.H., Shyne, A.W., Sherman, E.A., Haring, B.L.: *Factors Associated with Placement Decisions in Child Welfare.* New York: Child Welfare League, 1973. *Page 199.*

Polansky, N.A., DeSaix, C., Sharin, S.A.: *Child Neglect: Understanding and Reaching the Parent.* New York: Child Welfare League Publ. #618, 1972. *Pages 24, 251.*

Polier, Hon. J.W.: Professional Abuse of Children: Responsibility for the Delivery of Services. *American Journal of Orthopsychiatry*, 45(3):357, 1975. *Pages 166, 273.*

Pollock, C., Steele, B.: A Therapeutic Approach to the Parents. *Helping The Battered Child and His Family.* R.E. Helfer and C.H. Kempe, (eds.). Philadelphia: J.B. Lippincott, 1972, p. 10. *Pages 47, 49.*

Prugh, Dane, *et al.*: A study of the Environmental Reactions of Children and Families to Hospitalization and Illness. *American Journal of Orthopsychiatry*, XXIII, 1953, 70-106. *Page 65.*

Prugh, D.C., Harlow, R.G.: Masked Deprivation in Infants and Young Children. In *Deprivation of Maternal Care: A Reassessment of Its Effects.* Public Health Papers, No. 14. Geneva: World Health Organization, 1962. *Page 153.*

Quay, H.C., Werry, J. (eds.): *Psychopathological Disorders of Childhood*, New York: John Wiley and Sons, 1972. *Page 134.*

Rheingold, H.L., Eckerman, C.O.: The Infant Separates Himself from His Mother. *Science*, 1970, 168:78-83. *Page 130.*

Ribble, M.A.: *Rights of Infants: Early Psychological Needs and Their Satisfaction.* New York: Columbia University Press, 1943. *Page 153.*

Rice, E.P., Ekdahl, M.C., Miller, L.: *Children of Mentally Ill Parents.* New York: Behavior Publications, 1971. *Page 150.*

Richards, M.P.M. (ed.): *The Integration of a Child into a Social World.* London: Cambridge University Press, 1974. *Page 129.*

Richmond, J.B.: The Family and the Handicapped Child. *Clin. Proc. Child Hosp.*, 1973, 29:156-164. *Page 30.*

Richmond, J.B., Eddy, E., Green, M.: Rumination: A Psychosomatic Syndrome of Infancy. *Peds.*, 1958, 22:49. *Page 65.*

Ringler, N.M., Kennell, J.H., Jarveila, R., Navojoski, B.J., Klaus, M.H.: Mother-to-Child Speech at Two Years—Effects of Early Postnatal Contact. *J. Pediatr.*, January 1975, 86:141-144. *Pages 32, 73, 98.*

Robertson, J., Robinson, J.: Young Children in Brief Separation. *Psychoanalytic Study of the Child*, 1971, 26:264-315. *Page 65.*

Rosenthal, P.A., Mosteller, S., Wells, J.L., Rolland, R.S.: Family Therapy with Multiproblem Multichildren Families in a Court Clinic Setting. *Journal Amer. Acad. Child Psychiat.* 13:126-142, 1974. *Page 259.*

Rutter, M.: Children of Sick Parents: An Environment and Psychiatric Study. *Maudsley Monog. No. 16.* London: Oxford University Press, 1966. *Page 150.*

Rutter, M.: *The Qualities of Mothering: Maternal Deprivation Reassessed.* New York: Aronson, 1974. *Pages 33, 76.*

Rutter, M., Graham, P., Yule, W.: *A Neuropsychiatric Study in Childhood.* Philadelphia: J.B. Lippincott Co., 1970. *Page 143.*

Ryan, J.: Early language development—Towards a Communicational Analysis. In Richards, M.P.M. (ed.), *The Integration of a Child into a Social World.* London: Cambridge University Press, 1974. *Page 131.*

Sandgrund, A., Gaines, R.W., Green, A.H.: Child Abuse and Mental Retardation: A Problem of Cause and Effect. *Journal of Mental Deficiency*, 1975. Vol. 19, No. 3, 327-330. *Pages 2, 30, 95.*

Sattin, D.B., Miller, J.K.: The Ecology of Child Abuse within a Military Community. *Am. J. Orthopsychiatry* 41:675-678, 1971. *Page 155.*

Schmitt, B., *et al.: Child Abuse Primer for Multidisciplinary Teams.* Forthcoming, 1976. *Pages 182, 252.*

Schmitt, B., Kempe, C.H.: Neurological Aspects of the Battered Child Syndrome. In Vinker, P.J., Bruyn, G.W. (eds.), *Handbook of Clinical Neurology.* Amsterdam: North Holland Publishing Co., 1974. *Page 1.*

Schmitt, B., Kempe, C.H.: The Battered Child Syndrome. In Kelley, V.O. (ed.), *Brennemann-Kelley Practice of Pediatrics.* New York: Harper & Row Publishers, Inc., 1974. *Page 1.*

Schmitt, B., Kempe, C.H.: Child Abuse. *The Encyclopedia Americana*, 1974. *Page 1.*

Schmitt, B., Kempe, C.H.: The Battered Child Syndrome. In Gellis, S.S., Kagan, B.M. (eds.), *Current Pediatric Therapy.* 6th ed. Philadelphia: W.B. Saunders Co., 1974. *Page 1.*

Schmitt, B., Kempe, C.H.: Child Abuse—The Battered Child Syndrome. *A Folia Traumatologica Monograph*, Basle, Switzerland: Ciba-Geigy, Ltd., 1974. *Page 1.*

Schmitt, B., Kempe, C.H.: Neglect and Abuse of Children. In Vaughn, V.C., McKay, R.S. (eds.), *Nelson's Textbook of Pediatrics*, 10th ed. Philadelphia: W.B. Saunders Co., 1974. *Page 1*.

Schmitt, B., Kempe, C.H.: The Pediatrician's Role in Child Abuse and Neglect. *Current Problems in Pediatrics* monograph, Chicago: Yearbook Medical Publishers, Inc., Vol. 5(5), 1975. *Page 1*.

Schneider, C., Helfer, R.E., Pollock, C.: *The Predictive Questionnaire in Helping the Battered Child and His Family*. Kempe and Helfer, (eds.), Philadelphia: J.B. Lippincott Co., 1972. *Page 27*.

Scrimshaw, N.S., Gordon, J.E.: *Malnutrition, Learning and Behavior*. Cambridge, Mass.: M.I.T. Press, 1968. *Page 149*.

Sherman, E.H., Neuman, R., Shyne, A.W.: *Children Adrift in Foster Care: A Study of Alternative Approaches*. New York: Child Welfare League, 1973, #F46. *Page 199*.

Skinner, A.E., Castle, R.L.: *Battered Children: A Retrospective Study*. United Kingdom: National Society for the Prevention of Cruelty to Children, 1969. *Page 48*.

Smith, S.M., Hanson, R.: 134 Battered Children: A Medical and Psychological Study. *Brit. Med. Journal*. 14 September 1974, pp. 666-670. *Pages 30, 48, 83*.

Smith, S.M., Hanson, R., Noble, S.: Parents of Battered Children: A Controlled Study. In A.W. Franklin (ed.), *Concerning Child Abuse*. New York: Churchill-Livingston, 1975. *Page 15*.

Solnit, A.J.: A Study of Object Loss in Infancy. *Psychoanalytic Study of the Child*, 1970, 25:257-272. *Page 65*.

Somerhoff, G.: The Abstract Characteristics of Living Systems. In Emery, F.E. (ed.), *Systems Thinking*. London: Penguin Books Ltd., 1969. *Page 134*.

Sperling, M.: The Clinical Effects of Parental Neurosis on the Child. Chapter 26, pp. 539-570 in Anthony, E.J., Benedek, T. (eds.), *Parenthood: Its Psychology and Psychopathology* Boston: Little, Brown & Co., 1970. *Page 151*.

Spinetta, J.J., Rigler, D.: The Child Abusing Parent: A Psychological Review, *Psychol. Bull.*, 1972, 77:296-304. *Page 16*.

Spitz, R.A.: Hospitalism: An Inquiry into the Genesis of Psychiatric Conditions in Early Childhood. In the *Psychoanalytic Study of the Child*, Vol. I, 53-74. New York: International University Press, 1945. *Pages 73, 107, 153*.

Spitz, R.A.: *A Genetic Field Theory of Ego Development*. New York: International University Press, 1959. *Page 80*.

Spitz, R.A.: The Effect of Personality Disturbances in the Mother on the Well-being of Her Infant. Chapter 24, pp. 501-524, in Anthony, E.J., Benedek, T. (eds.), *Parenthood: Its Psychology and Psychopathology* Boston: Little, Brown & Co., 1970. *Page 150*.

Spitz, R.A., Wolf, L.M.: Anaclictic Depression: An Inquiry into the Genesis of Psychiatric Conditions in Early Childhood. In *The Psychoanalytic Study of the Child*, Vol. II, 323-342. New York: International University Press, 1946. *Pages 73, 107, 153*.

Steele, B.: *Working with Abusive Parents: From a Psychiatric Point of View*. U.S. Dept. H.E.W.—Office of Child Development #OHO75-70, 1975. *Pages 13, 254*.

Steele, B.F., Pollock, C.B.: A Psychiatric Study of Parents Who Abuse Infants and Small Children. In Kempe and Helfer (eds.), *The Battered Child, 2nd Edition.* Chicago: University of Chicago Press, 1974. *Pages 46, 48, 251, 254, 257.*

Stone, H.D. (ed.): *Foster Care in Question.* New York: Child Welfare League, 1972. *Page 199.*

Stone, L.J., Smith, H.T., Murphy, L.B.: *The Competent Infant.* New York: Basic Books, 1973. *Page 11.*

Stroufe, L.A., Wunsch, J.P.: The Development of Laughter in the First Year of Life. *Child Development,* 1972, 43:1326-1344. *Page 131.*

Stutsman, R.: *Guide for Administering the Merrill-Palmer Scale of Mental Tests.* New York: Harcourt, Brace & World, 1948. *Page 77.*

Talbot, N.B.: Has Psychological Malnutrition Taken the Place of Rickets in Contemporary Pediatric Practice? *Pediatrics* 31:909-918, June 1963. *Page 153.*

Templin, M.C., Darley, F.L.: *The Templin-Darley Tests of Articulation, Second Edition.* Iowa City: University of Iowa, 1969. *Page 84.*

Terman, L.M., Merrill, M.A.: *Stanford-Binet Intelligence Scale Manual for the Third Revision, Form L-M* Boston: Houghton Mifflin Co., 1960. *Pages 77, 202.*

Terr, L.: A Family Study of Child Abuse. *Amer. J. Psychiatr.,* 1970, 127:125-131. *Page 34.*

Thomas, W.: *Child Victims of Incest* Denver: American Humane Association, Children's Division, 1968. *Page 152.*

Tinbergen, N.: Functional Ethology and the Human Sciences. *Proceedings of the Royal Society* (B), 1972, 182:385-410. *Page 137.*

Tizard, J.: The Upbringing of Other People's Children. *Jour. Child. Psychol. & Psychiat.* 15:161-173, 1974. *Page 198.*

Tobach, E., Aronson, L.R., Shaw, E. (eds.): *The Biopsychology of Development.* London: Academic Press, 1971. *Page 137.*

Van Hooff, J.A.R.A.M.: Structural Analysis of Chimpanzee Social Behaviour. In Von Cranach, M., Vine, I. (eds.), *Social Communication and Movement— Studies of Interaction and Expression in Man and Chimpanzee.* London: Academic Press, 1973. *Page 130.*

van Rees, R.: The Triangle: A Therapeutic Social Center. Unpublished manuscript, 1975. *Page 236.*

Wechsler, D.: *Wechsler Intelligence Scale for Children.* New York: The Psychological Corporation, 1949. *Page 202.*

Werner, E., Simonian, K., Bierman, J.M., French, F.E.: Cumulative Effect of Perinatal Complications and Deprived Environment on Physical, Intellectual, and Social Development of Preschool Children. *Pediatrics* 30:490-505, 1967. *Pages 148, 155.*

Weston, J.T.: The Pathology of Child Abuse. In *The Battered Child,* R.E. Helfer and C.H. Kempe (eds.). Chicago: University of Chicago Press, 1968. *Page 48.*

Winnicott, D.W.: The Mother-Infant Experience of Mutuality. Chapter 9, pp. 209-244 in Reference #35. *Page 34.*

Wolins, Martin: *Selecting Foster Parents.* New York: Columbia University Press, 1963. *Page 194.*

Wortis, H.: Poverty and Retardation: Social Aspects. In Wortis, J. (ed.): *Mental Retardation.* New York: Grune and Stratton, 1970. *Page 148.*

Wortis, J.: Poverty and Retardation: Biosocial Factors. In Wortis, J. (ed.): *Mental Retardation.* New York: Grune and Stratton, 1970. *Page 148.*

Yarrow, L.J.; Maternal Deprivation—Toward an Empirical and Conceptual Reevaluation. *Psychol. Bull.* 58:459-490, 1961. *Page 152.*

Zager, Ruth: The Pediatrician and Preventive Child Psychiatry. *Clin. Pediat.* 14:1161-1167, Dec. 1975. *Page 212.*

✳ *Appendix C*

Subject Index

Contributors

Helen Alexander, MSW
Coordinator, Circle House Family Residential Treatment Facility
The National Center

Peter L. Appleton
Dept. Child & Family Psychiatry
Bethel Hospital
Norwich, United Kingdom
(Formerly Park Hospital, Oxford, U.K.)

Patricia Beezley, MSW
Assistant Director,
The National Center
Instructor Pediatrics,
University of Colorado Medical Center

Florence Berman Blager, Ph.D.
Chief, Speech Pathology and Audiology
JFK Child Development Center
University of Colorado Medical Center

Brian G. Fraser, J.D.
Staff Attorney, The National Center
Instructor Pediatrics,
University of Colorado Medical Center

Jane Gray, M.D.
Assistant Clinical Professor Pediatrics
University of Colorado Medical Center

Ruth S. Kempe, M.D.
Psychiatrist, The National Center
Assistant Professor Psychiatry and Pediatrics
University of Colorado Medical Center

C. Henry Kempe, M.D.
Director, The National Center
Professor of Pediatrics and Microbiology
University of Colorado Medical Center

Margaret A. Lynch, M.R., C.P., D.C.H.
Park Hospital for Children
Oxford, England

Harold Martin, M.D.
Associate Director, JFK Child Development Center
Associate Professor of Pediatrics
University of Colorado Medical Center

Mary McQuiston, BA
Coordinator, Child Care Facility
The National Center

Tobie Miller, OTR
Staff Occupational Therapist
JFK Child Development Center
University of Colorado Medical Center

Joan Mirandy, BA
Head Teacher, Playschool
The National Center

Martha Rodeheffer, Ph.D.
Psychologist, The National Center
Asst. Professor of Clinical Psychology
University of Colorado Medical Center

About the Author

Harold Martin grew up in Hannibal, Missouri. It was at that state's University in Columbia, Missouri that he completed medical school and his pediatric training. He then studied child development for two years at the University of Colorado Medical Center in Denver. He has been in training at the Denver Psychoanalytic Institute since 1971.

Doctor Martin is presently Associate Professor of Pediatrics at the University of Colorado Medical School. Since 1969 he has been the Associate Director of the JFK Child Development Center on that same campus. His clinical work and research with abused children dates back to 1966. He is affiliated with the National Center for Prevention and Treatment of Child Abuse and Neglect in Denver, Colorado.